12/2

W9-AAG-582

ABOVE AND BEYOND

ABOVE

THE STORY OF THE

AND BEYOND

CONGRESSIONAL MEDAL OF HONOR

By Joseph L. Schott

G. P. PUTNAM'S SONS   NEW YORK

FOR ELEANOR AND ROLF

Acknowledgments

THIS book could not have been written without the assistance of several extremely cooperative individuals in the armed services of the United States. The following were most helpful:

Major R. F. Prentiss, Magazine and Book Branch, U.S. Army.

Major James F. Sunderman, Chief, U.S. Air Force Book Program.

Lieutenant Commander F. A. Prehn, Head, Magazine and Book Branch, U.S. Navy.

My special thanks go to World War I flyers Bill Moore of Fort Worth, Texas, and William E. Barrett of Denver, Colorado. Bill Moore told me a lot in general about World War I flying and William E. Barrett furnished valuable documentary information about the Fiftieth Aero Squadron and the Lost Battalion.

I wish to thank Samuel I. Parker of Concord, North Carolina, past Secretary of the Congressional Medal of Honor Society of the United States of America, for answering so well all sorts of questions, personal and otherwise, about the Medal and its winners.

I wish to acknowledge a debt of gratitude to all those diligent people in the National Archives and the Library of Congress who dug around for all the books and dusty bundles of papers and then pushed them in on the little carts.

Final gratitude is due Norene Titus and Katherine Bradley of Fort Worth, and Patricia Morris of Grand Prairie, Texas, for heroism in line of the typing profession in struggling gallantly with index cards and manuscript in a manner far above and beyond the call of duty.

Contents

"Sometimes a very very thin line exists between an award of the Medal of Honor and a trial by court-martial. . . ."

—SECOND LIEUTENANT SAMUEL I. PARKER,
*winner of the Medal of Honor,
Soissons, France, 1918*

Introduction

THE late General George S. Patton, observing the award of the Medal of Honor to a soldier at Casablanca in 1943, said enviously, "I'd give my immortal soul for that decoration!" The devil apparently was not stirred by the Faustian invitation. Patton fought well in two of America's wars and displayed gallantry and courage on many occasions. He won many military honors—but never the Medal of Honor—the highest military award the United States can bestow.

This book is an informal history of the Medal of Honor—Army, Navy, and Air Force—a volume of remembrance dedicated to American heroes. It is not only a history of the Medal awarding system from the time of its origin during the Civil War to the present day, it is in great part a series of vignettes of many of the men, and of the one woman, who have won Medals of Honor.

Our history of awarding medals for brave deeds is as old as our country. One dark September night in 1780, on a lonely road near Tarrytown, New York, three American militiamen leaped from a covert beside the road and threw themselves on a passing horseman. Dragging their quarry from his horse, they searched him thoroughly, finding what they sought in his boots. This was no ordinary act of brigandage. The horseman was Major John André, British spy, and the documents in his boots were traitorous messages from the American general Benedict Arnold at West Point to the British commander in New York. As a result of this capture, André was hanged as a spy and Arnold fled to the British to die in exile.

Later that year the three militiamen, John Paulding, Isaac Van Wart and David Williams, were awarded special medals by Congress in recognition of their service in capturing the spy.

These, the first medals in our history awarded to common soldiers, are known as André Medals. Prior to these awards Congress had awarded special gold medals to Revolutionary generals George Washington, Horatio Gates and Henry "Light Horse Harry" Lee for outstanding leadership in defeating the British in battle.

But these six Revolutionary medals were individual awards and no effort was made to perpetuate them as standards for similar acts of bravery and service.

In 1782 General George Washington tried to establish two permanent decorations for his troops. In setting forth the conditions for the Badge of Military Merit, or Purple Heart, he stated: "The General, ever desirous to cherish a virtuous ambition in his soldiers, as well as to foster and encourage every species of military merit, directs that whenever any singularly meritorious action is performed, the author of it shall be permitted to wear on his facings, over his left breast, the figure of a heart in purple cloth, or silk, edged with narrow lace or binding."

Three men received this award in 1783. No others are on record as having received the Purple Heart as originally constituted. However, on February 22, 1932, the two hundredth anniversary of Washington's birth, the Purple Heart was reestablished and since that time has been given to members of all services wounded in conflict with the enemy.

Washington also established the Badge of Military Distinction—"a narrow piece of white cloth on an angular form, to be fixed on the left arm of the uniform coat." Given only during the Revolution, the badge could be worn by enlisted personnel who had served more than three years with "bravery, fidelity, and good conduct."

Then in 1847, during the Mexican War, Congress established the Certificate of Merit, a printed or written document, signed by the President, which was presented to Army enlisted men who performed "meritorious" services. As originally conceived, the Certificate of Merit was not a medal nor in any sense a decoration. It would, however, become a full-fledged medal in 1905, and further evolve into the Distinguished Service Medal in 1918.

In addition to the early Certificate of Merit awards, heroic or meritorious deeds performed prior to the Civil War were

recognized by being "mentioned in dispatches" or by the award of a temporary "brevet" promotion. But the documents and dispatches and brevet promotions were not medals to be worn proudly on the breast as public reminders that on some occasion in the past the wearer had performed a brave or gallant act and had been recognized for it.

The Medal of Honor, born in the smoke and tumult of the Civil War, was for many years the only authorized American military medal.

Mainly the Medal has been a decoration for battle deeds, for conflict with a human enemy. There have been exceptions to this rule and they will be explored at the proper time. But mainly battles are named in the citations: Bull Run, Antietam, Fair Oaks, Fort Fisher, Gettysburg, Little Big Horn, Apache Pass, Wounded Knee, El Caney, San Juan Hill, Samar, the Tartar Wall, Vera Cruz, Haiti, Belleau Wood, the Argonne, Guadalcanal, the Coral Sea, Anzio, Bastogne, Crucifix Hill, Pusan, the Chosin Reservoir, Pork Chop Hill . . .

The truth is there, behind the myths and legends, buried in the dusty archives. The names of the three thousand and more winners and what they did to get their Medals are all in the citations, scribbled and printed on yellowing old lists and general orders. The requirements for winning the Medal, different at different times, are all set forth in Congressional acts, Presidential executive orders, and the whimsical correspondence of certain Secretaries of War and Adjutants General.

Many provocative questions arise from the old records:

Who won the first Medal of Honor? The first awarded were Army Medals which went in a group to six survivors of a daring raid carried out against Confederate railroads in April of 1862. The true identity of their leader was never known.

Has anyone ever won the Medal twice? Yes. There were five Army double-winners and nine Navy double-winners and five immortal Marines who won both Army and Navy Medals of Honor.

Has anyone ever won the Medal and had it revoked? By all means. How many? Nearly a thousand people.

Did a woman who dressed like a man ever win the Medal of Honor? Yes.

Was the Medal ever won for throwing a well-timed bucket of

water? For crowning a cursing sailor with a hand holystone? For rescuing a woman from a burning hotel? As a mere "souvenir of memorable times now past"? Yes for all of these, but never again for the same reasons.

Was the Medal ever awarded for shooting an assassin? Yes— three times.

Why, exactly, is this decoration commonly called the "Congressional" Medal of Honor?

Do special awards, made solely on Congressional initiative, tend to degrade the Medal? What about Charles Augustus Lindbergh, the Lone Eagle, who got the Medal from Congress for flying the gray Atlantic alone in 1927? What about Richard E. Byrd? Floyd Bennett? Adolphus W. Greely? Did Billy Mitchell get a real Medal of Honor?

If the above individuals got the award, why did not such personages as Commander Alan Shepard and Lieutenant Colonel John Glenn, America's first space men, get Medals of Honor?

The Medal inspires many contradictions. General Dwight D. Eisenhower once said, "I would rather have the right to wear this medal than be President of the United States." Then he refused to be considered for the Medal when Congress offered it to him in 1945, and yet accepted the nomination for the Presidency in 1952.

Is the policy of making the Medal extremely hard to win a good policy? This may sound like a silly question, but there is a sober, logical and well-documented point of view which expresses the belief that the Medal, as awarded today, is much too difficult to attain.

What does it take to win the Medal of Honor? What separates one exploit from another in being considered worthy of the highest recognition? How far above and beyond the call of duty must one go to deserve it? Why did Samuel Parker, a Medal winner, say, with all due respect to the decoration, that sometimes the line between the Medal award and a court-martial trial was very very thin?

One fascinating bypath of the Medal of Honor legend lies in the widespread myths that certain American heroes are Medal winners who never got it at all. Without in any way attempting to detract from their exploits, it must be said to keep the record straight that Army flyer Colin Kelly, Marine hero Ira Hayes,

and the four military chaplains on the ill-fated troop transport *Dortchester* did not win Medals of Honor in World War II. Nor did Father Duffy, immortal chaplain of the "Fighting Sixty-ninth" in World War I, win the Medal.

Many flyers and Marines almost unknown to the public did win Medals, however. And of course a fire-eating Navy chaplain of the carrier *Franklin* won the Medal in World War II.

In summing up the hundred-year history of the Medal we may say this. The Medal is, and always has been, a peculiarly American award, whimsically bestowed perhaps on occasion, but nevertheless designed to fulfill the age-old military function of rewarding bravery. The original concept was broad in scope, covering many degrees of bravery. But do not forget that for many years the Medal of Honor was the only military medal authorized. No lesser awards existed.

We may wish to smile now at such deeds as a Marine refraining from shooting a woman, and a sailor's smashing the Johnny Reb head with the holystone because of abusive language. We may wish to smile, but when we soberly consider what it took to win the Medal at Bull Run, San Juan Hill, Château-Thierry, Omaha Beach and Pork Chop Hill, the strongest inclination will not be to smile, but to rise and salute. For the most common characteristic of the winners throughout history was courage—courage above and beyond the call of duty.

ABOVE AND BEYOND

I

Discord and the Foul Spirit of Secession

WASHINGTON, D.C., November 1861.
In the gray afternoon the capital city, called by contemporary observers the "dirtiest and most ill-kept borough of the United States," was more depressing than usual. Rain had been falling in a gray cloud for the past several days and had ceased temporarily, leaving the streets canals of liquid mud almost three feet deep. At the intersections near the base of the rise toward Capitol Hill, the muddy torrents moved in a steady flow downhill.
Lieutenant Colonel Edward D. Townsend, Adjutant General of the United States Army, strolled along Pennsylvania Avenue, glad to be free of his stuffy office long enough for a breath of air, the progress of the war much on his mind. The Union defeat at Bull Run during the summer had set a despondent keynote. The latest dispatches from Missouri were gloomy with news of more Confederate victories and harassments.
Passing before a group of loiterers in front of Willard's Hotel, Townsend was greeted by several clumsy salutes from newly recruited officers. One of them, a militia major, snapped to attention and saluted smartly, without removing his cigar from his mouth. The others, mostly foreigners in gaudy uniforms with bright medals on their tunics, did not deign to salute. They were mostly opportunists, soldiers-of-fortune, still a bit shocked by their crude surroundings: the duckboard sidewalks, the muddy streets and the uncouth atmosphere of the capital city of the Union.
Was this scramble to recruit professional officers abroad a good policy? Certainly these foreigners had not come uninvited. The Secretaries of State and War had sent a swarm of agents

abroad to comb the world for officers. And here many of them were, standing disdainfully on the wooden sidewalk in front of Willard's Hotel, looking down their noses at the mud and the half-finished buildings. Garibaldi himself had been offered a commission but had been unable to accept, because of prior commitments in Italy. The demands of some of the foreigners far exceeded even those of the native-born politicians seeking appointments as brigadiers. General George Klapka, a hero of the 1849 Hungarian Revolution, had laid down noteworthy terms: $100,000 in advance, a salary of $25,000 a year, appointment as chief of staff until he learned English, after which he would become General in Chief, replacing George B. McClellan. To an army that paid its brigadier generals only one hundred and twenty-four dollars a month, the terms were shattering.

But the foreigners were impressive, no question about that. They drew more spectators than a team of dancing bears. Townsend skirted the group gawking at the foreigners, keeping clear of the muddy edge. On the opposite side of the group, on sudden impulse, he grasped the shoulder of a drummer boy who stood there teetering on his tiptoes, trying to see over the heads of the crowd. The boy, barely fourteen, looked up with surprise at the imposing bearded officer.

"Drummer boy," said the Adjutant General, staring seriously at his quarry, "are you watching that crowd of foreign officers in front of the hotel?" He motioned with his dress sword at the group.

"Y-yes sir," said the boy.

"What catches your eye about them the most?"

The boy looked at Townsend in surprise, almost disbelief. "Why, the medals, sir. It's all the medals they have."

Townsend released the boy and walked on, deep in thought. "The medals," he said to himself, "the medals." Townsend was a man who believed in his hunches. That very afternoon, back in his office, he wrote a report to his superior, Edwin M. Stanton, the Secretary of War, on the subject of creating an American medal of honor for gallantry and distinguished service. He mentioned the foreigners' medals specifically. "They are objects of envy to many of our young aspirants to glory," he said.

The following week Colonel Townsend conferred informally with Secretary of War Stanton on the subject. Secretary of the

Navy Gideon Welles was present. Secretary Stanton was cautious. "I am in favor of this medal proposal," he stated, "but we must proceed carefully. There will be detractors in high places. I understand that the old general has always opposed medals on the grounds they are too European."

The "old general" referred to by Secretary Stanton was Lieutenant General Winfield Scott, the highest ranking officer in the Army, seventy-five years old and sick with dropsy, recently removed as General in Chief but still an influential voice. General Scott had often expressed his disapproval both publicly and privately of the wearing of military medals.

Gideon Welles smiled at his cautious colleague. "Proceed cautiously if you like, Mr. Stanton, but I am in favor of such a medal and will make inquiries at once of Congress to have a bill passed creating one for the Navy. General Scott shall exert no undue influence over sailors." Secretary of Navy Welles bowed to the Secretary of War and his Adjutant General and excused himself.

Thus, the Navy medal came first.

The original act creating the Navy Medal of Honor was introduced in the Senate by Senator James W. Grimes of Iowa. It was signed by President Lincoln on December 21, 1861. The Army would not have its Medal of Honor for another six months.

Because of this initial legislation the Medal has been referred to through the years as the "Congressional" Medal of Honor. Congressional legislation created the Navy Medal in 1861 and the Army Medal in 1862, empowering the individual departments to make their own awards. Congress can make individual awards of the Medal on its own initiative and has done so on several occasions, but these are exceptions to the general rule. From the very beginning Medals of Honor were generally awarded on the sole initiative of the military service involved.

The original piece of legislation, approved as law December 21, 1861, was called "The Act to Promote the Efficiency of the Navy." Section Seven of this act authorized the Secretary of the Navy to prepare two hundred Medals of Honor "with suitable emblematic devices." The original number authorized for manufacture proved to be conservative. The Navy ultimately awarded three hundred and twenty-seven Medals—three hun-

dred and ten to sailors and seventeen to Marines—for services in the Civil War.

This act stated that the Medal might be bestowed upon petty officers, seamen, landsmen, and marines. (A landsman was a sailor who had never before been to sea; he became a seaman after his first voyage.) Officers were excluded on the grounds that gallant conduct was merely part of their duty as officers and gentlemen, and need not be rewarded. The requirements for winning were "gallantry in action and other seamanlike qualities," and the last phrase was to open the door to a number of awards not connected with heroism at all.

The following is an extract from "The Act to Establish and Equalize the Grade of Line Officers of the United States Navy," approved by the President July 16, 1862.

> Section 10. And be it further enacted, That . . . seamen distinguishing themselves in battle or by extraordinary heroism in the line of their profession may be promoted to forward warrant officers or acting master's mates, as they may best be qualified, upon the recommendation of their commanding officer, approved by the flag officer and the Department. Upon such promotion they shall receive a gratuity of one hundred dollars and a medal of honor to be prepared by the Navy Department.

This section gives an insight into the thinking at the time regarding the Medal. The "medal of honor" was a third-place, tail-end appendage to a promotion and a prize of one hundred dollars.

The original Navy design was a five-pointed star, tipped with trefoils, containing a crown of laurel and oak in the middle of thirty-four stars, the number of states in 1862. The goddess Minerva, personifying the United States, stands with left hand resting on fasces (authority) and in her right hand holds a shield blazoned with the U.S. arms. Minerva is in the act of repulsing Discord, represented by snakes, and her militant attitude prompted one ardent Unionist to say, "She repulses Discord and the foul spirit of secession."

These original Medals were designed and engraved at the United States Mint in Philadelphia and were originally manufactured by William Wilson and Sons of that city.

The Army soon followed the Navy in initiating Medal of Honor legislation.

On February 17, 1862, Senator Henry Wilson of Massachusetts rose in the Senate to introduce a resolution for the creation of an Army Medal of Honor to be presented to privates of the Army of the United States who distinguished themselves in battle. On May 13, 1862, Senator Wilson reported on his resolution, which in the interim had been amended. The resolution now called for presentation of medals to "enlisted men of the Army [not just privates] and voluntary forces who have [already] or may [in the future] distinguish themselves in battle during the present rebellion . . ." Officers were excluded under the original act and the Medal was temporary, created only for "the present rebellion," meaning the Civil War. The original resolution specified that the Medal would be awarded "for gallantry in action and other soldierlike qualities," and the last phrase was to haunt all decisions relating to Army awards for years to come. It was much broader and less specific than the phrase in the Navy act which allowed the award for heroic acts done "in line of profession."

This resolution was approved by the President July 12, 1862, and was amended to make Army officers eligible for the award on March 3, 1863.

During July of 1862, the head of the Philadelphia Mint furnished a drawing of the design approved for the Navy Medal to Secretary of War Stanton with the suggestion, prompted by thoughts of economy, that the same Medal design might be used for the Army. The design was accepted by the Army, with the modification that the Army Medal was to be topped with an eagle rather than an anchor.

From the very beginning the Army had a more lavish concept of how frequently the Medal was to be awarded. Whereas the Navy first ordered two hundred Medals manufactured, the Army's first order was for two thousand. Ultimately the Army issued over twenty-one hundred Medals during the Civil War as opposed to the Navy's three hundred and twenty-seven. The Army must have intended for the Medal to be a rather common decoration, for records show that in 1865 eight thousand additional Medals of Honor were ordered from the manufacturer. What ever happened to this huge inventory remains a mystery. There must have been several thousand of them left in stock somewhere when the Army changed its design in 1904.

The Congressional Act of March 3, 1863, was important not

only because it made officers eligible for the award, but also because in this act Congress appropriated $20,000 for the purchase of Medals from William Wilson and Sons. Since no Medals could be purchased prior to this act, none could be awarded. The Wilson Company contracted to manufacture the first two thousand Medals at a cost to the government of two dollars each. These Medals were delivered to the War Department in March of 1863. Thus—with the Civil War almost two years old—the services finally could award the Medal of Honor.

II

Armies and Flags

THE first Medals of Honor awarded were Army Medals issued personally by Secretary of War Edwin M. Stanton to six soldiers on March 25, 1863, just a few weeks after the first Medals were purchased. The recipients were six survivors of the Andrews Raid, a group of twenty-one volunteers led by a mysterious spy calling himself James J. Andrews, who in April of 1862 penetrated nearly two hundred miles south into Confederate territory and captured a railroad train at Big Shanty, Georgia. In the wild railroad chase which followed, they attempted to destroy bridges and tracks between Atlanta and Chattanooga. When their fuel ran out, they had to forsake their train and take to the woods. All were captured by Confederate cavalry. Seven, including James J. Andrews, were executed. The remaining fourteen stayed in a Confederate prison until October 1862, when eight escaped. The six remaining in prison were paroled on March 17, 1863, and made their way to Washington. These six were the ones who got the first Army Medals. Nineteen of the raiders ultimately received Medals. James J. Andrews, the civilian leader, never won the award.

The atmosphere in the Secretary of War's office for this first presentation of awards was quite informal. Stanton seemed especially taken with Private Jacob Parrott, the youngest mem-

ber of the group, who could not read or write. The Secretary offered to pay for his education. Parrott answered that while the war lasted he did not wish to go to school, but would rather go back and fight Rebels.

Stanton smiled and brought out the Medals, and handed them around. "Congress has by a recent law ordered medals to be prepared on this model, and your party shall have the first to be given in the war."

In addition to a Medal, Stanton gave each of the six a present of one hundred dollars from the Secret Service Fund. This gratuity was not called for in the Congressional act establishing the Army Medal, as it was in the act for the Navy, and this was one of the few times that a cash gratuity accompanied the award of an Army Medal of Honor.

The Andrews Raid occurred during April of 1862. The first Civil War deed to be later honored with the Medal had occurred almost a year before, on May 24, 1861, when the war was scarcely a month old. The Eleventh New York Infantry Regiment had arrived in Washington during the middle of May, and on May 24th crossed the river into Virginia to man defenses south of the capital. Alexandria, Virginia, just across the river, was a hotbed of Rebel intrigue.

As the Eleventh New York—natty in their new Fire Zouave uniforms—marched through Alexandria, there were scattered jeers and catcalls from the crowds lining the street. Suddenly a loud cheer burst forth. A Confederate flag fluttered to the top of the pole on the roof of the Marshall House, a hotel, one of the tallest buildings in town. Now the flag waved gaily in the breeze, a hated symbol of rebellion to the Union troops.

Colonel Ephraim E. Ellsworth, the hot-tempered commanding officer of the regiment, leaped from his horse and ran up the steps of the hotel closely followed by his batman, Private Francis E. Brownell. As the halted troops and bystanders watched, Colonel Ellsworth appeared on the hotel roof, shinnied up the pole and tore down the flag. The troops cheered when the colonel reappeared on the hotel steps, carrying the captured banner in his arms. The rejoicing was short-lived. A shot rang out. Colonel Ellsworth toppled forward, the flag still clutched to his breast, shot through the brain by an assassin later identified as a man named Jackson.

Private Brownell, the batman, whirled and fired, felling the

assassin. Then, charging forward, he dispatched the fallen man with his bayonet. Thus died the assassin and Colonel Ephraim E. Ellsworth, the first Union officer killed in the Civil War, a Rebel flag clutched to his chest.

Brownell's Medal was not awarded until 1877, over ten years after his deed, and then at his own instigation. He applied to the War Department for a Medal of Honor in July of 1874 and was turned down. Then he interested his congressman in his case and was subsequently awarded the Medal on January 26, 1877. Brownell was the first man to receive the Medal for killing an assassin, but he would not be the last.

The Civil War has been called the last old-fashioned war. Due to the short range of weapons, it was fought up close. With no automatic weapons fire, there was less creeping and crawling than in modern warfare. Attacks were simple and direct. Exposed men ran forward behind their flags and standards in close-order ranks. When the man carrying the flag fell, there was a scramble to pick it up. Carrying the colors was an honor and the worst disgrace that could befall a unit was to have its colors captured.

Because flags were so important to the Civil War soldier, the most common Medal-winning acts involved them. The citations display an almost monotonous repetition:

"Planting national colors on enemy works"
"Taking guidon from hands of fallen color-bearer"
"Capturing enemy flag"
"Recapture of flag"
"Captured standard bearer, his horse and his equipment"
"Capture of flag and Confederate general with horse and equipment" (Note that the general is secondary to the captured flag.)
"Gallantry as a color-bearer."

When Lieutenant Tom Custer of the Sixth Michigan Cavalry leaped his horse across the barricade at Sailors Creek in April of 1865 to capture the enemy's regimental colors, there was a resounding cheer as he galloped back with the captured colors fluttering out behind. The ovation was no less resounding when he repeated the feat the next week at Namozine Church. He was awarded two Medals of Honor for these deeds. And he wore both of them on formal occasions, to the slight chagrin of his older and more famous but un-Medaled brother, General

George A. Custer. The general once noted with a touch of acid in correspondence with his wife that "Tom appeared at formal mess last evening wearing both of his baubles."

Sergeant John G. Merritt of the First Minnesota Volunteers found out at the First Battle of Bull Run that capturing Confederate colors was serious business. He and a companion saw a Confederate carrying a flag about thirty yards away. They slipped forward quietly and grabbed the colors from the hapless Rebel's hands. Then Merritt and his companion fled, laughing and whooping. There was a sudden, angry screech from the woods and a large band of Confederates burst forth, firing and giving forth their bloodcurdling yells. Merritt's companion pitched forward, the top of his head blown off. Merritt, wounded twice in the leg, managed to outdistance his pursuers and brought the flag back to his own lines. His leg had to be amputated, but he survived to wear his Medal for capturing the flag.

One of the daring flag deeds was accomplished by Major General Galusha Pennypacker, the youngest of the Civil War's general officers. Pennypacker, born June 1, 1844, was still too young to vote at the war's end. At Fort Fisher in 1865, Pennypacker commanded the brigade that attacked the fort from the land side while sixty warships struck from the sea. As his brigade faltered under the heavy fire from the fort, Pennypacker grabbed the colors of his former command, the Ninety-seventh Pennsylvania, and galloped forward waving the colors, calling for his old regiment to follow him. The men of the Ninety-seventh responded with great spirit and streamed after their youthful leader.

Pennypacker galloped his lunging horse up the fifth traverse and planted the flag at the top of the fort, the first Union colors on the works. Suddenly Pennypacker groaned and reeled from his saddle, rolling down the sharp incline of the battlements. A minie ball had struck him in the side, fracturing his pelvic bone. The wound was apparently fatal. A coffin was ordered for the young commander. When the coffin arrived, a surgeon, making a quick check before sending the body away, found him still alive. He was very much alive indeed, and stayed on active duty in the Army until retired in 1883. He died at age seventy-two in Philadelphia in 1916.

A Rebel mule won one Yankee first sergeant his Medal of

Honor during the Civil War. First Sergeant Francis Marion Cunningham, a descendant of the famous Swamp Fox, was a member of the First West Virginia Cavalry in the heavy fighting at Sailors Creek, Virginia, in April of 1865. While he was leading the last four men of the company, Cunningham's horse was shot out from under him. Stomping about on sore feet, he came upon a Confederate mule loose and wandering in a field. Cunningham threw his saddle on the mule and charged the Confederate works, his four men galloping along behind. Cunningham grabbed the Confederate colors and galloped back, bullets whizzing about his ears like angry bees.

General George A. Custer, who had observed the action, sent the sergeant to Washington the following month to present the colors to Secretary of War Stanton. Stanton in turn presented the sergeant a Medal of Honor.

Of course there were many other types of medal-winning deeds. The rescue of wounded officers and comrades was deemed important, as was continuing to engage in battle after being severely wounded. Then there were cases unique in themselves.

There was Major Harry E. Tremain of the U.S. Volunteers at Resaca, Georgia, in May of 1864, who rode between the lines while two Union brigades were firing at each other, each mistaking the other for the enemy. They were so set on shooting each other that Major Tremain had to ride down the length of the first ranks, knocking down their muskets with his sword.

Then there was Private Delano Morey of the Eighty-second Ohio, who won his Medal while his regiment was retreating before the onslaught of a superior Confederate force at McDowell, Virginia, in May of 1862. Morey saw two Confederate sharpshooters fire into the column and then begin to reload. Loading and firing a Civil War musket required eleven separate motions. Even with the most adept, loading took at least twenty seconds. Morey dashed up to the two Rebels as they frantically poured powder and rammed patches, and leveled his own piece at them. Grudgingly they surrendered. When Morey delivered his prisoners to his captain, the officer patted him on the head. "You're a good lad, Delano," he said. Morey was just sixteen years old. Later he found that in the excitement of capturing the two Confederates he had overlooked a small matter—his own gun had been unloaded at the time.

In that same campaign Brigadier General O. O. Howard won

the Medal for leading a charge at the Battle of Fair Oaks. As he galloped into the wild melee a bullet shattered his forearm. He did not stop. A few minutes later, another bullet smashed the elbow of the same arm. He fought on grimly, not seeking medical aid until the enemy was on the run. The surgeons at the field hospital amputated the shattered right arm.

In the hospital Howard was visited by General Phil Kearny. The wounded Howard was humorous even in his intense pain. "We must buy our gloves together now, General," he said. General Kearny smiled and agreed. He had lost his left arm in the Mexican War.

J. C. Julius Langbein was the rather pretentious name of a small and cherubic fifteen-year-old drummer boy of the Ninth New York Infantry. His girlish countenance caused many of the boisterous members of his regiment to call him "Jennie," a name which made him redden with acute discomfort. Langbein charged with his regiment at Camden, North Carolina, on April 19, 1862, rolling his drum smartly as he trotted after the colors. Casualties were so heavy that the charge was broken, and most of the survivors sought cover in a ditch along the road. A sergeant named Mossman, one of Langbein's most persistent teasers, wounded in the head, wandered dazedly in a field across the road, under heavy fire. Langbein sprang forward and grabbed the stricken man by the arm. Too small to carry the sergeant, Langbein piloted him slowly back to the Union lines in a whistling hail of bullets. At the field hospital a harassed and blood-spattered surgeon looked at Langbein's charge briefly and shook his head. "He's nearly dead and not worth while to remove." Langbein refused to leave the wounded sergeant, and stayed with him even after the Confederates attacked in force and the Union regiment began to retreat. Langbein staggered several miles along the road, the large wounded man leaning on him, until a sympathetic driver gave them a ride in a wagon. Langbein saw the sergeant safely to the Federal hospital at Roanoke before leaving him. The sergeant, who later recovered from his wounds, recommended the fifteen-year-old drummer boy for a Medal of Honor and it was subsequently awarded.

A group award of Medals of Honor was made at Vicksburg for an action occurring May 21, 1863. The siege of Vicksburg had begun May 19, and every assault had ended in great disaster. One of the principal obstacles was a defensive ditch

twelve feet wide and six feet deep. A one-hundred-and-fifty-man company of the Second Division volunteered to build a bridge across this ditch, thus enabling attacking waves to cross. As the volunteer company moved forward, laden with tools and timbers, the whooping Confederates opened an intense fire. Half of the volunteer bridge builders crumpled in their tracks. The remainder, taking shelter at the bottom of the ditch, fought back until darkness fell. Fifty-three survived, and all fifty-three received Medals of Honor.

Sixty-two Medals of Honor went for various deeds at the Battle of Gettysburg. One recipient was Major General Daniel E. Sickles, commander of the Third Corps at Devils Den. On July 2, 1863, when the feared Confederate General Longstreet, dubbed "The Bull of the Woods" by his contemporaries, made his famous charge, Sickles' Third Corps bore the brunt of the attack. General Sickles himself toppled from his horse, one knee shattered by grapeshot. The rumor spread among the troops that Sickles, an extremely popular commander, was dead. Well aware of Longstreet's deserved reputation for toughness and fearing lest his own troops crack, Sickles, notwithstanding his great pain, ordered a stretcher and had himself carried about the front lines where he gaily smoked a cigar and encouraged his men. The Union lines held firm and repulsed the assaults which followed.

The Civil War was the first American conflict in which chaplains of the various religious faiths served as commissioned officers in the United States Army, and during the Civil War three Army chaplains won Medals of Honor. Chaplain John M. Whitehead of the Fifteenth Indiana Infantry won his in December of 1862, at Stone River, Tennessee, by carrying wounded soldiers to the rear under heavy fire, and Chaplain Francis B. Hall of the Sixteenth New York Infantry performed similar valorous feats at Salem Heights, Virginia, the following May. Chaplain Milton L. Haney of the Fifty-fifth Illinois Infantry laid aside his non-combatant role at the Battle of Atlanta, July 22, 1864. When his unit reeled under an onslaught of Confederates, Chaplain Haney grabbed a musket from a fallen foe and led the charge that turned the tide and recaptured the Federal position.

The bemedaled foreign soldiers who had first dazzled the callow Union troops with their bright medals added several

names of the roster of Medal winners. Count Luigi Palma de-Cesnola, an Italian who had fought in the Crimean War, joined the Union Army as a lieutenant colonel in 1861. He won his Medal of Honor at the Battle of Aldie on June 17, 1863, while technically under arrest. Angered when a subordinate was promoted over him, the volatile Italian had challenged the upstart to a duel. General Judson Kilpatrick ordered Colonel deCesnola disarmed and placed under guard. When the battle began, deCesnola's regiment, the Fourth New York Cavalry, refused to charge without its commander. Ignoring his guards, the unarmed deCesnola galloped to the head of his troops and led them in three gallant charges against the enemy works. As deCesnola formed his regiment for the fourth and final charge, which would overrun the Confederate position, General Kilpatrick galloped forward and handed the Italian his own sword. Although his final charge was successful, deCesnola was shot from his horse and captured. He spent a term in Libby Prison, but was later exchanged in time to fight again for the Union in the Shenandoah campaign.

Swedish Baron Ernst von Vegesack was a major and aide-de-camp on the staff of General Daniel Butterfield, U.S. Volunteers, himself a Medal winner. At Gaines Mill, von Vegesack assumed command of the Twentieth New York, whose commander had been killed, and led them in a wild charge against the Rebel center. He refused to lower the high-flying colors of the regiment even when told they were drawing intense enemy fire. "The flag is our glory!" he reportedly shouted. Von Vegesack won the Medal of Honor for his gallantry in taking over command at a time of great crisis.

Another colorful foreign winner of the Medal was the Irish General Thomas Meagher. As a youthful participant in one of the Irish uprisings against British rule he had been condemned to death. Then, instead, he was sentenced to "transportation for life" to Tasmania. He escaped from Tasmania and came to America in 1852 to become one of the most widely known Union military leaders.

Several native Americans who later became famous military men won Medals during the Civil War.

Perhaps the most famous was General Arthur MacArthur. Failing to get an appointment to crowded West Point in 1861, MacArthur at seventeen was posted as First Lieutenant and Ad-

jutant of the Twenty-fourth Wisconsin Infantry. A year later he was a colonel. Commanding a regiment at the bloody battles of Resaca and Franklin, he was three times wounded. He won his Medal of Honor at Missionary Ridge, November 25, 1863, when he seized the colors at a critical moment and planted them on the captured works at the crest of the ridge. Entering the regular army after the Civil War, he retired as a lieutenant general in 1909. Arthur MacArthur was the father of General Douglas MacArthur of World War II fame, who won the Medal of Honor on Bataan. The MacArthurs are the only father and son Medal winners in history.

Another famous military name on the Civil War Medal list was General Nelson A. Miles, who won his Medal as a colonel in the Sixty-first New York Infantry for picket-line action at Chancellorsville in May of 1863. Miles, who made a colorful reputation as a fighting young officer with the Twenty-second Massachusetts early in the war, came to the Sixty-first New York in an unusual way. Determined to have a fighter to lead them into battle, the men of the Sixty-first New York kidnapped the dashing young captain from Massachusetts and made him their colonel. By May of 1864, when he was twenty-six years old, Miles was a brigadier general, one of the youngest in the Union Army. He served thirty-eight years more, achieved a colorful reputation as an Indian fighter and retired in 1902, as a lieutenant general.

The Civil War has been credited with many unique firsts. Among these were the first successful submarine, the first iron-clad ship, the first workable machine gun, and the first appearance of the wigwag signal code in battle. But by far the most amazing first of the Civil War appeared at the office of Lieutenant Colonel Edward D. Townsend, Assistant Adjutant General, in 1863. It was a woman, dressed like a man in dark gray trousers and black swallowtail coat, with a masculine face and short black hair parted in the middle—Dr. Mary Edwards Walker, who would be a thorn in the flesh of Townsend and other hapless members of the Washington military bureaucracy for years to come.

Dr. Walker presented documents and credentials showing that she had graduated from a recognized medical college in

Syracuse, New York, in 1855, and since that time had engaged
in the practice of medicine.

"I wish to volunteer my services as an assistant surgeon to a
regiment in the field," she stated.

Here was a pretty thing. It was strange enough that a female
would brave the unpleasantries of medical college and engage
in the practice of medicine—other than perhaps midwifery—
but to volunteer as a military surgeon! Colonel Townsend had
visited the battlefield after Bull Run and seen surgeons wielding their knives and bloody saws, like butchers in a vast slaugh-
terhouse. He had seen the gaping, jagged holes left by the minie
balls and smelled the burning flesh and heard the screams of
the writhing victims as the cauterizing irons were applied to
jagged stumps of arms and legs. A woman do that kind of work?

But the decision was not his. "I must refer you to the Surgeon
General," he said.

"Quite correct," said Dr. Walker, "but could I trouble you
for a letter of introduction to the Surgeon General?"

Colonel Townsend hesitated, then reached for pen and paper.

"And would it be too much to ask," Dr. Walker said, "to say
in the letter that there is nothing in the Army regulations
against the appointment of a woman as a surgeon?"

Colonel Townsend could think of no regulation against it.
And the woman apparently wanted to help the Union cause
. . . Townsend scribbled the observation as she requested. It
was a matter for the Surgeon General, anyway.

Dr. Walker's career with the medical department was stormy
from the beginning. Despite the absence of a disqualifying regulation, the Surgeon General refused to appoint her Assistant
Surgeon in the Army, with the accompanying rank of a commissioned officer, and reluctantly she went to work as a nurse in
an Army hospital, meanwhile continuing her efforts to become
a commissioned surgeon. During her time as a nurse she was a
constant source of annoyance to the male surgeons, addressing
them as equals, adamantly refusing to be relegated to the
menial position of female swamper and linen changer.

In November 1863, frustrated by the male fraternity of the
medical department, she wrote a letter to Secretary of War
Stanton asking permission to raise a regiment of men for war
service to be called "Walker's U.S. Patriots." She said she would

enlist men with criminal records who would volunteer for "the duration of the war." Apparently she intended to find most of her "patriots" in prisons and jails. She added at the end of the letter that her only stipulation regarding the officer personnel was that she would be the regimental surgeon.

Secretary Stanton declined the offer, voicing regret that more men did not have the militant spirit of this female doctor, and then, for some reason known only to him, sent her to General William T. Sherman, commander of the Army of the Tennessee, with the request that Sherman use her as a doctor in some way. Sherman, slightly amazed at the request, assigned her to a hospital. Within a short time she stood before him with a complaint.

"The men are making unseemly remarks about my attire," she said.

"Then why don't you wear a dress?" he asked.

"The male attire is more practical for my work," she said.

General Sherman refused to heed her complaint and sent the obstreperous female on her way. He later said to his adjutant, "Would you believe it, that damn fellow Stanton sent that woman out here just to bother me."

In March 1864, Dr. Walker appeared at the headquarters of General George H. Thomas, "The Rock of Chicamauga," then commanding the Army of the Cumberland. She volunteered for "special service" with the Fifty-second Ohio, a unit commanded by General Daniel McCook, then in close contact with the enemy. To volunteer for special service in the Civil War meant to work as a spy. General Thomas failed to find any reason to object. She might be useful, and an army could not have too many spies. There was one slight problem. The female doctor wanted to be posted to the Fifty-second Ohio as a commissioned assistant surgeon, as a "cover" assignment.

General Thomas agreed to send her, but made it plain her cover would be as an assistant *contract* surgeon—a civilian appointment—not as a commissioned surgeon.

Mary Walker would contend later with great tenacity and bitterness that her appointment had been in nature of a *commission,* not a contract. But that was not General Thomas's intent nor was it General McCook's understanding of her status when she reported to the Fifty-second Ohio later on in March. In her War Department file is a handwritten letter executed by

McCook, dated March 17, 1864, which says in part, "The female Doctor, not being a commissioned officer, cannot give a
valid receipt for property furnished her." The note went on to
authorize the quartermaster to furnish her with a horse and
saddle, despite the fact she could not execute a valid receipt.

While operating behind Confederate lines during April 1864,
Dr. Walker was captured. After being held prisoner for four
months at Libby Prison, she was exchanged from Castle Thunder, Richmond, for a Dr. Lightfoot from Tennessee in August
1864.

A few days after her release she strode into the office of the
Adjutant General in Washington. Colonel Townsend must have
greeted her with a melancholy premonition. Her problem was
one that he would hear about interminably in the years ahead.
Dr. Walker was without funds, and she felt there was money
due her from the government.

Townsend telegraphed General Thomas, asking him to clarify
the female doctor's status so that a settlement could be made
with her. Thomas telegraphed back the information that Dr.
Walker had gone on duty as an assistant contract surgeon on
March 11, 1864, and suggested she be paid for her service at the
standard rate of $80 a month from that date to the present.

Dr. Walker was unhappy with the arrangement. She was
positive that she had been given a commission and now it was
being taken from her. As a compromise she accepted a post as
head of the Female Prison at Louisville, Kentucky, until her
case could be acted on by the War Department.

At Louisville Dr. Walker began feuding immediately with
Dr. Brown, the male doctor in charge of the male military
prison. He insisted on visiting her wards and prescribing for
her patients. She managed, however, to obtain an order from
the local military commander which successfully enjoined him
from doing this. She did not savor her triumph long, however.

Chagrined by the female upstart, Dr. Brown recommended
she be examined by a military medical board, to determine
whether or not she was really qualified to practice medicine.
The Surgeon General was happy to oblige. From the perspec-
tive of the present—and in all fairness to Dr. Walker—it ap-
pears that the examining board was stacked against her.

A letter signed by Dr. Gross, the chief examiner, to the Surgeon General is blunt to the point of rudeness. The board found

her "utterly unqualified for her position." During the examination "she displayed ignorance of all branches of medicine." Her practical acquaintance with remedies was found to be "not greater than most housewives possess." As an afterthought, the board mentioned she did seem familiar with obstetrics and recommended she be employed as a nurse.

Dr. Walker fumed with anger, but to no avail. A month after the war ended in April 1865, her contract was terminated and she was paid the sum of $766.16 in settlement of all her claims against the government. The Civil War had ended, but to Mary Edwards Walker the hostilities had just begun.

Armed with testimonial letters from politicians throughout the country, she demanded that the War Department recognize her war services by commissioning her as a surgeon with the rank of major. She wrote not only Stanton and Townsend, but also Generals Sherman, McCook and Thomas. The recipients, forced to answer letters of inquiry from legislators and politicians about her, became so confused that several referred to her in correspondence as Major Walker. Thus was an illusion created that at one time she actually had been a commissioned officer in the Army.

Finally, she assaulted President Andrew Johnson himself with her correspondence. When the President appeared sympathetic, Dr. Walker was inclined to make a concession. She promised that if the President would confer the coveted rank of major on her, she would resign it at once, and never again ask for back pay.

President Johnson, sincerely interested in her case, felt that her services should be recognized in some way. He referred the matter to the Judge Advocate of the Army to see if a brevet commission might be conferred on her.

The Judge Advocate returned the opinion that conferring a brevet commission was impossible in her case. The brevet was an honorary promotion based on some substantive military rank, the legal officer stated. Since Mary Walker had never had a substantive military rank, then there was nothing on which to base a brevet.

After receiving this adverse opinion, President Johnson directed the Secretary of War to think of some way of recognizing her services.

Stanton reluctantly complied. There is a memorandum in the record dated November 13, 1865, from Colonel Townsend to John Potts, chief clerk of the War Department. "Secretary of War directs you have a Medal of Honor engraved by tomorrow for Dr. Mary E. Walker."

Thus Dr. Walker became an immortal female, the only one of her sex ever to win the Medal of Honor.

The Medal, along with a parchment commending her for duties during the Civil War, was presented to her by Colonel Edward D. Townsend on January 24, 1866. The citation read: "for services during the war from 1861 to 1865." The exact nature of these services was not set forth.

Once again, however, Colonel Townsend would find only temporary respite from Dr. Mary Walker.

III

Ships of Wood and Iron

THE mission of the United States Navy in the Civil War divided into three broad phases. First was the blockade of Southern ports, the thirty-five hundred miles of coastline extending from the Potomac to the Rio Grande. Then there were the campaigns on the great river systems within the country, the responsiblity of the mortar flotilla, the steam sloops and the gunboats. Finally, there was action on the high seas, a second blockade to stop leaks in the coastline watch.

The first Navy Medal-winning action in the Civil War was that of John Williams, Captain of the Maintop on the U.S.S. *Pawnee* in the attack on Mathias Point, Virginia, on June 26, 1861. This deed is cited with several others in General Order Number Eleven, dated 3 April 1863. As leader of a raiding party in a landing boat, Williams, who was ironically a native of New Orleans, was seriously wounded in the thigh but retained control of the boat. When the flagstaff was shot away, he

proudly held the flag aloft by the stump during the entire landing operation. Thus the symbol of the flag was as important in
the Civil War Navy as in the Army.

Two Navy men, Coxswain John Cooper and Boatswain's
Mate Patrick Mullen, won two Medals of Honor each for
deeds performed during the Civil War. Cooper won both of
his in different actions at Mobile. He was a gunner on the U.S.S.
Brooklyn during its battle with the Confederate ram *Tennessee*
in Mobile Bay on August 5, 1864, and manned his gun with
such skill and courage throughout the furious battle that he was
awarded his first. Serving as quartermaster on the same ship
the following April 26, 1865, he landed in a shore party. An intense fire was raging in the city and there were many wounded.
At the risk of being blown to pieces by exploding shells, he entered a burning building and rescued a wounded man, carrying
him on his back to a place of safety. This second deed also won
him a Medal.

Mullen served as boatswain's mate on the U.S.S. *Don.* During an expedition up Mattox Creek on March 17, 1865, he won
his first Medal for killing a score of Rebels with his howitzer
and causing their retreat. The following May 1st, he won another for rescuing an officer from drowning after a picket boat
swamped.

The famous battle between the first of the ironclads, the
Monitor and the *Merrimac,* was the background for another
Medal of Honor award. The battle between the two ironclads
had raged for over three hours, during which the *Monitor* was
struck twenty-two times by heavy shells from the Rebel ship—
nine times in the turret, eight times on the side armor, three
times on the deck and twice in the pilot house. The first time the
pilot house was struck, Peter Williams, a slight and wiry veteran
seaman who had boarded the *Monitor* in the Brooklyn Navy
Yard out of curiosity and found himself impressed as a steersman, was hurled to the deck stunned, but staggered back at
once to grasp the spinning wheel.

Then there was a sudden, stunning blast and blinding flash,
as the pilot house caught a direct hit. Williams found himself
on his hands and knees coughing in the smoke and fumes. The
pilot house was filled with light, for its roof had been blown off.
The captain writhed on the deck, covering his eyes with his
hands. "I'm blinded!" he gasped. "Call the first officer!"

Williams lunged back to the wheel, brought the staggering *Monitor* back on course, and continued to maneuver against the adversary. The *Virginia,* as the *Merrimac* had been rechristened, bore directly down on the Federal ship to ram her with the iron beak. Williams grimly turned the *Monitor* to meet the attack prow to prow. The two ironclads came together with a tremendous crash, and again Williams and the others in the pilot house were hurled to the deck.

After that tremendous onslaught, the *Virginia* backed away groggily. Unbeaten, but leaking badly and minus her iron beak, she limped back for sanctuary at Norfolk, and the bruised and blackened crew of the *Monitor* voiced a loud cheer. Peter Williams, the "volunteer" steersman on the *Monitor,* won the Medal of Honor for his part in the battle.

But the converted *Virginia* was not the last Confederate ironclad that would threaten the Federal blockade. Toward the end of the war in 1864, a menacing little monstrosity called the *Albemarle,* one hundred and twenty-two feet long and forty-five feet in the beam, stuck her iron beak down the Roanoke River in North Carolina. She was sheathed in heavy planks but had a raised octagonal shield amidships plated with four inches of iron. Her ramming beak was a heavy oaken pole, covered with iron and ground sharp as a spear. She was propelled through the water by two engines of four hundred horsepower each. She first wallowed down-river in April 1864, and sank or damaged several Yankee ships by crashing her deadly beak into them broadside. The effect of heavy shot on her was described by an observer. "The solid shot would bound from the roof into the air like marbles. Fragments even of our one-hundred-pound rifle shots, at close range, came back to our own decks." After wreaking a considerable amount of havoc, the *Albemarle* turned ponderously and steamed back up-river to drop anchor off the town of Plymouth. The Rebels built a floating cordon of chained cypress logs around her, as protection against torpedo attack. As additional security, a picket schooner was anchored fifty yards down-river to stand between the enemy and the deadly little ram.

During the next few months the *Albemarle* made several more forays down-river and into Albemarle Sound, sinking and crippling many Federal ships and menacing the blockade. Several daredevil attempts were made by individual Union sail-

ors to blow up the ram by swimming or paddling up-river past the picket boat with explosive charges. All of these attempts were frustrated by alert Rebel pickets, but three of the sailors won Medals of Honor for their unsuccessful attempts. One of this group was Charles Baldwin, Coal Heaver, U.S.N., of the U.S.S. *Wyalusing,* who tried to swim in under cover of darkness towing two large torpedoes. The Rebel picket boat put out flares and Baldwin had to cut loose from his torpedoes and splash frantically back down-river in a hail of rifle fire.

On the night of October 27, 1864, Lieutenant W. B. Cushing led a volunteer party to destroy the *Albemarle.* Under cover of darkness he steamed up-river in a thirty-foot launch, towing a cutter filled with armed sailors who were to deal with the Rebels on the picket schooner if the launch was challenged. Attached to the prow of the launch was a long spar-torpedo.

Cushing's party crept past the picket schooner—within thirty feet—without being challenged. Now he began to hope that he could board the ram with his men and take over with pistols, cutlasses and bombs. But the way was blocked by the chained log-boom. Then there was a sudden shout and a huge bonfire on shore flared up, flooding the scene with a bright, flickering light.

Casting off the cutter to fend for itself, Cushing drove the launch forward with a full head of steam for the barrier. As he stood at the helm his coat was ripped by enemy fire and he was wounded in the hand. He drove the launch crashing into the barrier. As he had hoped, the cypress logs were slimy and the little launch lurched up over them, approaching to within ten feet of the Rebel ironclad. Lowering the torpedo boom under the prow of the ram, Cushing pulled the lanyard. There was an earsplitting crash as the charge blew up almost in his face. Torrents of water and bits of broken logs and chain rained down.

Cushing shucked his clothes and leaped into the water. He was twelve miles up-river from the Federal fleet. Somehow he made it back, almost freezing in the river, and once ashore crawling on hands and knees past Rebel sentries. When he finally hailed a Union picket boat the next night, he had to argue to convince the sentry he was not a Rebel spy. His whole party was thought to have perished in the explosion of the ram. When word spread through the fleet that he had survived, the

men cheered and sent up rockets. Seven Medals of Honor were ultimately awarded to the crew of the launch which crashed the barrier and blew up the ram. Cushing, the leader, probably the bravest of all, was not, as a Navy commissioned officer, eligible for the award.

The Naval ratings of many of the Civil War Medal winners are amusing to the present-day reader. There were landsmen, coal heavers, and a jack o' the dust or two. James Machon, who won the Medal on board the U.S.S. *Brooklyn* at Mobile Bay on August 5, 1864, was listed as "Boy, USN." Then there were captains of the foretop, captains of the maintop, and captains of the forecastle. One of the most unusual ratings was that assigned to Robert Blake, an escaped Negro slave, who was awarded the Medal of Honor for serving his rifle gun bravely in action against the enemy aboard the U.S. Steam Gunboat *Marblehead* on December 25, 1863. Blake was rated in the citation as "contraband, USN."

Several of the deeds listed in the citations had humorous overtones. For example, Robert T. Clifford, Master-at-Arms on board the U.S.S. *Shokokon,* slipped ashore off Wilmington, North Carolina, on August 22, 1863, and "gallantly crept into the Rebel camp and counted the men who outnumbered his party three to one." What he did with this intelligence is not set forth. Probably he decided, rationally, not to attack.

Then there was the case of Christopher Nugent, Orderly Sergeant, USMC, the leader of a landing party on the Crystal River in Florida in June 1863. Nugent drove a group of eleven Rebels into the swamp "while gallantly withholding fire to prevent harm to a woman among the fugitives."

Then there was John Smith, Captain of the Forecastle on the U.S.S. *Lackawanna* in Mobile Bay in August 1864. In close fighting alongside the Rebel ironclad *Tennessee,* "Smith threw a hand holystone into one of the ports at a Rebel using abusive language against the crew of the ship."

The Medal was given a sailor in the Civil War for tossing a well-aimed bucket of water. Seaman Thomas Barton on board the U.S.S. *Hunchback* on October 3, 1862, was helping to man a howitzer in the attack on Franklin, Virginia. "When an ignited shell, with cartridge attached, fell out of the howitzer

upon the deck, Barton promptly seized a pail of water and threw it upon the missile, thereby preventing it from exploding."

Disposing of a hot bomb or shell has a long tradition as a Medal-winning act. Ordinary Seaman James K. L. Duncan won his Medal on the U.S.S. *Ft. Hindman* during the Civil War in this way. "Following a shellburst at one of the guns which started a fire at the cartridge tie, Duncan immediately seized the burning cartridge, took it from the gun and threw it overboard, despite the immediate danger to himself."

The case of Ordinary Seaman Philip Bazaar was unique among the Navy Civil War awards of the Medal. Bazaar, as a member of the crew of the U.S.S. *Santiago de Cuba,* distinguished himself during the assault on Fort Fisher on January 15, 1865. He was awarded his Medal in General Order One Hundred and One, dated 15 June 1914, nearly fifty years after the act. But late Civil War awards, which would cause so much criticism in the Army, were rare in the Navy.

One of the great sea battles of the Civil War occurred June 19, 1864, in the English Channel off Cherbourg, France, far from the blockaded coasts of the Confederacy. The ships involved were the Confederate raider *Alabama* and the Yankee battleship U.S.S. *Kearsarge.*

During the battle the ships made seven turns of the circle, guns firing so rapidly that smoke often hid them from spectators lining the cliffs on the French coast. In the midst of the grapeshot and flying iron, Quartermaster William B. Poole and Steersman James Saunders stood calmly at the helm of the *Kearsarge,* maneuvering the ship in response to orders from the bridge. They remained unmoved when an eight-inch shell struck the wooden sternpost beneath them and miraculously failed to explode.

The spectators ashore noted the difference in firing. The *Kearsarge*'s gun flashes were livid with flame, while the *Alabama*'s were densely black. The Yankee gunners shot for the waterline of the raider, opening great holes, and swept the deck and rigging with iron canister. The deck of the Confederate was littered with mutilated bodies. The deadly and efficient work of the Yankee gun crews was recognized in Medal awards

after the engagement. Thirteen of the fifteen Medals awarded
went to gunners, spongers, loaders and crew captains. Poole
and Saunders received the only other awards. The award came
at a fortunate time for Saunders. A few days before the battle
he had gotten drunk in Flushing, Holland, and wrecked a local
bar. He had been released temporarily from the brig to join in
the battle. His punishment was canceled because of his distinguished service in combat.

The ages of the Navy Medal winners of the Civil War were
not generally set forth in the records but one of the youngest
must have been George Hollat, third-class boy on the gunboat
Varuna at the capture of New Orleans by Admiral Farragut in
1862. Hollat was fifteen years old, a proud member of the crew
of the midship's gun, a smoothbore muzzle-loader which bore
the proud painted red letters "Red Rover."

Working a muzzle-loading Civil War gunboat cannon was no
job for a weakling. Stripped to the waist and barefoot, with
bandannas knotted on their heads, the crew sanded the decks
carefully before going into battle. Sand helped keep your
footing when the decks became slippery with blood. In battle
the crew had to show speed and muscle. After firing, they ran
the gun in with tackles so the muzzle could be serviced inside
the bulwark of the ship. A huge sponge, dripping with water,
was shoved in first to extinguish any remaining powder fire.
Then powder charges in bags were rammed home, and finally
the shell. Straining mightily, the sweating crew ran the loaded
gun out to the limit of the tackles and then the gun captain
thrust the priming wire through the vent hole in the breech
to pierce the powder bags, so that the flame from the primer
could make direct contact with the charge. The gun was fired
by the gun captain who sighted the gun and pulled the lanyard.
The crew then cowered back in the narrow confines as the belch-
ing monster kicked backward on the recoil ropes. God help
them all if the ropes broke. When that happened, the recoiling
gun crashed through to the opposite side of the ship, crushing
and killing everyone in the way.

As the Union fleet entered the mouth of the Mississippi that
night in April 1862, the Confederate forts along the river gave
them a warm reception. The defenders lit huge bonfires on

shore to light up the scene for their artillery and sent fire rafts, blazing hotly with burning pitch, down-river against the invading fleet.

As the *Varuna* closed with the Rebel gunboat *Morgan,* Red Rover took a direct hit, just as she was being run out to fire. The gun exploded, bursting the recoil ropes and smashing out the opposite side of the ship through a gaping hole. With blood-curdling Rebel yells the triumphant crew of the *Morgan* prepared to board the stricken *Varuna.* Hollat, the only surviving member of the Red Rover crew, grabbed a cutlass and led the defense, chopping away frenziedly at the boarders. The *Varuna,* sinking and almost helpless, collided with the *Morgan,* but the defenders were able to fight off the boarding party and get her to shore. There she was tied to trees with a bowline and the survivors taken from her by other ships of the Union fleet.

George Hollat, fifteen years old, won a Medal of Honor for his part in the action.

One of the last of the Navy Medal-winning acts of the Civil War was that of Landsman Aaron Anderson of the U.S.S. *Wyandank,* who was a member of a boat crew attempting to clear a creek of Confederate snipers on March 17, 1865. As Anderson pulled at his oar, a sniper shot it in two. Obtaining another oar, Anderson managed only two more strokes before the sniper shot that one in two. Seeking to eliminate his tormentor once and for all, Anderson grabbed a musket and aimed at the sniper's hiding place. Before he could fire, the Rebel sniper shot the barrel off Anderson's musket. Apparently, Anderson was awarded his Medal of Honor for dogged perserverance in the face of great adversity.

IV

The Bloody Years on the Plains

HISTORIANS today have a tendency to look disparagingly upon the Army awards of the Medal of Honor during the

Indian Wars. Little formal investigation was made of claims for the award. Detachment commanders, after observing a member of their command perform a heroic or gallant act, wrote a letter to the War Department and sometimes a Medal was issued. Presentations were certainly informal. A dusty mail rider delivered the Medal by registered mail at the isolated outpost, and if the winner happened to be absent on a scout, the first sergeant signed for the package and threw it on the soldier's bunk.

Sometimes the winner was no longer there by the time the Medal arrived. He might lie in an unmarked grave on the prairie or have been transferred to another post. Or his enlistment may have expired and then he had just drifted on, disappearing forever over the horizon in a cloud of dust, the way a man could in those days. Perhaps he was hiding from the law or a deserted wife back in the States and had enlisted under a false name. Then when he drifted on, no photograph or fingerprints being on record to identify him, the Medal would be returned to Washington and the bureaucratic paper shuffling begun as War Department clerks dipped their quill pens and started the endless correspondence in longhand to find the winner or his heirs, or someone who could legally sign for the troublesome registered package.

Army historians generally classify the period of the Indian Wars as extending from 1861 to 1898. During this period the Army awarded four hundred and sixteen Medals of Honor. With two exceptions—the first and last exploits, respectively— all these Medals were awarded for events occurring between March 25, 1865, and December 30, 1891.

The first deed chronologically which won an Army Medal of Honor for action against Indians was, in fact, the first deed *chronologically* to win any Medal of Honor, either Army or Navy. On February 13-14, 1861, before the Medal was even created by Congress, Assistant Surgeon Bernard J. D. Irwin, a graduate of New York Medical College and a commissioned officer, voluntarily led a rescue party to the aid of a troop of U.S. Cavalry surrounded by hostile Apaches near Apache Pass, Arizona. The rescue attempt was successful. Irwin ministered to the numerous wounded of the troop and then led a fighting dash that broke through the encircling ring of Indians. Thirty-three years after the deed—in 1894—Irwin, by that time a colo-

nel in the Army, made application for the Medal of Honor for this deed, and the Medal was awarded.

The most famous surgeon Medal winner of the Indian Wars was Leonard Wood, who was twenty-six years old and Assistant Surgeon with the Fourth U.S. Cavalry when he won his Medal. Wood joined the Army after graduation from Harvard Medical School and was sent to the Arizona Territory. In May 1885, he volunteered to carry dispatches on a hundred-mile trip through country teeming with hostiles. He made the trip, seventy miles during the night while mounted and thirty miles the next day on foot. Later on in the campaign he showed his superiors he knew more about military matters than just probing and bandaging wounds and spooning out castor oil and quinine to the troops. Taking command of an officerless infantry detachment, he led his men gallantly in several skirmishes.

The citations for Indian War awards were inconsistent, ranging from full descriptive paragraphs to the single word "bravery." Individual units turned out distinctively stereotyped phraseology. Harassed and overworked adjutants followed the standard Army practice of pouncing on a phrase that had worked before in getting the Medal and then beating the phrase soundly to death. In the 1860's the standard phrase for the Eighth Cavalry, on duty in Arizona, was "bravery in scouts and actions against enemy." During 1873, when the Eighth was on duty at Fort Selden, New Mexico, the standard phrase was "services against hostile Indians." In the late 1870's the phrase common to many of the units stationed in Arizona was "gallant conduct during campaigns and engagements with Apaches."

Certain basic disputes appeared for the first time, disputes which have not been fully resolved to this day. In 1869 a number of Medals were recommended and subsequently awarded for troopers of the Eighth Cavalry with the non-specific citation, "bravery in scouts and actions against Indians," the period specified vaguely as "from August to October 1868," and the locale as "Arizona." One of the most unusual citations on record was that for Sergeant Frederick W. Gerber of the U.S. Engineers who received the Medal on his retirement from the Army in 1871. His citation reads, "Distinguished gallantry in many actions and in recognition of long, faithful, and meritorious service covering a period of thirty-two years."

Twelve Indians won Medals of Honor during the Indian Wars. These were Indian scouts on active duty with the Army. They had military status, as opposed to the white scouts, contract surgeons, teamsters and packers, who retained civilian status. They are carried on the rolls by single names such as Rowdy, Blanquet, Chiquito and Jim. An unusal citation was the one for Co-rux-te-chod-ish, a sergeant in the Pawnee Scouts commonly known as "Mad Bear." His deed was the first of the Indian scouts, occurring July 8, 1869, on the Republican River in Kansas. From the facts set forth in the citation it is hard to say just why he was awarded a Medal, other than perhaps to soothe ruffled feelings. The citation stated that Co-rux-te-chod-ish ran out from his own command in pursuit of a dismounted hostile Indian and was shot down and badly wounded by gunfire from his own men. That was all. The disgruntled Indian may have acquired the name "Mad Bear" on the spot in a display of fury at being shot down by his brother redskins.

Ten of the Indian scout Medal awards had identical citations: "Gallant conduct during campaigns and engagements with Apaches." These were given for action during the winter of 1872-73 in the Arizona Territory when the Apache chief Cochise was finally subjugated. Cochise began his depredations in 1860. Operating from his stronghold in the Dragoon Mountains, he murdered more white men than any other Indian leader. The nemesis of Cochise was General George Crook, a well known Civil War general sent to the frontier in 1870 to campaign against Indians. Crook's appearance was not prepossessing. He was a slouchy-looking bearded man, who generally wore an old black hat and a long cotton duster covering a civilian suit of clothes. Many of the men who served under him on the frontier never saw him in military uniform until he was dead and lying in state in his coffin. The plain-clothes general had a natural bent for fighting Indians and a gift of knowing how to pit them against each other. Within the tribes there was constant and bloody feuding between individual bands. During the summer of 1872 and the following winter, Crook used Indian against Indian to such good advantage that Cochise sued for peace. Ten of the Apache scouts who fought with Crook were awarded Medals of Honor. All these Medals were issued August 12, 1875, and presented to the winners at Fort Bowie, Arizona Territory.

Famous battles of the Indian War period naturally generated large numbers of awards. No Indian War battle is more famous than the one on the Little Big Horn, Montana Territory, in June 1876, sometimes called Custer's Last Stand. In this battle, Custer and his two hundred and sixty-four men were surrounded by about three thousand Sioux led by Sitting Bull, and the Custer command died to the last man. The Battle of the Little Big Horn is part of the Custer legend, but it is also part of the history of the Medal of Honor. While the yellow-haired General Custer, who had never won the Medal of Honor, and his brother Tom, who had won two, fought their last fight against the hordes of painted savages, the rest of the Seventh Cavalry just two miles away was also under attack. This portion of the Seventh fought Indians for three long days. A section of the prairie was ablaze, cutting off the beleaguered group from water. The waves of heat from the blazing sun and the burning grass were intense. The troopers, crouched behind their supply wagons and the corpses of their dead horses, fired grimly at their attackers, blinking red-rimmed and burning eyes in the stinging smoke. Everywhere the wounded writhed and cried weakly for water. Somehow, in spite of the burning prairie and the Indian bullets and arrows, a few of the troopers managed to make it to the river and bring back water. Peter Thompson, one of the volunteer water carriers, was wounded in the head, but staggered to and from the water point twice more.

Others who carried water to the wounded were Privates Neil Bancroft, Abram B. Brant, and Theodore W. Goldin. Blacksmith Henry Mechlin took up a position on the stream bank and fought off the Indians who tried to shoot the carriers as they filled their buckets.

Suddenly in the shattering melee of screeches, curses and gunfire, an Army pack mule loaded with ammunition bolted from the perimeter and stampeded into the encircling ring of Indians. Sergeant Richard P. Hanley put the spurs to his unwounded horse and galloped after the fleeing mule, making a wild chase among the surprised Indians. Hanley pursued the mule for over ten minutes, knocking over Indians and trampling them. He finally caught the mule and led it back to his own lines without ever being scratched. Hanley and the water carriers ultimately received Medals of Honor for their deeds.

After the battle, Brigadier General Alfred A. Terry, Depart-

ment Commander, was appalled by the great number of rec-ommendations made by the company commanders for Medal awards. General Terry wrote to Colonel Samuel F. Sturgis, com-mander of the Seventh Cavalry, that it seemed "company com-manders have recommended every man . . . that behaved ordinarily well during the action . . ." General Terry rejected the entire list. He directed Colonel Sturgis to convene a board of officers and review the recommendations, approving only those whose acts "far exceeded any just demand of duty."

The review board was convened, the first of its kind in his-tory, and twenty-two soldiers were approved for Medals. The list was approved by Colonel Sturgis, General Terry and finally by Lieutenant General Phil Sheridan. On August 29, 1878, over two years after the Battle of the Little Big Horn, these twenty-two soldiers were awarded Medals. This first Army dec-orations board set a precedent in raising the standard required for winning the award.

During the 1890's two old troopers, Privates Thomas J. Callan and Theodore W. Goldin, veterans of the battle, de-cided they had been overlooked and submitted applications for Medals of Honor directly to the War Department, describ-ing their deeds as water carriers. They were awarded Medals, making the grand total of awards for the Battle of the Little Big Horn twenty-four in all.

In Indian War citations one name appeared again and again. "For bravery in action against Geronimo." "For gallantry in pursuit of Geronimo." "For gallant conduct in a campaign against Geronimo." The name Geronimo was terror in Arizona and Mexico. Among his pursuers was First Lieutenant Marion P. Maus, a man who, unlike many of his colleagues, actually caught up with Geronimo and lived to tell about it.

The year 1885 in Arizona witnessed the greatest Apache break-out in history from the reservations around Fort Bowie. Early that spring the Chiricahua medicine man Goylothay—called Geronimo the Orator by the Mexicans—led four hun-dred of his tribe off the reservation and south to the "ghost line," as the Indians called the Mexican border, firing their rifles at the pursuing Indian police. Once across the border, the renegades drifted south toward the Sierra Madre Mountains, believing themselves safe from pursuit in Old Mexico.

But unknown to Geronimo, the United States had negoti-
ated a "hot trail" treaty with Mexico, enabling troops of either
country to cross the border when in hot pursuit of Indians. So
the blue-clad Long Knives ignored the ghost line and galloped
deep into Mexico after the Apaches. But to no avail. The ragged
Apaches on their gaunt little ponies vanished like puffs of
smoke before the thundering cavalry. By November it was
painfully clear that the campaign of 1885 was a failure.

Then the bloodthirsty Geronimo, unscathed but angered by
the defiance of the ghost line and the unwillingness of the other
Apaches in Arizona to follow him, sent his dark angel Josanine,
a youthful chief, with ten warriors back across the border to
wreak vengeance against whites and his cowardly red brothers
as well. The dwarfish raiders, naked-legged and wearing only
dirty twisted breechcloths, scuttled along the rocky ridges,
avoiding troops and preying on the unwary. They slew thirty-
eight whites, mostly women and children on isolated ranches,
gutting them and building fires on their faces. Then, with coun-
tenances painted horribly black and yellow, they fell on their
old reservation, killing twenty-one of their people, mostly
squaws and children, in a fierce, bloody raid. Josanine and his
men covered twelve hundred miles in four weeks, eating liz-
ards, snakes, rabbits and their own horses. They slipped un-
spied through country guarded by forty-three companies of infantry, forty troops of cavalry, and hundreds of Apache scouts,
without once being seen by anyone who lived to tell about it.
Then the band disappeared back into Mexico as mysteriously
as it had come.

General George Crook, the old plain-clothes general, was ordered back from his campaigns against the Sioux in the Dakotas to command again the Department of Arizona. Crook felt
he had no choice. The bloody raid must be avenged in blood
but regulars had proved ineffective in trailing the renegades
into Mexico. He would send Apache scouts, commanded by
white officers, down to the Sierra Madres to search out Geronimo and his band. Crook picked his officers carefully. In command he put Captain Emmet Crawford, a meticulous young
West Pointer in mustache and goatee, a veteran of several Indian campaigns. The second in command was First Lieutenant
Marion P. Maus, a stocky bulldog-type officer, who had fought
the Sioux with Crook on the Rosebud. Two young second lieu-

tenants were also detailed to go, as well as an assistant surgeon.

A week later the white officers inspected their ragtag army with mixed feelings. They found it hard to share their general's enthusiasm for Indian troops. A hundred White Mountain and Chiricahua Apaches trooped past in a straggling line on barebacked ponies. Issued complete Army uniforms that morning, they now wore only the undershirts and tunics, having thrown away the trousers and shoes. They rode with dangling, bare legs ending in high boot-topped moccasins. Each scout carried a Winchester or Springfield rifle and wore two bandoliers of cartridges crossed on his chest. Each wore his personal "medicine" or lucky piece—a tuft of cardinal feathers, the head of a quail, the wings of a woodpecker, the feet of a prairie dog, a bright button, a piece of broken glass, the charred splinter from a tree that had been struck by lightning.

On December 1, 1885, the column straggled south out of Fort Bowie. From the first, Captain Crawford proved to be of a distant and detached turn of mind, expecting Maus, his second in command, to handle routine command functions. Maus and the two young shavetails tried to keep the unruly army in some sort of military formation. Behind the column stretched a lengthening string of heliograph stations. General Crook wanted to maintain contact with the flashing mirrors as long as possible.

The column crossed the Mexican border at Nacori, leaving behind the last heliograph station perched high on the sawtooth ridge above the town. When the expedition disappeared over the horizon from that hill, they were cut off from all contact with friendly authorities north of the border.

Mostly the Indian scouts were docile. On rest days they roasted and ate the leaves of the century plant and danced, firing their rifles into the air. The white officers winced at the waste of ammunition, but said nothing. As the column straggled past villages, the peons watched fearfully. Apaches of any sort were demons from hell to the villagers.

The expedition spent Christmas Day 1885 at Huásabas, an oasis in the desert at the foot of the Sierra Madres. The scouts found mescal in the village and a wild orgy of drunkenness ensued. An Apache scout, staggering back to the village to get more of the fiery liquor, came suddenly on a village policeman. Shocked by the wild apparition of the drunken Apache, the jit-

tery policeman threw up his muzzle-loader and fired, killing the Indian instantly. When news of the killing reached camp, the Apache scouts began a drunken war-dance.

In Huásabas the villagers gathered at the church and prayed. They were defenseless against a hundred heavily armed Apaches. Muttering to each other apprehensively, the white officers sat up in their bedrolls all night, fingering their weapons. If the Indians fell on the village in a frenzy, the mood of awakened blood-lust might cause them to massacre the white officers as well.

Lieutenant Maus was busy elsewhere. He filled the biggest barrel that he could find in the village with mescal and brought it to the Indian camp on a cart. Then he spent the night forcing it on the Indians in huge dollops and encouraging them to dance. The gamble paid off. By daylight all of the Indians had passed out cold. When they awakened from their drunken orgy the dead comrade was forgotten in the misery of their hangovers.

At the edge of the mountains they picked up the trail of Josanine. The going was exhausting. The winter mountains were foggy and cold and full of bottomless canyons and high ridges. Captain Crawford began to weaken under the grind and offered no objection when Maus volunteered to take a party ahead to locate Geronimo's village. Two nights later Maus's group, far ahead of the main party, saw many camp fires on the ridges high in the clouds. It was Geronimo's camp. Anxiously they awaited the arrival of the main party.

On January 3rd Crawford and the main body dragged up, gasping in the thin air of the high altitude. Crawford's face was drawn and weary and even the Apache scouts were stumbling with fatigue. But the bulldog Maus was still bounding with energy, and, dividing his men into four groups, he led them to surround the Indian camp.

As dawn broke, two curious burros, nibbling the scant grass at the edge of the camp, spotted one group and ran into the camp, braying the alarm. Thus the battle was set off prematurely before all groups were in position.

The engagement was short and violent. Most of the braves, including Geronimo, managed to gallop off through a bottleneck canyon. The attacking scouts fired wildly into the milling crowd of squaws and children, inflicting many casualties.

When hostilities ceased, the attackers found they had captured the main camp and the supplies, along with most of the women and children, but no Geronimo. He and his fighting braves had escaped.

That night the victorious scouts, after looting the camp, made a bonfire of Geronimo's supplies and raped the captured women. The white officers, too exhausted to interfere, slept on the ground in the glare of the bonfire, deaf to the wails and screams of the violated squaws.

Next day as the officers argued hotly among themselves as to who was to blame for the premature attack, scouts ran in with startling news. A Mexican army was approaching! The discord ceased abruptly.

The approaching army was a group of Tarahumare Indians commanded by Mexican officers, ludicrously similar to the American group, except that the Tarahumares, unlike the Apaches, had not thrown away their uniform trousers. They wore the trousers around their necks like scarves, the legs tied together at the throat.

Bristling like angry dogs, the two packs of Indians stood off from each other muttering a mutual hatred. Apaches and Tarahumares were traditional enemies.

As Captain Crawford and Maus tried to parley with the Mexican officers in an open space between the two armies, firing suddenly broke out. Captain Crawford slumped forward, shot through the head. Maus picked up the stricken captain and ran back to his own group. The Mexican officers beat a hasty retreat to their side.

Crawford had a gaping hole in his head but was barely alive. After leaving him with the surgeon, Maus turned doggedly and walked back toward the Mexican group to parley again. The Mexican officers wanted the American pack mules, which Maus angrily refused.

Suddenly, from a high crag above and behind the Mexican force, a huge booming voice joined the argument. It was Geronimo, calling to his brother Apaches with the Long Knives to unite with his forces and destroy the common enemies, the Tarahumares.

Maus knew if Geronimo got control of his scouts, they would be lost forever and might turn on the white officers after the Tarahumares were taken care of. He turned grimly to the un-

nerved Mexican officers and threatened to accept the Apache's proposition. There ensued a mad scramble and a thunder of hoofs as the Mexican group galloped away.

As the common enemies left the area, Geronimo became more placating. He wanted to powwow with the white officer. Sensing that the loss of the women and supplies had made the old renegade receptive to argument, Maus moved forward with his interpreter.

Geronimo had the appearance of a sinister vaudeville character, wearing a sack coat so tight it pulled up under his arms and nothing below except a dirty breechcloth and boot moccasins. His skinny bowed legs were bare. He wore a bright orange bandanna around his straggling hair and his face had been rubbed with ground galena until it shone like black shoe polish.

As Maus had surmised, the old renegade wanted the squaws and children back. The old warrior kept shaking his head doggedly, his men still had their guns and would fight for the women and children. Maus listened somberly. His command was miles south of the border in a hostile territory and almost out of ammunition. His dead were numerous and the captain had a mortal wound.

Finally, Maus laid down his terms. Geronimo would get the squaws and children back but he had to agree to a meeting with General Crook the following March at the Cañon de los Embudos, just south of the border. And to insure good faith and the safe passage of the column back to the border, Geronimo must give hostages.

The old warrior grunted and complained, but finally gave in. When the American column pulled out, Natchez, the hereditary chief, and several of the minor chiefs rode along as hostages. Geronimo refused absolutely to give up Josanine or his band.

Captain Crawford, carried on a litter, died January 11, 1886, on the long road back. He was buried in a temporary grave at Nacori, just north of the ghost line. The heliograph, high on the sawtooth ridge, flashed the word of the column's return to to General Crook at Fort Bowie.

As a result of the expedition, Geronimo met with General Crook the following March at the Cañon de los Embudos as Maus had arranged. The old renegade reluctantly agreed to

cross back into American territory and cease his depredations. Thus one of the great Indian campaigns ended in victory for the Long Knives. Geronimo spent the rest of his life in Army custody and First Lieutenant Marion P. Maus was awarded the Medal of Honor. When the Medal was pinned on, the White Mountain and Chiricahua Apache scouts of his command beat the ground with their feathered prayer sticks and crooned a guttural song. The star of the Great White Father was strong medicine, they sang, stronger than the wings of a woodpecker or the feet of a prairie dog, stronger even than the beak of the sacred owl, or even the hands of Geronimo.

Not all of the Indian War Medal awards, strangely enough, involved actions against Indians. The citation of Private Allen Walker, Company C, Third Cavalry, is peculiar and certainly ambiguous. "While carrying dispatches, he attacked a party of three armed men and secured papers valuable to the U.S." This incident occurred in Texas in December of 1891. Who were the men he attacked and what were the papers, "valuable to the U.S."? The records do not say. And of course the men referred to in the citation were whites. If they had been Indians, under the universal custom of the day, they would have been designated as Indians.

Another non-Indian, Indian War Medal award was described in detail in the citation of Sergeant James Fegan, Company H, Third U.S. Infantry, awarded his Medal for a deed near Plum Creek, Kansas, in March of 1868. "While in charge of a powder train en route from Fort Harker to Fort Dodge, Kansas, [Sgt. Fegan] was attacked by a party of desperadoes, who attempted to rescue a deserter in his charge and to fire the train. Sergeant Fegan, singlehanded, repelled the attacking party, wounding two of them, and brought his train through in safety."

Five men in history have won two Army Medals of Honor. All five won them either in the Civil War or Indian War periods of history. The story of Lieutenant Thomas W. Custer who won two Medals in the Civil War has been previously told.

First Lieutenant Frank D. Baldwin won one Medal in the Civil War and one during the Indian Wars, the only winner to get one in each period. He won his first at Peach Tree Creek, Georgia, on July 20, 1864, by capturing two Confederate offi-

cers and their guidon, and the second at McClellans Creek, Texas, on November 8, 1874, by rescuing two white girls from a large force of hostile Indians. The record shows he was issued both Medals the same date, December 3, 1891.

Sergeant William Wilson of the Fourth Cavalry won a Medal at Colorado Valley, Texas, on March 28, 1872, and at Red River, Texas, September 29, 1872. The first was for "gallantry in pursuit of a band of cattle thieves from New Mexico." The second was for "distinguished conduct in action with Indians."

First Sergeant Henry Hogan of the Fifth Infantry won two Medals in 1877, the first at Cedar Creek, Montana, on January 8th for gallantry in action and the second at Bear Paw Mountain on September 30th for carrying a severely wounded officer from the field of battle under heavy fire. Hogan received both Medals seventeen years later on June 26, 1894.

The case of Army double-winner Patrick Leonard points up the fact that possession of the Medal was no safeguard to rank. He won his first as a sergeant in the Second Cavalry at Little Blue, Nebraska, on May 15, 1870, for "gallantry in action," and the second with the lesser rank of corporal in the Twenty-third Infantry on April 28, 1876, near Fort Hartsuff, Nebraska, for "gallantry in charge on hostile Sioux." Each of these Medals was awarded during the year earned.

Colonel Edward D. Townsend, with the brevet rank of Major General, continued as Adjutant General of the Army for some years after the Civil War. In 1869 he was approached by the publisher of a widely read periodical called *The Soldier's Friend* for a copy of a list of those winners who had legitimately won the Army Medal up to that time. Townsend was glad to comply, not only to dispel the doubt as to who were the actual winners, but also to attempt to locate certain individuals who had been awarded Medals but had never applied for them. Some of them were dead, he realized, but others did not know they had received the award. Thus the Medal of Honor list was published for the first time.

Colonel Townsend had always thought that when the Civil War ended, many of his problems would also end. Some of them did, but he still had Dr. Mary Walker. During the latter part of 1871, he received a brief and polite letter from her re-

questing he send a letter to the Commissioner of Pensions stating that she had served as a "contract surgeon" with the Army during the Civil War. Townsend complied, sending a terse letter to the effect that she had served briefly with the Army as an "assistant contract surgeon."

The next year he received a letter from her requesting a letter addressed "to whom it may concern" stating that a Medal of Honor and parchment had been granted her by the President, commending her for her duties during the war. It soon became painfully clear that what Dr. Walker wanted was a government pension and she had the energy and tenacity to work at it tirelessly. During the years 1873, 1874 and 1875, she flooded the War Department and a host of government bureaus with requests for testimonial letters, copies of military orders and regulations, legal opinions, and innumerable questions for answering. Officials would cringe when they saw the bulky missives arrive, addressed in the familiar black scrawl. It was Dr. Walker's contention that she had somehow suffered injuries during her government service and a pension was owed her.

It became a sport for Colonel Townsend to refer the correspondence to agencies. The other victims squirmed and fought back. An official in the Department of the Interior wrote him during 1876, "In the name of humanity! Why saddle Dr. Walker on me?"

In May of 1876, Colonel Townsend noted with some satisfaction that Dr. Walker was beginning to harry Congress directly. That year she bullied and cajoled a congressman into introducing a bill before Congress for her "relief." The bill demanded a settlement of $10,000 on her "for money expended and injury received in the late war." This bill died in committee, but Dr. Walker pressed on.

In November 1876, after a tireless ten-year campaign against the male conspirators in the government bureaus who were out to deprive Dr. Walker of her rights because she was a female, she managed to get herself on the pension rolls for the first time. She was awarded a pension of $8.50 a month for "atrophy of the nerves of the eyes" arising from her government service. It seemed that during her time as a Confederate prisoner in Libby Prison she had ruined her eyes by straining them while rendering medical aid to fellow prisoners in the

dim and flickering light of candles. Her claim could not be proved or disproved, and she had her sheaf of testimonials from many prominent politicos. The Commissioner of Pensions threw up his hands and granted her one-half disability. Full disability from this affliction would have paid her only $17 a month. It was a small beginning, but a beginning nevertheless.

During the 1880's she continued her barrage of correspondence, now demanding alleged "arrears in pay." Colonel Townsend retired in 1880, to devote the remainder of his life to religious work. His contacts with the "insidious female doctoress," as she was called in correspondence from the reactionary male doctors of the Surgeon General's office, may have made a retreat into the realm of the spiritual world most relaxing. Townsend's successors then took her on.

Soon after he took office as Secretary of War in 1881, Robert Todd Lincoln, son of the dead President, received a letter from a member of Congress stating that Dr. Mary Walker had informed him that Secretary of War Lincoln had "personal knowledge" of the important services she had rendered the Union cause during the Civil War. The congressman said that since he was the member of a committee considering a pension bill which had been introduced in Dr. Walker's behalf, any information the Secretary of War could give would be most helpful in getting the bill passed.

The Secretary of War informed the congressman that he had no knowledge, personal or otherwise, of any service, important or otherwise, that Dr. Mary Walker had ever performed, during the Civil War or at any other time.

This adverse letter helped kill that bill, but Dr. Walker did not cease her campaign. In 1887 she forced another harassed congressman to introduce a bill for her "relief." By now Dr. Walker was active in the Women's Suffrage movement, and in her militant demeanor and fiery glare, the politicos could envision the wrath to come when she and her ilk won the vote. This bill called for a pension of $50 a month. It languished in committees for years, with Dr. Walker following its progress constantly, spouting correspondence with a machine-like rapidity.

During this period she was arrested several times in Washington and in other cities for appearing in public dressed in male attire. On these occasions she displayed a document purported to be a "Congressional permit" to wear the clothes. No

record was ever found in Congress of issuance of such a permit to her.

In 1888, after the resignation of the baleful Robert Todd Lincoln, she demanded a letter from his successor stating she had been the only female contract surgeon ever employed by the Army in history. Apparently, she feared that some of the militant members of her own sex might someday try to steal her thunder by declaring they too had been Army doctors during the Civil War. The Secretary of War complied, stating she had been the only woman employed in this capacity, but noting that she had been an assistant contract surgeon.

In a War Department Circular dated February 11, 1892, the Adjutant General's Office defined for the first time the distinction between the Medal of Honor and the Certificate of Merit. The Medal of Honor should be awarded to officers and enlisted men "for distinguished bravery in action," while the Certificate of Merit was to be awarded only to enlisted men "for distinguished service, whether in action or otherwise, of a valuable character to the United States." Thus a differentiation was made for the first time between heroism in battle and an act benefiting the government.

The decade of the 1890's is looked upon generally by historians as the Dark Ages in the history of the Medal of Honor. The old veterans of the Civil War were on the march, storming the halls of Congress in their old black slouch hats and pestering the overworked clerks in the War Department. They wanted recognition for deeds they claimed they had accomplished long ago at Bull Run, Fair Oaks or Elkhorn Tavern. They wanted Medals of Honor. Most made no attempt to explain why they had delayed so long in making application. A half-hearted explanation was voiced by Colonel Eugene A. Carr, commander of the Third Illinois Cavalry in the Civil War, when he submitted his application for a Medal of Honor in 1893. "Since many soldiers have received medals on my recommendation," he wrote, "it occurred to me I might be entitled to one." Then he went on to describe an incident at Pea Ridge, Arkansas, which had occurred in March of 1862, over thirty years before. Colonel Carr was issued his Medal the following year. Later, apparently, Colonel Carr yearned to join the ranks of the double-winners. In 1907 he applied for an-

other Medal of Honor for something he had done in an Indian fight in the 1870's. When it was denied, he asked again in 1908 and again the second Medal was denied.

The awards picked up momentum as the decade of the 1890's progressed. In 1890, twenty-two Civil War Medals were approved; in 1891, forty-one; in 1892, sixty-six; in 1894, one hundred and twenty-seven. . . . Over six hundred Medals in all for Civil War service were awarded during the 1890's. The trouble was that the original act and the ensuing regulations had not stipulated a time limit for applying for the Medal. For as long as a Civil War veteran was steady enough to hold a pen and send a letter off to the War Department, he was eligible to apply for a Medal of Honor.

President William McKinley, an Army veteran of the Civil War himself, ordered a revision of the regulations in 1897. For the first time a list of requirements was set forth.

Effective June 26, 1897, all applications for the Army Medal of Honor had to fit into one of three chronological categories: (1) For military service from the outbreak of the Civil War to December 21, 1889; or (2) for services between January 1, 1890, and June 26, 1897, the date of the new regulation; or (3) for cases "that may arise for service performed hereafter." Hereafter meaning the period from June 26, 1897 on. Eyewitness supporting accounts were made mandatory. For categories (2) and (3) the application could not be made by the candidate himself, but had to be made for him by his commanding officer or some individual who had personally witnessed the deed of gallantry.

The regulation stated further that for category (3) recommendations would have to be made within one year after "performance of the act for which the award is claimed."

Thus, the basic modern requirements for seeking the Medal —a time limit for applying and submission of affidavits of eyewitnesses—appeared for the first time. But these affected only categories (2) and (3).

The reforms did not block the flood of Civil War claims, the insidious category (1). The horde of black-hatted old G.A.R. veterans surged on. One hundred and twenty Civil War Medals were awarded in 1896, one hundred and eighteen in 1897, sixty-one in 1898.

Imitations of the Medal and its ribbon also proved trouble-

some in the 1890's. Unscrupulous veterans and impersonators of veterans used the Medals and their imitations to seek charity or patronage consideration for jobs. Imitation Medals could be seen even on the bosoms of sidewalk beggars in the cities.

To complicate matters further, several cities and states struck medals for their heroes after the cessation of hostilities. Most of them were remarkably similar in design to the Medal of Honor. Some could not be told from the real thing even by close inspection.

In November 1896, in an attempt to frustrate the imitators, the War Department changed the color of the Medal of Honor ribbon from a design of narrow, vertical red and white stripes extending from a blue upper-band, to a design of broader red, white and blue vertical stripes. Also the Department authorized the wearing of a rosette or knot of the same combination of colors as the ribbon, on the coat lapel in lieu of the Medal.

Early in 1897 a familiar female figure in male attire appeared at the office of R. A. Alger, Secretary of War. It was Dr. Mary Walker, first to demand her new Medal of Honor ribbon and rosette. Secretary Alger informed her testily that the ribbons and rosettes, although authorized, had not been manufactured yet. Medal holders would be notified in the public press when the ribbons were ready and she could apply at that time.

"I want my ribbon and rosette without unnecessary delay," Dr. Walker advised him in no uncertain terms and strode out.

Dr. Walker was residing at The Crosby, a hotel for females in Washington, between her lecture tours made in the cause of Women's Suffrage. When nervous females shrieked at the sight of the apparition in male attire in the sacred upper halls of the hotel, Dr. Walker informed them that she had been given the right to wear male attire by Congress for her services during the Civil War. Then she displayed her Congressional "permit" to wear the attire. Also, she made it known that it was right and proper for the employees and guests at the hotel to refer to her as "Major" Walker.

When the War Department announced that the new Medal ribbons and rosettes were ready, Dr. Walker ordered hers at once and thereafter wore the rosette in the flower buttonhole of the cutaway coat, even when she was wearing her Medal. In

1898 her persistent attacks on Congress finally paid off again. On July 7, 1898, she was awarded an additional pension of $20 a month for her services during the Civil War by a special act of Congress. Her old enemy, the Commissioner of Pensions, fumed but paid that one too.

Dr. Walker continued to harass the government bureaus as the period of the Indian Wars came to a close. She would have been glad to learn that the last Medal of Honor deed for actions against Indians was performed by a medical person, Private Oscar Burkard, Hospital Corps, on October 5, 1898, at Leech Lake, Minnesota, during a belated uprising of Chippewa Indians. Burkard courageously risked his life in rescuing wounded comrades under heavy fire and was cited for "bravery in action against Indians." His Medal was awarded August 21, 1899, less than a year after the event.

Not a Single Spanish Ship Escaped

By 1898 the ramshackle old Spanish empire in the New World had almost completely disintegrated. Misgovernment and oppression had spurred incipient nationalism in all its colonies. By 1898 all that Spain owned in the New World were the Philippines in the Pacific, and Cuba in the West Indies. Cuban trade with the United States, at that time an estimated value of one hundred million dollars a year, fanned Spanish resentment, and anti-American demonstrations broke out.

In January 1898, President William McKinley ordered the battleship *Maine* to Havana to protect United States citizens and property. By February 15, the tension seemed to have eased. Mob demonstrations had abated and Americans could walk the streets without fear of being cursed and spit upon. On the evening of that day the *Maine* rode quietly at her moorings in the harbor. In his cabin, Captain Sigsbee was writing a re-

port to his superiors in Washington. Suddenly, without warning, the ship rocked with a great roar. The lights winked out
and the darkness was filled with clatter of falling wreckage and
a cacophony of minor explosions. Then came the crackle of
flames and the cries of the wounded as the great ship keeled
over on her side and began settling to the floor of the harbor.
Two hundred and sixty officers and men died on the *Maine*.
A Navy board of inquiry later found that she had been sunk
by the explosion of a submarine mine. A wave of anger swept
America. An American battleship had been destroyed and many
American lives lost. War on Spain was declared the following
April 24th.

The Secretary of the Navy at once cabled Commodore
George Dewey, commander of the American Asiatic Squadron
at Hong Kong, "War has commenced between the United
States and Spain. Proceed at once to Philippine Islands. Com-
mence operations particularly against the Spanish Fleet. You
must capture vessels or destroy. Use utmost endeavor."

On May 1, 1898, the great white ships of the American Asiatic Squadron, with the flagship *Olympia* leading the van,
slipped through the early morning mists past the forts on Cavite and trapped the Spanish fleet in Manila Bay. Commodore
Dewey, pacing the bridge, turned formally to the captain of
the *Olympia*. "You may fire when ready, Gridley," he said.
When the range had been closed to two and a half miles, Captain Gridley did fire, with great accuracy and effect, as did the
other ships of the squadron. By the time night fell, not a single Spanish fighting ship remained afloat in Manila Bay.

After the defeat of the Spanish fleet, Dewey's squadron
blockaded Manila until August 13th, when the city surrendered after Dewey threatened a bombardment. In this Pacific
phase of the Spanish-American War, only four Medals of
Honor were awarded, three to crew members on the U.S.S.
Concord off Cavite, Manila Bay, May 21, 1898. They were
William A. Crouse, Water Tender, and Firemen First Class
John W. Ehle and James L. Hull. These men won their Medals
fighting live steam rather than the human enemy. The three
citations are identical in wording and appear in the same General Order. "Following the blowing out of a lower manhole-
plate joint on boiler B of that vessel [the *Concord*], . . . as-
sisted in hauling the fires in the hot, vapor-filled atmosphere,

which necessitated the playing of water into the fireroom from a hose."

While Dewey was at grips with the Spanish enemy at Manila Bay, the Cuban theater of operations was active. For weeks, the American North Atlantic Squadron, under the command of Admiral W. T. Sampson, searched vainly for the Spanish fleet, while amphibious operations were carried out against the Cuban coasts. On May 11, 1898, forty sailors and twelve Marines from the cruisers *Nashville* and *Marblehead* rowed close to shore to cut an important submarine cable which connected Cienfuegos with the outside world. Using hacksaws they worked for an hour and a half under heavy small-arms fire from shore to cut a two-hundred-foot length from each strand of the double cable. All fifty-two of these men received Medals for participating in this action. Most of them were listed in the same General Order, Number Five Hundred and Twenty-one dated 7 July 1899. Five of them, apparently overlooked in the first order, received their Medals later. All their citations were brief and identical in wording. "Facing the heavy fire of the enemy . . . set an example of extraordinary bravery and coolness throughout this action."

On May 29, 1898, while Admiral Sampson's flagship *New York* was anchored outside the reef at Key West hastily re-coaling from lighters for the run to Cuba, a young naval constructor named Richmond P. Hobson reported on board to give the admiral the benefit of some of his ideas. Sampson had just received intelligence that the Spanish fleet was hiding in the bay of Santiago de Cuba and he had much on his mind, but he gave the young officer a few minutes. Hobson had a plan to take Havana by using a so-called "unsinkable" iron ship of his own design to run the mine-filled channel leading to the harbor.

Sampson wasn't interested. His own plan called for a sinkable, rather than an unsinkable ship, to be sunk in the narrow channel leading to Santiago harbor, thus bottling up Admiral Cervera and his fleet. Whereupon the bright and versatile Hobson suggested that one side of a ship be lined with torpedoes on the outside below the waterline, then that the ship be swung crosswise in the channel, the anchor dropped and the torpedoes fired off. Furthermore Hobson volunteered to lead the daredevil mission.

And so it turned out on the night of June 2, 1898, a cloudy night ominous with fitful lightning, that Naval Constructor Hobson found himself in command of his first ship, the condemned collier *Merrimac*. On board was a volunteer group of seven sailors. Ten torpedoes which could be fired electrically were secured to the port side, riding flush against the plates about twelve feet below the waterline. A lifeboat was towed astern.

The old ship crept slowly through the night toward the dark outline of the hostile shore. The plan was to slip past the guns of Morro Castle, and enter the harbor channel. At the narrowest point Hobson and crew planned to swing the *Merrimac* crosswise, drop anchor, open her valves, blow the torpedoes and then leap overboard to escape in the lifeboat.

At 3:30 A.M. on the morning of June 3rd with Coxswain Deignan at the helm the *Merrimac* entered the channel under the guns of Morro Castle. The shore guns were silent and this seemed ominous to Hobson, standing by the pilot. Surely they must have been seen by now. It was too late to turn back. "Full speed ahead!" he barked and the old collier lunged down the channel. Suddenly, a gun flamed from shore and there was a whistling crash on the port side. They were in for it now. The shells began whistling down on them in great numbers.

The old *Merrimac* shook from the pounding and flames leaped from the ricocheting shells. Suddenly, a ship's length from her planned sinking position, she began to slip out of control. "Rudder's shot away, sir!" Deignan reported to Hobson.

Hobson swore in frustration. They were in a narrow section of channel but not crosswise. They merely angled slightly across. But there was no other alternative. "Fire the torpedoes!" he shouted above the crashing uproar of the incoming shells.

There was a frustrating wait and then only two of the torpedoes exploded. The shelling had broken the electrical connections. Now a floating wreck, the *Merrimac* began drifting around slowly in the channel as she sank. Undersea mines began exploding and the old collier started breaking to pieces.

As she became immobile in the channel, firing from the shore ceased. Spanish picket boats swarmed out from shore. The lifeboat had been destroyed, so the crew and their leader,

clad only in life jackets and underwear, had to cling to a raft in the water. The old collier bubbled her last protesting breath and stuck on the bottom, angling across the channel but leaving a narrow clear channel past her prow.

Blue with cold and with teeth chattering, the crew clung to the raft for over an hour until sunrise. Then they were picked up by a Spanish steam-launch. Young Hobson climbed aboard with the assistance of a distinguished-looking Spanish naval officer who wore a neat white beard. Hobson found to his amazement that it was Admiral Cervera, commander of the Spanish fleet, himself.

Hobson and his entire crew survived their ordeal and were held prisoners of war for slightly more than a month. On July 6, 1898, they were exchanged for some captured Spanish officers and welcomed back to American lines as heroes. Hobson rode a horse in the lead and the crew rode behind in an army wagon. American troops saluted and cheered as they passed by. Their daredevil effort to block the channel had failed, but their example would become part of American naval tradition.

The crew members were awarded Medals of Honor for their part in the action, their citations all appearing in General Order Five Hundred and Twenty-nine, 2 November 1899. They are all identical in wording and brief: "Despite heavy fire from the Spanish batteries, . . . displayed extraordinary heroism throughout this operation."

As a commissioned officer, Naval Constructor Hobson was ineligible for the Medal in 1898. However, he did receive a glowing letter of commendation from the Secretary of the Navy.

Most Navy Medals in the Spanish-American War were "group" awards but one unusual individual deed was performed by Sergeant John H. Quick of the Marines. Quick was a member of the Marine battalion which landed to capture Guantanamo Bay on June 10, 1898, the first United States troops to invade the island. On June 14th his platoon became involved in a deadly skirmish with Spanish troops on a high ridge overlooking the coast. The gunboat *Dolphin*, in an attempt to support the land forces with cannon fire, undershot its target and dropped shells in the midst of the hapless Marine platoon. Quick improvised a semaphore flag from a large ban-

danna attached to a long stick and leaped to the crest of the ridge where he could be seen by the gunpointers on the *Dolphin*. Standing in the full view of the enemy only two hundred yards away, he braved their bullets, calmly wigwagging the Navy gunboat to cease firing. After completing his message and having it formally acknowledged from the ship, Quick dropped to the ground unhit.

Quick's deed was observed by Stephen Crane, the famous author then in Cuba as a war correspondent. Crane described the deed in a news dispatch. Quick, written up widely in the newspapers, was awarded the Medal of Honor.

The Naval blockade on Santiago harbor was maintained until Sunday morning July 3rd, when the Spanish fleet, now cut off from the shore installations by the advancing American Army, tried to break through the blockade in a vain attempt to escape to the open sea and thus save the fleet. With the flagship *Maria Teresa* in the lead, the Spanish ships—the *Viscaya*, the *Cristóbal Colón* and the *Almirante Oquendo*—steamed for the open sea.

The American squadron was cleared for action and ready. Drawn up in a semicircle six miles from the harbor entrance, they blasted the enemy ships with shattering broadsides. Within a few hours the sea battle was over. Not a single Spanish ship escaped. As the burning hulks floated dead in the water, filled with the minor explosions of boilers and ammunition and the screams of the wounded, American sailors rowed out from their ships to rescue the Spaniards struggling in the water. Thus ended the Navy phase of the Spanish-American War in Cuba.

The United States had a twenty-six-thousand-man regular Army when hostilities with Spain began April 25, 1898. The entire country was so enraged over the insult to the national honor in the blowing up of the *Maine* that citizens flocked into military service, and before the war ended, the United States forces numbered more than three hundred thousand.

There were many minor annoyances for the eager warriors. For one thing, there were not enough summer uniforms available for the troops, so most had to go to the tropics in heavy, blue-woolen uniforms, suitable for winter wear in the Dakotas. Also, the Army had just changed from the old Springfield to

the Krag-Jorgenson rifle. Since there were not nearly enough new rifles to go around, some troops had to carry the old Springfields. This made for a confusing assortment of ammunition.

The eager Americans ignored these minor problems and looked proudly at their armament, especially their rapid-fire Gatlings and their "dynamite" guns which would throw sticks of dynamite at the enemy. But no one told them that the Spanish troops had smokeless powder and they did not. The troop ships steamed gaily down to Cuba with lights burning brightly at night and bands blaring, to land at Daiquiri on June 22nd.

The Army fighting which began on June 22 with the landing at Daiquiri ended after twenty steaming days of jungle fighting with the Spanish surrender at Santiago. The Army's war was mostly an infantry battle, foot soldiers charging entrenched Spanish positions. The two principal generals made an odd pair. Nominally in command was General William R. Shafter, winner of the Medal of Honor as a Union lieutenant during the Civil War at Fair Oaks. Shafter was afflicted with gout and so fat he had to be boosted onto a horse. Generally he rode in a spring wagon. In camp he was most often found prostrate in his hammock panting in the heat. His second in command was General Joe Wheeler, also a Civil War veteran. Wheeler had been a general in the Confederate Army at twenty-five and when the Spanish-American War broke out, he joined the United States Army to become a general again. During the twenty-day campaign in Cuba, the wiry little general, with his bright eyes and white beard, was never far from the front lines. When he cracked the Spanish resistance near San Juan Hill, the old Rebel yelled, "Come on, boys, we've got the Yankees on the run!"

The Army awarded thirty Medals of Honor to soldiers on Cuba in the Spanish-American War. The citations were generally brief, mostly describing acts of gallantry in the rescue of wounded. Most of them were awarded for deeds performed during the attacks on San Juan Hill and El Caney blockhouse on July 1, 1898.

Of the thirty Medal winners, only six were officers. One officer was Captain Albert L. Mills, Assistant Adjutant General of the Volunteers. He suffered a severe head-wound during one attack and temporarily lost his sight, but refused to be evacu-

ated and remained at his post to encourage his men. Mills recovered and later became a brigadier general.

Three sergeants, three corporals, and seventeen privates were winners. One musician won the Medal. He was Herman Pfisterer of Company H, Twenty-first Infantry, who laid down his bugle and helped rescue the wounded under fire at El Caney.

Five members of the all-Negro Tenth U.S. Cavalry won Medals of Honor in Cuba during the Spanish-American War. They were Sergeant-Major Edward E. Baker and Privates Dennis Bell, Fitz Lee, William H. Thompkins and George H. Wanton. These would be the last Negroes to win Medals of Honor until the Korean War of the 1950's. Prior to the Spanish-American War, several Negroes had won Medals in the Civil War and the Indian Wars.

On September 3, 1898, after hostilities had ceased in Cuba, the War Department in a General Order set out the rules for the award of the Army Medal of Honor for services in the Spanish-American War and thereafter, a manifestation of further tightening of policy. This General Order completely omitted any consideration of "soldierlike qualities" as a basis for the award. In fact this order began in a severely negative fashion by stating that the "Medal of Honor will not be awarded to officers or enlisted men except for distinguished bravery or conspicuous gallantry . . . manifested in action by conduct that distinguishes a soldier above his comrades, and that involves risk of life, or performance of more than ordinarily hazardous duty."

In addition, the order stated that the Medal recommendation could be made only by an officer, either the officer in command during the action or an officer having personal cognizance of the specific act for which the Medal was requested. The recommendation had to be accompanied by a detailed recital of circumstances and certificates of officers or affidavits of enlisted men who were actually eye-witnesses. There had to be at least two eye-witnesses to the specific act or acts. And the facts of the case had to be further attested by "official reports of the action, record of events, muster rolls and returns and descriptive lists."

One obvious effect of this General Order was manifest in the

citations for the Medal written after the Spanish-American War. These citations grew progressively more detailed and specific as time went on.

VI

Brush Fires and Banana Republics

ALTHOUGH Commodore Dewey and the Asiatic Squadron had made short work of the Spanish fleet at Manila Bay in May 1898, and occupied the city of Manila itself the following August, the Philippine Islands were far from subjugated. Nationalist insurgent forces under Emilio Aguinaldo and vicious Mohammedan Moros fought the invading Americans as fiercely as they had the Spanish. Attacks against American forces and Filipinos who cooperated with them continued, even within the city of Manila itself, until 1913. This period of guerrilla fighting in the Philippines is known to history as the Philippine Insurrection.

The role of the Army and the Marines during this period was to "pacify" the insurgents, generally by the sword. The Navy's role was to furnish transport and artillery support for the Army and Marine ground operations, as well as to patrol coastal waters and inland rivers with gunboats.

The Army awarded seventy Medals of Honor to soldiers for deeds in the Philippine Insurrection. These Medals were awarded according to the standards set forth in the General Order issued in September 1898, requiring recommendations by officers only and the signed statements of eye-witnesses corroborated by the official records. All the Army Medals went for acts involving jungle skirmishes with the insurrectos.

One of the first Army Medal deeds was by Sergeant Charles W. Ray of the Twenty-second Infantry Regiment on October 19, 1899. Sergeant Ray, leading a two-man squad as advance scouts ahead of the main body of troops, came to a bridge guarded by a small force of insurrectos. Ray and his men

killed the guards in a swift attack and captured the bridge. Sending back one of the men to bring up the main column, Ray and his companion played "Horatius at the Bridge" for almost an hour, defending it against a large body of attackers until the other Americans arrived at the scene.

The Navy awarded nineteen Medals of Honor for heroic actions during the Philippine Insurrection. Eight of these went to Marines. Two of them went to the first Marine officers in history to perform Medal-winning acts. Colonels Hiram I. Bearss and David D. Porter were young Marine captains when they led their troops in the great battle with the Moros on Samar in the Philippine Islands on November 7, 1901.

"Moro" was a name to strike terror in the Philippines at the turn of the century. A runty bloodthirsty crew of fighters, the Moros massacred most of Company C, Ninth Infantry Regiment, on Samar on September 28, 1901. The few survivors lived on as deadeyed zombies from the memory of the terror. For years afterward in the old Army when one of the survivors appeared in a strange mess, the command would ring out, "Gentlemen rise! This man served in Samar."

Samar is the third largest of the Philippine Islands. The coastline is broken and irregular, with many shallow water bays and inlets to hide the small sailing craft of the fierce Moros. The Moros were Moslems, an island people of mixed Malayan extraction, who sailed across the Sulu Sea to the Philippines, years before, to fall with bloody violence upon the Christianized island natives, whom they considered infidels. They had fought the Spaniards with great dedication and gusto, and now they fought the invading Americans. By 1901, they had taken refuge on the island of Samar to fight to the death.

Moro headquarters on Samar was a fortified stronghold on high cliffs at the junction of the Cadacan and Sohoton Rivers. These cliffs were several hundred feet high of soft pumice-like volcanic stone. Honeycombed with caves, they offered natural cover for defenders, and the wily Moslems had spent three years in making them impregnable to attackers. The caves were filled with stores of rice and ammunition and on the cliff faces huge woven nets of vines held tons of rocks suspended, ready to be dropped on any attackers from below. The fanatical Moros were determined to defend their stronghold from any infidel attack with a dedicated religious zeal.

In the middle of November 1901, the United States Navy put ashore two bodies of troops by small boats through the surf of Samar's coastline. Once ashore they moved in two columns through the jungle to converge at the Moros' stronghold. The mission was to take the cliff fortifications by assault and break Moro power on Samar once and for all.

The commanding officer of the assaulting columns was Marine Captain David Dixon Porter, twenty-four years old, a grandson of the famous Commodore David Porter, Navy hero of the War of 1812. The second in command of the columns was another young Marine captain, just two years older than Porter, Hiram Iddings Bearss of Peru, Indiana. Both would live on to become Colonels in the Corps, and Bearss would earn the sobriquet of "Hiking Hiram" in various campaigns in the "banana republics" prior to World War I. In this November of 1901, the chances of living a long full life for either of the young officers did not seem especially bright.

The trails leading through the steamy jungle to the river valleys were fraught with hidden dangers. The dense foliage hid ambushers who would fire suddenly on the column with muzzle-loading rifles and then burst screaming down upon the troops in a frenzied suicidal charge, cutting and slashing with a razor-like bolo knife. Then the old Krag breech-loading rifles and the .45 caliber Colt Navy revolvers would boom, trying to knock down the fanatic before he got within slashing distance of the column. On the trail floor were pits, covered cleverly with vines and foliage. And the pit floors were lined with poisoned spear heads.

On November 17th, Captains Porter and Bearss led the columns in the assault on the cliffs. Leaving half of the force on the floor of the river valley to lay down a covering fire, the two officers led their groups, carrying bamboo ladders, to the base of the cliffs. Then they began the laborious job of scaling the face of the cliffs, using these ladders. The Moros, taken by surprise, died by the score in the withering fire from below as they tried to slash the vine cables at the cliff edge to loose the heavy swollen webs of rock. Some of the deadly loads were precipitated down the cliff face, but none near the climbing attackers. In a final lunge up the last twenty feet of cliff, the invaders swarmed over the top and met the Moros hand to hand in a brief, deadly onslaught. As the rest of the Americans from the

valley below swarmed up the ladders, the Moros' impregnable stronghold was overrun.

The citations of these two Marine officers are almost identical in wording and are different from other citations of this period in that they contain a detailed description of the deeds performed. But, of course, the citations were written years later. Porter and Bearss were not awarded their Medals of Honor until 1934.

During the unpleasantness with the Moros in the Philippines, American forces were also engaged with enemy forces on the mainland of China. A native patriotic society, with an anti-foreigner gospel, began uprisings all over China. The name of the society, translated literally as Fists of Righteous Harmony, was called colloquially the Boxers. Foreign governments had exacted humiliating territorial concessions from the Manchus, causing a loss of face. The construction of foreign railroads had thrown thousands of Chinese boatmen out of work. Foreign missionaries interfered in Chinese courts when the fates of native Christians were at stake. The foreigner also made a convenient scapegoat for the vast multitude of the discontented, being blamed for flood, famine or drought. For every problem, the Boxers had a simple answer—kill the foreign devils.

By April 1900, old China hands in Peking noted alarming developments. The price of knives in the native markets was soaring. Rude epithets were tossed at foreigners by coolies in the street. Then a sinister poster began to be seen on public walls: "The will of heaven is that the telegraph wires be first cut, then the railways torn up, and then shall the foreign devils be decapitated."

To timid Chinese, who had a natural fear of the foreign devils' guns and bullets, the Boxers had another simple answer, rather reminiscent of the creed of the American Indian messiah Wowoka, that precipitated the disastrous Battle of Wounded Knee. The Boxers could not be hit, was the answer. Instead of Wowoka's ghost shirts, the Boxers wore a yellow sash to lend the aura of immortality. The true believer would be protected, the high priests of the Boxers told the ignorant Chinese. Then the priests bravely faced firing squads and survived and the coolies were quickly convinced, unaware that the shots at the priests by the firing squads were blanks.

In the latter part of May, the telegraph wires around Peking

began to be cut mysteriously, and on May 28th the main railway station was set on fire. The Americans had no commercial interest in the telegraphs or railroads, but they had numerous missionaries in China. In the hills around Peking at various mission schools, the Boxers carefully removed the missionaries' glasses before they chopped their heads off.

In the early dawn of May 29, 1900, an international fleet of seventeen warships—American, British, French, German, Japanese, Italian and Russian—steamed into the Chinese harbor of Tientsin. As daylight broke, a flotilla of barges, lighters and cutters swung away from the international fleet and headed for shore. The warships then laid off behind the sandbar and pointed their big guns toward the three Chinese forts, ready to lay in the broadsides if the forts fired on the shorebound flotilla. In the boat from the U.S. cruiser *Newark* were fifty Marines and four sailors, with orders to proceed with the troops of the other nations to Peking, one hundred and ten miles inland.

On the late evening of May 31, the international force—numbering three hundred and forty men—arrived at the railroad terminus outside Peking and marched in formation past sullen torch-lit crowds, past the forty-foot-high Tartar Wall and into the Legation District where eleven nations maintained diplomatic missions.

The legation guards had arrived none too soon. Within the next few weeks the railways were destroyed by howling Boxer fanatics and the remaining foreign telegraph lines were leveled. Mysterious fires began breaking out in the city. When Baron von Ketteler, the red-bearded German minister, set out on June 20th in his sedan chair to lodge an official protest with the old painted Manchu Empress, he was shot down in the street. All the foreigners in the city now saw that flight was out of the question and crowded into the Legation District, an area about three quarters of a mile square, bounded on one side by the Tartar Wall, by the pink-tiled parapet of the Empress's Imperial City on two sides, and by a two-hundred-foot-wide street on the fourth side. That same day the old Empress officially put in with the Boxer movement and notified the foreigners they must leave China within twenty-four hours. It was a manifestly absurd order. The foreigners would have gladly departed except for the hordes of maddened Chinese surrounding them. American Minister Conger informed his Marine guard:

"I have been promised we will be relieved by friendly troops, but I don't know when. We must therefore fight until we are relieved, or . . ." he hesitated, "until we are dead."

That afternoon at 4:00 P.M., a Boxer rifle cracked from a rooftop opposite the French Legation. A French marine toppled from the wall. The siege had begun.

In the days that followed, attack after attack swirled around the beleaguered Legation District. There were at least twenty thousand attacking Chinese in all, composed of dedicated Boxers, rabble volunteers, and a few units of trained military groups. The Boxers were wildest of all, and easiest to kill. Screaming curses and waving old muskets, spears, swords or sticks, they would dash forward in plain view, believing themselves invulnerable in their yellow sashes. The cracking Lee and Mauser rifles of the defenders brought them down by the score, but still other fanatics took their places.

The fifty Marines and four sailors in the American Legation guard gave a good account of themselves. Most of their citations state generally that they distinguished themselves "by meritorious conduct" during stated periods without specifically describing their acts. Others cite the winners generally for assistance "in the erection of barricades."

One of the Marines winning a Medal at Peking during this siege was Private Daniel Joseph Daly, a twenty-seven-year-old rookie, just five feet five inches tall and weighing a scant one hundred and twenty-five pounds. Daly would have a thirty-year career in the Corps, win a second Medal of Honor, be recommended for a third, and become a tradition in the Marines of the same sort that Sergeant Alvin York became in the Army.

Daly's citation for his first Medal of Honor stated: "In the presence of the enemy during the battle of Peking, China, 14 August 1900, Daly distinguished himself by meritorious conduct." His deed was quite noteworthy.

On the night of July 14th a critical situation had developed for the American group. The German company on one flank had been driven from their position leaving that side dangerously exposed. It would be necessary for a Marine volunteer to crawl forward alone on the Tartar Wall, a hundred yards away from the rest, and try and hold off the attackers while the rest worked frantically to erect a barricade. Daly volunteered, crawling away in the darkness, pushing his rifle ahead of him.

For the rest of the night, while the work went on behind him, Daly was a very busy Marine. Whenever pigtailed heads appeared over the parapet, he would blast them with his rifle. It was a long deadly night. During one attack, three attackers came close with swinging swords. The pint-sized Daly bayoneted two of them and sent the third hurtling from the wall with a smash of rifle butt. No Chinese got past him. The first light revealed a tangle of dead Boxers around his position.

The citation of Joseph Mitchell, Gunner's Mate First Class, USN, states he "distinguished himself by meritorious conduct" —another masterpiece of understatement. Along with his courage Mitchell brought mechanical talents to the defenders. They were woefully short of artillery. The Italians had an antiquated one-pounder that was wildly inaccurate and the British had an 1887 Nordenfelt howitzer that jammed every fourth round with clocklike regularity. One afternoon Mitchell made a pleasant discovery in the rubble of an old blacksmith shop. It was an old Chinese artillery gun barrel, vintage of 1860. Old as it was, the bore was clear and unpitted and the metal had a solid ringing sound when Mitchell hit it with an iron maul. With a Welsh Marine named Thomas as his assistant, Mitchell built a new cannon. And a mixed breed of cannon it was—Chinese barrel, Italian mounting, Russian powder and shot, British and Yankee crew. The formal British referred to the homemade masterpiece as "the international gun." The less formal Yanks called her "Old Betsy" or just "the old crock." Her performance was rather hair-raising for both attackers and defenders and her accuracy left much to be desired. The recoil dismayed even her iron-nerved inventors, but she had a devastating roar, and a lot of power. Her first cannon ball crashed through three walls.

On July 12th, while helping man Old Betsy on the British Legation wall, Mitchell deserted his gunnery duties long enough to engage in a tug of war. The Chinese troops had the effrontery to lean their banner against the wall. Mitchell leaned over and grabbed the enemy flag. A burly Chinese soldier grabbed the end of the pole just in time, and for the next few minutes all firing ceased while both Chinese and Europeans gaped at the tug of war. Cursing and holding his end of the flagpole with one hand, Mitchell threw fistfuls of dirt and rock down on the dogged Chinese below. Finally, the enemy

soldier, half-stunned by the heavy pelting, had to let go. Amid the cheers of the defenders Mitchell plunged back into the compound, clutching the tattered banner to his bosom.

Relief came to Peking with an Allied Army on August 14, fifty-five days after the siege began. During the siege five hundred defenders had held off a Chinese horde of over twenty thousand. Up until the last day, the Boxers attacked the island of foreign devils viciously. On August 13th, the day before deliverance, Old Betsy, the international gun, took a direct hit from a heavy cannon-ball. The gun was not seriously damaged, but Gunner's Mate Mitchell fell to the ground, his arm shattered.

The Navy awarded a total of fifty-six Medals of Honor for heroic acts performed by members of the China Relief Expedition. Twenty-two went to sailors and thirty-four to Marines. Most of the Medals went to those who suffered through the fifty-five-day siege of Peking, but over a dozen went to Marines and sailors who fought their way from the coast to liberate the beleaguered garrison.

The Army awarded only four Medals of Honor to participants in the China Relief Expedition. Two went to officers and two to enlisted men. All were members of the Ninth Infantry Regiment. On July 13th, while the Army column was still in Tientsin getting ready to proceed to the relief of Peking, Captain Andrew W. Brewster saved two of his men from drowning while fording a canal to engage some enemy snipers. The same day at Tientsin First Lieutenant Louis B. Lawton won the Medal for carrying a message under fire.

During the long march to Peking, the column was continually harassed by snipers and enraged groups of the fanatical Boxers. Private Robert H. Von Schlick, while on a solo foraging party, was ambushed by a group of the enemy. Badly wounded, he nevertheless fought a stubborn one-man stand until rescued, killing several of the attackers. He was awarded the Medal.

When the column reached the outer walls of Peking on August 14th, the two companies of the Fourteenth Infantry attacking the Tung Pien Gate met hot resistance. Calvin P. Titus, a musician of Company F, scaled the almost vertical wall without the use of ropes or ladders and reached the top, where he immediately came under intense enemy fire. Ignoring the bul-

lets, Titus shouted for his companions to come up the same way. Following his example, a group scaled the wall and soon outflanked the gate and subdued the resistance. Titus, after winning the Medal of Honor, later won an appointment to West Point.

While soldiers and Marines fought their battles in the Philippines and in China, many changes were taking place at home.

The appointment of the distinguished lawyer Elihu Root as Secretary of War changed the course of Medal of Honor history. Shortly after his appointment in 1899, he convened a board of general officers of the Army to study Medal of Honor policies and make suggestions that would be the basis for new legislation.

The first problem was the vast number of imitation Medals in the hands of the public. "With few exceptions," said General Theophile F. Rodenbough, who had won the Medal of Honor as a captain during the Civil War, "these have no national, official significance." The War Department thereafter announced it would consider proposed designs for a new Army Medal that would make the old Civil War model obsolete.

Brigadier General George L. Gillespie, Army Chief of Engineers, who had won the Medal for carrying dispatches at Bethesda Church during the Civil War, submitted the winning design. This Medal was also a star, but the star was gold and was surrounded by a distinctive laurel wreath of green enamel. The center of the star displayed the head of the goddess Minerva, personifying the United States. In addition to the design, General Gillespie also furnished the War Department a method of protecting the new Medal against unscrupulous imitators and jewelry manufacturers. Gillespie applied for, and received, a patent on his design. On December 19, 1904, he assigned the ownership of the patent "to W. H. Taft and his successor or successors as Secretary of War of the United States of America." For the first time in history the Secretary of War had full legal control of the Medal of Honor design.

The Gillespie design of the Army Medal of Honor, accepted by the War Department in 1904, is the one presently in use by both the United States Army and Air Force. Occasional attempts have been made to change this design, but none have been successful.

In 1905, several months after the acceptance of the Gillespie design by the War Department, Secretary of War William Howard Taft, an obese lawyer sometimes called "the great buttertub" by his detractors, received an unannounced caller at his office. "I am Doctor Mary Walker!" rang out a commanding voice from the doorway, and indeed it was. Time had grayed her hair and hardened her features. The fifty percent "atrophy of the nerves of the eyes," for which she still drew a pension, did not prevent her from fixing the Secretary of War with a purposeful stare. "I have come for my new design of the Medal of Honor."

The Secretary returned her gaze with a countenance that was bland and Budda-like. He knew Dr. Walker by reputation. In 1901 she had joined with Carrie Nation and other militant members of the Suffrage Movement in vilifying the dead President McKinley, shot down by an assassin. Dr. Walker had gone even further than most of them. Once in a railroad station soapbox speech she had stated it was no worse for the assassin Czolgosz to kill McKinley than for the state of New York to execute Czolgosz. She blamed the assassination on Theodore Roosevelt, McKinley's Vice-President. "He would do anything to become President," Dr. Walker announced. The local police had to rescue her from a raging mob after that observation. Now, here she was, demanding her new Medal in no way dismayed that her enemy, Theodore Roosevelt, was in the White House.

Secretary Taft informed her that the design had been approved but that the Medals had not been manufactured. Dr. Walker demanded to be informed when they were ready and strode from the room.

Although not a Medal-winner himself, President Theodore Roosevelt concerned himself greatly with raising the dignity attached to the award of the Medal of Honor. On September 20, 1905, he signed an executive order directing that the Army award "will always be made with formal and impressive ceremonial," and the recipient "will, when practicable, be ordered to Washington, D.C. and the presentation will be made by the President . . ."

It was most edifying to the President that the first winner to receive his Medal at the White House under this executive order was a former Rough Rider who had served with T. R. in

Cuba. This was Assistant Surgeon James Robb Church of the First U.S. Volunteer Cavalry, awarded his Medal by the President, January 10, 1906.

The Civil War kept furnishing applicants for the Medal even into the twentieth century and some approvals were made. James M. Seitzinger, who had been a private at Cold Harbor in 1864, and John C. Sagelhurst, a sergeant of cavalry at Hatcher's Run in 1865, were awarded Medals in 1906, over forty years after the actual fighting took place. Then, in 1907, J. Monroe Reissinger, who had fought as a corporal at Gettysburg, won the award.

In 1907 the War Department received a letter from the inmate of a sanitarium in Oswego, New York, a letter written in a familiar irate scrawl. Dr. Mary Walker was ailing, but could still grasp a pen. She had never received her Medal of the new Gillespie design and now she demanded it, with no further delay. Her congressman had informed her the Medals were ready.

In answer the War Department coldly informed her she must appear in person in Washington to identify herself as a winner in order to get the new Medal.

But Dr. Walker, an old Washington hand and seasoned baiter of bureaucrats, was not deceived by this ruse. "There is a simple form available, I know very well," she said. "Send me the form without further excuses and I will execute it before a justice of the peace. Otherwise, I shall consult my congressman."

The Department wearily sent her the form and after it was returned properly executed they sent the "insidious female doctoress" her new Medal.

On April 6, 1914, a peaceful attempt by a boat from the U.S.S. *Dolphin* to purchase fresh fruit during a visit of the U.S. fleet at Tampico almost precipitated another war with Mexico. A Navy commander named Earle and his shore party were haggling with native vendors on the dock through an interpreter when they were suddenly surrounded by Mexican soldiers and hustled away through the streets to police headquarters for questioning. A protest was registered quickly by the fleet commander, Rear Admiral Mayo. He demanded release of the Americans and an apology. Commander Earle and his group were released after being held several hours and allowed

to return to the *Dolphin* in their boat, but no apology was forthcoming. The Mexican authorities also refused to honor Admiral Mayo's flagship with the traditional twenty-one-gun salute.

President Wilson and the rest of the United States were angered by the incident. The President appeared before Congress and asked for its approval in using troops "to maintain the dignity and authority of the United States . . . amidst the distressing conditions now unhappily obtaining in Mexico." Congress approved the use of military force, disclaiming any hostility toward the Mexican people.

Thereafter, proceeding on Presidential order, Admiral Frank F. Fletcher led a naval squadron composed of American warships *Prairie, Utah* and *Florida* into the harbor at Vera Cruz, Mexico, and landed a regiment of Marines and two seaman battalions. Under sporadic artillery and small-arms fire, the landing party seized the customhouse and armory on the water front, and then moved cautiously toward the center of the city against stiffening resistance. A strong point developed at the Naval Academy not far from the pier. Machine guns chattered from sandbagged cellar windows and an occasional one-pounder roared. A runner was sent hurrying to the dock to request artillery support. The cruiser *Prairie* swung around smartly and gave the resisters in the Naval Academy a taste of her three-inch gun battery. After a good five-minute pounding, a white flag blossomed from an upstairs window of the building. The sailors and Marines cheered and pushed on into the city.

By noon of April 23rd, the city was cleared, firearms and ammunition dumps had been confiscated, and captured Mexican troops penned behind barbwire. In the three-day battle for the city, fifteen Americans had been killed and fifty-six wounded.

The fighting at Vera Cruz was important in the history of the Medal of Honor mainly because of a piece of legislation passed by Congress March 3, 1915, almost a year after the action took place. An extract reads as follows. The italics are the author's. "The President of the United States is hereby empowered to prepare a suitable medal of honor to be awarded *to any officer of the Navy, Marine Corps, or Coast Guard* who shall have distinguished himself in battle or displayed extraordinary heroism in the line of his profession."

The Navy and Marine officers immediately came forward to grab a share of the Medals. Of the fifty-five Medals of Honor awarded for deeds performed during the three-day action at Vera Cruz, twenty-nine went to Navy officers and nine went to Marine officers. Seventeen Medals went to enlisted sailors, but not one single Medal of Honor was awarded an enlisted Marine.

One of the most colorful officers in the Marine Corps' long history, Smedley D. Butler, won his first Medal of Honor as a major commanding a battalion at Vera Cruz. He was cited for "distinguished conduct in battle" and "exhibited courage and skill in leading his men through the action of the Twenty-second in the final occupation of the city."

Butler was born in West Chester, Pennsylvania, July 30, 1881, and appointed a second lieutenant in the Marine Corps in 1898, while still in his teens, for the war with Spain. He was a fire-eating Marine from the very beginning. Serving with distinction in the Boxer Rebellion in China, he was promoted to captain by brevet for distinguished conduct in the presence of the enemy near Tientsin. Wounded in battle on July 13, 1900, he was invalided home. Not yet twenty years old and already a combat-scarred Marine captain, Butler was presented a sword by the townspeople of West Chester in recognition of his heroic actions in the Boxer Rebellion.

The fetid green-hell of Haiti was the background for several Medal-winning acts performed by Marine heroes of legendary stature. By 1915 a series of revolutions had carried that country to a state of anarchy. Leaders of various jungle-bands warred on each other constantly for power. Yet power in Haiti was deadly. Since liberation from the French in 1804, fifteen of its twenty-eight presidents had left office via the assassination route, seven between 1910 and 1915. After a particularly brutal massacre on July 26, 1915, following the usual president assassination, American business interests on the island howled frantically to Washington for aid; and so the Marines landed, "to get everything well in hand," as they said so often in those days.

The commanding officer of the Marine detachment (two thousand men) which came ashore from the U.S.S. *Connecticut* and other ships of the fleet was none other than Major Butler and with him was a sawed-off veteran gunnery sergeant, now almost white haired, Daniel Joseph Daly—both Butler and

Daly were winners of the Medal of Honor, and both were legends in the Corps.

During the Haitian Campaign of 1915, six Marines won Medals of Honor in the course of two different engagements with Caco bandits. Butler and Daly won repeats as two of the six awarded.

On October 22, 1915, Butler led a twenty-seven-man mounted patrol into the jungle to reconnoiter a Caco stronghold called Fort Dipitie. The ramrod-straight Butler was every inch a horse-marine, but the city-bred Daly jounced along painfully on his mount. Most of the way led through a thick jungle of matted vines and creepers. They chopped their trail with machetes and axes, the horses and pack animals sometimes having to be led, plunging and bug-eyed, across the swamps and sink holes. The jungle seemed to be alive with mysterious hidden movements. Although twenty years older than most of his men, the white-haired Daly lent a hand to the laggards, packing their rifles and ammunition cases while they led the skittish horses.

On the evening of the second day they reached the banks of a broad, sluggish river and started to cross. The clinging mist of a light rain was falling. As the outfit stretched out in a long line, splashed in midstream, heavy rifle-fire broke out from the mist-filled underbrush around them. The jungle-wise Cacos had caught them in a pretty ambush. Horses screamed and kicked wildly as bullets thudded into them. The men thrashed around in the water in near panic. Daly cursed and herded the men across, pushing and shoving.

Forming on the opposite bank, Butler found he had lost twelve horses in the melee, but miraculously not a single Marine. "Set up the machine gun over there," he barked at Daly, pointing at a swell of high ground that commanded the river bank.

"Sorry, sir, it's on one of the dead mules at the bottom of the river," Daly said.

There was an interval of silence and the jungle seemed to draw in closer around them. Without the machine gun, they could be overrun by a frenzied all-out attack. "Then we'll just have to do without, sergeant," said Butler quietly.

Daly had other ideas. He resolved to have the gun or die trying. Removing all his equipment except a knife, he headed

back through the jungle to the river. Legend has it that he killed several Cacos on the way with his knife and hid their bodies in the jungle. On reaching the river he splashed about in water over his head, trying to find the dead mule with the machine gun. Night had fallen but a full moon lighted the surface of the river bright as day. After repeatedly diving into the river, Daly found the machine gun and then spent half an hour diving and hacking away at the water-soaked ropes and leather lashings that secured the gun to the dead mule. Laboriously he carried the heavy gun to shore and then the tripod. Then, after a lung-bursting straining effort, he brought to the surface three cans of thirty-caliber ammunition, one at a time, and landed them on shore. Strapping the gun and tripod on his back and carrying the ammunition cans in his hands, the one-hundred-and-thirty-pound Daly staggered with his two-hundred-pound load back through the jungle to the patrol perimeter.

It was an amazed Major Butler who received the sergeant's gasping report. "Machine gun mounted and ready, sir!"

At dawn when the Cacos came again in a frenzied all-out attempt to overrun the Marine perimeter they were met by the deadly chattering machine gun which mowed them down by the dozen. When they fell back into the jungle they left behind over fifty of their number dead in front of the Marine position. Presuming that the enemy would not expect his crippled group to continue the advance on Fort Dipitie, Butler did just that the next day. He and Daly led the scaling party over the walls of the old French bastion-fort.

Sergeant Daly and two officers, Captain William P. Upshur and First Lieutenant Edward A. Ostermann, won Medals for actions on the six-day reconnaisance which ended in taking Fort Dipitie. Butler, as commanding officer of the shore forces, made the recommendations and they were approved. The following month, November 1915, Butler led the attack on Fort Rivière, another old bastion-fort in the jungle, held by Caco bandits. Throughout the hand-to-hand fighting, he was conspicuous for his bravery and leadership. Rear Admiral Caperton, senior Navy officer of the American squadron, recommended a second Medal of Honor for Butler for leading the assault. Butler, in turn, recommended two enlisted men of his command, Sergeant Ross L. Iams and Private Samuel Gross,

for Medals for their actions at Fort Rivière. All three were approved by the Navy Department.

Butler and Daly were the only Marines in the history of the Corps to win two Navy Medals of Honor.

VII

The Good Losers

FULL-SCALE discussions of the Medal were carried on in Congress in 1914. The clouds of war in Europe hung ominously close, encouraging a militant attitude in all branches of the government.

The Congressional discussions in 1914 and 1915 developed ultimately into the act of April 27, 1916, which provided for the creation of a Medal of Honor Roll. This act provided that when a Medal of Honor winner, either Army or Navy, reached age sixty-five, he would have his name recorded on the Roll and be entitled to a special pension of $10 a month for the rest of his life. There was a catch to it, though, buried deep in the legal phraseology. To be placed on the Roll, the winner must have won his award as an officer or enlisted man of the military service for an action involving actual conflict with the enemy, distinguished by conspicuous gallantry or intrepidity at the risk of life above and beyond the call of duty.

This act was further implemented by the National Defense Act of June 3, 1916, which ordered the Secretary of War to call a special Army board consisting of five general officers on the retired list to investigate and report on all past awards of the Army's Medal of Honor. In any case in which the board found that the Medal had been awarded for any cause other than specified above, the name of the recipient was to be permanently stricken from the Medal of Honor list. The act said further that it would be a misdemeanor for any stricken recipient to wear or publicly display his Medal.

Accordingly, between October 16, 1916, and January 17, 1917, the Army board reviewed all the papers pertaining to the two thousand six hundred and twenty-five Army Medals that had been awarded up to that time. On February 15, 1917, the board struck nine hundred and eleven names from the official Medals of Honor list. Those stricken were the names of the eight hundred and sixty-four members of the Twenty-seventh Maine Infantry Regiment, and the names of forty-seven other individuals whose Medals, the board decided, had not been properly awarded.

Why did the Twenty-seventh Maine receive the awards in the first place, and then why were they stricken from the list?

By the middle of 1862, President Lincoln could see with melancholy foreboding that the conflict was going to be protracted and wearisome. In the first flush of optimism in the spring of 1861, Northern troops had been asked to volunteer for terms of only three months. Thus it was that at the first Battle of Bull Run in July of 1861, many of the Union troops were fighting after their service had expired or at a time when their terms were about to expire. This made for discord and dissension in the ranks. Many of these units volunteered to remain and fought gallantly, but others were laggard and left the field for home as Rebel cannons boomed ominously in the distance.

On August 15, 1862, the President ordered a draft of three hundred thousand militia to serve enlistment terms of nine months. A quota was assigned each state, and Maine's quota was nine thousand six hundred and nine. The eight hundred and sixty-four members of the Twenty-seventh Maine Infantry were part of this draft.

The Twenty-seventh Regiment was raised in the county of York and joined the great rendezvous of militia at Camp Abraham Lincoln, Portland, on September 10, 1862. On September 19th the regiment elected officers and organized itself for service. On September 30th it was mustered into the Federal forces by swearing the oath. The term of service, as stated, was nine months.

The Twenty-seventh arrived in Washington by train on October 22, 1862, camped for a few days on East Capitol Hill, and then were assigned to bivouac on Arlington Heights, Lee's old estate. For the next few months the Twenty-seventh labored on the fortifications.

By June of 1863, as the enlistment term was coming to a close, General Lee began moving his army ominously north. A creeping hysteria spread through Washington. What were Lee's intentions? Did he intend to outflank and isolate the nation's capital? The city itself was almost unguarded, since most Federal troops were in the field or manning picket lines south of the city. Nervous civilian clerks patrolled the city and guarded Long Bridge.

In the midst of this tense situation, the nine-months men of the Twenty-seventh Regiment and the other Maine units became restive. They were farmers and needed to get back home and harvest their hay crops. When not released on June 10, nine months after going to camp, they sent a delegation to ask when they would be released and issued an informal ultimatum that if not released by June 30, nine months after their mustering date, they would go to Congress with the charge that the President had shown bad faith.

Beset with dire warnings from spies and other intelligence sources that Lee was now moving into Pennsylvania, Secretary of War Stanton on June 25th sent a frantic letter to Congressman D. E. Somes of Maine, asking that the congressman use his influence with the Maine troops to have them remain in service a short time longer, until the emergency had passed.

Congressman Somes made a personal appeal to the troops but they eyed him with country stubbornness. Lee might be moving into Pennsylvania, but the hay crop had to be harvested in Maine, and an agreement was an agreement with the New Englanders.

Then Colonel E. D. Townsend, the Army Adjutant General, issued Army General Order Number One Hundred and Ninety-five, dated June 29, 1863. Conceived in anxiety and born in a fleeting moment of hysteria, this general order would haunt the history of the Medal of Honor from then on.

The general order read in part as follows: "The Adjutant General will provide an appropriate medal of honor for the troops who, after the expiration of their term, have offered their services to the Government in the present emergency . . ."

On June 30, 1863, the Twenty-seventh Maine was called into formation on Arlington Heights and asked for a show of hands from those who would volunteer to remain until the emergency

was past. Three hundred and twelve officers and men volunteered to remain. Then the bulk of the Twenty-seventh Maine, over five hundred men, departed from Washington by train the morning of July 1, arriving home July 3. As the large group departed gaily for home, the three hundred volunteers grimly shouldered their muskets and trudged back south into the defenses below the Potomac.

The great battle at Gettysburg, Pennsylvania, raged from July 1 through 3, 1863. Until the very last day the issue was in doubt. But at last Lee's great lunge at the capital was repulsed, and the Confederates fell back, sustaining thirty percent casualties. By the evening of July 3, Washington could breathe a vast sigh of relief. The battle was unquestionably over. Lee's army was beginning a slow retreat southward.

The three hundred volunteers of the Twenty-seventh Maine were released July 4, and departed by train the same day. They arrived in Portland on July 6. The entire regiment was mustered out formally as a group on July 17, 1863.

Almost two years later, in 1865, the Adjutant General's office in Washington sent eight hundred and sixty-four Medals of Honor to Governor Samuel Cony of Maine for the Twenty-seventh Regiment, with a note stating the Medals were to be distributed "to the soldiers entitled to receive them." Official records show that it was the intent of the Federal Government to award Medals only to those who had volunteered to remain during the emergency. But official records did not show the names of those who volunteered and those who did not. Governor Cony, with a politician's dislike for stirring up needless controversy, and with no official notice from Washington to guide him, issued the Medals to all those mustered out with the Regiment on July 17, 1863—whether they had volunteered to remain in defense of Washington or not.

In the first report sent by the 1917 Army board to the Adjutant General only the five hundred and fifty-five members of the Twenty-seventh Maine who did not volunteer were cited as those who should be disqualified for not performing distinguished service. But in the end, all eight hundred and sixty-four regimental names were stricken from the Medal of Honor list.

The next largest group-award stricken from the list numbered twenty-nine. These were the members of Lincoln's Body

Guard who accompanied the body of the dead President on its last journey to the cemetery in Springfield. This group, composed of one captain, three subalterns and twenty-five first sergeants, were selected by Headquarters, Department of Washington, from members of the Veterans Reserve Corps, and were described as "the best and most reliable men in the command." They were awarded Medals of Honor on May 20, 1865, in recognition of their services in the guard after their return to Washington. The Army board felt that such an assignment, while worthy of some sort of recognition, did not constitute distinguished service.

The board struck the names of five members of the Twenty-seventh New Jersey Infantry as being commendable but not distinguished, and that of one Robert Storr, whose only citation was "a British subject who died in Union service." The board also struck the name of James M. Hawken, storekeeper in the Quartermaster Department, who had been awarded the Medal for extinguishing a fire in a government storehouse during the Civil War.

The board looked down its nose at the name of Asa B. Gardiner who during the Civil War had been captain of Company I, Twenty-second New York State Militia. The file showed that in April 1872, Gardiner wrote a letter to the Secretary of War requesting he be awarded a Medal of Honor "as a souvenir of memorable times now past." The board noted with horror that a Medal had been issued Gardiner with no further documentation, the citation stating vaguely "distinguished service performed during Civil War." Gardiner's name was stricken from the list.

In its first report the board noted that the law of June 3, 1916, prescribed that if the stricken winner were still in the Army, he must return his Medal for cancellation. The board said in its report this contingency did not apply, since none of those stricken were still in the Army. The board was wrong. Asa B. Gardiner was very much alive in 1917 and still on active duty in the Army. But there is no record that the old soldier was tracked down and stripped of his "souvenir" Medal.

The cases of five civilian scouts who had received Medals of Honor plagued the board. Three of them were considered almost immortal as Indian fighters by a large section of the hero-worshipping public.

Only one of the scouts was of Civil War vintage. He was William Woodall, a scout attached to General Sheridan's headquarters, who won a Medal at Appomattox in the spring of 1865 for capturing the headquarters flag of Brigadier General Banninger, the commander of a brigade of North Carolina cavalry.

The other four scouts won their Medals for gallantry in action against Indians in the 1870's. They were Amos Chapman, William Dixon, William F. Cody, and one Dozier, first name unknown, who had been a citizen-guide attached to the Army in action on the Wichita River in Texas, in 1870. Although the identity of Dozier was not known, the other three Indian scouts were too well-known for the comfort of the board. Amos Chapman, the hero of the Buffalo Wallow Fight, had been a legendary scout and Indian fighter when many of the board members were young shavetails doing their service on the frontier. Billy Dixon was the hero of the Battle of Adobe Walls when the buffalo hunters fought Chief Quanah Parker and his painted braves south of the Cimmaron in 1874. And William F. "Buffalo Bill" Cody, ye gods, he was an immortal! What would the youth of America say, especially the Boy Scouts—Buffalo Bill was one of its sponsors—when that fabled character was scratched from the list?

The board mulled the problem at great length and could find but one answer. Section One Hundred and Twenty-two of the law of June 3, 1916, was specific in restricting the award of the Medal of Honor to "an officer or enlisted man," and the scouts had all been civilians. In its report relating to the scouts, the board said "they rendered distinguished service and fully earned Medals." The board expressed the rather forlorn hope that the law of 1916 might be "modified" in some way to let the scouts keep their Medals.

There was but one slightly comforting circumstance relating to scouts, as far as the board was concerned. They were all dead. Buffalo Bill, the last to go, had died just two months before. The aging frontiersmen could not appear in person to haunt the waking hours of the board members.

Debate marked many of the board meetings and there had been differences of opinions regarding various individual awards. But the opinion of the board was unanimous in one case, that of Dr. Mary Edwards Walker, awarded the Medal

during the Civil War, the only woman on the list. There is "no evidence of distinguished gallantry on the part of this female contract surgeon," the board said. There was but one loudly dissenting voice, Dr. Walker herself, still very much alive and capable of wielding her venomous pen.

Early in 1916, months before the board was appointed to pass on the awards, Dr. Walker had written in to apply for the special Medal of Honor pension. She was seventy-four years old and residing at 304 Indiana Avenue, N.W., in Washington, keeping close tabs on all pending legislation.

The Secretary of War informed her tartly that as of that time, April 1916, the pension bill had not yet been approved by the President.

The following month, after the President had signed the bill into law, she wrote again, stating that her possession of the Medal was proof of her valor and she wanted the pension at once, and no nonsense about it.

There was an ominous note in the Secretary's next letter to the female doctoress. He stated that the benefits of the act— the pension—were restricted to persons whose military status had complied with the regulation embodied in the act. Mere possession of the Medal was not enough. The Secretary advised that since her assignment at the time of the award had been that of an assistant contract surgeon—a position ruled "civil" rather than "military"—she could not possibly qualify as an officer or enlisted man as the law required and her name would be stricken from the list.

And so the hosts of the male Philistines had triumphed at last. Dr. Walker's chariot was smashed, but she still had a broken sword to wave at her tormentors. "Notwithstanding such infamous regulations," she wrote the Adjutant General regarding her Medal, "I shall wear it, and one of them I will wear every day, and the other I will wear on special occasions!" For of course Dr. Walker had two, the old original one bestowed through the sympathy of Andrew Johnson in 1866 and the new Gillespie model, bullied out of the War Department in 1907.

There was one award on the record, however, that might have afforded Dr. Walker ammunition in her fight to retain her Medal had she known of it. That was the "special" Congressional award made to Major John O. Skinner, U.S. Army

Retired, in April 1915. Skinner was given the Medal for rescuing wounded soldiers under heavy fire in action against Indians at the Lava Beds in Oregon on January 17, 1873. At the time he performed his deed, Skinner was a contract surgeon. His name was not stricken from the official Medal of Honor list by the board in 1917.

With the year 1917 came the last of the awards to Civil and Indian War veterans, nine Medals awarded during March and April of that year. These were the last of the old timers with their memories of Bull Run and the Little Big Horn. The last Indian War Medal went to Leander Herron, onetime corporal in the Third U.S. Infantry, who won the award for an action against Indians at Fort Dodge, Kansas, in 1868, forty-eight years before. The last two Civil War Medals of Honor went to Henry Lewis and Henry C. Peters, both former members of the Forty-seventh Ohio Infantry, for deeds performed fifty-four years before at the Battle of Vicksburg.

VIII

A Fellow Can Get Killed This Way

THE great purge of the Army list in 1917 was only the beginning of a sweeping revision of Medal of Honor procedures. In June of that year Secretary of War Newton D. Baker wrote his views on proposed legislation to Senator G. E. Chamberlain of the Committee on Military Affairs. "I am against making provision in the law for awards for past deeds," Secretary Baker wrote bluntly, "other than for cases in which the Certificate of Merit has already been granted. The evidence for such awards is too irregular, casual and verbal. It is impossible to do justice to those who come up for consideration." Secretary Baker obviously desired to cut off once and for all the nagging requests for Medals by veterans of the Civil and Indian Wars.

The Congressional act which became a law on July 9, 1918,

was everything the Secretary might desire in clarifying the awards system. In addition to answering all questions about the Medal of Honor, the law also established three lesser decorations: the Distinguished Service Cross, the Distinguished Service Medal and the Silver Star.

This 1918 law applied only to Army decorations. A law for the Navy was not passed until the following year.

The 1918 law said the Medal of Honor would go "only to each person who, while an officer or enlisted man of the Army, shall hereafter in action involving actual conflict with an enemy, distinguish himself conspicuously by gallantry and intrepidity at the risk of his life above and beyond the call of duty." Thus the law made it clear that civilians were not eligible and armed conflict was a necessary condition.

Some attention should be given to the lesser awards since they were established to support the Medal of Honor at the apex of the so-called pyramid of honor.

The law provided that the Distinguished Service Cross could be awarded by the President, but not in the name of Congress, "to any person . . . serving in any capacity with the Army of the United States . . . who displayed extreme heroism in connection with military operations against an armed enemy."

Also, the President could award the Distinguished Service Medal, not in the name of Congress, "to any person . . . serving in any capacity with the Army of the United States . . . for exceptionally meritorious service to the Government in a duty of great responsibility, and also to any enlisted man of the Army to whom a Certificate of Merit had been awarded in the past."

The Distinguished Service Cross and the Distinguished Service Medal were placed on the same plane of importance to make an honorable but distinct separation in the awards system between outstanding acts of heroism relating to armed conflict and equally outstanding acts of meritorious service of great benefit to the Government, not necessarily related to armed conflict.

The third decoration established by this law was the Silver Star. In World War I this award was generally called a "citation star" and was worn on a campaign ribbon. It was awarded for gallantry in action by the order of a headquarters commanded by a general officer.

Enlisted men winning the Medal of Honor, DSC or DSM received $2 extra a month in pay for each medal while on active duty. Officer medal holders did not receive this pay. Only one medal of each type could be awarded winners. Any additional awards of the same medal were represented by bars. Enlisted men received the extra $2 a month for each bar. A widespread myth later grew that enlisted winners of the Medal of Honor were entitled by law to a salute. This was never the case, the salute story being just one part of the legend that grew up about the Medal.

The law set identical time limits for recommendations and issuances of all these awards. Recommendations had to be made within two years of the deed and the award itself had to be granted within three years. There was one exception to this time limit. As a consolation to those previously recommended for the Medal of Honor in full compliance with former regulations for services which did not fully justify the Medal under the new law, it was stated that the DSC or DSM might be awarded, if the services justified these lesser awards. The three-year limit could be waived in these cases, but all evidence of the deed had to be obtained from official records of the War Department. No more hazy verbal recollections would be accepted.

This law empowered only the President to make the awards of the top three medals and only the Medal of Honor was presented "in the name of Congress." But the law said the President could delegate the power to make the awards, if he desired, to commanding generals of separate armies or higher units in the field.

The United States Army awarded ninety-five Medals of Honor in World War I. This number included six to Marines, five of whom also received Navy Medals as duplicate awards, and four to Army Air Service flyers.

No Medals of Honor for World War I service were actually awarded until after the Armistice, November 11, 1918. Only four were approved before the Armistice. Two went to Lost Battalion officers: Major Charles W. Whittlesey, a New York lawyer, and Captain George McMurtry, a former Rough Rider. The other two were to First Lieutenant Samuel Woodfill of the Fifth Division, called by General Pershing "the greatest sol-

dier in the A.E.F.," and Private Thomas C. Neibaur of the Forty-second Rainbow Division.

Of the ninety-five Medals of Honor awarded by the Army in World War I, thirty-nine went to noncoms: twenty-seven to sergeants and twelve to corporals. Twenty-one went to privates and privates first class. Company grade officers took a lion's share of the officer awards. Seven captains and sixteen first and second lieutenants got Medals. Lieutenant colonels and majors received three each. No officer above the rank of lieutenant colonel won the Medal in World War I. Although according to legend, Generals John J. Pershing and Douglas MacArthur won Medals of Honor in World War I, MacArthur did not receive his until Bataan in World War II and General Pershing never got the award.

Several of the Army Medal winners of World War I became famous and remain either famous or well known to this day. Practically everyone has heard of Eddie Rickenbacker, Chairman of the Board of Eastern Airlines; William J. Donovan, New York corporation lawyer; and Alvin York, the Tennessee backwoodsman.

Rickenbacker's story will be told with the other Air Service winners. Donovan's story is so well known it will not be repeated in detail. He won his Medal in World War I as an officer of the Forty-second Rainbow Division for leading several assaults after being severely wounded. His command in the Forty-second was the old Sixty-ninth New York Regiment, better known as "The Fighting Sixty-ninth." Legend has it that the chaplain of this regiment, the immortal Father Francis P. Duffy, also won the Medal of Honor. This is not so. No chaplain, either Army or Navy, won the Medal of Honor in World War I. Father Duffy won the Distinguished Service Cross.

Lieutenant Colonel Donovan was one of the most decorated heroes of World War I, receiving the French Legion of Honor and Croix de Guerre, the Order of the British Empire, the Belgium Order of Leopold, and many many others. As a major general in World War II he headed the cloak and dagger Office of Strategic Services. Success followed this Medal winner in all his undertakings.

In contrast with the Donovan saga of perennial success is the career of Alvin York, mountaineer. He was perhaps the most famous hero of World War I and his personal tragedy became a

sort of national disgrace. As a youth York cursed and caroused and followed the ways of sin. Then one fateful day—January 1, 1914—the Lord showed him His face, as York has said, and converted him to a denomination called the Church of Christ of Christian Union.

When the war came in 1917, York was twenty-eight years old, a rawboned six feet two inches, weighing two hundred and ten pounds, and barely literate. His main livelihood was hunting foxes for $35 a pelt, shooting them cleanly through the head so as not to spoil the fur. At first he refused to enter military service on religious grounds, as a conscientious objector. Then something changed his mind and he joined up as a doughboy in the Eighty-second Division. On October 8, 1918, on Hill Two Hundred and Twenty-three in the Argonne, Corporal Alvin York displayed the marksmanship of a Tennessee fox hunter to a German battalion. After killing twenty-eight Germans—all shot through the head as cleanly as had been the foxes—the remainder of the battalion, one hundred and twenty-eight men and four officers, surrendered to the lanky mountaineer.

When York returned to the States he was a sergeant and a hero. In New York he got the big ticker-tape parade and the suite at the Waldorf Astoria. He helped found the American Legion. In Washington he listened to the applause of Congress. Then he went back to the place where he had been born, the Valley of the Three Forks of the Wolf River near Pall Mall, Tennessee.

Sergeant York became a big man in his own country. In Jimtown, the county seat of Fentress County, practically everything was named after him: the Alvin York Highway, the Alvin York Agricultural Institute, the Alvin York Bible School.

He made a lot of money on the lecture circuit, putting all his earnings into the York Institute, an organization he founded to bring modern farming methods to the backward mountain folks of his area. In 1941 Hollywood made a movie of his life called *Sergeant York* and York's share for the Institute was over $200,000.

Tragedy struck in 1954—cerebral hemorrhage. The old soldier shuddered like a tree struck by lightning and came crashing down. Then the Bureau of Internal Revenue moved in and said he owed the government $25,000 in back income taxes. As one mountaineer said, "By God, it ain't easy to be a hero now

with all these taxes." The old soldier was almost destitute in his mountain home, "riding the bed," as he put it. The $25,000 tax debt to the government was paid off by public subscriptions, and there was some money left over to pay medical bills. Although still almost penniless from giving everything away, Sergeant York could rest a bit easier in the Valley of the Three Forks of the Wolf.

In contrast with the famous York, there was another type of winner.

On Armistice Day 1921, three years after the cessation of hostilities, the United States buried the body of the Unknown Soldier at Arlington National Cemetery. General John J. Pershing selected three outstanding heroes of World War I to be among the pallbearers. He chose Colonel Charles Whittlesey of the Lost Battalion, Sergeant Alvin York of Pall Mall, Tennessee, and Sergeant Samuel Woodfill of the regular Army. News reporters looked puzzled when Pershing made this announcement. "Who's this Woodfill?"

The old general smiled. "Just the greatest soldier in the A.E.F."

When World War I started, Samuel Woodfill was a veteran of seventeen years' Army service. He had served in the steamy Philippines against the insurrectos and in frigid Alaska against the Kodiak bears and the long winter tedium. He was as fine a sharpshooter as York and because of his long military experience was twice the soldier. He never received as much publicity as the "civilian" soldier-heroes and apparently never sought any. Given a temporary wartime commission at the outbreak of the war, Woodfill served during World War I as a company commander in the Fifth Infantry Division.

After being commended in dispatches for gallantry in action on several different occasions, Woodfill, on October 12, 1918, in the Cunel sector, singlehandedly cleaned out five German machine-gun nests, one at a time with his rifle and automatic pistol. Attacked fiercely by the survivor of the last nest, Woodfill, his guns unloaded, beat his adversary to death with an entrenching tool.

The damp weather and poison gas did what the enemy fire could not do. Gasping with pneumonia, Woodfill was evacuated to the base hospital at Bordeaux. The mustard gas had affected his eyes severely and on his release from the hos-

pital, the medics refused to certify him for combat duty. The Army put the greatest soldier in the A.E.F. in charge of a delousing station. He was serving in this exalted capacity when called to A.E.F. Headquarters to receive the Medal of Honor.

In 1919, about to be mustered out of the Army, Woodfill requested permission to remain on active duty until 1923 so he could draw the full retirement pension for his long years of service. The chairborne brass cogitated about that for a while and finally decided that Woodfill was a good soldier all right but not really a gentleman and could stay on active duty only by taking a reduction in rank to sergeant.

As one disrespectful wag said later, "Woodfill's Medal of Honor and a nickel entitled him to ride on any subway in New York."

But Woodfill, the career soldier, accepted the sergeancy and retired from the Army in 1923 to a farm in Indiana. During World War II he served briefly as a major. He died in 1951 and is buried in Arlington National Cemetery.

Most of the Medal of Honor winners of World War I are as unknown today as Sam Woodfill. As examples take Gumpertz and Mallon. The military saga of First Sergeant Sydney Gumpertz and his company commander Captain George Mallon during the First World War displayed some of the characteristics of the Jewish-Irish vaudeville teams that flourished during that period.

Sydney G. Gumpertz was born in Stockton, California, in 1879, the son of a Jewish storekeeper. His people had come west with the covered wagons in 1850, peddling from packs during the day and helping fight off the fierce Indian raids during the long nights. In his high school days in Stockton, Gumpertz was a sergeant in the cadet corps. Always afterward he had a frustrated yearning to be a soldier. Leaving school he worked for several years as a newspaper bum in Chicago, Washington and San Francisco. In 1917, when the United States declared war on the Central Powers, Sydney Gumpertz was six feet tall and muscular. But he was also thirty-eight years old and married. Safe from the draft because of his age and marital status, he nonetheless volunteered to fight for his country.

Gumpertz went to training camp at Camp Logan, Texas, with the Second Illinois, which now became the One Hundred and Thirty-second Infantry Regiment of the Thirty-third In-

fantry Division. In the Division Headquarters company, Gumpertz rose quickly to sergeant, and when a first sergeancy became vacant in a line company, he volunteered for it and became First Sergeant Sydney G. Gumpertz of Company E, One Hundred and Thirty-second Regiment.

When Company Commander Captain George H. Mallon and Gumpertz first came on the scene, Company E had the reputation of being hard to handle, but that soon changed. Breaches of discipline brought company punishment, swift and inevitable, and after a while none of the company had much energy left for devilment because of the exhausting training program enforced by the rugged captain and his first sergeant.

The Thirty-third Division landed in France in May 1918, and were first brigaded with a British division which was regrouping from the ravages of the winter offensives. The outfit got its baptism of fire in the Somme and saw its first dead bodies, the grisly remains of men who had fallen months before, and were still unburied.

On the day of Yom Kippur in September of 1918, Gumpertz and the other Jews of the division were just preparing to go to Bar-le-Duc to attend services in the synagogue, when the long-awaited advance order came. All leaves were canceled. The division was moving out. The big push on the Argonne had started.

For the next several days they hiked along the French roads at night and tried to hide out all day, sleeping in barns and under camouflage nets. On the night of September 25th, Gumpertz' company relieved French troops in the trenches near a hill with the ominous name of Le Mort Homme—Dead Man's Hill. At two-thirty A.M., the Allied artillery began its preparation barrage.

At five-thirty A.M., a whistle sounded shrilly in the American trenches and they scrambled over the top, stumbling forward in a thick fog across the open ground, behind the rolling barrage. Sergeant Gumpertz leading the fourth platoon could hear other platoons to his right and left, but could not see them. Everyone was moving blindly forward, guided by the luminous dials of wrist compasses. Somewhere up ahead in the darkness, behind the rolling barrage, the enemy waited, playing possum in their holes.

Occasionally an incoming shell would explode with a violent

baroom, leaving a brief eerie glow in the dimness. Bullets whispered through the fog. Occasionally, a soldier would grunt and fall and then those coming behind would stumble over him and continue on. The medics might find him later, lightly wounded but trampled to death.

The breaking of day gave them a scene that caused the platoon a grim laugh. The laugh was at the expense of a corporal named Prazak. Loaded down with bandoliers of rifle ammunition, Corporal Prazak wore also around his waist a belt of ammunition festooned with half a dozen hand grenades. Suddenly, as the platoon trotted down a sudden hill, Corporal Prazak became the object of an enemy sniper's attention. Several bullets, almost spent, struck his ammunition belt, popping cartridges like firecrackers. Impressed with the danger of having the grenades explode on him, the erstwhile slow-moving Corporal Prazak suddenly went into a wild acrobatic dance to free himself of the grenade belt. He leaped about like a mad striptease artist, struggling with his tangle of belts and bandoliers. The rest of the platoon, including Sergeant Gumpertz, roared with laughter at his desperate antics.

"Goddamn it, men," said Corporal Prazak resentfully to his tormenters after finally freeing himself of his lethal belt ornaments, "it ain't that funny! A feller can get killed this way."

His words were prophetic. Prazak was killed later that day.

It was daylight now but clouds of heavy smoke and some of the remaining fog swept around in patches, obscuring the outfits to the right and left. Sergeant Gumpertz kept an eye out for greenish-colored clouds that might be poison gas.

At the base of a hill was a narrow stream and Gumpertz led them across, holding their rifles high above their heads. Shells dropping in the stream set up vaporing geysers of water. The water had been waist-deep and they clambered up the far bank with soaked pants and their heavy shoes full of water, all except the ones who died in the brook.

At the sunken road that was their first objective, they rested fifteen minutes. Sergeant Gumpertz, ever the conscientious noncom, ordered that shoes be removed and dry socks be put on. After exactly fifteen minutes—the rest that had been pre-ordered—Sergeant Gumpertz picked up his pack and waved the platoon to their feet. They were still on schedule. Fifteen minutes later they were held up by an enemy machine-gun nest.

Ahead of them the hidden machine gun chattered in the fog, bullets kicking up dirt in the intervening field. The enemy gunner was arcing an area, traversing the field about knee-high so that the bullets would knock an approaching enemy down on the first traverse and then as he lay on the ground, polish him off on the second sweep. The enemy gunner could not see the platoon for the fog, but on the other hand, Gumpertz and his men, faces in the dirt, could not see the gunner.

Followed by two volunteers, Sergeant Gumpertz trotted toward the sound of the machine gun. Clutched in his right hand was his forty-five pistol. There was no use in weaving or dodging in the fog, they all just ran headlong toward the sound of the gun.

Suddenly, they were charging up an incline and then almost fell headlong into the machine-gun nest. "I had not known I was so near the nest," said Gumpertz later. "It opened right under my feet."

Before the gunner could tilt his gun upward or grab his own sidearm Gumpertz fired his pistol with devastating accuracy. In a second the gunner, his loader, and assistant loader were sprawled across the gun and the other German crew members had their hands up trying to surrender.

They took fourteen prisoners and sent these to the rear with their hands up. Looking at his watch, Gumpertz saw they were behind schedule and ordered the platoon forward again.

Ten minutes later they were halted by another machine-gun nest. Gumpertz swore futilely, lying on his face with the others, pinned down by the arcing fire. To make matters worse, the enemy artillery had come alive and shells now began dropping among them.

Again calling for two volunteers, Gumpertz leaped forward, his two men following at five-yard intervals, the prescribed "artillery formation."

Again they could not see the machine gun because of the fog but could fix its position by the chatter of its fire. After a scant thirty yards, a shell burst among the advancing three and they flew about like tenpins. Paul Siclar, one of the volunteers, was killed instantly, his head blown off. Sebastian Emma, the other, was mortally wounded. He spoke briefly when Gumpertz crawled back to him and then died.

Through a rift in the fog, Gumpertz saw suddenly the spit-

ting muzzle of the machine gun, just twenty yards away. The gunner saw him at the same time and swung the muzzle around, but a drifting shard of fog hid Gumpertz as he staggered grimly toward the gun, pulling the pin of a grenade. He threw the grenade where he thought the gun was, waited until the explosion and then charged, praying that his blind throw had been accurate.

The nest was a shambles. A German noncom was trying frantically to pull the dead body of the gunner off the machine gun. Gumpertz shot him and then two more Germans who charged through the fog.

The rest of the platoon, summoned by the sergeant's yells, ran forward. They took sixteen more prisoners along with two heavy machine guns and sent the prisoners to the rear. After disabling the guns by smashing the bolts, Gumpertz hurried them on, trying to keep up with the schedule. By now he looked like a blackened scarecrow. He had lost his helmet and his uniform was shot and torn to shreds.

Reaching the edge of the Bois de Forges, they knew they were getting close to the final objective, but they were held up by yet another machine gun. This time it was in a pillbox on the edge of a clearing, the machine gun firing from a narrow slit. Gumpertz crawled off in a flanking circle. While the sergeant crawled up on the blind side of the pillbox, the platoon kept up a covering fire. Lying just under the slit in the pillbox, Gumpertz pulled the pin of a grenade, counted a couple of seconds slowly to burn up the fuse and delicately flipped it into the slit. There was a dull muffled roar and the iron door at the rear of the pillbox blew off from the inner concussion. Peering in through the smoke, Gumpertz could see that everyone was dead inside, so they hurried on.

Gumpertz said later that during this stage of the advance he had been in high hopes of beating Captain Mallon to the objective on the Meuse. But that was not to be. As Gumpertz led his platoon on the run up to an emplacement of four huge one-hundred-and-fifty-five-millimeter guns, he saw that Captain Mallon was already there interviewing the captured German artillery officer. Captain Mallon was standing in a position of parade rest and the German officer was lying on the ground holding his head. Captain Mallon had personally captured the

battery by charging singlehandedly and flattening the German officer with a blow of his fist.

The Mark IV tank of World War I was a ponderous lozenge-shaped monster weighing thirty-one tons. The clanking rigid track suspension propelled the tank at less than four miles an hour. The range was only fifteen miles on seventy-five gallons of fuel. And yet despite their shortcomings, these primitive tanks were effective weapons in no man's land. They could cross a ten-foot trench, climb a twenty degree slope or a vertical wall four feet high. They advanced ponderously and inexorably on enemy machine-gun nests, firing as they came, and then crushing the enemy gunners like bugs if they did not flee.

During an attack the inside of a tank was like a small corner of hell. Pistons clanked and small-arms fire hammered deafeningly on the steel sides. The air inside was chokingly full of fumes: hot oil, gasoline and cordite from the six-pound cannons.

Two tankers won Medals of Honor in World War I. Both were members of the Three Hundred and Forty-fourth Tank Battalion, Tank Corps, commanded by the youthful Lieutenant Colonel George S. Patton, who would have given his immortal soul to win a Medal of Honor, but never did.

The first tanker winner was Corporal Donald M. Call. When his tank suffered a direct hit from a German artillery shell, Call rescued a wounded officer from the burning tank and carried him under heavy fire for over a mile to bring him to safety.

Corporal Harold Roberts, a tank driver, won his Medal of Honor at Montrebeau Woods on October 4, 1918. Roberts fought his guiding handles grimly as the huge Mark IV rocked and slid across the steep terrain, recently deluged with rain. As the tank slewed sideways out of control down a steep slope, Roberts saw with horror at the bottom of the slope a huge shell hole, ten feet deep and full of water. As the tank teetered ponderously on the edge, Roberts gasped to the gunner beside him, "Only one of us can get out." He shoved the gunner out the back door just as the tank tipped over the edge and sank into the water-filled crater. Roberts, drowned in the submerged tank, was awarded the Medal posthumously.

Only five men in our history have won both Army and Navy Medals of Honor. All of them won their Medals during World

War I and all of them were Marines. They received their Army Medals first and their Navy Medals later as duplicate awards for the same deeds.

When World War I broke out, the Fourth Brigade of United States Marines was detached from the Navy to serve with the American Expeditionary Forces in France under the command of Army General John J. Pershing. The Brigade consisted of two rifle regiments, the Fifth and Sixth. The cadre were old timers drawn from ships' guards and shore stations all over the world. They were the old breed who had seen service in the Legation Guard in Peking, the Fleet Marine Force, Samar, Vera Cruz, Nicaragua, Haiti and the Dominican Republic. Smedley D. Butler, Dan Daly, and other Marine Medal-winners were there. The units were filled out with gangling boisterous recruits from every state in the Union, and soon the recruits were kicked into line and took on the character and color of the old breed.

Arriving in France in February 1918, the Marine Brigade was part of the Second Division of the United States Army. They fought with the Second Division during the war and returned with it when the division came home in August 1919.

All five of the Marine double-award winners had something in common in that their deeds involved charging enemy machine-gun nests.

Gunnery Sergeant Ernest August Janson, serving in the Corps under the name Charles Hoffman—a touch of personal mystery here that was never explained—won his Medal June 6, 1918, during the attack on Hill One Hundred and Forty-two. Janson was attempting to dig in on the north slope when his platoon came under fire from a German squad with five light machine guns. Charging the enemy squad, Janson bayoneted two of the gunners and put the remainder to flight.

Sergeant Louis Cukela, an Austrian-born resident of Minnesota, won his Medal during the action in the Forest de Retz, near Villers-Cotterêts, France, on July 18, 1918. When an enemy strong point held up the advance of his platoon, he crawled out on the flank in the face of heavy fire and worked his way to the rear of the enemy position. Then, bounding to his feet, he rushed the key machine-gun nest of the strong point and killed most of the crew with his bayonet, driving off the rest. Then he bombed out the rest of the emplacement with Ger-

man hand grenades captured in the nest. By the time the rest of the platoon got there, the show was over.

Sergeant Matej Kocak, another native-born Austrian in the same rifle company as Sergeant Cukela, won his Medal the same day, July 18, 1918, in the Villers-Cotterêts section. When a hidden machine-gun nest halted the advance of his battalion, he too went forward alone and unprotected, working his way to the flank of the German position under heavy fire. Then he too took his enemy position with the mad charge and the bloody work with the bayonet. Later the same day he organized some French colonial soldiers who had become separated from their unit and led them in the successful attack on another machine-gun nest.

Corporal John Henry Pruitt of Faderville, Arkansas, was awarded the Medal posthumously for his actions on October 3, 1918, in the Battle of Blanc Mont Ridge, a key German defense point in the Rheims sector. The ridge was an old battleground, scarred with deep trenches and covered with concrete fortifications and masses of barbwire entanglements. It had been battered and blasted for years by artillery and mortar without success in evicting the stubborn defenders. In the midst of this ravaged landscape Corporal Pruitt found an enemy machine-gun nest and captured it with a singlehanded charge, killing two of the enemy. Then he captured forty prisoners in a dugout nearby. An hour later, he was killed by enemy artillery fire while sniping at the enemy from an isolated position far in advance of his own lines. The one-man vendetta was over.

Another Marine received an Army Medal of Honor for actions during a gas attack. The Germans had first used chlorine gas against the Allies at Ypres on April 22, 1915. Early that morning the members of the Eighty-seventh French Territorials observed what seemed to be a greenish-yellow cloud floating toward them on the light breeze. As it came closer, the cloud seemed to turn an ice-blue. Suddenly, from one of the forward outposts, a sergeant stumbled, clutching his throat and emitting agonizing screams. The whole group in the forward echelon began coughing and choking and tearing at their tunic fronts. They sank to their knees and in their last throes, rolled over and kicked the air. Some tried to escape the cloud in dugouts and trenches. It was no use. The gas was two and a half times as heavy as air and quickly filled all ground cavities.

Five thousand men died during this first gas attack.

Although the Allies developed effective gas masks and certain defensive techniques, gas remained the largest single casualty maker of World War I. In that war the gas toll was ninety-one thousand one hundred and twenty-eight deaths and one million two hundred and five thousand, six hundred and fifty-five serious injuries.

On June 14, 1918, the Ninety-sixth Company of the Sixth Marine Regiment, of which Gunnery Sergeant Fred Stockham was a member, was in action at Belleau Wood. The desperate Germans fired gas shells and a favorable wind quickly carried the deadly cloud to the attacking Marines. Sergeant Stockham gave one of the wounded men in his platoon his gas mask, and then stayed on maskless in the gassed area, helping get the wounded out. Late that afternoon he collapsed choking. After suffering horribly for several days in a field hospital, he died from the effects of the deadly cloud.

Sergeant Stockham was the only Marine serving with the Army in World War I who won an Army Medal of Honor and was not issued a Navy Medal as a duplicate award for the same deed.

IX

A Question of Coordinates

DURING World War I, the story of the Lost Battalion was publicized widely in the newspapers. Its stand in the Argonne was compared at various times with the defense of the Alamo, and the Battles of New Orleans and the Little Big Horn. Eight members of the Lost Battalion won Medals of Honor. Three of the winners were Major Charles W. Whittlesey, Captain George McMurtry and Captain Nelson M. Holderman. It might be noted that Captain Holderman was named for General Nelson A. Miles, a Civil War winner of the Medal.

There was another unit whose destiny became enmeshed with that of the Lost Battalion. The story of this unit has never been widely told. This unit was the Fiftieth Aero Squadron. The Army Air Service won four Medals of Honor during World War I, and practically everyone has heard the names of two of the winners: Captain Eddie Rickenbacker and Lieutenant Frank Luke. But few people have heard of Lieutenants Harold E. Goettler and Erwin R. Bleckley. They were members of the Fiftieth Aero Squadron and won their Medals by their efforts to locate the Lost Battalion and furnish the beleaguered battalion supplies by the first air-drop in history.

The Lost Battalion was composed of units of the Seventy-seventh "Statue of Liberty" Division, a New York outfit. The Fiftieth Squadron originated far away in Texas, formed at Kelly Field near San Antonio on August 6, 1917. Their destinies would not become involved until September 1918, when the great battle for the Argonne Forest began.

The most glamorous flying role in World War I was piloting the one-seater "pursuit" planes. This was the type of ship the "aces" flew. This was the type that got in all the newspapers. Shortly after the Fiftieth Aero Squadron was formed at Kelly Field, they got the bad news. They would be issued two-seater planes and would perform the unglamorous mission of reconnaissance and infantry-contact patrol.

One hundred and forty-nine men reported for duty in the original outfit. Nobody knew what his job was going to be. They had one characteristic in common, a virgin ignorance about flying. And for a while it looked as if they were never going to do any flying. They spent their time doing the shake-down chores of military life: close order drill, barracks scrubbing and kaypee. After a while they drew planes and a small percentage passed, or survived, flight training. The others became mechanics, riggers and armorers.

The Fiftieth trained at Kelly Field; Garden City, Long Island; Winchester, England; and finished up at St. Maixent and Amanty in France. In France First Lieutenant Daniel F. Morse became commanding officer. Morse scorned the idea that pursuit was the most important branch of the Air Service. To him the most important mission of war aircraft was observation work, and pursuit planes existed only to protect the larger aircraft.

The outfit adopted the popular Dutch Girl cleanser trademark as its insignia. The squadron motto was "cleaning up Germany." But, despite the brave trademark and motto and the remarks of Lieutenant Morse, the pilots and observers had certain trepidations about the two-seater DeHavilland Four planes they flew. This aircraft was popularly known as the "flying coffin" because the unarmored gasoline tank was located between the two cockpits. The pilot and the observer burned almost instantly when a good burst of incendiaries hit the tank. Also the landing gear, being too light, was known to buckle on rough landings. And many of the Liberty engines were defective and spark plugs of the era were consistently bad. Diving in to zoom low over enemy positions to photograph gun emplacements was fatal when the plugs failed to fire and the engine conked out suddenly.

Observation work in the cranky planes was a ticklish business. Sometimes they had to fly just a few feet off the ground looking for enemy and friendly units on the fog-shrouded terrain. American ground troops were notoriously uncooperative. They objected to displaying identification panels for their own patrol planes. The doughboys said the panels told the enemy aircraft where they were and the enemy had a lot more planes in the air than the Allies. When any plane came over, the tendency on the part of ground troops was to lie in their holes and play possum. This possum attitude frustrated Corps artillery which needed to keep track of the ever-shifting line positions in order not to rain shells on Allied troops. Sometimes the observation planes had to fly low enough to look at uniforms. Then if the troops were enemy, the planes would be harassed with small-arms fire.

On September 22, and 23, 1918, the Fiftieth Squadron moved from their field at Behonne near Bar-le-Duc to Remicourt. The move was made with an air of great secrecy during a heavy rain. They knew something big was in the wind. On September 26th the great battle for the Argonne Forest began.

The Argonne Forest was twenty miles wide and ten to twelve miles deep. During almost four years of war the Germans had laced it with barbwire and fortified it with a complex of trenches and pillboxes. Standing squarely in the path of the Allied advance, it had to be smashed before winter set in.

The offensive, as usual, began with a great artillery barrage,

the heaviest of all barrages up to that time. The shells fired outnumbered all those fired by the Northern armies in the entire Civil War. But the enemy was by no means destroyed or visibly subdued by the barrage. When the Allied infantry attacked, they were met with machine guns, mortars and poison gas. The attack slowed and finally stalled to a full halt. Then orders came down from Pershing, "Objectives are to be gained regardless of losses."

Major Charles W. Whittlesey, commanding officer of the First Battalion, Three Hundred and Eighth Infantry, Seventy-seventh Division, received the bad news with the other battalion commanders. His orders were slightly worse than the others. His battalion was to advance on the left flank of the offensive, straight north through the German lines, across the Charlevaux Valley and then up the far slope of the valley to where a little road ran east and west from Charlevaux Mill. He was to dig in along the road and await further orders. The joker was that if he reached his objective, his outfit would stick out like a finger into enemy territory with no flank protection.

Whittlesey, a lanky New York lawyer, blinked solemnly through his steel-rimmed spectacles. "Well, I don't know if you'll hear from us again," he said. Whittlesey had been given the unenviable flank position during an advance several weeks before and had almost been cut off from the main body. He knew what the hazards were.

At 12:30 P.M. on October 2, 1918, the gawky Whittlesey led his command into the murky gloom of a wooded ravine leading north. He slogged along in front with his sergeant major, carrying a forty-five automatic and a large pair of wire cutters. Behind him came his support, the Second Battalion under the command of Captain (acting major) George G. McMurtry and several sections of the Three Hundred and Sixth Machine Gun Battalion. Whittlesey had scouts out and there was light resistance, just a few snipers and some scattered artillery shells bursting high in the trees.

In the middle of the afternoon, they captured a group of sixty German prisoners, and sent them back with guards along the connecting file of runner posts that had been set up. Major Whittlesey began to breathe more easily. Maybe this was going to be an easy offensive after all.

By 5:15 P.M. Whittlesey led the advance elements of the

First Battalion down the slope of the Charlevaux Valley and across a narrow plank foot bridge spanning the stream that ran along the valley bottom. Their objective, the mill road, ran just above them on the north slope. Whittlesey deployed his troops along the road in a position about three hundred yards long and sixty yards deep. Here they dug in and prepared to spend the night. They had plenty of ammunition and grenades but were short of rations and blankets. Shivering in their holes, the men smoked Bull Durham or the tailor-made Piedmonts.

In the gray dawn of early morning, they were heartened by reinforcements. Captain Nelson M. Holderman, commanding officer of Company K of the Three Hundred and Seventh, led his company up to the position. He had come in along the line of runner posts. Whittlesey was glad to see Holderman, a stolid silent type of officer, known to be a good combat soldier.

Enemy artillery began coming in about 8:30 A.M., but the Americans were protected by the reverse slope of the road above. Whittlesey found the silence to his right and left ominous and sent out scouts. The news they returned with was not heartening. The French unit that was supposed to be on the left was not there. But the Germans were. The Three Hundred and Seventh, supposed to be on the right, was not there. Just some more Germans. Then small-arms fire began sounding from the rear, along the connecting file of runner posts. Whittlesey sent Captain Holderman and his company back to reconnoiter. Holderman returned in a few hours with the news that the Germans had captured the high ground behind them.

Shortly after noon on October 3rd, the situation became sickeningly clear to Whittlesey. He and his five hundred and fifty men, crammed into a little four-acre pocket, were surrounded by the enemy in the Argonne Forest. What he did not know at the time was that out of all the fifty thousand attacking troops, his group had been the only one which had broken through to its assigned objective.

Whittlesey conferred with McMurtry and Holderman in a hole. They made a strange trio, the lanky bespectacled lawyer, the stolid Holderman with the air of a solemn scout-master, and the hearty bulldog McMurtry who had been a Rough Rider during the Spanish-American War and could call practically every man of his battalion by his first name.

Then Whittlesey sent the message that was to cause the heart-break and the dissension in the years to come. "I'll send our position back to Division headquarters," he said. The battalion was beyond the reach of telephone wires and there was no radio available in that war. But the battalion had brought seven crated carrier-pigeons with them. The system was to write the messages on rice paper, insert the message in the metal capsule on the pigeon's leg and let the bird flap away to the home loft in the rear. Whittlesey set out the coordinates of his position, locating his unit at 294.6-276.3 on the battle map. He requested artillery support. These coordinates would later become an important part of the controversy.

At 3 P.M. that afternoon came the first organized enemy attack on the pocket. A heavy Minenwerfer opened up from about six hundred yards away and began to rain mortar shells on the position. From the ridge above came the sudden shower of hand grenades that presaged a full-scale infantry attack. The green-clad infantry advanced through the murky woods, firing from behind trees and hurling grenades. The battalion chaut-chaut gunners on the periphery fought them back.

Within a few hours the besieged group was reduced to about two hundred and fifty fighting men. Food ran out and then bandages. The wounded began using their wraparound leggings to bandage their wounds. Whittlesey sent back another carrier-pigeon message, a plea for more ammunition and some artillery support.

About noon of the next day, after enduring a cold and sleepless night, there was a lull in the German fire. Many of the defenders crawled out of their holes to stretch and take a breather. Suddenly, the outfit was galvanized by the sound of explosions on the ridges to the south. It was artillery support at last.

The barrage crept slowly down the slope and across the marshy valley, blowing up volcanoes of earth, trees and underbrush as it came on, inexorably, closer and closer to the pocket of American troops.

There was a hoarse cry of horror and outrage, and the shells began bursting in the midst of their position, blasting and killing with explosive ferocity.

The officers frantically struggled to control the panic-stricken troops. Major Whittlesey stalked about grimly, seemingly un-

mindful of the holocaust, trying to quiet the panic. Captain McMurtry leaped about from hole to hole, shouting encouragement and bandaging wounded.

The slaughter was shocking. With shaking fingers, Whittlesey reached for his message pad. This was the message he sent with the last pigeon: "We are along road parallel to 276.4. Our own artillery is dropping a barrage directly on us. For heaven's sake stop it." The last pigeon circled the position with maddening confusion and then perched obstinately on a tree branch. One of the defenders got it in the air again by throwing a rock. Finally, the bird, pursued by enemy gun fire, flew away toward the rear.

Picking up the story back at Seventy-seventh Division Headquarters, a United Press correspondent sent back to the States a short squib about the American unit trapped in the Argonne Forest. His editor in New York, smelling a good human-interest story, wired back: "Send more on Lost Battalion."

Newspapers picked it up at once, headlining the story. Out of the millions of men fighting on the Western Front, the "Lost Battalion" was singled out for vivid dramatic treatment. It mattered not that the name and entire concept were erroneous. It was not one battalion, but two battalions along with units from others. And the outfit was not lost—the coordinates sent out by Whittlesey later proved to be slightly off, but the general location of the unit was known. Still, the outfit became the Lost Battalion in the headlines and also in history.

On October 4th orders came for the Fiftieth Aero Squadron to supply Whittlesey and his men by air-drop. A DH-4 was loaded heavily with supplies and Lieutenants Floyd M. Pickerell and Alfred C. George flew the mission. Lieutenant Dean Morse, the Fiftieth C.O., furnished them with the map coordinates sent out by Whittlesey. Pickerell and George flew over the designated position and dropped the food and medical supplies. Ground fire was heavy, but they failed to see any American troops. Other planes followed, dropping supplies.

The Fiftieth Squadron received Whittlesey's last frantic message about artillery barrage on October 6th, with orders to find the unit before dropping any more supplies. They started the task immediately.

Lieutenant Harold E. Goettler, pilot, with Lieutenant Erwin R. Bleckley, as observer, took off in their heavily loaded DH-4

on the morning of October 6th. Using the Charlevaux Mill as a point of reference, they winged down low over the ravine. So much mist and smoke shrouded the terrain that they dropped to five hundred feet to make a run, then made another at three hundred. The enemy on the floor of the ravine cannily held their fire to conceal their positions, but the Germans on the heights above the ravine blasted away at the low-flying aircraft with machine guns and rifles. Even at three hundred feet the searching plane could see no troops in the tangled undergrowth. Circling at a thousand feet, they fired Very lights, but received no answering signal from the ground.

Down they went along the long roller coaster, wings vibrating and struts whining, skimming the tops of the trees at less than two hundred feet. As they roared the length of the ravine, the plane was actually lower in altitude than the German gunners on the heights. Fire rained down on them, but they ran the gauntlet, still without seeing any troops. Back at the drome the pair looked over their plane. There were forty holes in the DH-4. Two of them were gaping shrapnel gashes in the wings.

As plane after plane of the Fiftieth joined in the search for the Whittlesey group, the German accuracy on the heights of the ravine improved. Two planes were shot down that day, crashing in no man's land. Another limped home with a wounded, bloody pilot grimly fighting the controls.

Goettler and Bleckley, the pair who had started the day, volunteered for one more trip. They decided this time they would fly so low they would draw fire from the floor of the ravine. They thought they might locate the American position by process of elimination. It was a reckless idea. But the airmen suspected that the isolated command was so closely surrounded that they dared not move around to lay out panels or shoot Very lights.

Harold Goettler informed Lieutenant Dan Morse prior to the take-off, "Erv and I have decided we're going to find that bunch of doughboys or die trying."

It was one of those fateful prophecies, taken lightly at the time, which come back later with heavy import.

There on the ground in their isolated little four-acre pocket of hell, Major Whittlesey, and Captains McMurtry and Holderman, citizen soldiers and amateur officers all, were learning the fearful and lonely responsibilities of command. Especially

Whittlesey. The lanky scholarly lawyer, by nature a sensitive and retiring person, sat among the starving and thirst-maddened wounded, presenting an image of calm confidence. "There are a million Americans behind us," he told them. "It won't be long. Just hang on a little while longer . . ."

One maddening aspect of the position was that a stream of clear water flowed in the ravine not far away. But the approaches to the stream were covered by enemy machine gun and mortar fire. Trying for the stream to bring back water was sure death. But the die-hards kept trying. "I'm going to shoot the next man that leaves his position to get water," Captain Holderman announced quietly.The men knew that the solemn one was not kidding. They looked beseechingly at their idol, the convivial McMurtry. The glad-handing Rough Rider smiled at them grimly. "Right," he said, "and I'll shoot the second one." The men stayed in their holes and endured their thirst.

Late in the afternoon of October 6th, the members of the Lost Battalion watched one of the most daring air shows of the war. It was another one of the American two-seater planes with the Dutch Girl insignia on the side. Skimming in above the tree tops, the cumbersome plane almost touched the ground in the open spaces, zoomed to clear the trees again and then pivoted to come doggedly back almost along the floor of the ravine.

The Germans on the floor of the ravine could not resist the temptation. They opened fire on the harassing plane with machine guns and rifles. Bleckley, the observer, carefully noted the position of the enemy fire, marking off an area on the map where he felt the lost group must be. Goettler, the pilot, confident that only the enemy was firing from positions on the floor of the ravine, strafed methodically with the forward machine gun. To make the run a second time was suicidal but Goettler brought the ship about and came down again. As the plane roared again through the merciless barrage of ground fire, the pilot's windscreen and the instruments on the dash disintegrated. Bleckley was hit and slumped over his Lewis gun. With bloody hands, Goettler lifted the nose of the crippled DH-4 up over the ridge to the west. With a loud crash the DH-4 pancaked flatly in front of the French lines and skittered to a sideways halt.

Miraculously the plane did not catch fire before the French patrol got there. Goettler the pilot was dead. Bleckley was dying but pressed his map into the hand of the French officer. Clearly outlined on the map was the area where he knew the Lost Battalion had to be because of the lack of ground fire there.

As result of Bleckley's map location of the unit, deliverance came with unexpected suddenness. At 7:07 P.M. next day Whittlesey and McMurtry were in the command hole, wearily talking. McMurtry was suffering from a jagged wound in his back caused by a German grenade.

A runner panted up. "Major, there's an officer wants to see you! He just came in."

It was Lieutenant Richard Tillman with a patrol from the Three Hundred and Seventh Infantry. The Lost Battalion had been found.

The outfit was welcomed back to the Seventy-seventh Division as heroes. Whittlesey received a promotion to lieutenant colonel and McMurtry to major. With Holderman they received Medals of Honor for their actions with the Lost Battalion.

Then came the dissension that could have caused the tragic ending of Whittlesey's life. It had to do with the pigeon message of October 3, 1918. Reporting the unit's position on that date, Whittlesey located himself at coordinates 294.6-276.3.

On October 7, 1918, after the battalion had been found, Lieutenant W. J. Rogers, observer of the Fiftieth Aero Squadron, reported the correct coordinates as 294.9-276.3.

Captain Daniel P. Morse, Jr., commanding officer of the Fiftieth Aero Squadron, later made this observation, "This small difference, however, made all the difference between life and death . . ."

In the question of the coordinates lay the personal tragedy of Lieutenant Colonel Charles W. Whittlesey, prominent Manhattan lawyer. It trapped him eternally in that hellish four-acre pocket in the Argonne Forest. The public never let him forget the experience. He was harried and harassed for speeches, always on the same subject—the happenings during the five days of the "Lost" Battalion. In 1921 it became too difficult to bear. He committed suicide by jumping over the rail of a cruise ship at night on a trip to Havana.

Thus three of the Medal winners were dead, their destinies enmeshed in the mystery of the Lost Battalion and its position: Goettler and Bleckley the airmen, and Whittlesey the ground commander, hounded by his memories.

Captain Nelson M. Holderman became Commandant of the Veterans' Home of the State of California. He had received seven wounds during the five-day siege and in the heat of the action had been described by numerous witnesses as propping himself up on two rifles as crutches, firing his forty-five and whooping and yelling like a madman. But back in civilian life, he reverted to his own silent self, refusing to talk about any of his actions during the siege.

The gregarious McMurtry, the former Rough Rider, lived on to be eighty-two years old, a successful and wealthy New York stockbroker. Until his death in 1958, he financed the annual reunion luncheon in New York City of the Lost Battalion survivors. He always kept in mind what Charles Whittlesey told him the day they walked down the ravine after being relieved: "George, no matter where we go or what we do, we will never be in finer company."

X

The Cowboy and the Racing Driver

Two Army Air Service pursuit pilots won Medals of Honor in World War I. The most mysterious and controversial of the two was Frank Luke. He swaggered out of Arizona in the tradition of an airborne Wyatt Earp or Wild Bill Hickok, had his brief and violent fling, and then he was gone, to an end that became almost as mysterious and legend-ridden as that of another youthful gunman, Billy the Kid.

Frank Luke was born in Phoenix, Arizona, May 19, 1897, which was about thirty or forty years too late for a man with his natural talents. Had he been a young man in the Arizona Territory in the 1870's and 1880's he would have been a hellion in

the tradition of the Earp brothers and Texas John Slaughter. But by the time he was a young man the age of the gunslinger was past and he exercised his wonderful talent for marksmanship by shooting at wolves and coyotes with a thirty-thirty Winchester. In school he was a poor student, but a good athlete, winning letters in baseball, football and track. He was a natural born scrapper. At seventeen he got into the ring with a touring professional prize fighter named Haney and knocked him out in one round. And on September 25, 1917, in Tucson, he enlisted as a private in the Signal Corps and requested flying duty.

He had many of the natural qualities of a good combat pilot: keen eyes, good coordination, lightning reflexes, steady nerves, and practically no imagination at all. The most outstanding thing about his performance, however, was not his ability to fly as much as it was his ability to shoot. Firing a machine gun, even from the balky yawing training planes, his accuracy was uncanny. He was commissioned second lieutenant January 23, 1918.

Like most replacement pilots, Luke went to the Aviation Instruction Center at Issoudun where he took advanced training under veteran combat pilots. Frank Luke was not impressed. He had several narrow escapes in the training planes but his confidence in himself never wavered. Perhaps it was this cocksure attitude that caused his superiors at Issoudun to send him to the ferry pool at Orly, rather than to a fighting squadron at the front.

Luke made no secret of the fact that he felt ferrying new planes from Orly to the front was beneath his abilities as a pilot. He flaunted authority and took off on solo jaunts of his own in the new planes that were badly needed at the front. When admonished by his superior officers, he said sullenly, "I came here to fight, not ferry."

On July 26, after one of his solo jaunts, the commanding officer finally had enough of his insubordination and sent him as a replacement pilot to the Twenty-seventh Aero Squadron commanded by Major Harold E. Hartney. The Twenty-seventh was one of the four squadrons comprising the First Pursuit Group. The other squadrons were the Ninety-fourth, Ninety-fifth, and One Hundred and Forty-seventh.

When Frank Luke stepped out of the sidecar with his kit bag

at the Twenty-seventh drome, twenty-five miles south of Château-Thierry, he was still not impressed. The landing field was
"L" shaped with muddy, uneven turf. An unsightly group of
buildings fronted the field: shacks, decayed canvas hangars,
and cookhouses with crooked tin chimneys.

In the mess, Luke immediately made a name for himself.
"I can't imagine," he observed, "how some of you guys have
stayed up here so long and still haven't knocked down your
five planes to become aces."

A certain noticeable chill fell over the room after that.
There were several veteran pilots present who had risked their
lives on many sorties over the lines but still had not shot down
the required number of planes to qualify as aces.

They were further disillusioned with their swaggering replacement when Major Hartney took him up next day for a
mock dogfight in the rear area. The veteran Hartney found
that Luke was so green as a combat pilot that he could not
elude the most elementary combatant tactics. "I'll tell you one
thing though," he said to his executive officer in the privacy of
his quarters, "that boy can shoot. If he can live long enough to
learn any acrobatics he may become an ace himself."

Notwithstanding that observation by the veteran Hartney,
Luke was considered an incompetent loudmouth by the other
pilots and ignored. He continually flouted orders by taking off
on solo patrols. The only one who would have anything to do
with him was a pilot named Joe Wehner, who made it a point
to be agreeable to Luke. Luke responded to his advances and
for once he had a friend.

From his first day at the front, Frank Luke had noticed balloons hanging like swollen and misshapen blobs in the sky behind the enemy lines, without being particularly drawn to
them. Swinging baskets, attached to these balloons, held artillery observers with powerful field glasses and oversized parachutes who were ready to hit the silk if a pursuit plane made a
pass at them.

Observers were not the menacing things about balloons.
Balloons were surrounded by anti-aircraft gun emplacements
and ground-mounted heavy machine guns. All the guns were
zeroed in on the area surrounding the bag and any attacking
plane had to brave a merciless ring of fire. Also, on landing

fields near balloons, enemy pursuit planes were always warmed and in readiness to fight off attackers of their gasbags.

Early one September morning Luke and Wehner took off from the field, one at a time, the little Spads clawing into the air with their yawing sideways climb. Luke led because he knew where there was an enemy balloon near Marieulles. Circling high above, they looked down at the bloated bag straining on its cable. Luke had not devised any complicated plan. Waving at Wehner, he peeled off, roaring down on the target. With the bag enormous in his Aldis sight he pressed his triggers, the incendiary bullets streaking out. His fire seemed to have no effect, the balloon kept looming larger and larger, even though the crew was pulling it in desperately. Suddenly, the sky seemed to explode all around him in jarring black puffs of archie and buzzing machine-gun bullets. Grimly ignoring the distractions Luke steadied his wildly jumping plane and let his guns go again. Suddenly the huge bag blew up, emitting a black hell of smoke and red flame almost in his face. The explosion bounced the Spad all over the sky. Luke pulled out of a shallow dive just off the ground and made it back to his own lines, flying less than fifty feet above the earth.

Over Berzy the next day a flight from the Twenty-seventh watched the Arizona cowboy break another balloon. As Luke dived away from the formation down on the bulbous blob, Joe Wehner clawed for altitude above to act as lookout. The flight watched with horrified fascination as Luke zoomed straight for the bag, unmindful of the flaming concentric rings of archie and machine-gun fire. As he closed to within a few hundred yards he pressed his triggers and let the long chattering burst of incendiaries stream out. He zoomed upward just in time as the balloon dissolved into a mound of flame.

Ignoring the fact that the Twenty-seventh flight had been engaged by a superior group of enemy Fokkers, Luke headed away on his own. There was another balloon near Boinville and he was going after it. He had to dive on it six times and his plane was practically shot to shreds before this bag collapsed.

Back in the squadron mess that night Frank Luke was accepted for the first time with something like cordiality. After all, how many squadrons had pilots who could shoot down two

balloons in a single day? The cordiality brought an invitation for Luke to participate in the evening crap game for the first time and this brought out another irritating facet in Luke's personality. The cowboy was a fabulously lucky crap shooter and reveled in his gambling victories as much as he did in his air victories. Flushed and loudly belligerent, he covered bets all around the board and won them all.

Charging bull-like straight at balloons through the rings of protective fire was Luke's direct method of knocking them down. Apparently he lacked imagination to conceive that someday the percentages would catch up with him and the archie would get him. He was supremely confident that his luck would hold. But Joe Wehner was shrewder and more calculating. And the cowboy would bend his ear when Wehner spoke. "How about catching the bags at dusk, just before they haul them down? We can see them against the sky a lot better than the ground can see us. And there won't be as many Fokkers around."

That made sense to the hunter in Frank Luke. In the dusk of evening on September 16, Luke and Wehner crossed the field to their planes. The C.O. nervously informed the two that there were two distinguished visitors at the field that evening, Colonel Billy Mitchell, Chief of the Air Service, and Lieutenant Eddie Rickenbacker, America's leading ace.

"Great!" said Luke. "Tell them the first balloon will go up at exactly 7:15 and the next at 7:19."

The C.O. shook his head and rejoined his distinguished visitors in the mess. The cowboy was nutty as a squirrel, but he would call Mitchell and Rickenbacker from the mess anyway.

As the three stood peering into the fading light, they could just make out the dark blobs of the balloons against the sky. At exactly 7:15 one of them suddenly burst into a bright star of flame. They watched the luminous dials of their watches. Seven nineteen came and passed. Nothing happened. Then at 7:20 another new star of flame blossomed in the east.

Back at the drome Luke was more insufferable than ever. Now he had the eye of the Chief of the Air Service. Everyone knew how Frank Luke, the loudmouth cowboy from the Twenty-seventh Squadron, had made his brags in front of Colonel Mitchell and won. Everyone knew about it, because if they

had not heard it before—or even if they had—Frank Luke himself would tell them about it.

From then on it was a sort of crazy whirl. On the day his friend Joe Wehner was killed, Frank Luke knocked down two balloons, two Fokkers and an enemy Halberstadt observation plane! Five victories in one day. Then the next day he received three delayed confirmations of victories. His official score was now posted at fourteen, twice the number Eddie Rickenbacker had on his record at the time. Frank Luke, the cowboy from Arizona, was the leading ace of the American Air Service.

His last flight was an attack on three balloons over the Meuse River near Dun. Ever the show-off, Luke dropped low over the American Balloon Headquarters at Souilly and dropped in a cylinder. "Watch out for those three nearest balloons at D-1 and D-4 positions," he wrote, giving them the coordinates.

Eyes straining in the darkness toward the designated positions were soon rewarded. At brief intervals three vivid explosions blossomed in the sky. Then came the silence and the waiting.

Frank Luke never came back. It was as simple as that. The whole story was not learned until the war was over. Then it came in the form of an affidavit signed by fourteen French citizens of the town of Murvaux who had witnessed his passing from this earth.

With his Spad badly crippled from ground fire after blasting the third balloon, Luke yawed and see-sawed over the small town of Murvaux, barely missing the church steeple. As he settled lower and lower over the road, he fired burst after burst of incendiary bullets at the enemy ground-troops, killing a dozen of them. He managed to land the crippled plane in a field near the edge of town. Staggering from the plane, coughing from the fumes, he got to a small stream and took a drink of water. It was there the German patrol found him, to their sorrow. As they converged on him, calling out a command to surrender, Luke crouched and went for his forty-five automatic. Before he collapsed under the hail of fire, he had shot dead three members of the German patrol. Even at the end he could not conform to the common idea that flyers fought only in the air and were supposed to surrender on the ground.

The German patrol stripped his identification from his body

and buried him in an unmarked grave in the Murvaux cemetery. The spectacular seventeen days of Frank Luke were
over. That was September 29, 1918. Since September 12th he
had won eighteen air victories, knocking down eleven balloons
and seven aircraft.

He was awarded the Medal of Honor posthumously, his sister Eva appearing in Washington to accept the Medal on his behalf. "I am very proud that he died for his country," she said.

When the word came down from First Pursuit Group Headquarters that First Lieutenant Eddie Rickenbacker had been
appointed the new commanding officer of the Ninety-fourth
Pursuit Squadron, there was a certain amount of grousing and
bellyaching. The Ivy Leaguers were especially incensed. Here
was a guy with practically no education and immigrant family
background who had been made an officer and gentleman in the
United States Air Service by act of Congress. And that was not
enough. Now he was going to be the C.O.

Rickenbacker, at twenty-seven, was years older and ages
wiser than his Ivy League squadron mates. As far as he was concerned the sooner they got the romantic nonsense about the
glamour of flying and the manure about being officers and gentlemen out of their heads and became aerial gunmen, the better he would like it. If he could change his name from Richen-
bacher to Rickenbacker and give up a $40,000-a-year income as
a racing driver to help in the war effort, they could damn sure
buckle down and become flyers.

On the morning of September 25, 1918, his first day as commanding officer of the Ninety-fourth Squadron, his first official
act was to shape up the mechanics and maintenance personnel.
The Twenty-seventh Squadron—with the balloon-busting
Frank Luke running hog-wild—was leading the First Pursuit
in victories and Rickenbacker had decided that leadership was
going to cease.

At a formation in the main hangar, he informed the mechanics in no uncertain terms that all planes mechanically unable to
fly had to be reported to him immediately, with the reason why
they could not fly. He would check the plane personally and if
his analysis of the difficulty did not coincide with that of the
mechanic, it was going to be tough as hell on the mechanic.
The mechanics quivered with apprehension. Rickenbacker

could listen to the sound of a balky engine from fifty yards away and shout at you what was wrong with it.

Then, later that same morning, Rickenbacker folded his lanky six-foot-two frame into the cockpit of his Spad and took off on a solo flight over the lines to illustrate graphically the kind of combat flying he expected from his pilots, and incidentally to win the Congressional Medal of Honor.

Riding high in the sun over Étain, the two-hundred-and-thirty-five-horsepower Hispano-Suiza engine purring smoothly, Rickenbacker spotted two enemy L.V.G. two-seater machines below him, obviously on an observation mission over Allied lines. Rumbling along, fat as a pair of cows, they looked inviting, but Rickenbacker looked cagily about for protective escort. Sure enough, there were the Fokkers, five of them, above and behind the observation planes.

His position high in the sun had enabled him to escape their notice. When he was well to their rear and above them, he shut down his engine and screamed down on the rearmost Fokker.

The enemy pilot never knew what hit him. Dead in the first burst, he slumped over the side of the cockpit and his Fokker made a twisting, wailing descent, crashing into a field just south of Étain.

It had been Rickenbacker's original intention to knock off one Fokker and then get the hell out of there by zooming upward into the sun. But to his amazement, the remaining four Fokkers scattered in all directions, undisciplined as a flock of wild ducks. Rickenbacker dived on through their formation and descended on the cowlike observation planes.

The two-seaters, noting the attack of the American plane, turned and headed for home. Rickenbacker pursued grimly, revving up to a hundred and thirty miles an hour, determined to bag at least one of them. But he had caught a pair of tartars. Flying parallel and drawing apart, the pilots gave their rear seat gunners the opportunity to blast away at the pursuing Spad. As he bore down on them from behind and slightly above, they gave him a good spraying. Diving under the nearest machine, he zoomed up quickly at him from below. Kicking his tail around, the German pilot gave his gunner another good blast at Rickenbacker. In the meantime, the second observation plane had sneaked in behind him and tracers from the German's forward guns began streaking past.

Zooming out of that trap, Rickenbacker continued feinting maneuvers, keeping a weather eye out for the return of the Fokker escort. Then he spotted his chance, as the two-seaters flew parallel to each other, less than fifty yards apart. Descending in a screaming sideslip, Rickenbacker leveled his Spad and let go with a long burst, just as the nearest plane passed through his line of fire. Bursting into flame, the two-seater began its screaming descent.

Just in time, Rickenbacker roared upward into the sun. The Fokker escort, with guns flaming, had returned belatedly to the scene. But the new C.O. made it back home safe, with some bullet holes in the leading edges of his wings as testimony of the skill of the German rear-gunners.

The news of his two victories beat him back to the drome. Most of the squadron was waiting for him as he taxied the Spad carefully across the lumpy field. He got out of the plane, calmly pulling off his gloves. Then he began telling the mechanics how to repair the plane. The Ivy Leaguers marveled at his coolness, but then it came to them that to a man with ten years' experience on the dirt tracks, crashes and sudden death were nothing new. Finishing with the mechanics, he turned to the group of pilots. "Afternoon patrol at fifteen hundred hours," he said crisply. "Remember, we're still behind Twenty-seven Squadron." The bunch saluted and watched their lanky C.O. walk to the orderly room, stopping occasionally to pick up bits of unsightly paper or string from the area. He had a passion for neatness.

The Ivy Leaguers watched with a new respect. The new C.O. might be an immigrant and a grease monkey, but by God he could fly a pursuit ship in anybody's air service. Walking back to the mess, they occasionally bent over and picked up a scrap of paper or a cigarette butt. The new C.O. liked to keep the place clean.

Eddie Rickenbacker was not awarded the Congressional Medal of Honor until 1931, thirteen years after the events transpiring on September 25, 1918, his first day as commanding officer of the Ninety-fourth Aero Squadron. The citation read in part: ". . . For conspicuous gallantry and intrepidity above and beyond the call of duty in action against the enemy near Billy, France, 25 September 1918. While on a voluntary patrol over enemy lines, Lieutenant Rickenbacker attacked seven en-

emy planes . . . Disregarding the odds against him, he dived on them and shot down one of the Fokkers . . . He then attacked one of the Halberstadts and sent it down also."

By Armistice Day—November 11, 1918—Rickenbacker had a record of twenty-six confirmed victories, which made him by far the leading ace of World War I.

XI

Medics, Marine Flyers and Sub-chasers

THE Congressional act authorizing the Navy to present Medals of Honor for service in World War I was not passed until February 4, 1919, and so no Navy Medals for World War I deeds were awarded until the year following the cessation of hostilities. The act also provided the Navy with lesser awards. It established the Navy Cross for "extraordinary heroism in connection with military operations against an armed enemy," and gave the Navy a Distinguished Service Medal, a decoration on the same plane as the Navy Cross, but awarded for "exceptionally meritorious service to the Government in a duty of great responsibility" rather than for heroism. Thus the Navy too made the honorable but definite distinction in the awards system between acts of heroism and acts of meritorious service.

The Act of 1919 did not amend or supersede former Congressional acts applicable to Navy awards of the Medal of Honor. The Navy could still award Medals for acts of heroism performed "in line of profession," acts having no connection with armed conflict.

The Navy Medal of Honor design of World War I is a source of confusion to many. For World War I deeds involving conflict with the enemy the Navy awarded a distinctive design of the Medal of Honor, completely different from the original. This was a gold cross pattée designed by Tiffany & Co., which bore the legend "United States Navy 1917-1918." This design

was not awarded for non-combat heroic acts performed in line of profession during World War I. The traditional design was awarded for those deeds. This design was formally discontinued later, and except for this brief aberration, the Navy has always used the original Civil War five-pointed star design of the Medal of Honor.

In general, the Navy role in World War I was three-fold. Destroyers and cruisers protected the east-bound troop and cargo convoys from marauding enemy submarines, delivering them safely to such ports as Brest and Saint-Nazaire and then steaming back to the States for others. The second mission was that of the splinter fleet of small wooden sub-chasers, equipped to fight U-boats with depth charges. Manned largely by reserves with little seagoing experience, they suffered many casualties, and many disappeared in the stormy North Atlantic without a trace. The third role was laying the thousands of antenna-mines which closed the North Sea to U-boats from the Orkney Islands to the tip of Norway.

During World War I the United States Navy awarded twenty-eight Medals of Honor. Twenty-one of these went to sailors and seven to Marines. Of the seven Marines receiving the Navy Medal during World War I, five also received Army Medals of Honor duplicate awards for the same heroic acts as the Navy award, and their stories have been already told. The two Marines not receiving duplicate Army Medals of Honor were flyers, Lieutenant Ralph Talbot, pilot, and Sergeant Robert G. Robinson, Talbot's observer, both members of Squadron C, First Marine Air Division, in France. On October 14, 1918, on a raid over Pitthem, Belgium, Talbot's plane became cut off from the main group and was immediately attacked by twelve enemy planes. Sergeant Robinson shot down one of the enemy planes before being severely wounded in the arm. Then his machine gun jammed. While Talbot maneuvered acrobatically to gain time, Robinson worked on the gun with one hand. After clearing the jam Robinson fired until hit twice more, once in the stomach and once in the hip. Then he collapsed over his gun. Talbot attacked an enemy plane with his forward guns and shot it down. Then, with his motor failing, Talbot dived for the earth, crossing to his own lines just fifty feet over the German trenches. Landing near a field hospital he

left the severely wounded Robinson, and then took off in the plane to fly it back to his own aerodrome.

Six Navy medics serving with Marine units in the battle lines won the Medal of Honor in World War I.

Lieutenant Commander Alexander G. Lyle, Dental Corps, USN, on April 23, 1918, under heavy shellfire, rushed to the assistance of Corporal Thomas Regan who was seriously wounded. Unmindful of the bombardment, Lyle staunched the flow of blood from Corporal Regan with a tourniquet and saved his life.

There is a photograph in Navy Records showing winner Lieutenant (JG) Weedon E. Osborne as having a deceptively babyish face. A member of the Dental Corps, USN, Osborne was assigned as a medical officer to the Fifth Regiment of the United States Marines. During the advance on Bouresches, France, on June 6, 1918, he threw himself recklessly into the work of rescuing the wounded. The enemy fire was merciless and Osborne was wounded himself several times. He was killed by the explosion of an enemy mortar shell while carrying a wounded Marine officer on his back through the woods to his dressing station.

Another medic with the Fifth Regiment, U.S. Marines, was Lieutenant Orlando H. Petty, Medical Corps, USN. During the attack in the Bois de Belleau on June 11, 1918, Lieutenant Petty was knocked to the ground by an exploding gas shell and his gas mask was badly torn. He courageously continued his medical work despite the presence of gas. When his dressing station received a direct hit, he personally carried a wounded Marine officer through the shellfire to safety.

Pharmacist's Mate John H. Balch exhibited exceptional bravery in establishing an advanced dressing station under heavy shellfire in the action at Somme-Py on October 5, 1918.

Lieutenant Joel T. Boone, later Vice-Admiral, a Navy surgeon, won his Medal while serving with the Sixth Regiment, United States Marines, in the vicinity of Vierzy, France, on July 19, 1918. With disregard for his personal safety, he left his dressing station in a protected ravine to venture forth onto the open battlefield on a motorcycle to aid the fallen wounded. Despite the heavy small-arms and artillery fire and the explosion of gas shells, Lieutenant Boone tended the wounded Marines. Running out of bandages and medical supplies, he rode his

motorcycle back to the rear area, returning shortly with a side-car load of the needed supplies, bouncing across the rough terrain seeking out and aiding the wounded. Again exhausting his supplies, Lieutenant Boone rode his motorcycle to the rear and again returned to the field of battle to continue his work. Untouched by bullets, Boone was also unharmed by the gas. During his labors, he completely forgot to put on his mask. "I was too busy to breathe," he remarked later.

Hospital Apprentice David E. Hayden, attached to the Sixth Regiment of Marines, at Thiaucourt on September 15, 1918, crossed an open field swept by machine-gun fire to give medical aid to a wounded corporal. Finding the noncom bleeding profusely, Hayden dressed the wound while still under intense fire, then picked him up and carried him to a place of safety.

The brunt of anti-submarine warfare was borne by the splinter fleet of wooden sub-chasers, manned chiefly by naval reserves. The principal weapon used against the U-boats were "garbage can" depth charges, fired from "Y" guns or simply rolled over the side. When not actually mounted for use, the cans were securely lashed to the deck. When accidents occurred, and one or more of the sensitive cans broke loose to roll with lethal aimlessness around the deck, there was hell to pay.

On the gray morning of December 17, 1917, the U.S.S. *Remlik*, on anti-submarine duty in the North Atlantic, was plunging along in a heavy gale. There was a sudden warning shout from the bridge, "Depth charge free aft!" The depth-charge box on the taffrail aft, containing a Sperry depth charge, had been washed overboard by a high wave, leaving the depth charge itself free to roll inboard on the deck. Chief Boatswain's Mate John MacKenzie, one of the few Navy veterans aboard, ran aft on his own initiative and sat down on the charge, bracing it against the taffrail with his body, holding it motionless for some twenty minutes until the plunging little ship could be headed up into the sea and the charge secured with another box.

Ensign Daniel A. J. Sullivan of the U.S. Navy Reserve gave a good account of himself in action aboard the U.S.S. *Christabel* on May 21, 1918. In closing with a submarine, his eager crew dropped a charge so close to their own craft they almost

blew themselves out of the water. A number of loose depth charges began rolling about. Ensign Sullivan threw himself across the loose charges, holding them almost motionless with the weight of his body until they could be secured. He was credited with saving the ship from certain disaster.

Gunner's Mate Osmond K. Ingram was one of the heroic failures that mark the history of Medal awards. He was a failure in the sense that his heroic act did not succeed in preventing disaster and the loss of life. While his ship, the *Cassin*, was engaged in the search for a U-boat raider on October 15, 1917, Ingram on lookout at the rail, saw a torpedo coming directly at the ship. Realizing the torpedo might strike aft in the section where depth charges were lashed, Ingram ran to release the charges before the torpedo struck. The torpedo struck the ship with a violent explosion before Ingram could complete his task. Ingram was killed. He sacrificed his life in a vain heroic attempt to save the ship and lives of his shipmates.

The predatory U-boat captains of World War I were not averse to surfacing and slugging it out with ships of the splinter fleet on occasion. The U.S.S. *Ticonderoga* was attacked by an enemy U-boat on October 4, 1918. The sub opened fire with its deck gun at a range of five hundred yards and sent shells crashing into the bridge and forecastle. One of the two forward guns on the sub-chaser was disabled by the second shot. The duel continued for nearly two hours.

Lieutenant Commander James J. Madison, a Navy Reserve officer in command of the *Ticonderoga*, was severely wounded in the first salvo. Refusing to be carried below, he ordered a chair to be placed on the bridge and remained in command during the entire action. His last order, before losing consciousness from loss of blood, was to abandon ship. Lowered into a life boat he survived with thirty-one others, all that remained of a total crew of two hundred and thirty-six. Lieutenant Commander Madison was awarded the Medal of Honor for his heroism.

Chief Gunner's Mate Oscar Schmidt, Jr. of Philadelphia, Pennsylvania, received the Medal for extraordinary heroism while a member of the crew of U.S.S. *Chestnut Hill* on the occasion of an explosion and fire aboard the U.S. sub-chaser 219, on October 9, 1918. Standing by a rail of the *Chestnut Hill*, Chief Schmidt saw a crewman of the sub-chaser, his legs partially

blown off, hanging from a line on the bow of the 219. Skinning out of his shoes and jacket, Schmidt leaped over the rail and swam to the sub-chaser. Disengaging the wounded man from the bow of the sub-chaser, Schmidt swam with him to the stern where he was able to hoist the wounded man to the deck by a bowline. On the deck of the sub-chaser, Schmidt attempted to pass through the searing flames amidships to rescue another crewman who was badly burned. This he was unable to do, but when the man fell overboard, Schmidt leaped back into the water and brought him aboard the afterdeck of the sub-chaser.

The saga of Navy Lieutenant Edouard V. M. Izac, Medal of Honor winner from World War I, is in a class by itself. It is a tale of pursuit and hairbreadth escapes. Lieutenant Izac was an officer aboard the U.S.S. *President Lincoln* on convoy duty in the Atlantic. On the dark night of May 31, 1918, returning from France, the *President Lincoln* was attacked by the notorious German submarine raider, the U-90. Struck in the vitals by three torpedoes, the *President Lincoln* sank within a few minutes.

Half an hour after the ship went down, the crew of the raider, now on the surface gloating over the kill, pulled from the water a dripping oil-smeared survivor of the American ship. His identification tag showed that he was Lieutenant Edouard V. M. Izac. This was indeed a good catch, the U-boat commander decided. Interrogation of the American Navy officer by German Naval Intelligence should prove very fruitful.

But to the U-boat captain's disappointment, the prisoner appeared to be a blockhead or in a state of shock from the explosion on the American ship. He lay in his bunk most of the day staring vacantly at the steel bulkhead or wandered about aimlessly in the confined area of the sub. During the remaining two or three weeks of the voyage, before dropping the prisoner with German Navy authorities at Kiel, they ignored him, letting him have the run of the ship.

Unknown to the U-boat captain, his prisoner was not in a mental daze at all, far from it. And also unknown to the submariners, the prisoner was fluent in the German language and could understand all the conversation that went on around him. During his period as a prisoner aboard the sub, Lieutenant Izac gained a wealth of first-hand knowledge about the move-

ments and tactics of the German U-boat fleet. He determined to escape at the first opportunity.

Arriving in Germany, Izac was sent under guard by train to the American and Russian officers' prison camp at Villingen. Locking himself in a washroom on the train, while it was clicking along at a fast clip, he pried open the window and leaped out. He sprained an ankle in landing on the opposite railroad track and for that reason was unable to outrun the guards who appeared on the double after the train had been brought to a sudden halt.

For this escape attempt he was brutally pistol-whipped by his guards and given two weeks' solitary confinement. When he finally joined the group at Villingen he looked like a walking skeleton, but his spirit was unbroken and his desire to escape burned brightly as ever.

Utilizing his engineering skill, Lieutenant Izac devised a method of short-circuiting all the electrical circuits in the prison camp to extinguish the floodlights used by the machine gunners in the guard towers to watch for escaping prisoners. With the aid of some American Army officer prisoners, Izac blew all the fuses in the camp on the night of October 6, 1918, and cut his way out through the barbwire fences. The machine gunners in the guard towers laid down a withering searching fire, but Izac escaped in the dark.

For seven days and nights he skulked through the woods traveling a wary and disjointed course over the mountains toward the Rhine. Crawling past the guards on the river bank, he slid silently into the water on a moonless night. He swam silently through the strong current to the other shore.

Two days later, still damp and bedraggled, he presented himself at the American Legation in Berne, Switzerland. Lieutenant Izac had made good his escape. Four weeks later, he was back in Washington writing a report on his U-boat information. Just as he finished the lengthy report that could be so vital, he heard the news that made it all unnecessary. An armistice had been declared. The war was over.

XII

A Stone from Floyd Bennett's Grave

IN THE peaceful era between the two World Wars, practically all the Navy Medals awarded went for deeds of heroism performed "in line of profession." (However, two Marines won Navy Medals in Haiti during this period and two in Nicaragua for "conflict with the enemy" actions.) Rescue was the type of deed most common to the period—rescue from submarines, from steam-filled boiler rooms and from burning ships or aircraft.

To tell the full story of the Medals awarded for submarine rescues, we must hark back to the sinking of the U.S.S. F-4 which went down with all hands off Honolulu on March 25, 1915. This was the first in the series of Medal of Honor acts relating to stricken submarines, a series which extended through the 1930's.

The F-4, with twenty-one men aboard, stood out of the harbor at Honolulu for a practice run at 9:15 A.M. that fateful March 25th with her sister subs F-1 and F-3. It was a peaceful spring Thursday morning. The sister subs returned on schedule in an hour or so, but the F-4 did not come home for five months and four days and then it returned with a crew of dead men.

On March 26th the grapnels of searching tugs located the stricken F-4. She was resting on the bottom of Mamala Bay, three hundred and four feet straight down. An emergency cable was sent for the Navy's experimental diving unit in New York. By the time they arrived all hope for the F-4 crew would be gone, but it was necessary to raise the sunken vessel to determine exactly what had caused the sinking. Navy submarines were in their infancy and weaknesses in construction had to be determined at all costs.

In 1915 the Navy had divers trained for shallow-water work, but the regulations forbade them to go beyond sixty feet. The experimental unit, in their deep-water tank, had reached simulated depths of two hundred and fifty-six feet. One member of

the unit had actually gone down to two hundred and seventy-four feet in Long Island Sound. But the F-4 was three hundred and four feet down. Attaining great depths in the standard diving rigs of that day was fraught with dangers. The bends could cause terrible pains if a man were brought to the surface too quickly, or the squeeze at great depths could force a man's body up into his diving helmet. The squeeze occurred when the air supply was cut off by accident or an air hose was cut. The air pressure in the helmet would then revert to normal atmospheric pressure of slightly more than fourteen pounds a square inch and then the sea pressure—forty-five pounds a square inch at only a hundred feet—would crush the hapless diver.

On April 12th the six-man Navy diving team, composed of five gunner's mates and a Navy surgeon, reported at Honolulu to go down for the F-4. Frank W. Crilley, thirty-one years old, of Trenton, New Jersey, the smallest of the five, was picked to make the first dive. At 7:45 A.M. on April 14th, he coolly checked his lines, waved once to the rest of the crew on deck, and backed down the ladder into the sea. Five minutes later he stood on the bottom at three hundred and four feet. He had broken the depth diving record and now plodded laboriously in his heavy iron shoes surveying the stricken F-4 in the clear water. After staying on the bottom twelve minutes he was pulled to the surface in slow stages to offset the bends, the upward journey taking an hour and forty-five minutes.

After Crilley had shown it could be done, the others followed, performing the slow laborious task of looping the stricken sub with steel cables so that she could be tugged to shallower water.

On April 17th the diving crew had its first accident. Gunner's Mate Bill Loughman started up from the bottom and got his lines hopelessly fouled and tangled at two hundred and fifty feet. Frank Crilley put on his diving gear and went over the side. On reaching Loughman, Crilley found that the current had whirled and twisted him, winding his air pipe several turns around his shot line and both around one of the wire hawsers connected to the wreck. For more than two hours the crew waited grimly on deck while Crilley worked furiously under the sea to save his friend. Leaks developed in Loughman's air hose and air flasks servicing him would last only five minutes.

Spare flasks were rushed from a nearby sub-tender. At one point Loughman passed out and went limp in Crilley's arms. Finally, Crilley managed to work the stricken diver free and they were hauled to the surface. Loughman, due to having been exposed to high pressure for over four hours, suffered a severe case of the bends. Then he contracted pneumonia and almost died. He finally pulled through, but never dived again.

The diving efforts of Crilley and his mates were finally successful in salvaging the F-4, five months after she disappeared.

Crilley was awarded the Medal of Honor by the Navy for his heroism in saving Loughman's life, receiving the award in 1928, thirteen years after the deed occurred.

The Navy continued its policy of awarding Medals of Honor for peacetime feats relating to submarine wrecks through 1939.

On the morning of October 28, 1923, the U.S. Submarine 0-5 collided with the steamship *Abangarez* and sank in less than a minute. When the collision occurred, Henry Breault, Torpedoman Second Class, was in the torpedo room. On reaching the hatch, he saw the ship was sinking rapidly. Instead of leaping overboard to save his own life, he ran back to the torpedo room to make sure that his shipmate, a seaman named Brown, had gotten out. Brown was unconscious on the floor, and before Breault could lift him, the torpedo room began flooding. Breault closed the torpedo-room hatch, trapping himself in the stricken boat to save the unconscious man. They remained trapped in the compartment until rescued by the salvage party thirty-one hours later. Breault received his Medal at the White House from President Coolidge in March of 1924.

At noon on Saturday, December 17, 1927, the U.S. Submarine S-4 put out from Provincetown Harbor to run a series of speed and maneuverability trials on the measured mile course just off Wood End. She was not new, being a World War I submarine, but she had been subjected to various improving modifications. She was considered a safe boat, with a double hull and four bulkheads which divided her internally into five watertight compartments: the torpedo room, battery room, control room, engine room, and small motor room.

At 3:37 P.M. that afternoon the S-4 collided with the U.S. Coast Guard destroyer *Paulding*, and sank almost immediately in one hundred and ten feet of water. The *Paulding* had

been engaged in an off-shore patrol looking for rumrunners in that Prohibition year of 1927.

The rough sub-freezing December weather made rescue operations exceedingly hazardous. The rescuers, however, were spurred on with the knowledge that a group in the watertight torpedo room on the sub remained alive. The officer in charge of that section could be heard tapping out messages in Morse code with a wrench against the metal hull of the boat.

One of the veteran divers rushed to the scene was Chief Gunner's Mate Thomas Eadie of Newport, Rhode Island. Eadie, a taciturn Scotsman forty years old, was one of the best divers in the business. Another diver was Chief Torpedoman Fred Michels, also a veteran.

In the teeth of a rising gale, Michels went down to the sub on December 18, in an attempt to connect an air line to the sub to furnish oxygen to the men trapped in the torpedo room. It was eight o'clock at night as Fred Michels walked laboriously along the hull of the submarine, carrying a one-thousand-watt lamp and struggling with an extra hundred feet of air line, necessary to compensate for the bucking and heaving of the salvage ship above on the stormy surface. Without a lot of slack, his line would have snapped off in short order.

At 8:35 P.M., Michels gasped laboriously over the telephone, "Line fouled. Con't get . . . loose. Tell Eadie . . . bring . . . heavy . . . wire . . . cutter . . . " Then his voice faded out.

In the bunk room of the salvage ship Eadie was deep in the sleep of exhaustion, having already put in a full shift on the ocean floor below. But when they told him of Michels' plight, he wearily pulled on the heavy wool underwear and socks and headed for the diving-gear room. A few minutes later he was sliding down through the icy depths on Michels' shot line.

On the deck of the sub Eadie saw Michels' lamp glowing dimly. It was not moving. Then he found the stricken diver, lying face down in a jagged tangle of wreckage on the sub deck near the conning tower, his line hopelessly snarled. Turning Michels over, Eadie saw that he must still be alive, although weak, because his eyes blinked under the glare of Eadie's light. Eadie clomped about on the sub hull in the frozen gloom, working frantically with a hacksaw to cut Michels loose before they

both froze to death. Occasionally he could hear a faint, lonely knocking from the poor devils trapped in the steel tomb beneath.

Just as Eadie got Michels completely free, he ripped the trouser leg of his diving suit on a sharp piece of steel. He could feel water creeping into the suit and up to his waist. It was numbingly cold. His line tautened slightly from above. "Don't pull me up!" he yelled into the phone, "pull up Mike!" Eadie's line went slack and Michels began rising in the ghostly gloom.

"Tom, are you all right?" The words crackled faintly from above reaching Eadie's numbed brain.

"Yes," he gasped, "pull me up." His body was almost completely numb with cold and there was a viselike pressure squeezing his temples together. Then he began rising slowly as the line tautened.

Both divers were pulled immediately to the surface with no pauses along the way and placed immediately in the recompression chamber. The diving suits and layers of heavy underwear were cut from their contorted bodies, and the pressure built up to sixty pounds, as much as it had been on the deck of the sub below.

Eadie and Michels survived their ordeals although none of the men from the S-4 did. All attempts to attach air lines to the stricken sub failed. She was not raised until March 17, 1928, almost three months from the day she went down.

For his rescue of Michels, Eadie received the Medal of Honor "for display of extraordinary heroism in the line of his profession above and beyond the call of duty . . ."

The year 1939 was a black one for submariners all over the world. That year the Japanese submarine I-63 sank in the Bungo Channel, killing eighty-one officers and men. In June of that year there were two major sub disasters. The British *Thetis* went down in the Irish Sea with a loss of ninety-nine aboard and two weeks later the French submarine *Phénix* dived into the depths of the sea off Indo-China taking sixty-three with her, never to return. The United States Navy had been miraculously lucky up until this time. Not since 1927 when the S-4 sank had the United States lost a submarine, and then the *Squalus* went down.

On May 23, 1939, the U.S. submarine *Squalus* was a brand-

new five-million-dollar boat, busy making her test runs before joining the fleet. On reaching her testing grounds off Hampton Beach, New Hampshire, about 8:40 A.M., she radioed "Preparing to descend for one hour." Then came the silence.

That afternoon the lookout in the conning tower of the searching submarine *Sculpin* saw a plume of red smoke leap suddenly from the choppy gray sea off the New Hampshire coast. It was a distress signal from the stricken *Squalus*. She lay on the bottom, her stern sunk in blue mud, two hundred and forty feet down. Four of her compartments were flooded. Half of her complement of fifty-nine officers and men were already dead. The Navy rushed all available rescue units to her aid.

In the twelve years since the S-4 went down, although the Navy had lost no more submarines, Navy experts had made many advances in rescue and escape procedure and equipment for stricken undersea craft. The most important of these was first tested at the scene of the *Squalus* disaster. This was a steel rescue chamber, a huge ten-ton bell, shaped something like a pear, that could be lowered down a steel line and clamped over an escape hatch in the deck of the sub. Theoretically, small groups of survivors could be taken one at a time into the bell and then the bell, resealed, could be raised to the surface. It had never been put to actual use. Whether it was practical or would kill everyone inside had never been proved.

On May 24th a line was attached to the ring on the *Squalus*'s escape hatch and the diving bell lowered down from the salvage ship. In the bell were two volunteer divers, Chief Machinist's Mate William Badders and Torpedoman First Class John Mihalowski. On them depended the lives of the men trapped in the submarine. The bell had actually two chambers, one above the other. Around the rim of the lower chamber was a heavy rubber gasket which seated itself around the hatch. Once seated, air was pumped into the lower chamber to force out the water, giving the men in the upper chamber access to the hatch.

There was a tense moment as Badders began turning the hatch wheel. Would the pressure between sub and bell equalize properly? Or would a sudden burst of pressure blow them off the side of the sunken sub, killing rescuers in the bell and the men in the sub compartment?

There was a slight hiss, like pulling the lid from a bottle of soda pop, and suddenly the hatch was open. The men trapped

in the darkness of the submarine compartment blinked in the bright light from the bell. The bell was obviously a success.

Thirty-three officers and men were rescued from the *Squalus* by use of the rescue chamber. Nine was the largest number the chamber could carry each trip, so several nerve-wracking trips had to be made to get them all. Chief Boatswain's Mate Orson L. Crandall and Chief Metalsmith James H. McDonald made the last trip in the bell that brought up survivors. This trip almost ended in disaster when the raising cable jammed on the winch. The line fouled immediately and the chamber hung helplessly one hundred and fifty feet below the surface. For four hours Crandall and McDonald fought to maintain the exact air-buoyancy inside the bell to prevent it from popping to the surface and smashing against the side of the salvage ship or sinking like a rock to join the *Squalus*. Divers around the bell, dangling with no support for their feet, finally unfouled the line and the last rescue trip was made successfully.

The Navy awarded four Medals of Honor to the operators of the diving bell. These went to Chiefs Badders, Crandall, and McDonald and to Torpedoman First Class John Mihalowski. These four were the last Medals of Honor awarded by the Navy for participation in peacetime submarine rescue operations.

Five Navy Medals were awarded by special acts of Congress during the period from 1920 to 1940. One of the deeds—that of Naval Constructor Richmond P. Hobson who led the group trying to sink the *Merrimac* in Santiago channel in the Spanish-American War—has already been described. He had been ineligible, as a commissioned Navy officer, prior to 1915, but he appeared hale and hearty and glad to get his Medal from the President at the White House in 1933, after Congress gave him the award by special legislation. Two awards were given posthumously to Ensign Henry Clay Drexler and Boatswain's Mate First Class George R. Cholister, both of whom served on the U.S.S. *Trenton* on October 20, 1924, when powder ignited during a firing practice. Both were burned to death in trying to smother burning bags of powder with their own bodies. Congress awarded their Medals on February 3, 1933.

Two of the special awards of Navy Medals by Congress were for acts of great national achievement in Arctic exploration.

They went to Commander Richard E. Byrd and Warrant Machinist Floyd Bennett for flying over the North Pole in an airplane in 1926. The fame of Richard E. Byrd as an explorer is great, but the public generally knows little or nothing about the man who was his assistant and close friend, Floyd Bennett.

Bennett, born in Warrenburg, New York, in 1890, was two years younger than Byrd. A skilled mechanic, he enlisted in the Navy for World War I service in 1917. Within two years he had attained the rank of Chief Machinist's Mate, Aviation, and successfully completed the flying course for enlisted pilots at Pensacola. Byrd said later that Bennett was a genius as a flyer, a mechanic and a shipmate. As an outstanding Navy pilot, Bennett was chosen in 1925 to accompany the MacMillan Expedition to the Arctic. On this expedition he first served under Lieutenant Commander Richard E. Byrd.

In the spring of 1926, three Arctic expeditions—those led by Byrd, Amundsen and Wilkins—were competing in a dramatic race to be the first over the North Pole in aircraft. Amundsen was readying his giant dirigible, the *Norge*. Wilkins, who had made an unsuccessful bid the year before in flying boats, was waiting for clear water to take off again.

On May 9, 1926, Byrd and Bennett took off from King's Bay, Spitzbergen, in a big blue tri-motored Fokker equipped with two-hundred-horsepower Wright engines. The plane was named *Josephine Ford* in honor of the young daughter of auto magnate Edsel Ford, who had contributed funds to the expedition. The sky was clear but the cold was intense. Byrd and Bennett estimated they had fuel for twenty-five hours. The earth they flew over was a desolation of ragged pressure ridges and craters of open water. They knew they would not survive long if forced down.

Byrd and Bennett alternated as pilots. While Byrd was at the controls, Bennett carefully refilled the gasoline tanks from auxiliary cans. It was a ticklish business, handling the volatile gasoline in the close confines of the plane cabin.

Over the ice cap, just sixty miles from the Pole, the right-hand engine coughed and began throwing oil, spattering the cowling and window on that side. Grimly, they went on, determined to continue the flight with only two engines if necessary. Miraculously, the leak never worsened and the engine continued functioning.

Over the Pole, they circled several times so that Byrd could verify their position with instruments and drop markers. After a final circle, they turned and headed back for King's Bay.

In 1909 the Peary Expedition—the first to the North Pole—had reached their goal by dog sled, after being out of touch with civilization for four hundred and twenty-nine days, an ordeal which culminated in a final thirty-seven-day lunge across the pressure ridges and open water to the final victory. In 1926 Byrd and Bennett made the same journey by aircraft in a flight of fifteen hours and fifty-one minutes.

The public reception to this successful flight was hysterically enthusiastic. The Washington *Daily News* chanted this triumphant refrain:

"First to fly at all . . . First to fly across the Atlantic . . . First to fly across the Pacific . . . First to fly around the world . . . First to fly over the North Pole.

"When better stunts are done in the air, Americans will do them!"

It was a great stunt all right, but Byrd was modest about it. "Floyd Bennett deserves the credit," he said.

By special acts on January 5, 1927, Congress promoted Byrd to commander and Bennett to officer rank as a warrant machinist. So, as brother officers they rode down Broadway together in the open touring-car, in the cloud of ticker tape. On February 19, 1927, Congress awarded them Medals of Honor for their historic flight.

Bennett's life ended tragically, that same year. After a successful tour of forty-four cities in the big Fokker used in the polar flight, Bennett sustained serious injuries in the crackup of an experimental plane he test-flew for the Navy in March 1927. In April, still not fully recovered from his injuries, Bennett volunteered to fly to the relief of three European trans-Atlantic flyers, forced down in Newfoundland. On this flight he contracted pneumonia of the most virulent type and died in a hospital in Quebec.

Byrd, at Bennett's bedside when he died, wept unashamedly. "He was a man in a million, a man in a million!"

Byrd never forgot his friend. He called his expedition to the South Pole in 1929 "The Floyd Bennett Memorial Expedition." The airplane he used on this expedition was named the *Floyd Bennett*. As he circled over the South Pole on this historic

flight, Byrd dropped an American flag to mark the spot. The flag was weighted with a stone from Floyd Bennett's grave.

XIII

The Most Ambiguous and Misleading Citation of All

DURING the period from 1920 to 1940 all but two of the Army Medals of Honor awarded went for armed conflict deeds performed during World War I. The three-year limitation on issuing Medals of Honor for these exploits, as provided by the statute, ran out in 1921. On several occasions during the 1920's and 1930's Congress extended the time limit so that later awards for World War I could be made. One Army Medal of Honor for World War I service was awarded as late as 1936, almost twenty years after the hostilities ended. This was to Lieutenant Samuel I. Parker for heroic action at Soissons in July 1918.

The Army issued six Medals of Honor to the Unknown Soldiers of the United States and allies of World War I. The Medal went to the United States Unknown in 1921, to the Unknowns of Belgium, Great Britain, France and Italy in 1922, and to the Unknown of Rumania in 1923.

Small details of Medal of Honor designs mark the period just after World War I. The Gillespie patent expired November 21, 1918, and again the Army Medal design was thrown into the limbo of the public domain. In 1923 Congress passed a law forbidding imitation of any United States military decoration, thus protecting all U.S. medal designs.

The two Army Medals awarded during this period for deeds other than World War I service were special awards, voted by Congress for acts of great public renown having no connection with armed conflict. One went to a young Air Corps reserve captain and the other to an ancient retired general officer of the United States Army.

In 1927 the young Air Corps reserve officer—and air mail pilot—Charles Augustus Lindbergh made the first solo non-stop trans-Atlantic flight from New York to Paris. All over the country victrolas began playing, "Oh, Lucky Lindbergh, what a flying man is he . . . Oh, Lucky Lindbergh, his name will live in historee . . ." He became Lucky Lindy and the public idolized the gangling young airman.

On December 14, 1927, Congress passed a public law authorizing the President to present Captain Charles A. Lindbergh of Little Falls, Minnesota, with the Medal of Honor for his hostoric flight. President Coolidge pinned the Medal on him at the White House the following year. His citation read as follows: "For displaying heroic courage and skill as a navigator, at the risk of his life, by his nonstop flight in his airplane, *The Spirit of St. Louis*, from New York City to Paris, France, 20-21 May 1927."

Years later, in 1941, Lindbergh opposed the entry of the United States into World War II. He resigned his commission as colonel in the Air Corps Reserve after being verbally attacked by President Roosevelt for his isolationist views. There was some talk on the floor of Congress about "taking away" his Medal of Honor. This was never done. No Medal of Honor has been taken from any winner since the time of the great purge of the Army list in 1917. In regard to Lindbergh's military status it should be stated that he was tendered and accepted a commission of brigadier general in the Air Force Reserve in 1954 and presently holds this rank.

The second special award by Congress of the Army Medal of Honor is one that the public knows little about. It went to Major General Adolphus Washington Greely in 1935. His citation read as follows:

"For his life of splendid public service, begun 27 March 1844, having enlisted as a private in the United States Army on 26 July 1861, and by successive promotions was commissioned a major general 10 February 1906, and retired by the operation of law on his sixty-fourth birthday."

This was the most ambiguous and misleading citation that ever accompanied the award of a Medal of Honor. The words did not even vaguely allude to the specific act for which the Medal was actually awarded.

It was true that Adolphus W. Greely enlisted in the Union

Army as a private in July 1861, at the age of seventeen, and had a distinguished record during that war—wounded in action three times and emerging with the brevet rank of major. After the war he elected to remain in the Army.

In 1881, as a first lieutenant in the Army Signal Corps, he led an exploration party composed of twenty-four Army volunteers to the Arctic. The Greely party ultimately reached a point eighty-three degrees and twenty-four minutes north, forty-one degrees west—further north than any explorers had ever gone before. After supply ships, trapped in the ice, failed to reach him, Greely floated his party on an ice floe down to Greenland to await aid.

Just why he was not sent aid right away was never made clear. The War and Navy Departments began a bitter argument, each assigning the other the responsibility of rescuing the Greely party. While the services at home quarreled, Greely and his men ate mossy lichens and their own boiled moccasins, and slowly starved to death in the frozen north.

Finally, three years after the Greely expedition had sailed for the Arctic, Congress stepped into the inter-service debate and dispatched a relief ship, the *Bear,* to rescue the party. When help finally arrived, Greely and six skeletal survivors were all that were left of the original party of twenty-five.

On arriving in New York, the weakened survivors found to their consternation that the public looked upon them not as heroes but as ghouls. Sensational newspapers of the day had seized upon unsubstantiated reports of cannibalism by the survivors and written lurid headlines. Greely, the leader, bore the brunt of the grisly insinuations.

Robert Todd Lincoln, Secretary of War, was apparently not disposed to hurry in absolving Greely of blame in the matter. Perhaps the Secretary felt the press hullabaloo attacking Greely for the alleged cannibalism was better than a press hullabaloo attacking the War Department for allowing eighteen members of the party to starve to death without turning a hand. During the long-drawn-out investigation, Secretary Lincoln ordered Lieutenant Greely to be passed over for promotion several times.

Steadfastly maintaining his innocence of any wrongdoing, Greely remained in the Army. The investigation never turned up anything derogatory about his personal conduct on the

expedition and gradually the hubbub died. As a pioneer in wireless telegraphy, Greely went on to have a distinguished career in the Army, attaining the rank of major general as Chief of the Signal Corps. He retired from the Army in 1908, at the mandatory retirement age of sixty-four.

Despite his successful Army career, Greely and certain colleagues always felt the War Department had tarnished his reputation by the protracted cannibalism investigation, and had tried to make him the goat of the Department's own disastrous mistake in not rescuing the Arctic expedition.

Influential friends, including Rear Admiral Richmond P. Hobson, who had been awarded the Medal by special act in 1933, and General Billy Mitchell, who would be awarded the Medal in 1946 long after his death, petitioned Congress on Greely's behalf. Precedent was certainly there since Congress had previously awarded Medals of Honor to Richard E. Byrd and Floyd Bennett for deeds relating to Arctic exploration.

Congress made the award on March 19, 1935. The old explorer was not deceived by the ambiguous wording of the citation. He knew that his award of the Medal was meant in a sense to make amends for the undeserved disgrace arising from the Arctic expedition investigation. The old man was still irritable about it. "I was up there out of the world for three years and when I got back I found I had been demoted through political pull," he said when told that Congress had made the award.

And so it turned out on March 27, 1935, the ninety-first birthday of Major General Adolphus W. Greely, that a troop of the Third Cavalry clattered along O Street in the old Georgetown section of Washington and wheeled smartly to a parade front before the small white frame house where the aged hero lived. A color guard was posted on the front lawn and the regimental band played "Ruffles and Flourishes," and then the National Anthem. The old gentleman himself, with a shawl around his shoulders, sat on the front porch in a rocking chair.

Then Colonel Beckham, an old friend, read the citation and Secretary of War George H. Dern presented the Medal. Among those present were Billy Mitchell, Richmond P. Hobson, and Brigadier General David L. Brainard, the only other surviving member of the Greely Arctic Expedition of 1881-83.

The old explorer had little in way of comment. He rocked

in his chair. "When you're ninety, little medals and things don't matter much."

Adolphus W. Greely died the following October and was buried in Arlington National Cemetery. At the funeral he was accorded the thirteen-gun salute of the major general.

The last World War I award of the Medal was made the following year in 1936 to Samuel I. Parker, formerly a second lieutenant in the First Infantry Division. During the Battle of Soissons in July 1918, Lieutenant Parker found himself in a front-line position with one flank exposed to heavy enemy machine-gun fire from a rock quarry on high ground. The enemy gun position was technically in the French sector and orders were strict forbidding the invasion of an ally's sector. Disregarding the standing orders, Lieutenant Parker led his depleted platoon and some leaderless French colonial troops in a mad rush up the hill to take the enemy position by storm. Parker's charge resulted in the capture of six machine guns and forty prisoners.

Parker said later that his main concern at the time was not the thought of getting a decoration, but the fear that some canny superior would recommend that he be court-martialed for leaving his own sector. Parker was awarded the Silver Star for this action at the time and this decoration was "upgraded" by an Army board in 1936 to a Medal of Honor.

XIV

The Navy Brass Won Most of the Medals

THE United States Navy awarded one hundred and thirty-eight Medals of Honor to its heroes in World War II. Fifty-seven of these Medals went to Navy personnel, and eighty to Marines. One lone Medal of Honor was awarded a member of the United States Coast Guard.

The Navy Medal of Honor in World War II, as far as sailors were concerned, was predominantly an officer's award. Twice as many went to officers as enlisted men, a change from World War I when the Navy Medals were almost evenly divided between the brass and the ranks.

This preponderance of awards to Navy officers in World War II pointed up a Navy policy in awarding the Medal that differed from that of the Army and the Marine Corps. The Navy made many awards to officers for executing their command responsibilities in a courageous manner, far above and beyond the call of duty. The Army and Marine viewpoint was, generally speaking, that courageous leadership was to be expected of officers and should not necessarily be rewarded by the highest decoration. Whether or not to award the Medal for courageous command has long been a controversial question in all the services.

Immediately after the declaration of war on December 8, 1941, General George C. Marshall, Army Chief of Staff, advocated a policy of "prompt recognition" for Army heroes. He formed a War Department Decorations Board which operated under two principles: (1) to recognize valor promptly; (2) to make no unmerited awards of the Medal of Honor. The strict requirements of the Congressional Act of July 9, 1918, were followed, but the procedure was different in World War II in that awarding Medals was not delayed until the cessation of hostilities. The Navy followed suit in both the "prompt recognition" and the strict requirements policy.

World War II began for the United States with the Japanese air attack on Pearl Harbor, Hawaii, December 7, 1941. Fourteen Medals of Honor were awarded by the Navy for actions on this first day. Therefore, these fourteen were the first Medalwinners of World War II.

Eight of the awards went to officers and six to enlisted men, but two of the enlisted winners survived to become Navy officers.

The Japanese air attacks began at 7:55 A.M. that peaceful sunny Sunday morning at Pearl Harbor. It was the first weekend since July 4th that all the battleships—nine in all—were in the harbor, clustered around Ford Island. Moored parallel to shore in a double line on the east side of Ford Island were the *Nevada, Arizona, West Virginia, Oklahoma,* and *California.*

Alongside the *Arizona*, Admiral Kidd's flagship, was the ancient and venerable Navy repair-ship *Vestal*. On the west side of Ford Island lay the battleship *Utah*. These are the important ships to this history, because members of these ships' companies won Medals of Honor.

The first blow came when a single dive bomber screamed almost straight down out of the blue at the seaplane ramp at the southern end of Ford Island. A Navy commander, busy in his office on the island, thought it was a young Navy pilot doing a little stunting. He frowned and ran from his office to record the culprit's plane number. The commander and the duty officer were too late to see the plane. As they searched the sky vainly, a shattering blast followed by a geyser of dirt and smoke burst from the shore end of the ramp.

That was how it began. Within five minutes the sky over the harbor was filled with planes dive-bombing the sitting battleships and sweeping in like deadly low-flying gulls to launch torpedoes.

On board the *West Virginia*, Captain Mervyn Bennion was interrupted at his breakfast by his Marine orderly informing him that the harbor was under attack by the Japanese. Captain Bennion laid down his napkin carefully and reached for his gold-encrusted cap. "This is certainly in keeping with their history of surprise attacks," he remarked calmly and headed for the bridge.

As Captain Bennion clambered up the crowded gangways trying to get to his bridge, the *West Virginia* was rocked by two crashing torpedoes in one-two order. Lights flashed on and off and steel lockers tumbled over. Captain Bennion made it to the open bridge and began calmly giving the orders to minimize the chaos. As an "outside" ship in the mooring line, the *West Virginia* began taking a frightful beating. Torpedo planes buzzed in, dropped their deadly fish and zoomed away, leaving the ship shuddering and trembling from the ensuing explosions. Below decks there was chaos. Telephone lines were dead. Lights were out. Fumes filled the crowded quarters. When someone hysterically shouted "Abandon ship!" a wild stampede ensued. Thick clouds of yellow smoke began pouring from rents in the deck seams.

Pale but composed on the bridge, Captain Bennion directed damage control from one of the few phones still operating.

When the ship began to list heavily from the great holes in her side, he gave the orders to counter-flood the opposite holds and then the *West Virginia* settled down solidly in the harbor mud on an even keel.

With the *West Virginia* an obvious casualty, the dive bombers began concentrating on her inboard companion, the *Tennessee*. A mass of steel splinters from the suffering *Tennessee* swept the bridge of the *West Virginia*, and cut down Captain Bennion. The captain slumped across the sill of the starboard signal-bridge door with a great wound in his stomach. An ensign looked vainly through a medical locker for morphine. Then he sat down beside the dying captain, holding his head, and tried to anesthetize him with a can of ether. Captain Bennion, conscious to the end, kept asking questions. Were the ship's guns still firing? Was the ship badly hit? As the flames crept closer, several of the officers carried the dying captain to a more sheltered spot behind the conning tower. He ordered the men remaining on the bridge to leave him where he was and save themselves. Captain Bennion was awarded the Medal of Honor.

On the *Arizona*, moored inboard from the old repair-ship *Vestal*, Admiral Isaac C. Kidd and Captain Franklin Van Valkenburgh shared the bridge. Both of them career Navy officers in their fifties, they surveyed the carnage grimly, but without panic, and tried to organize some sort of a defense. The moment of calm and fortitude was not long, for early in the attack the *Arizona* blew up, killing everyone on the bridge and becoming a twisted steel tomb for one thousand one hundred and two men. Afterward, some observers said a bomb went right down the stack, but this observation was later disproved. The bomb crashed through the deck and set off the forward magazines. A huge black ball, laced with fire, leaped five hundred feet in the air, accompanied by a resounding "Whoom!" The concussion was tremendous. Both Kidd and Van Valkenburgh received Medals of Honor posthumously.

From his command post on the bridge of the old repair-ship *Vestal*, moored outboard of the *Arizona*, Commander Cassin Young was blown overboard by the blast. With the captain gone, the crew of the *Vestal* began leaping into the water wildly, abandoning the ship.

Climbing grimly back aboard, Commander Young was sop-

ping wet and dazed from shock but certainly not ready to give up. From the gangway he yelled for the splashing swimmers to come back. "We're not giving up this ship yet!" he yelled. The swimmers turned and began splashing back.

With most of his crew back aboard, Young ordered the hawser anchoring the *Vestal* to the doomed *Arizona* cut. Although strafing and bombing planes swept his ship and set her afire, Commander Young directed a Navy tug in towing the *Vestal* across the harbor and beaching her on the coast near the Aiea landing. His action saved the valuable repair-ship and the lives of the men on board her.

Commander Young's award was one of the few non-posthumous Pearl Harbor awards. He lived to wear the Medal and be promoted to captain, but was killed in November 1942 as commanding officer of the *San Francisco,* when a blazing enemy plane crashed onto his bridge during the Battle of Guadalcanal.

The *Oklahoma,* the outboard ship alongside the *Maryland,* was struck by five torpedoes in quick succession. The first two put out her lights and the next three ripped off her whole port side. When this happened a weird phenomenon occurred, something that was just not supposed to happen to a battleship. The *Oklahoma* began turning upside down. Inside the ship water swirled in, floating many survivors wearing life belts about like corks. In their dazed buoyant state many of them did not realize that the ship was turning over. As they floated around in air pockets many were puzzled by the tile ceiling. They could not for the life of them recall what part of the ship had tile ceilings. What they thought was the ceiling was really the floor.

On the open deck the situation was simpler. As the *Oklahoma* slowly turned over, most of the men crawled over the starboard side and walked against the roll, ending up on the ship's bottom. During this turning over two Medals of Honor were won.

As the ship began its slow ponderous roll, the emergency lights went out. The hysterical men jamming the ladders were trapped in darkness. In their precariously slanting world, they could not see how to get out. Ensign Francis C. Flaherty and Seaman First Class James R. Ward remained in a turret holding flashlights so that the trapped men could see to escape. Flaherty and Ward, staying too long, failed to escape.

The *Oklahoma* continued rolling until she was bottom-up, her mast and superstructure jammed down into the mud, a tragic and slightly ludicrous spectacle.

Just before the attack began at 7:55 A.M., the band leader on the *Nevada* had gathered his group to play morning colors. The first Jap torpedo-plane skimmed across the harbor just as the band crashed into "The Star-Spangled Banner." It was unthinkable to stop in the middle of the National Anthem, so during the first of the attack the director kept conducting and band kept playing, standing in formation until the last note sounded. Then the men scattered for cover.

Incredible as it may sound, the *Nevada* managed to get up steam within forty-five minutes after the attack started and made ready to pull out of the line of battleships. Chief Boatswain Edwin J. Hill climbed down to the mooring quay, cut loose an ammunition lighter alongside, and cast off. As the *Nevada* drifted out with the tide. Hill leaped into the water and swam after the retreating ship. He had been in the Navy twenty-nine years and was not going to abandon his ship in her time of peril.

As the *Nevada* steamed slowly south, heading for the channel to the open sea, she came under intensive enemy air-attack. The Japs obviously hoped to sink her in the channel and bottle up the whole fleet. Navy shore headquarters signaled frantically with flags for the *Nevada* to stay out of the channel. The commanding officer of the ship regretfully nosed her into Hospital Point on the south shore and grounded her.

Chief Boatswain Hill, who had performed the perilous casting-off operation less than half an hour before, now dashed forward to drop anchor. As he worked the chain, a wave of enemy planes dived on the grounded ship. Three bombs landed near the bow and Hill vanished in the tremendous blast. He was another posthumous Medal-winner.

During the *Nevada*'s short jaunt across the harbor, Lieutenant Commander Donald K. Ross was officer in charge of the forward dynamo room. As the room filled with smoke, steam and flame, his men coughed and retched miserably and tried to carry on. Finally Ross ordered all the men out of the dynamo room and performed all the duties himself until he fell, blinded and unconscious. On being dragged out and resuscitated, he staggered back to the dynamo room where he again took charge

until he was again overcome by exhaustion and smoke. Recovering a second time, he returned to the dynamo room and remained in charge until the order came to abandon ship. He became one of the living winners of the Medal of Honor.

Four Medals, the most to any ship during the battle, went to personnel on the *California*. Moored at the southern end of the row of battleships, the *California* caught her first torpedo at 8:05 A.M., then several more in quick succession. In anticipation of an inspection on the following Monday, most of the manholes leading to her double bottom were open. Water swirled in, knocking out the power plant. With the power gone, crews tried desperately to perform tasks ordinarily done by machines. A long chain of men passed powder bags and shells up from an ammunition room far below. Stifling fumes filled the passages, and then flames. Chief Radioman Thomas J. Reeves stayed alone in a burning passageway passing ammunition by hand until he was overcome by smoke and flames and died.

On the second deck Ensign Herbert C. Jones organized a party to pass ammunition to the anti-aircraft battery on the open deck. When the *California* took a bad hit at 8:25, Jones fell, severely wounded. As two men attempted to lift him from the path of the flames, he fought them off weakly. "I'm done for," he gasped. "Get out of here before the magazines go off!" He died at his post.

Machinist's Mate First Class Robert R. Scott was in charge of an air compressor on the *California*. The machine was one of the few left working on the ship after the attack started. When a torpedo struck nearby and his compartment began to flood, Scott ordered the other personnel out, but refused to leave himself. He said grimly, "This is my station and I'll stay and pump air as long as the guns are going." He never made it topside again.

On the third deck Gunner Jackson C. Pharris was in charge of an ordnance repair-party when the first torpedo struck the *California* almost directly under his station. Pharris survived the attack and lived to have his Medal pinned on after his promotion to lieutenant, but his future did not look rosy at the time. The concussion of that first torpedo bounced him to the ceiling and back to the deck like a basketball. Quickly recovering, he set up a hand-supply ammunition train for the ack-ack

guns. As the ship began to list heavily to port as result of the second torpedo strike, Pharris ordered the shipfitters to counter-flood the opposite holds. Twice rendered unconscious by fumes and wounds, Pharris persisted in handling ammunition supply. Several times he entered flooded compartments to drag out unconscious shipmates being slowly submerged in oil. Pharris was later credited with being principally responsible for keeping the *California* in action during the attack.

The ancient battleship *Utah,* now demoted to target ship, was moored on the opposite side of Ford Island from the row of active battleships. Under the hail of bombs and torpedoes, she began listing drunkenly to port. Seeing the port rail disappear under water convinced the captain that the ship was going to capsize, so he ordered all hands topside to prepare to abandon ship. Although informed that orders were to report on deck, Chief Water Tender Peter Tomich remained at his post in the boiler room to see that all his crew got out and that the boilers were secured against explosion, before he checked out himself. The ship capsized before Tomich could make it topside.

During the attack a special shore target of the dive bombers was the Kaneohe Naval Air Station on Oahu. There twenty-six PBYs were lined up by a ramp and four more sat in the bay. As the bombs exploded, blazing gasoline splashed the ramp from the parked planes. Chief Aviation Ordnanceman John W. Finn ran far out on the ramp, set up a fifty-caliber machine gun on an instruction stand and began firing back. Finn, like Gunner Pharris on the *California,* survived the battle to wear his Medal and became a Navy lieutenant. Standing in the shower of blazing gasoline on the ramp, hammering away at the strafers with his machine gun, he looked like a goner. A bullet clipped his heel and he was severely scorched by the burning gas, but his gun kept chattering. The station commander finally ordered him off the ramp to seek medical attention. After being bandaged at the infirmary, Finn returned to his post at the Naval Air Station and although in great pain from wounds and burns, took charge of the rearming of returning planes.

The backbone of the United States Navy was almost smashed at Pearl Harbor. Eighteen big ships had been sunk or seriously damaged. Over two thousand Navy men were killed. After

this disaster, the first victories over enemy ships by United States surface craft went to PT Boats. Two Medals of Honor were awarded captains of these fragile but deadly craft.

PT boats, technically known as Motor Torpedo Boats, were plywood speedboats, boasting not an ounce of armor, seventy-seven feet long. Powered by three fourteen-hundred-horsepower Packard engines, they had a maximum speed of fifty knots and were highly maneuverable. Their armament was four twenty-one-inch torpedo tubes mounted on deck and four fifty-caliber machine guns.

Lieutenant Commander John Duncan Bulkeley was commanding officer of Motor Torpedo Squadron Three, operating in the Philippine Islands on December 7, 1941. A quiet, competent career Navy officer, Bulkeley became a dedicated nemesis to Jap shipping. On the night of January 20, 1942, Bulkeley's command boat stole into the mouth of Binanga Bay and spotted Japanese transports unloading troops. Despite the heavy fire of enemy machine guns and a three-inch artillery battery on shore, Bulkeley sped to the attack through the withering fire and sank a five-thousand-ton Japanese supply ship with torpedoes before wheeling sharply and streaking back.

During the first four months of the war, Bulkeley led his group in destroying a large number of Japanese planes, combat and merchant ships, and harassed landing parties unmercifully. It was the battered remains of Bulkeley's group that took General Douglas MacArthur on the first leg of his historic withdrawal from the Philippines to Australia.

The other Medal of Honor awarded a PT Boat commander went to Lieutenant Arthur Murray Preston, a reserve officer from Maryland. Lieutenant Preston was commander of Motor Torpedo Boat Squadron Thirty-three, operating off Halmahera Island in the Pacific in September 1944. On the afternoon of September 16th, a Navy pilot was shot down in Wasile Bay, less than two hundred yards from the strongly defended Jap-held island. The pilot's squadron mates and a PBY plane were unsuccessful in rescue attempts. Volunteering for the perilous rescue mission, Lieutenant Preston led two of his PT Boats through sixty miles of heavily mined waters, down an eleven-mile strait leading to the bay under heavy shore-fire, and then into the restricted confines of the bay itself. Aided by an aircraft-laid smoke screen, Preston picked up the pilot less than

one hundred and fifty yards offshore. Then he cleared the area, sinking a small enemy cargo-vessel on the way. Streaking back through the strait, Preston and his crew experienced an exciting shell-splashed twenty minutes before reaching the open sea. The two boats had been under continuous shell fire for two and a half hours, but neither was damaged seriously.

In addition to Admiral Kidd, two other Rear Admirals won Medals in World War II. They were Admirals Daniel J. Callaghan and Norman Scott. Admirals Callaghan and Scott received their Medals for "inspiring leadership" during the naval action against Japanese forces off Savo Island, during the night of 12-13 November 1942. This action was part of the bloody Guadalcanal campaign and both admirals died in bombardments while directing close-range operations against the enemy.

Two other Navy captains besides Franklin Van Valkenburgh at Pearl Harbor won Navy Medals of Honor in World War II.

Captain Albert H. Rooks was commanding officer of the U.S.S. *Houston* during the Battle of Madoera Strait in 1942. Seriously damaged during the battle, the *Houston* was steaming under cover of darkness along the Java coast when she ran into the midst of a strong Japanese naval force. The frenzied night battle that followed has been described by experts as "one of the most gallant in the history of the sea." Ringed at close range by fifty-eight enemy warships of all sizes, the *Houston* fought valiantly for more than an hour. Her sister ship, the *Perth,* went down immediately under the terrific concentration of fire. Then big Japanese cruisers on the outer rim of the circle pumped shell after shell into the lone target. Enemy destroyers closed in, firing deck guns and launching torpedoes. The *Houston* fought gamely, sinking two loaded transport-ships and scoring damaging hits on the attacking destroyers.

On the bridge, Captain Rooks set an example of calm courage in the midst of chaos. The intercom was flooded with voices, a confused babble announcing targets, fires and damage. A salvo smashed the after engine-room and burst the steam lines, scalding the engine-room crew to death. Geysers of live steam spouted through ragged rips in the deck, drenching the gun crew. A second torpedo hit the *Houston* and she listed drunkenly to starboard. In the eerie glare of dropping flares, the crew

fought on, inspired by their captain still visible on the bridge.

Shortly after midnight, Captain Rooks turned to his signal-man and said, "We're going to beach and fight our way into the hills." The order was never given. The next Japanese salvo wrecked the bridge, killing Captain Rooks. The captain went down with his ship a few minutes later. Only three hundred and sixty-eight of her complement of eight hundred and eighty-two survived.

The *Houston* had been christened in her namesake city of Houston, Texas, in September 1929. On Memorial Day of 1942, several months after the courageous death of the ship and her captain, a thousand young men stood in an impressive twilight ceremony on a downtown street in Houston and took the Navy oath, volunteering to replace the complement of the lost ship. The *Houston* and her captain were not to be forgotten.

America's war fish played a deadly game with the enemy during World War II, especially against the Japanese in the Pacific. Seven submarine commanders were awarded Medals of Honor. All went for actions in the Pacific theater. Three of the awards were posthumous, the winners failing to return from their war patrols. Since submarine operations were always shrouded in a veil of secrecy for security reasons, the exploits of most of these men did not become known until long after the war was over.

Captain John P. Cromwell, the third Navy captain to win the Medal in World War II, was commanding officer of a submarine attack group operating in the enemy-controlled waters off the Japanese stronghold of Truk, in November 1943. This patrol was principally a reconnaissance for the first large-scale offensive in the Pacific. Captain Cromwell bore a secret gnawing responsibility. He alone in the attack group knew the secret plans regarding fleet movements and the projected attack. While scouting the enemy-patrolled waters close to Truk, his command submarine, the *Sculpin,* came under severe enemy attack. Rocked and battered by depth charges, the *Sculpin* dived deeply but could not escape. She was in danger of becoming a tomb for the entire crew. Captain Cromwell ordered the *Sculpin* to surface and engaged the enemy in a gunfight to enable as many of the crew as possible to escape. On the surface, as the crew leaped into the water, Captain Cromwell refused to

leave the stricken submarine. He was determined to sacrifice himself rather than risk capture and the possible betrayal of secret plans under torture. He went down with the ship, preserving the security of his mission at the cost of his own life.

The case of Commander Howard W. Gilmore was somewhat similar to that of Captain Cromwell. Gilmore was commanding officer of the U.S.S. *Growler* during her fourth war-patrol in the southwest Pacific during January and February 1943. An enemy gunboat surprised the *Growler* on the surface the night of February 7th and dashed in close to ram her. Commander Gilmore, on the bridge, daringly maneuvered the *Growler* to miss the prow of the onrushing vessel and then rammed the attacker himself, crashing the *Growler* into the gunboat's port side at seventeen knots, ripping off the enemy's plates. In the scathing fire of the sinking gunboat's machine guns, Gilmore gave the orders to clear the deck. Remaining to be the last off the bridge, the sub commander collapsed under a fusillade of bullets. Commander Gilmore gave his last order to the officer of the deck. "Take her down!" he gasped. The *Growler* dived, seriously damaged, but under control. She made it safely to port, leaving the body of her courageous captain somewhere in the waters of the southwest Pacific.

Commander Samuel D. Dealey, a quiet Texan, was, like all the submarine winners, a professional Navy career man. After graduation from the Naval Academy in 1930, Dealey divided his time between surface ships and the pigboats of the Submarine School at New London, Connecticut. He became one of the legendary fighters of the submarine service in World War II. Commanding the U.S.S. *Harder* in her fifth war-patrol, he found himself pursued rather than the pursuer. Surprised on the surface in bright moonlight, the *Harder* was suddenly attacked by an onrushing enemy destroyer escort. Instead of diving to a safe depth and sweating out a few charges, Dealey dived merely to periscope depth and waited for the enemy to come within close range. Then he opened fire at the prow of the onrushing destroyer, sinking the enemy with the third torpedo.

Shortly thereafter he sent another enemy destroyer down, tail first, with a devastating direct hit amidships.

Prowling onward down the coast he entered the confined waters off Tawi Tawi, and bushwhacked two patrolling destroyers in quick succession. Both of these were "down

the throat" shots, the torpedoes fired with the enemy bearing directly down on the *Harder*.

Next day, under attack by another Jap destroyer, Dealey tried another "down the throat" shot, firing three bow tubes at an attacking enemy as it loomed huge in his periscope. As the *Harder* crash-dived beneath the onrushing destroyer, the sub was rocked terrifically and almost sunk by the ship exploding just above.

The destruction of five destroyers in such short order was overwhelming to the Japs, who were convinced that a huge wolf-pack of submarines was working in the area. As a result, they pulled most of their fleet out of Tawi Tawi, withdrawing the ships to the home islands.

The *Harder* made it safely back from her fifth war-patrol. She failed to return from her sixth, the gallant commander and crew disappearing in the depths of the sea. In her brief career, the *Harder*, under Commander Sam Dealey, sank twenty enemy ships, including seven destroyers.

There were several instances of Navy officer awards for types of bravery that did not fit into any sort of pattern. One of these was the case of Lieutenant Richard Nott Antrim of the U.S.S. *Pope*.

The end came for the *Pope* during the Battle of the Java Sea in 1942. Attacked by a horde of enemy planes and surface vessels, she quickly became a crippled, unmaneuverable wreck. The order came to abandon ship and a small party managed to escape in a lifeboat before the ship was sunk by point-blank fire from a Japanese cruiser.

Lieutenant Richard Nott Antrim, executive officer of the *Pope*, commanded the single lifeboat. He organized the one hundred and fifty survivors into a disciplined group. Under his leadership no casualties resulted from the strafing. Every wounded man survived. Every man received his share of food and water while they drifted for three days in hostile waters. An enemy destroyer captured them and delivered them to Makassar on the island of Celebes.

The *Pope* survivors joined twenty-five hundred other prisoners of war at Makassar. They found themselves in the hands of cruel and barbarous captors, kicked and beaten unmercifully at the slightest provocation. Finally Antrim had enough.

As a frenzied Japanese guard clubbed a helpless prisoner, Antrim intervened, attempting to persuade the Jap to stop beating the prisoner. Ignoring the officer's pleas, the Jap continued raining blows on his helpless victim with a heavy hawser. Antrim then grabbed his arm and volunteered to take the remainder of the punishment for the prisoner. The entire guard-force, thrown completely off-balance by this strange request, retreated in amazement, sparing the prisoner further beating. A roar of acclaim rose from the other prisoners. Antrim's fearless intervention saved the life of the prisoner and inspired a new respect for American officers and men in the camp. On release from the camp at the end of the war, he was awarded the Medal of Honor.

Unusual also was the case of Lieutenant (jg) Albert Leroy David. David was a member of the ship's company of the U.S.S. *Pillsbury* during an attack on the German submarine U-505 off French West Africa June 4, 1944. After a prolonged search by the task force, the enemy surfaced, obviously crippled from depth charges. As the enemy sub circled erratically at a speed of five or six knots, David led a boarding party to take control of the vessel. Acutely aware that the sub might momentarily sink or be blown up by scuttling charges, David dived through the conning-tower hatch and took possession. This was the first successful boarding and capture of an enemy man-of-war on the high seas by the United States Navy since 1815.

Unique because of the winner's branch of service, was the award to Signalman First Class Douglas A. Munro of the United States Coast Guard, the only member of this service ever to win a Medal of Honor. On September 27, 1942, a detachment of Marines was put ashore near the mouth of the Matanikan River on Guadalcanal. They encountered unexpectedly heavy opposition and were pushed back to the beach where they sweated out a rain of mortar fire. Sighting the seaplane tender *Ballard* offshore, the sergeant in charge of the Marine group signaled an urgent SOS to the ship. Although the *Ballard* was a maintenance vessel and not equipped to handle large-scale amphibious operations, she did happen to have five Higgins boats aboard. Douglas Munro, the signalman first receiving the distress signal from shore, volunteered to lead a rescue party.

As the little boats chugged shoreward from the *Ballard*, they

soon came within range of enemy small arms on shore. Enemy machine-gun fire was directed at them and then mortar shells began to explode around the boats.

On nearing the beach, Munro signaled the other boats to pick up the troops while he maneuvered his boat into a position between the landing party and the main source of enemy fire. He then returned the enemy fire with a light machine gun mounted on his boat. As the loaded boats put back out to sea, Munro followed behind, acting as cover. He was fatally wounded by enemy fire during the withdrawal. On being lifted back aboard the *Ballard* he was conscious only long enough to ask, "Did they all get off?" He was posthumously awarded the Medal of Honor.

The only chaplain in Navy history to win the Medal of Honor was Lieutenant Commander Joseph Timothy O'Callahan, a Jesuit priest on the U.S. Carrier *Franklin*. On March 19, 1945, the *Franklin* and the rest of Task Force Fifty-eight were cruising fifty-three miles west of Shikoku, Japan, waiting for daylight to launch the attack. Prior to that fateful day, the *Franklin* had been struck by enemy air bombs twice and survived. Many of the crew spoke forebodingly that a third time might be fatal. Adding fuel to the superstitious fires was the *Franklin*'s number as an Essex class carrier—CV Thirteen.

Chaplain O'Callahan pulled himself wearily from his bunk at five A.M. He had to make his rounds of the pilot's ready-rooms to say a brief prayer with them prior to take-off. The first strike was at 5:30. By seven o'clock the chaplain had finished his rounds and sat down at a table with other officers for breakfast. At 7:07 A.M. time had run out. The carrier was about to be struck by its third air bomb.

One minute O'Callahan was sitting at the table staring distastefully at his cold French toast and the very next there were two sudden shocking explosions and he was sprawling under the table with the others, his rimless spectacles hanging from one ear, his hands shielding his eyes and face from the flying glass of broken light fixtures. Then Chaplain O'Callahan had a thirty-second lull to voice a brief prayer before the first great holocaust rocked the ship.

A twin-engined Japanese plane, called a Judy in naval parlance, had zoomed down from a cloud over the bow of the *Frank-*

lin at seventy-five feet and dropped two bombs in quick succession. One bomb exploded in the hangar near the gasoline pumps. The other landed squarely in the middle of thirty Helldivers, gassed and loaded with bombs, on the flight deck.

Thousands of gallons of high-test airplane gasoline exploded, shooting a wall of fire the entire length of the hangar deck and leaving in its wake eight hundred charred corpses.

From then on for the next several hours, Chaplain O'Callahan was afforded a vivid dramatization of what hell was like. He groped his way through the smoke-filled corridors to the open deck and ministered to the wounded and dying amid the violently exploding bombs, shells and rockets. He knelt calmly with the wounded as burning fragments and debris rained down on the deck. Then he organized and led fire-fighting crews into the fire bowels of the ship, and helped in the jettisoning of live hot bombs which rolled helter-skelter on the decks.

As he led a hose crew splashing water on the flames near a group of wounded, a fountain of clear liquid began spouting from a vent on the deck. "Padre!" the captain shouted from the bridge. "For God's sake find out if that's gasoline! If it is, get the wounded away from there fast!"

For a second O'Callahan stared blankly at the voice from the bridge. If it did happen to be gas, where in the name of all the saints was he supposed to move the wounded to? But orders were orders.

Toiling up the slanted deck to the bubbling geyser, he thought numbly, I'll taste it to see if the stuff's gasoline. If it catches fire, I'll look like a human volcano. Cupping his hands he brought some of the foamy sprew to his lips. He made a face and spat. Salt water. It was just a burst water main.

Turning to the bridge the chaplain held his thumbs up, nearly doing a pratfall on the slanting deck. Waving a relieved acknowledgment, the captain growled to his navigator, "I'm going to put that Irishman in for a medal if he lives through this."

The Irishman lived through the carnage and the medal he got was the Medal of Honor.

Although no commissioned Navy medics got the Medal in World War II, seven enlisted Navy medics did. All seven were medical corpsmen attached to Marine ground-units dur-

ing the bloody assaults on Iwo Jima and Okinawa during the closing months of the war in the Pacific in 1945.

John Harland Willis was a Navy medic who believed in fighting for his patients. Attached to a rifle platoon of the Third Battalion, Twenty-seventh Marines on Iwo Jima in February 1945, Willis was wounded by shrapnel during the assault on Hill Three Hundred and Sixty-two, and was ordered back to the battle-aid station. After being bandaged, without waiting for official release, he returned to his company. During a savage hand-to-hand enemy counterattack he wriggled and squirmed to the very front position through mortar and sniper fire to aid a wounded Marine. As he administered blood plasma, a hostile grenade fell into the shell hole with him. He threw it back. And that was just the beginning. The Japs began to throw grenades. Willis threw back seven more before the ninth one exploded in his hand, killing him and his patient.

Robert Bush, a native of the State of Washington, was a medical corpsman attached to a rifle company in the second battalion of the Fifth Marines, Fifth Marine Division, when his outfit hit the beach at Okinawa in the spring of 1945. He won his Medal in action against Japanese forces on May 2, 1945. Bush was administering blood plasma to a wounded Marine officer skylined on a ridgetop when the enemy counterattacked in force. Holding the plasma-bottle high in one hand, Bush drew his forty-five with the other and fired into the enemy's ranks until the pistol was empty. An enemy bullet smashed the bottle of life-giving plasma and wounded Bush seriously, blinding him in one eye. Bush grabbed a discarded carbine and opened point-blank fire on the charging Japanese. He killed six of the enemy, which routed them. Despite his wounds he refused to be evacuated until his patient was carried back. He calmly administered another bottle of plasma, while waiting for stretcher bearers. He collapsed on his way back to the aid station, but survived to wear his Medal.

The Medal award to Boatswain's Mate Second Class Owen Francis Patrick Hammerberg was unique in that it was the only Navy Medal of Honor awarded during World War II for a deed not directly connected with action against the enemy.

Salvage operations on the ships sunk at Pearl Harbor were

still being carried on in 1945. Hammerberg's award was a post-humous one, made for his actions at West Loch, Pearl Harbor, on February 17, 1945. The following passage quoted from his Medal of Honor citation graphically describes what he did:

> Aware of the danger when two fellow divers were hopelessly trapped in a cave-in of steel wreckage while tunneling with a jet nozzle under an LST sunk in forty feet of water and twenty feet of mud, Hammerberg unhesitatingly went overboard in a valiant attempt to effect their rescue despite the certain hazard of additional cave-ins and the risk of fouling his life line on jagged pieces of steel imbedded in the shifting mud. Washing a passage through the original excavation, he reached the first of the trapped men, freed him from the wreckage and, working desperately in pitch-black darkness, finally effected his release from fouled lines, thereby enabling him to reach the surface. Wearied but undaunted after several hours of arduous labor, Hammerberg resolved to continue his struggle to wash through the oozing, submarine, subterranean mud in a determined effort to save the second diver. Venturing still further under the buried hulk, he held tenaciously to his purpose, reaching a place immediately above the other man just as another cave-in occurred and a heavy piece of steel pinned him crosswise over his shipmate in a position which protected the man beneath him from further injury while placing the full brunt of terrific pressure on himself. Although he succumbed in agony eighteen hours after he had gone to the aid of his fellow-divers, Hammerberg, by his cool judgment, unfaltering professional skill and consistent disregard of all personal danger in the face of tremendous odds, had contributed effectively to the saving of his two comrades.

The award to Hammerberg was the last Navy Medal of Honor award in history for an act of heroism done "in line of the Navy profession," having no connection with conflict with an armed enemy.

The Navy fought a war in the air as well as on the surface and under the sea. Six Navy flyers won Medals of Honor in World War II. All were commissioned pilots: two in fighters, two in patrol planes and two in bombers.

Lieutenant Butch O'Hare, a fighter pilot, saved the life of the United States Carrier *Lexington* to win his Medal. On February 20, 1942, the *Lexington*, steaming as part of a task force on Rabaul, was intercepted by Japanese bombers. The

carrier's fighters managed to disperse the first wave of enemy bombers, but when the second wave of enemy bombers roared in, only two American planes were left in the air to oppose them. They plunged in at the Japs, but the guns of one plane jammed.That left only Lieutenant Butch O'Hare in his little wasp of a plane between nine big enemy bombers and the task force with the precious carrier.

O'Hare, with guns blazing, attacked the rear of the enemy's arrow-tip formation. He blasted the starboard motors out of the two twin-engine bombers on the right flank of the enemy formation, and then zoomed upward from below the formation firing at a third bomber. It staggered and fell away, throwing smoke.

Two more bombers began to smoke under his raging attacks, and the enemy formation went to pieces. But four of them managed to get through and drop their bombs. O'Hare was waiting for them as they clawed upward for altitude. He shot all four of them down. In four minutes O'Hare had shot down five enemy bombers and seriously crippled three more.

Other Navy fighters from the *Lexington* overtook and knocked down the three damaged enemy bombers. Of the attacking formation of nine planes, only one escaped.

Lieutenant John J. Powers was pilot of a Dauntless dive bomber in the Coral Sea area during May 1942. On May 7 he led his section of three bombers in a screaming dive against an enemy carrier. In the face of heavy anti-aircraft fire he dived to an altitude well below the safety level in order to insure a hit on the carrier. His bomb struck the carrier in a vital spot, and the enemy blew up in a tremendous explosion and sank almost immediately.

Back on his carrier Lieutenant Powers, lecturing in his capacity as Squadron Gunnery Officer, advocated a low release-point for bombs to insure greater accuracy. He admitted, however, that the danger from enemy fire was great at a low altitude and also the danger of the attacking plane being engulfed in the bomb blast and the flying fragments.

Next morning as he prepared to take off, he remarked grimly to a mechanic, "I'm going to get a hit if I have to lay it on their flight deck." Later in the morning he led his section of dive bombers down on an enemy carrier from a height of eighteen thousand feet. A wall of bursting anti-aircraft fire came up to

meet him. He almost made good his boast to lay a bomb directly on the flight deck of an enemy. He released his bombs at an altitude of barely two hundred feet and attempted to pull out. He was too low. His plane exploded in the uprising mushroom of flame and debris from the stricken vessel.

XV

The Bloody Island Beachheads

EIGHTY Navy Medals of Honor went to Marines in World War II. Thirty went to officers and fifty to the ranks.

One Marine general received the Medal, Major General Alexander A. Vandergrift who won the award "for outstanding and heroic accomplishment above and beyond the call of duty as Commanding Officer of the First Marine Division in operations against enemy Japanese forces in the Solomon Islands during the period, 7 August to 9 December 1942." General Vandergrift was personally present on the Guadalcanal beachhead during those first dark days when it seemed that the resourceful enemy would push the outnumbered Marines back into the sea.

Among the Marine officers were two full colonels, three lieutenant colonels, five majors, eight captains, ten first lieutenants, and one lone second lieutenant. Sixteen of the awards, more than half of the total thirty, went to reserve officers. Fourteen of the Marine officer awards were posthumous.

The first Marine to win the Medal in World War II was an officer, First Lieutenant George H. Cannon. Cannon was a battery commander when the Japanese bombarded Sand Island in the Midway group on December 7, 1941. Mortally wounded by enemy shellfire, he refused to be evacuated from his command post until all of the men of his command, who had been wounded by the same shell, could be evacuated. Because of his refusal, he died from loss of blood shortly after arriving at the battle-aid station.

The late General Merritt A. "Red Mike" Edson, USMC, winner of the Medal as a colonel on Guadalcanal, was a slightly built Marine officer with a lopsided grin. He was a career officer of the old breed. From the days of his service in Nicaragua from 1927 to 1929, through Guadalcanal, Tarawa and Saipan in World War II, he was known as a top leader of guerrilla-type actions. Edson's Raiders, called the First Marine Raider Battalion after February 1942, were formed before Pearl Harbor. They practiced rubber-boat sneak landings, toiled through obstacle courses and sent members to attend British commando schools. When their time came to go into action on Guadalcanal, the raider group and their redheaded commanding officer, Colonel "Red Mike" Edson, were ready.

Edson's group—depleted to eight hundred men after several weeks of jungle fighting—was assigned to hold the ridge above Henderson Field, because the ridge was an inactive sector on the beachhead perimeter and the raiders needed a rest.

Hiking with his company commanders over the terrain of the ridge, Red Mike came to the conclusion that if the Japanese commander had any military ability, which Edson was sure he did have, then the defenders would not get much rest here. The most direct route of attack to Henderson Field, the island's indispensable airfield, was through Edson's position on the ridge.

Edson's foreboding was justified. That night a howling mob of Japs, three thousand strong, stormed the ridge. They quickly disrupted radio communications, cutting in on all channels with English-speaking radio men to broadcast confusing messages. Edson resorted to the primitive runner-system of World War I for carrying messages. Since the battlefield was small, he roamed all over it himself, taking charge where the action was the hottest, recklessly exposing himself to enemy fire. When asked to take cover, Red Mike always said "no Jap bullet is ever going to get me."

During the hottest part of the action, when it seemed the line must break, Edson called in artillery support immediately in front of his positions. The shells exploded so close that fragments rained into raider foxholes. Edson's own sweaty Marine jacket was ripped with shrapnel.

Major Kenneth D. Bailey, a company commander in Edson's Raiders, also won his Medal during the battle to hold the ridge

above Henderson Field. Major Bailey sustained a severe head-wound during the fighting, but refused to be evacuated and led his troops in hand-to-hand combat with the enemy for ten more hours. Major Bailey died in the battle to hold the ridge.

When the battle was over, the ridge line was still intact and more than one thousand Japanese were dead. Edson's defense against overwhelming numbers had saved Henderson Field.

The Marines struck Tarawa in the Gilbert Islands on November 21, 1943, in a brief and bloody assault. During the first seventy-six hours, one thousand twenty-six Americans were killed and two thousand five hundred and fifty-seven were wounded. Three Marine ground officers won Medals in the fighting. They were First Lieutenant Alexander Bonnyman, Jr., First Lieutenant William Dean Hawkins, and Colonel David M. Shoup. The first two were awarded posthumously, while Colonel Shoup, though badly wounded, survived to continue a brilliant career and ultimately became Commandant of the Marine Corps.

In all, fifty Medals of Honor were awarded to enlisted Marines for heroic actions during the amphibious assaults and the land fighting in the Pacific during World War II. No Marines fought in the European Theater. Of these fifty, thirty-two died in winning their Medals. Fourteen awards went to sergeants of all grades, eight went to corporals and twenty-eight went to privates and privates first class.

The awards to enlisted Marines showed a trend as to type of action, a trend as manifest almost as the "flag acts" of the Civil War. The most common act winning a Marine a Medal of Honor during World War II was to smother a live grenade with the body. Twenty-six, more than half of the total fifty enlisted Marines, won the Medal in this way. And as unbelievable as it may sound, three of the Marine-enlisted grenade jumpers survived the explosions—Corporal Richard E. Bush of Glasgow, Kentucky; Private First Class Jacklyn H. Lucas of Belhaven, North Carolina; and Private Richard K. Sorenson of Anoka, Minnesota.

Some critics of the Medal of Honor awards system in recent years have criticized awarding the Medal for this type of suicidal act. The questions was raised: was there time to make a heroic decision within the brief span between the arrival of the in-

coming grenade and the smothering, or was the leaping on the deadly charge an involuntary act of hysteria? Some psychologists have relegated this type of act to a manifestation of a latent "death wish." In any case, the Marines thought a lot of this act as Medal of Honor material during World War II, and so did the Army, as will be seen later.

The first enlisted Marine to win the Medal in World War II was Sergeant John Basilone, the famous "Manila John" who won his Medal on Guadalcanal.

Old residents in Raritan, New Jersey, recalled Johnny Basilone—one of the ten children of tailor Salvatore Basilone—as a skinny kid with a big shock of black hair, hustling beside the Italian peddlers' carts, hawking vegetables. They recalled that he was always hustling and that he always wore a happy grin as though life was a lot of fun to Johnny Basilone.

At eighteen, when Johnny was a tall weedy kid with jug ears, he joined the Army. It was 1934 and there was no civilian job to be had. He liked the Army and made a name for himself as an amateur boxer.

When Johnny Basilone joined the Army there were still a lot of old timers around who had served against Aguinaldo in the Philippine Insurrection, the Boxers in China and Pancho Villa in Mexico. The veterans were full of stories of the China Station and Manila. From them John Basilone acquired the vast fund of yarns that he would spin to Marine recruits on Guadalcanal, yarns mostly about Manila. Because of these Manila stories, he would receive the nickname "Manila John."

After a three-year Army hitch in the Philippines, John Basilone came home, a seasoned veteran with big tattoos on his arms. When the war clouds gathered in 1940, he joined the Marines. The Corps was glad to get an experienced veteran like Basilone. He was a natural soldier and leader. To the eighteen-year-old recruits in boot camp he was an oracle, a veteran who knew how to make a bunk and roll a tight pack. At night in the barracks they listened wide-eyed to his yarns of the old Army—the China Station, Schofield Barracks, Pearl Harbor, but mostly the Philippines. On the firing range they marveled at his skill with the thirty-caliber water-cooled machine gun.

During the latter part of August 1942, Mr. and Mrs. Basilone received a note written in their Marine son's round school-boy

hand on a scrap of brown wrapping paper from a place called Guadalcanal. "I have arrived safely," was all the note said.

The safety did not last long after arrival, however. On the night of October 24, 1942, Sergeant Basilone, in command of two machine-gun sections in the Lunga area, fought off wave after wave of attacking Japanese. It was like a fantastic five-minute news reel that repeated itself over and over again. First would come the entrance of a whirling, dervish-like puppet of a Jap officer screaming a battle cry and waving a long sword. Behind him followed the horde of dwarfish soldiers, their helmets grotesquely camouflaged with broom grass and vines.

"Banzai! Banzai!" the officer yelled and charged, flailing with the big sword.

"Banzai, yourself," said Manila John and pressed his trigger, his bursts sending the officer kicking and then chopping into the dwarfish followers.

Then the Japs would fall back to regroup and begin another charge. All night and into the dawn the machine gun chattered and all night and into the dawn the Japs died.

When the enemy withdrew, intelligence reports from the area were astounding. Dead Japanese were all over the place. Thirty-eight lay in one tangled mound. Basilone's one-man stand with his machine guns had annihilated the major part of a Jap infantry regiment.

Several months later Mr. and Mrs. Salvatore Basilone of Raritan, New Jersey, received this letter from their son in the Marines. "I am very happy for the other day I received the Congressional Medal of Honor, the highest award you can get in the armed forces."

In September 1943, John Basilone came home on leave. The tailor's son was a hero. Raritan proclaimed "Basilone Day" and turned out with a blaring high school band to meet his train at the station. He got the hero treatment and the grand tour to sell War Bonds. A comic strip called "Manila John" was written about him. The home folks presented him with a $5,000 War Bond for himself. Then he married a lady Marine, Sergeant Lena Riggi, in San Diego in July 1944. The Corps offered him a commission, but he turned it down. "I'm a plain soldier —I want to stay one."

Manila John now really had it made. He had a good-looking wife and a big bond and because of his Medal the Navy gen-

erally let him have the admiral's gig and eight sideboys to pipe him over the side. But Basilone yearned to get back to his outfit. "What will they say on Dewey Boulevard in Manila, if the Marines land and Manila John is not there?" he asked plaintively.

In September 1944 he kissed his wife good-by and headed back to the Pacific. From Pearl Harbor he sent his mother a photo of himself in dress uniform wearing his Medal around the neck, with a hand-written note: "Tell Pop his son is still tough." He was going back to the war.

On February 19, 1945, an American invasion force of eight hundred ships lay off a tiny evil-looking island in the Pacific on the sea road to Japan. Five and a half miles long by two and a half miles wide, it was a black, brooding hump rising out of the sea. The island was the blackened crystallized remains of volcanic eruption. The terrain was a bleak waste of rubble, boulders, gullies and ridges. This was Iwo Jima.

With an area roughly eight times as large as the Rock of Gibraltar, Iwo was full of underground tunnels, a maze connecting the hundreds of heavy-gun positions and pillboxes. When the American attack came, the Japanese defenders withdrew into their secret underground strongholds and each vowed to kill ten of the enemy before dying.

On the first day, Gunnery Sergeant John Basilone led an assault team of the Twenty-seventh Regiment, Fifth Marine Division, onto the beach of Iwo Jima. A shell with his name on it came out of the blue. His last words to his section were, "Get in there and set up those guns." He was twenty-eight years old.

Hugging the earth, the invaders had to crawl forward in pairs or alone toward each pillbox or camouflaged machine-gun nest. Every boulder had a sniper. It was man against man with grenades, bayonets, rifles or flame throwers.

During the twenty-six-day Iwo Jima campaign, twenty-six Medals of Honor were awarded Marines and hospital corpsmen. The invading forces sustained over twenty thousand casualties. More than forty-three hundred of that number were killed.

Five Marine officers won Medals of Honor on Iwo Jima, all for heroic acts in leading their attacking units up the cliffs of the volcanic island against the enemy in their rock-imbedded fortifications, but the most famous of the winners who made the beach at Iwo Jima remained John Basilone. According to many

Marines, Manila John did not really die, and when the Marines landed in the Philippines many of his shipmates swore they saw him there, firing his machine guns. His indomitable spirit has lived on in the Corps.

XVI

Nobody Calls Me Gregory Anymore

ELEVEN Marine flyers won Medals of Honor in World War II. All except one of the eleven were fighter pilots. The lone exception was Captain Richard E. Fleming who as a pilot of Marine Scout-Bombing Squadron Two Hundred and Forty-one won his Medal for a bombing action against the Japanese fleet during the Battle of Midway on June 4 and 5, 1942. As he dived on a Japanese battleship, his plane was set afire but he grimly continued the dive, releasing his bomb on his target at less than five hundred feet. Fleming was unable to pull out and crashed into the sea in flames.

The case of Captain Henry Talmage Elrod, USMC, a pilot of Marine Fighting Squadron Two Hundred and Eleven, was similar to that of World War I winner Frank Luke, Jr. Elrod, like Luke, did not believe he was supposed to quit shooting at the enemy just because his plane was shot down.

At Wake Island during the first days after Pearl Harbor, Elrod fought in the skies as long as the planes held out. On December 9, 1941, he engaged a flight of twenty-two enemy planes, knocking down two. On December 12th he inflicted mortal damage on an enemy vessel with his bombs during low-altitude runs, the first American to sink a major enemy warship by bombing in World War II.

When his last plane was disabled by enemy fire, Elrod crash-landed and walked away from the wreck. He assumed command of an infantry company on the island. As the howling invaders stormed through the surf and onto the beach, Captain

Elrod led his men in hand-to-hand combat with them. Capturing an enemy machine gun, Elrod personally accounted for over a dozen of the enemy. He fell, mortally wounded, on December 23, 1941.

With the exceptions of Fleming and Elrod, the remainder of the Marine air winners were of the "ace" variety, having long strings of enemy "kills" to their credit. Most of them were not awarded their Medals for single climactic actions, but were cited for outstanding leadership and bravery covering periods of weeks and months.

The best known of these Marine pilot winners were Bob Galer, Joe Foss and Pappy Boyington.

Major Robert Edward Galer, USMC, was born and raised in Seattle, Washington. Although only five feet ten inches tall, he was star basketball player at the University of Washington. In 1934 he scored one hundred and seventy-six points and set a new conference scoring record. He was team captain in 1935 and graduated that same year with a degree in engineering. Entering the Marine air service soon after graduation, Galer won a commission and pilot's wings. He saw peacetime duty in the Virgin Islands and served as squadron recreation officer in addition to his other duties. He was also a star tennis player on service teams.

As commanding officer of a Marine fighter squadron in the Solomons, Bob Galer soon became a star combat pilot. His citation read in part, for "individually shooting down eleven enemy bomber and fighter aircraft over a period of twenty-nine days." Galer was one of the Marine air winners who survived to wear his Medal.

Another Marine winner whose public life since winning the Medal has been crowned with success was Joseph J. Foss of South Dakota. After the war Foss served two terms as governor of his home state and then became President of the American Football League. His citation read in part as follows: "Engaging in almost daily combat with the enemy from 9 October to 19 November 1942, Captain Foss personally shot down twenty-three Japanese planes and damaged others so severely that their destruction was extremely probable."

The following January after returning from a bout of malaria in the hospital, Foss shot down three more enemy planes,

tying the Rickenbacker World War I record of twenty-six confirmed kills. Foss was the first American flyer of any of the services to tie this record.

Four of the eleven Marine air awards were posthumous. A
fifth award, that to Major Gregory "Pappy" Boyington, was
thought to be posthumous when made. Boyington has said that
the brass would never have given him the award had they
dreamed he would turn up alive to "embarrass" them. But
Pappy did turn up alive and has the same legendary status
among Marine flyers that Basilone has among the ground troops.

Gregory Boyington, who became the legendary leader of
the Black Sheep Squadron, was born December 4, 1912, at Cour
D'Alene, Idaho, the son of a dentist. His parents divorced when
he was three years old, and he was raised by his mother and
step-father on an apple farm near Okanogan, Washington.
Like Bob Galer, Boyington attended the University of Washington in Seattle, working his way through college parking cars
in a storage garage. After graduating with a degree in aero-
nautical engineering, he entered the Marine Corps in 1935 and
soon won his wings as a pilot.

Boyington was an excellent pilot, but a sloppy military man.
Naturally pugnacious and in the habit of drinking to excess, he
was a thorn in the flesh of his superiors. Turbulence marked
his domestic life as well. By 1941 he was divorced with the
custody of three small children.

In 1941, in an attempt to make money to pay his creditors, he
resigned from the Marine Corps and went to China as a member of Claire Chennault's Flying Tigers. After Pearl Harbor, he
resigned from the Flying Tigers to escape the ignominy of
being inducted into the Army Air Corps. Then he came home,
and to his great consternation, the Marines did not seem to
want him back.

And then the legend grew about Boyington in the yarns of
the pilots who flew with him in the Tigers and those later in
the South Pacific.

They tell how Boyington, an experienced fighter-pilot, with
six kills as a Flying Tiger to his credit, had to work parking
cars in a garage in Seattle for months before his irate telegram
to the Secretary of the Navy brought about his return to the
Marine Corps. The Marines still talk about the booze and the
brawling. They tell how their legend, a bull-necked, flat-nosed,

sawed-off little character, after his triumphal return to the Corps, loved to roughhouse and brawl in the officers clubs, to the great consternation of the top brass. They tell how, as the oldest active Marine fighter-pilot, he formed his Black Sheep Squadron from the rejects and misfits and turned it into the most enemy-feared air unit in the Pacific. They tell about how, on the long flights up the Slot which stretched from Guam to Bougainville, as his squadron rode herd on bombers, he would connect a weird network of rubber bands and bits of string to the flight controls, making a Rube Goldberg automatic pilot, and then settle down for a nap. His wing man would signal the message, "Keep a sharp lookout, Black Sheep, the old guy's taking a nap," then they would watch their ancient commanding officer—he was all of thirty-one years old—with fascination. If a wing dropped, the old boy would rouse slightly and tap a rubber band. The wing would rise slowly to even keel. If the Corsair started going uphill or downhill, the change in engine sound would stir him. Opening one eye he would fiddle with a string and the plane leveled off.

They tell how Boyington, when awake, always smoked cigarettes in his plane and they knew action was near when he pushed back his flap and tossed out the butt. They tell how he nearly went berserk trying to break Eddie Rickenbacker's record of twenty-six kills, and about the beer shampoos he liked to give in the Hotel de Gink on Guadalcanal. There is no end to the tales they tell about Boyington. But mostly they tell about the time over Kahili that he talked the Japs into the air and he and his Black Sheep flamed twenty of them.

By October 1943, the Americans held footholds in the Solomons on Guadalcanal, New Georgia, and Vella Lavella, and in the tiny Russells. In the air, the fragile Zeros had suffered heavy casualties from the heavily gunned American fighter planes and were wary and elusive, concentrating their fury on the slower, more vulnerable American bombers.

On October 17th over Kahili the weather was murky and overcast, not favorable for bombing. While Boyington's fighters circled watchfully above, the TBFs went down to ten thousand feet, unloaded their eggs in a perfunctory fashion, then headed for home. Not a single enemy fighter came up to challenge them. The whole situation began to prey on Pappy's mind. Just the night before in the Hotel de Gink on Guadalcanal his Black

Sheep had given him a beer shampoo, shouting, "Get us a Jappy, Pappy! Get us a Jappy!"

It was humiliating to Boyington that he could not furnish his Sheep with the sport they craved. He personally was the most desperate of the lot. At his age the brass would probably not allow him another tour as a fighter pilot. If he did not make his record twenty-six kills this tour, he was cooked.

Halfway back home, Pappy suddenly turned his outfit around and headed back up the Slot for Kahili. He had decided to give the Japs an imaginary squadron of unprotected bombers.

High above Kahili, he began jabbering over his radio, impersonating the leader of a bomber squadron. "This is Major Boyington. Close up, angels, and prepare for bomb run. Umbrella's gone. Look out for bandits. We've got to get out of here fast." The Black Sheep waited expectantly.

Suddenly over the radio came a query in almost too-perfect English. "Major Boyington, what is your position?" It was the kibitzing enemy ground-radio pretending to be an American fighter group in the vicinity. "Can we give umbrella?"

"Yeah, man," said Pappy. "Need it bad. Can you assist?"

"Can do. What is your position, Major Boyington?"

"Over Treasury Island," he said, "at twenty thousand feet."

"Major Boyington, what are your angels?"

Pappy shook his head in admiration. The Jap radio operator had the patter down to a tee. "We are twenty angels," said Pappy. "We are twenty angels, twenty thousand feet over Treasury Island."

"I hear you five by five," said the Jap operator precisely. "Hold your position and we will umbrella."

Boyington had given their exact position over Treasury Island, but had lied about the altitude. The Black Sheep were at thirty thousand rather than twenty thousand feet. A few minutes later they saw below them a formation of thirty Zeros, climbing in an easterly direction at twenty-five thousand feet. Apparently they were all looking down, hunting the bombers. Boyington cracked his hood panel and threw out his cigarette. Then he pointed his controls downward and led his twenty Corsairs roaring down the long roller-coaster.

When the enemy leader loomed so large in his sights that a crash seemed imminent, Pappy let go with his six fifty-caliber

machine guns at point-blank range. The Zero blew up in his face in a huge violent blossom of black smoke tinged with orange flame.

Then the long spiral downward began, like water swirling into a whirlpool. Boyington blasted a second Zero before he pulled out, just above the choppy sea. Then he flamed another just off the water. The Zero went into the drink with a sizzling column of steam.

Then, in a mad roaring climb for altitude, he led the outfit upward, trying to get back on top of the Jap formation. It was too late. The few remaining Zeros could be seen fleeing back toward Kahili.

Circling again over Kahili, Pappy went back on the radio. "This is Major Boyington. I am still waiting over Treasury Island. Where is my umbrella?"

But this time there was no answer. Twenty Zeros had gone down in flames because of the subterfuge of the humorous Major Boyington. The enemy would not forget his name.

The three kills over Kahili had brought his total to twenty-three, just three kills short of the magic Rickenbacker record. Time after time he led the Black Sheep over Kahili and other enemy strongholds hollering on the radio, "This is Major Boyington. Why don't you yellow bellies come up and fight?" But they never would. They just waited patiently for Major Boyington to come down to them.

By the beginning of January 1944, Boyington had twenty-five kills and was approaching immortality, but the twenty-sixth kill seemed to elude him like a phantom.

On January 3rd, flying at twenty thousand feet over Rabaul, New Britain Island, he saw Jap planes down near the water and peeled off. Just off the water he flamed one and dived on, anxious to get another that would beat the record. Zooming upward he was suddenly in the middle of twenty Zeros. Blasting through the roaring melee, he got another flamer and then tried to dive out, heading downward at full throttle. Pulling out of the dive at four hundred knots, barely a hundred feet off the water, his main gasoline tank exploded. Unsnapping his safety belt, he moved the ejection seat-lever. He had forgotten one small item: the canopy. He crashed through it in a shower of glass and landed in the water with a big splash. When the

Black Sheep last saw their ancient commander he was floating in St. George Channel off Jap-held New Britain Island, being irresistibly drawn shoreward by the tide.

Major Boyington was classified as missing in action and given credit for twenty-six planes. Three months after his crash he was awarded the Medal of Honor, "probably" posthumously, and during the next twenty months he became a legend.

But the ancient airman was not dead. When the war ended he turned up in a Jap POW camp. For some reason his captors had never notified the Red Cross he was alive.

The story of his captivity was grim. He was fished, badly wounded, from the waters of St. George Channel by a Japanese submarine. When the Japs found they had captured the famous radio-comedian Major Boyington they refused to treat his wounds and paraded him about for the benefit of the troops, working him over occasionally with a baseball bat. He barely survived.

On hearing about his award of the big medal, he was sophisticated and acted unimpressed. "Just a booby prize. Show me a hero and I'll prove he's a bum."

And that remark became part of the legend too, just like the Rube Goldberg automatic pilot, the smoking in the planes and the brawls in the Hotel de Gink on Guadalcanal. The bull-necked, flat-nosed, sawed-off little character was stuck with the hero label. He was a hero in the name of Congress.

In 1962 he changed his first name legally from Gregory to Pappy. "Nobody ever called me Gregory anymore anyway," he said.

XVII

Are the Best Soldiers in the Guardhouse?

SHORTLY after hostilities began in World War II, General George C. Marshall, Chief of Staff, created a War Department Decorations Board. In recommendations for the Medal

of Honor, theater commanders had to include the most specific information obtainable. Eyewitness affidavits had to be detailed. Maps and diagrams of terrain were requested. Closeness to the enemy and the degree of hazard had to be strictly defined.

The Army awarded two hundred and fifty-four Medals of Honor to ground troops in World War II. One hundred and eighteen went to officers and one hundred and thirty-six to enlisted men. Top brass got three of the awards. General of the Army Douglas MacArthur, whose father won the Medal as a first lieutenant during the Civil War, received a Medal of Honor in World War II. So did General Jonathan M. Wainright, who remained with the gallant defenders on Bataan, and Brigadier General Theodore Roosevelt, Jr., whose father as President of the United States had done more than any other to raise the dignity of the Medal.

Seventy of the Medals went to ground troops in the Pacific. The first Army Medal of Honor action in World War II—that of Second Lieutenant Alexander R. Nininger, Jr. during the battle of Bataan on January 11, 1942—occurred in the Pacific theater as did the last—Corporal Melvin Mayfield's one-man charge of a ridge near Pacdan in the Philippines on July 29, 1945. Between the first and last Pacific actions there was much smoke and blood. Five Army Medals were won on Bataan, three on Guadalcanal, eight on New Guinea, one on Bougainville, three on New Georgia—including the one to the legendary Rodger Young—one in the Aleutians, two on Saipan, nine on Okinawa, and thirty-six more on the triumphal return to the Philippines.

Alexander R. "Sandy" Nininger, Jr. graduated with his West Point class in June 1941. He was not the typical hardboiled career officer, being fond of music, art and good books. But, paradoxically, the decision to become a career soldier had been his own and he gained admission to West Point by the tough competitive examination route.

He arrived in the Philippines in October 1941, a brand new Infantry shavetail. He was assigned to the Fifty-seventh Infantry Regiment, Philippine Scouts. When war came on December 7th he was a platoon leader of Company A of the First Battalion. Nininger and the rest of the Fifty-seventh were in the field when the Japs hit the beaches and began blasting their way inland in a pincer movement on Manila.

On January 11th, leading a ten-man patrol against the enemy in the Abucay area, he infiltrated the enemy lines and began inflicting casualties in their rear. When ordered back, he refused and continued his advance. When the rest of his company broke through the enemy lines, they spotted Nininger at once, staggering along with his M-1 in pursuit of a fleeing enemy. Before they could reach him, three Japanese soldiers fell on him, stabbing him from behind with bayonets. Whirling, he killed them all with his pistol before expiring on the ground. Sandy Nininger, the sensitive art and music lover, was the first man of the Military Academy class of 1941 to die in the war.

There were many other Army Medal of Honor winners in the Pacific, most of them now forgotten in the rush of history. A two-man machine-gun squad of the Twenty-fifth Division won Medals on Guadalcanal in January 1943. Fighting waist deep in swamp water, Sergeant William G. Fournier held a light machine gun balanced on his back while Corporal Lewis Hall fired the weapon at the surrounding enemy. Hall and Fournier killed forty-six of the attacking Japanese before they were killed themselves.

Private First Class George J. Benjamin of the Seventy-seventh "Statue of Liberty" Division was a radio operator on Leyte in December 1944. When the platoon leader and ranking noncoms were killed, Benjamin took over to lead an attack. He led the platoon lugging a cumbersome, heavy radio and armed only with a forty-five caliber pistol. He fell mortally wounded. As he lay dying, he called the battalion tactical officer on the radio and reported the location of all the enemy positions in the area. When completely surrounded by the enemy and about to be overrun, he radioed the coordinates of his positions and called for artillery fire upon it.

Private First Class David M. Gonzales of the Thirty-second Infantry Division won a Medal on Luzon in April 1945. Five of the members of his squad were buried alive by the explosion of a five-hundred-pound airplane bomb. Gonzales was mortally wounded while trying to dig them out. He managed to rescue three of the trapped men before dying himself.

Another ardent digger was Second Lieutenant Donald E. Rudolph, member of the Sixth Infantry Division on Luzon in February 1945. Rudolph ripped a grenade slot in the roof of a Japanese pillbox with his bare hands, inserted a grenade which

killed everyone inside. Later that day he climbed on an enemy tank and dropped a white phosphorous grenade through the turret. He barely made it to the ground before the tank exploded and burned.

Slightly unusual citations for ground force awards in World War II were those of Lieutenant Colonel William J. O'Brien and Private First Class Martin O. May. Both citations cover periods of time, rather than climactic acts and both awards were posthumous. Colonel O'Brien, an officer of the Twenty-seventh Infantry Division on Saipan, was cited for performing a "series of gallant exploits" in the period between June 20 and July 7, 1944. Private May, a member of the Seventy-seventh Infantry Division in the Ryukyus, was cited for making a three-day stand with a machine gun against the Japanese, during the period May 19 through May 21, 1945.

During World War II no Army Medals of Honor went to commissioned physicians or surgeons. But ten enlisted medics won Army Medals—five in the Pacific and five in Europe. They were practically all privates and privates first class, and all were aid men attached to combat troops. Their deeds had mostly to do with ministering to the wounded while under heavy enemy fire. But the case of Private Harold A. Garman of the Fifth Division medics near Montereau, France, on August 25, 1944, was slightly out of the ordinary.

Late in the evening of that day, the main body of attacking allied troops were stopped on the south bank of the Seine River. Some of the division troops had gotten across the river earlier and encountered heavy enemy resistance. After darkness fell, Garman and his fellow medics were busy ferrying the wounded back across the river in assault boats. Garman's assignment was as a litter bearer on the south bank. Just as a boatload of wounded reached midstream, a German machine gun, barely a hundred yards away, opened up. All the occupants of the boat took to the water except one badly wounded man on a litter. Two others clung weakly to the sides of the boat. Ignoring the enemy machine gun, Garman kicked off his boots, swam directly into the path of the heavy fire and towed the boat with the wounded to shore. The Medal of Honor was pinned on him by an envious General George S. Patton.

In the Army ground forces, fifteen Medals were awarded soldiers who smothered live grenades with their bodies, as com-

pared with twenty-six Marines who won their Medals with this suicidal act. Two Army officers won the Medal for this deed as did one Marine officer.

One of the Army grenade smotherers was Private First Class Sadao S. Munemori, an American-born Japanese from Los Angeles serving in the all-Japanese One Hundredth Infantry Battalion in Italy in 1945. On April 4th of that year Private First Class Munemori was a member of an attacking force moving up the western slopes of the Appennino Mountains, with the immediate objective of capturing Hill "Georgia," near Sevarezza. Munemori was assistant squad-leader and took command of his group when the sergeant squad-leader fell wounded. Crawling ahead of his squad, he reconnoitered a mine field and stirred up some opposition by lobbing grenades into an enemy machine-gun nest. An enemy patrol spotted the squatty little GI and followed him back to his squad. Just as he was crawling into a hole with Privates Akiri Shishido and Jimi Oda, a grenade bounced off his helmet and fell into the hole with the men. Munemori immediately leaped on the grenade, smothering the blast with his body. He was killed, but his buddies Oda and Shishido were saved, although Oda was wounded in the eyes and Shishido came out of it partially deaf.

Private First Class Herman C. Wallace of the Seventy-sixth Division in Germany smothered an even larger explosion than a grenade. Advancing across a wooded area, he tripped an "S" mine, an anti-personnel mine of a type that leaped up several feet in the air to explode when tripped. The mines were commonly called "Bouncing Betties." When he tripped the Betty, Wallace leaped on it at once, smothering the explosion with his body. He was veritably blown to bits by the heavy mine.

But the Army man who voluntarily absorbed the biggest blast of all was First Lieutenant Bernard J. Ray of the Fourth Infantry Division. It happened on a cold sleeting November 17, 1944, in the Huertgen Forest near Schevenhutte, Germany. Company F of the Eighth Infantry Regiment had been stopped by what appeared to be an immovable barrier. The youthful company commander, Second Lieutenant Bernard J. Ray, studied the obstruction grimly through his binoculars.

The obstruction was a massive barricade of tangled barbwire nailed on railroad ties that blocked the single road leading through the thick forest. The road area in front of the ob-

struction was sown with land mines, and the wooded area on the flanks was full of anti-personnel "S" mines. The tangled maze, buttressed by the railroad ties and protected by mine field, effectively halted the advance of armor and heavy equipment in the whole sector.

"I got an idea about how to knock that thing out of the way," Ray said to his first sergeant. "I'm going to crawl up there with a load of H.E. and blow it up."

The sergeant was ten years older than his commanding officer and his sudden reaction bore it out. "You're nuts, lieutenant," he said.

Ray grinned sourly. "Maybe so, sergeant, but I'm going to get that thing out of the way."

A few minutes later Ray loaded himself down with bangalore torpedoes and stuffed his pockets full of explosive caps. He wrapped a twenty-foot length of primer cord around his waist. "That ought to be long enough," he said. Then he tucked a bundle of dynamite under one arm. "How do I look?" he asked.

"Like a human torpedo," said the sergeant.

Hugging the earth on his belly Ray began slithering across the open area toward the barricade. The German small arms and machine guns opened up, but could not seem to depress their trajectories enough to hit him. The slugs passed a foot over his head. It was difficult to stay that low because the bulky primer cord wrapped around his waist kept snagging on rocks and logs. Then the little fifty-millimeter mortars opened up and they came very close. There would be a distant "thunk" as the shell dropped in the tube and then the terrifying crescendo of the whistling shell coming in, culminated by the crashing explosion. Ray hugged the frozen ground and crawled on. Somehow, he made it to the wire maze and crawled under, pushing the bundle of dynamite ahead of him and cutting a path with a pair of wire cutters. It was slow, maddening work and he had to get up on his knees. A sudden burst of machine-gun fire knocked him flat.

"I'm coming after you, lieutenant!" shouted the sergeant from the edge of the clearing.

"No, stay back!" yelled Ray. "I won't be but a minute." Those were his last words. He jerked loose one end of the primer cord wrapped around his waist and fastened it to the

dynamite package. The other end of the cord he attached to the charger. Then, staggering up to his knees, he pushed down on the plunger with both hands.

The barricade and Lieutenant Bernard Ray disappeared in the great crashing roar of the explosion. Nothing was left of the barricade but blackened splinters and twisted, broken wire. No trace of Ray was ever found, but his heroic action had opened the way through the Huertgen Forest.

Bernard Ray's father received his son's posthumous award of the Medal of Honor at the White House. "Bernie was a good boy," was all he could say at the presentation.

Although most Army Medals during World War II were awarded to soldiers killed in performing their heroic acts, many of the winners emerged alive. Some of the survivals defy all reason. There was First Lieutenant Frank Burke, a battalion transportation officer in the Third Infantry Division, who won his Medal at Nuremberg on April 21, 1945. Pulling the pins on two grenades, he rushed an enemy-held building, with a grenade in each hand. As he heaved his bombs into a window, the Germans inside tossed a heavy "potato masher" grenade under him. The Germans were killed, but Burke got up after the blast, dazed but unhurt.

Then there was the case of Staff Sergeant Paul L. Bolden, winner of the Medal near Petit-Coo, Belgium, on December 23, 1944. After throwing two grenades into a house, he kicked in the door to find himself confronted by thirty-five groggy but dangerously alive SS men. Bolden emptied the clip of his submachine gun into the room, killing twenty Germans before he fell back to reload. When his call to surrender was refused, Bolden stormed grimly back with his deadly tommy gun and killed the remaining fifteen.

The deed of First Lieutenant Edward A. Silk has a bizarre quality that makes you wonder about the winner's state of mind at the time. Silk, a member of the One Hundredth Division, won his Medal near Pravel, France, on November 23, 1944. When his platoon was pinned down by intense enemy fire from a house, Silk dashed madly forward through a hail of lead. With blood-curdling yells, he threw in his grenades. Then when he ran out of grenades, he began heaving in rocks, still yelling like a mad man. His last act proved to be too much for

the enemy. Rather than be stoned to death twelve of them surrendered.

Then there was the one-man stand of Private First Class Alton W. Knappenberger, a Pennyslvania Dutchman, BAR man
of the Third Infantry Division. On the road to Cisterna, Italy,
on February 1, 1944, he fought a one-sided duel with his BAR
against an enemy twenty-millimeter anti-aircraft self-propelled
truck, called a flakswagon. With the flak whirring about his
ears, he aimed his BAR at the crew and disposed of them all.
During that day he fired six hundred rounds of ammunition
with his BAR and killed at least sixty enemy soldiers, halting
the advance of a German battalion. Returning to his company he found that most of the officers and noncoms had been
wiped out and he was in line for promotion to corporal. They
could not put a deal like that over on a real GI like Knappenberger. "Don't give me that corporal stuff," he said. "They
make you a corporal or sergeant and then you have to work."
Knappenberger retained his first class privacy.

Because the United States Army swelled to such huge pro-
portions in World War II, it was natural that most of the Medals of Honor were won by the amateurs: the National Guards-
men, the draftees, the ROTC officers, the ninety-day wonders.
An exception was winner Captain Bobbie E. Brown, an old
soldier who won his Medal on Crucifix Hill above Aachen, Germany, on October 8, 1944. Robert Evan Brown, Jr. had joined
the Army in 1922 at Columbus, Georgia, when he was fifteen years old. The Army needed men in those days and all
you had to do was look old enough. Nobody asked for a birth
certificate. Writing his name as "Bobbie" on the recruiting sergeant's book changed Brown's name. As far as the Army was
concerned Robert Evan Brown, Jr. became Bobbie E. Brown
from then on.

The fifteen-year-old found a home in the Army. He qualified as an expert in every infantry weapon: rifle, bayonet,
forty-five caliber pistol, BAR, and light and heavy machine
guns. He was an outstanding athlete, a six foot, hundred and
seventy-five pounder with a strong jaw. He won thirty-nine of
forty bouts as a light heavyweight boxer. He was a marathon
runner as well as a gifted performer in baseball, basketball,
lacrosse and hockey. In 1927 he made the all-Army football

squad. Three colleges offered him scholarships before they found he had never even finished grade school.

By 1939 he was a master sergeant, serving for a while as top kick of General George Patton's headquarters company at Fort Benning, Georgia. Brown and Patton were men turned out of the same mold, forged in the same furnace. Both were hardnosed disciplinarians of a type now almost extinct in the Army. The Army "book" was law and heaven help you if you fouled-up or gold-bricked. Brown went overseas with the Second Armored Division to North Africa in 1942 and was promoted out of the ranks to first lieutenant. In June 1943, he transferred to the foot infantry, the famous First Infantry Division, better known as the "Big Red One." He hit Omaha Beach as a platoon leader in that outfit the following year.

By October 1944, Company C of the Eighteenth Regiment of the Red One, commanded by Captain Bobbie Brown, was fighting in the area of the ancient city of Aachen. Hitler himself had said the city could not be taken. The city was defended by Crucifix Hill, a huge mass of rocky ground holding forty-three concrete and steel pillboxes. And the fortifications were all manned by seasoned veterans.

At four A.M. on October 8th Captain Brown got his orders. His outfit was to seize pillboxes seventeen, eighteen, nineteen, twenty, twenty-six, twenty-nine and thirty. His attack was not to begin until the air force had bombed the pillboxes for an hour between 12:15 P.M. and 1:15.

Fifteen minutes after the last P-47 had blasted the hill, Brown led his company from the graveyard at the bottom in a frontal assault. The air attack had not dented the pillboxes to any great extent, but apparently had dazed some of their occupants. Brown and his company reached a tank trap in front of pillbox eighteen before the gunners cut loose at them. The trap was about fifteen feet deep and they were safe as long as they stayed there, but the fire from the pillboxes had them pinned down.

Brown turned to the platoon sergeant. "Give me a couple of flame throwers and some pole and satchel charges," he ordered. A pole charge was a five-foot metal pole with sixty half-pound blocks of TNT attached to one end. A satchel charge was a handbag containing one hundred and twenty half-pound

TNT blocks. Both pole and satchel charges had three-and-a-half-second fuses.

Brown crept up to the first pillbox and was about to lean the pole charge against a viewing aperture when the steel door of the pillbox opened and a German soldier stepped out. Quick as a flash Brown knocked the soldier back through the door with a blow of his fist, threw in a pole and satchel charge, slammed the door shut and leaped back. He barely made it into the tank trap before the vents in the pillbox lit up like the eyes and mouth of a jack-o'-lantern from the heavy, rumbling internal explosion. Nothing moved inside. That took care of one pillbox.

With two more charges Brown crawled grimly the thirty-three yards uphill to pillbox number nineteen. Machine-gun bullets skimmed two feet above his head. Working his way behind the pillbox he pressed a pole charge against a twelve-inch aperture, pulled the fuse and dived into a hole. The explosion blew a gaping hole in the pillbox. Just to make sure, Brown threw in the satchel charge for good measure. That took care of the second pillbox.

Lying in the hole, Brown noticed his knee was covered with blood. He had no idea when he had been hit. Also he found a couple of bullet holes in his canteen.

Next was number twenty, the largest and most heavily armed pillbox on Crucifix Hill. This box was topped by a turret that revolved three hundred and sixty degrees. Mounted on the turret were a short-barreled eighty-eight-millimeter cannon, flanked by two thirty-caliber machine guns and two twenty-millimeter guns. The pillbox itself was studded with small-arms apertures. It had seven rooms and was manned by forty-five men. The walls were six feet thick.

Crawling behind the pillbox, Brown had a stroke of luck. A German soldier came out, leaving the back door open, and walked to an ammunition bunker several yards away. Brown started to shoot him, but thought better of it. When the soldier came back with his ammunition, he would have to leave the door open for a few seconds until he unloaded inside, Brown figured. He was right. As soon as the soldier disappeared in the door, Brown lunged forward. Jerking the fuses from satchel and pole charge he threw both of them through the

door, kicked the door shut, and whirled in the air like an adagio dancer to seek cover. Just as he landed on his face in a crater and wrapped his arms around his head, the earth rocked from the explosion. That took care of the third pillbox, and with the destruction of that pillbox, the enemy resistance on Crucifix Hill was broken.

Bobbie Brown, the old soldier, came home from the wars. He wears his Medal of Honor rosette, the tiny blue lapel ribbon dotted with white stars, at all times. He has also a pair of M-1 carbines. One of them is shattered from an enemy bullet that came too close. The stocks of both are notched in the manner of the Western gunslingers. There are forty-five notches on the stock of the shattered one and seventeen notches on the other. Each notch represents a dead German. These, naturally, do not count the enemy he killed with demolitions.

Brown retired from the U.S. Army as a captain in 1952, a thirty-year man at age forty-five. He lives in Flushing, New York, and works during the week as supervisor of Washington Hall at West Point. He has a son, Robert Evan Brown III, who is eleven years old. Bobbie III has already informed his father that he will enter West Point and make the Army his career.

Charles E. "Chuck" Kelly, who would later acquire the colorful nickname of "Commando" Kelly, was born and raised in the tough Twenty-third Ward on the north side of Pittsburgh. His military career contrasted sharply with those of professional soldiers such as Bobbie Brown, but nevertheless he won the Medal of Honor and deserved it as much as his illustrious colleagues.

The Kelly home was a dilapidated shack in the alley behind a tenement building, crowded with the parents and their nine boys. There was no electricity; kerosene lamps were used for light. There was no bathroom, you went to the toilet in a smelly privy across the alley, an outhouse shared with several other families. You took a bath in a big washtub in the kitchen. During the summers about the only time the kids bathed was when the sanitation department turned on a fire plug to wash out the gutters.

After finishing the grades, Chuck refused to go to high school. He did odd jobs in the neighborhood but mostly he

loafed on the street corners with his gang. When he could beg
or borrow a car, he liked to roar through the neighborhood,
yelling with excitement as the tires screeched around the corners. Naturally, the cops gave him a hard time about that. At
this time his greatest ambition was to be a truck driver but
the teamsters were not taking grown men, much less punk kids
with no driving experience.

December 7, 1941, when the war broke out, Chuck Kelly was
a slight, wiry youth of twenty, with a mop of dark wavy hair, a
beaky nose and a prominent Adam's apple. He did not look
especially tough unless you noticed the catlike movements and
the expressionless green eyes that never gave away anything.
Chuck was tough and he liked to brag about it. It got him a
few knocks in the Army but the knocks never broke the toughness.

Chuck joined the Army right after Pearl Harbor. The war
looked like it was going to be the biggest gang rumble of them
all. The day before he left for camp, he bragged to the cops on
the beat, "I'll go fight this war while you 4-F's guard the vege-
table wagons." Then he swaggered off, spitting tobacco juice.

Chuck Kelly's early Army career was not promising. Taking
infantry basic training at Camp Wheeler, Georgia, Kelly
made a name for himself as a sloppy soldier right away. His
bunk was always rumpled and his shoes never shined. He was
continually being gigged for chewing tobacco during close-
order drill.

His idiosyncrasies on the firing range unnerved his dogmatic
instructors. He shot his rifle from the right shoulder, but
sighted with his left eye. He leaned his head way over across
the rifle stock, a most peculiar stance. That he could shoot extremely high scores using this off-beat position, just made the
instructors madder than ever. The cadre noncoms put him on
KP and made him latrine orderly for days on end, but he still
would not change his sighting method with the rifle.

Also unnerving for the cadre was his happy-go-lucky attitude
toward explosives. He was continually fooling with grenades,
unscrewing the caps and pouring out the powder. And sometimes he would pull the fuse of a sixty millimeter mortar shell
and then shake the shell at his ear to determine if anything rat-
tled.

Regular infantry training was too tame for him. After completing basic, Kelly volunteered for paratrooper training at Fort Benning, a decision he was to regret.

At first everything went well in the paratroops and Kelly romped through the rough conditioning courses with ease and enthusiasm. Then one day he took a walk through the hospital wards, after visiting an injured friend. The place was full of guys with broken arms, legs and backs. A lot of them would never walk again; they would stay in braces and wheelchairs for the rest of their lives. The odds did not look too good, even for a daredevil like Kelly. He wanted to fight the enemy, not emerge from training as a gimp before even getting into combat. In a mood of depression he went AWOL to Pittsburgh.

His folks were glad to see him. He told them he had been granted leave. But after he had stayed home several weeks, they began questioning him with concern. The neighborhood with most of the old gang gone was not the same. He wandered around lost for several more days and then went back to camp to take his medicine.

He entered a plea of guilty at his court-martial and got twenty-eight days restriction and twenty-eight dollars fine. He was kicked out of the paratroopers and sent to a hayseed Texas outfit—the Thirty-sixth "Texas" Division—that was getting ready to go overseas from Camp Edwards, Massachusetts.

It was a strange outfit for a city boy but soon Kelly found a lot of kindred spirits among the Texans. They were just as cocky and boastful as he was, and twice as loud. They had never been to Pittsburgh, or any town bigger than Fort Worth or Abilene, but they knew all about a place called Fist City, and were continually ready to go there. They were much given to horseplay and knocking each other around. On the range Kelly found that the noncoms did not give a damn which eye Kelly used to sight his rifle. "You can aim it with yoh rear end, if you can hit the tawget thataway," his platoon sergeant said obligingly. The whole outfit, like Chuck Kelly, was spoiling for a fight.

September 9, 1943, found them off Salerno Beach on the coast of Italy, moving toward shore in landing boats. The noises of violent death filled the air. The German shore batteries had them zeroed in. The shells came in whistling and crashing in huge geysers of water among the boats. An occasional F-W 190

screamed in under the allied cover and strafed the boats heading for the beach.

Confusion was rampant on the beachhead. U.S. officers urged the milling GI's to hurry inland and form their outfits at their rendezvous points. An English-speaking German, via a high-powered amplifier, exhorted the American troops to throw down their arms and surrender. "We have you covered," the enemy informed them. "Come on, fellows, throw down your guns and surrender!"

Kelly felt very lonely suddenly, even in the middle of the crowded confusion. No one from his outfit was in sight. A shell exploded shockingly close. "Come on in, fellows," the German wheedled, "we've got you covered."

The first thing Kelly did, while crossing a field, was to jump headlong into a drainage ditch. Cursing, he sloshed about, feeling under the water for his BAR. Then he checked his wallet to make sure the photos of his family had not been ruined in the soaking. He was in a sort of daze. When an enemy machine gun began chattering ominously close by, he began crawling across the field, advancing. The going was hard, but from that time on, Kelly never stopped advancing in Italy.

Rejoining his outfit, he helped his first sergeant and a squad in knocking out two German scout-cars with a bazooka, Kelly firing the round that knocked out the first car. The next afternoon they entered the village of Altavilla. The enemy was still in town in force, their machine guns chattered from the rooftops. Mortar and artillery shells whistled in from an enemy-held hill nearby. L Company found a strongly built three-story house and moved in, stacking the place with arms and ammunition. They found out later that they had appropriated the mayor's house.

They barricaded the windows with mattresses and prepared for siege. Enemy artillery rained on the house, crashing into the thick walls and making the whole building shudder. Dust drifted down from the ceiling. Snipers and machine gunners directed fire on them. The house filled with smoke and the acrid smell of burned gunpowder. L Company coughed and rubbed stinging eyes.

American reinforcements were unable to climb the hill to the town now that the enemy had built up such artillery strength on Hill 315. L Company, in the mayor's house, was

completely surrounded, an American island in a sea of Germans. The casualties began to mount up. One room was now filled with wounded and slain.

The Germans brought up flame-throwers that night to burn them out. It was eerie and terrifying. The spouting flames cast huge shadows of the black figures behind. Kelly laid his head way over his rifle stock in the manner that had been the despair of the cadre at Camp Wheeler and drilled one of the cans on a flame-thrower's back. The enemy soldier blew up in a great gush of flame, lighting up the whole street. "Come on, you bastards!" he yelled. "Bring on some more of them hot cans!"

The tough kid from Pittsburgh showed them how to fight. When daylight came, he shot his BAR until the barrel turned red. Then he used a tommy gun while the BAR cooled.

Kelly liked to shoot the SS troops especially. They always attacked with hopped-up, fanatical fury. Scrambling across the courtyard wall they would run up to the house windows and spray away with their "burp" guns. They weren't chicken. They kept coming at you as long as they could move.

Yelling just as wildly, Kelly aimed his tommy gun down from his window and sprayed back. Soon the courtyard was covered with the sprawled bodies of the black-uniformed SS men. During the attacks Kelly paled with excitement, but his green eyes peering down the gun barrel were cold and expressionless. This was a rumble to end all rumbles.

As the cadre at Camp Wheeler had once predicted, Kelly almost blew himself to hell there in the courtyard of the mayor's house at Altavilla. During a lull he found an abandoned thirty-seven millimeter anti-tank gun and tried to figure out how to fire it. The first time he made it go off, his chin was too close to the recoil plate and he was almost knocked cold by the recoil. He shook his head groggily, but now that he knew how to fire the weapon he concentrated on aiming, lowering the barrel to what seemed to be a proper angle for his target, a church steeple. Then he threw a round in the chamber and pulled the lanyard.

Luckily, it had been an armor-piercing shell he fired and not one full of high explosive. The shell clipped the top of the wall a few feet from his head and sprayed him with rock and mortar dust. A high-explosive shell striking that close would have blown him and the gun right out of action. But Kelly, unfazed,

just raised the muzzle to miss the top of the wall and fired the anti-tank gun until he ran out of ammunition.

The German attacks intensified throughout the afternoon. When L Company ran low on grenades, the Germans swarmed into the courtyard, yelling and firing into the windows, and Kelly performed an experiment that the cadre at Camp Wheeler had always forbidden. He pulled the pin and safety lock from a sixty millimeter mortar shell and then tapped the shell carefully on the windowsill to free the secondary pin. When that pin dropped out, he lobbed the big shell down on the Germans below. The blast was deafening.

A sudden wave of panic swept the company in the house. The place must have been hit by a big shell. Then someone passed the word, "Take it easy. Chuck Kelly's dropping mortar shells on them."

Kelly's hand-thrown mortar barrage broke up the street and courtyard attacks. He killed over twenty Germans before they withdrew.

As darkness fell, the officers counted the men remaining. Only thirty were alive and many of them wounded. The brass decided to pull out that evening in groups of six at a time. Everyone who could walk had to go. The badly wounded had to be left behind.

Kelly crawled across the floor to the company commander, keeping well below the line of the windows. "Sir, I'll cover the rear," he said. The face of the wiry kid from Pittsburgh was blackened from smoke and his jaw was swelled from being hit by the recoil plate of the thirty-seven millimeter gun, but the green eyes were as cold and expressionless as ever.

"O. K., Kelly, good luck," said the company commander grimly.

In the dark alley behind the house, after the others had gone, Kelly held his BAR at the hip and waited for the enemy troops to come out the back door. When they crowded into the doorway, getting ready to disperse up the alley, he opened fire, blasting everybody in the door. With his last clip empty, he dropped the hot gun and took to his heels. The rumble had been great while it lasted, but now it was time to leave.

For his heroic actions at Altavilla, Technical Sergeant Charles E. Kelly was awarded the Congressional Medal of Honor. The smart-aleck kid from Pittsburgh was a hero. A

news correspondent hung the handle "Commando" on him and it stuck. The following May, Sergeant Kelly returned in Roman triumph to the grimy Twenty-third Ward of Pittsburgh. His new uniform was sharp and military, but there was still an unmilitary swagger to his walk and a lump of tobacco in his jaw. Nobody remembered that Chuck Kelly was supposed to be yellow because he refused to become a gimp in paratroop training.

The Medal brought financial reward to Kelly, along with the fame and adulation. *The Saturday Evening Post* paid him $15,000 for his life story and a Hollywood producer gave $25,000 for the rights to a movie about his war experiences. Kelly spent part of the money buying a new home for his parents, equipped with electricity and inside plumbing, and moved them out of the old alley tenement. Then he went down to Fort Benning and showed paratroopers how to lob mortar shells by hand. Even with the Medal and the noncom rank he still had a fixed idea about soldiers. "The best soldiers are in the guardhouse," he always said, "they are the best fighters."

The most decorated individual, soldier, sailor or Marine, in World War II—or any war in American history—was the baby-faced Audie Leon Murphy of Farmersville, Texas, whose family had eked out a bare living as share croppers in the cotton fields. He became practically a walking "pyramid of honor." There were seven medals for heroism awarded by the United States during World War II, and it is a simple way of beginning by stating that there were only two of the seven that Audie Murphy missed. One was the Distinguished Flying Cross—he was earthbound and did not participate in aerial flights—and the other was the Soldier's Medal, given for heroism not involving actual conflict with an enemy. Since conflict with the enemy was Murphy's main forte in the service, he simply never had the opportunity to acquire the Soldier's Medal.

In addition to the Medal of Honor, Audie Murphy won the Distinguished Service Cross, the Legion of Merit, the Silver Star and cluster, the Bronze Star and three Purple Hearts. He fought through Tunisia, Morocco, Sicily, Anzio, Salerno, invasion of Southern France, the Rhine, Colmar and Nuremberg, and, as a member of the Third Infantry Division, he was in the company of heroes. It was one of the proud boasts of the Third

that they fought the Nazis on all fronts during World War II
—North Africa, Sicily, Italy, France and Germany. Men of the
Third Division won thirty-five Medals of Honor in World War
II. But even in such company the baby-faced kid with the big
smear of freckles was outstanding.

On Pearl Harbor Day, December 7, 1941, Audie Murphy
was seventeen years old, working as a helper in a radio-repair
shop in Collin County, Texas. He was a slight kid, just five
feet seven, weighing about a hundred and thirty pounds, in appearance a typical freckle-faced poor-white kid. And buried
there was the deep-seated pride and the violently explosive
temper. This was the type of man who went up to Gettysburg
in the Civil War with Hood's old Texas Brigade, the type of
fighter that the Southern states have furnished in all of America's battles and skirmishes from Kings Mountain to the Yalu
River.

At the Army recruiting office the sergeant almost embraced
him when he volunteered for infantry. The sarge must have
been low on his quota for the month. He almost wept as he
filled out Audie's papers. "It does my heart good to enlist a real
fighter," he said.

Infantry basic training in the hot sun was harder than chopping cotton. After a two-hour session of close-order drill, Audie
Murphy closed his eyes and collapsed in a dead faint on the
dusty drill-field. As they carried him away, the leathery old
cadre sergeant shook his head. "How can we win the war with
these babies?" The sergeant recommended that Audie Murphy
be sent to cooks' and bakers' school.

Audie strode grimly into the company commander's office
and swore he would take the guardhouse before becoming a
cook. "I'm not going to cooks' and bakers' school," he said between clenched teeth. The officer looked at the scrawny recruit
drawn up in the tight brace and ruled in favor of a belligerent
spirit. "O. K., Murphy, but don't fall out on the hikes and don't
expect anyone to carry your pack . . ."

Somehow he made it, even the twenty-mile hikes, staggering
along pale and grim under the heavy pack, stumbling through
the obstacle courses, climbing the rope ladders up the side of
the simulated ship. In the late fall of 1942 he was at Fort
Meade, Maryland, a port of embarkation, ready for overseas
shipment.

At Fort Meade he was almost sidetracked again. A chaplain, horrified that such a babyish-looking recruit was being sent overseas to war, almost had him transferred to the permanent cadre. Audie Murphy suddenly found himself a clerk in the PX, selling cigarettes and shaving soap to the real soldiers who were going overseas. Daily he deviled his superiors for overseas orders and begged the chaplain to take the hex off him. Finally, in order to be rid of him, they shipped him to North Africa as a replacement in the Third Infantry Division. In due course he arrived in Company B of the Fifteenth Infantry Regiment. The heroic saga had begun.

North Africa was now almost a rear echelon. The last remaining pocket of Germans, in the Tunis area, surrendered without firing a shot shortly after Audie arrived. It was not until the outfit moved out for Sicily that Audie Murphy saw any combat.

Sicily was his baptism of fire; there he killed, for the first time, two nattily clad Italian officers trying to escape on white horses. His cold-blooded attitude unnerved his lieutenant. "Why did you do that?"

"That's our job," said the baby-faced Murphy grimly.

He made corporal on Sicily and got malaria, but after a week in the hospital he made it back to his outfit at Salerno. The mud and death of the Italian campaign dissipated his glorious concept of war as a glamorous undertaking. The banners failed to wave and the trumpets remained unblown. He knew now there would be war enough for everybody. All the GI's in Italy decided the war would last well into 1965, at least. Mignano. Monte Lungo. Cassino. Artillery, grenades, machine-gun fire. Dark nights and gray days in the mud and rain. Death. That was the way you left Italy: sewed in a mattress cover and piled up with your dead buddies like cordwood in a jeep trailer.

Malaria again in Naples. The usual week in the hospital and back to the outfit at Anzio. Entering Company B headquarters, a muddy cave dug in a hillside, the company clerk said, "Congratulations! You've just been promoted to staff sergeant."

"You take out the next patrol," the company commander said.

Mere survival became a problem on the Anzio beachhead. Artillery and heavy mortar shells kept raining into the foxholes and dugouts and if you stood up, a machine gun or sniper had you spotted. Beltsky, the platoon sergeant, caught a shell frag-

ment that sheared off part of his leg, whereupon the share-cropper kid from Texas became platoon sergeant. Audie Murphy would say later that there was a doomlike quality about the promotion. He said it made him feel like a fugitive from the law of averages.

Then the war was over in Italy for the Third Division and Audie was still a living fugitive from the law of averages. He was still with the outfit when they hit the beach of southern France in August 1944. There seemed to be a cloak of immortality about him. As he led a patrol near Besançon, France, an enemy mortar shell whistled in and blew him high in the air. The two men with him were killed in the blast. Audie was wounded slightly in the heel. After a few days in the hospital he was back at the front.

In November 1944 Audie Murphy was promoted to second lieutenant. The share-cropper kid was now an officer and gentleman. A weary colonel pinned the gold bars on him and then snapped, "Shave, take a bath, and get the hell back into the lines." That was the way the war was in the infantry.

One gray morning while leading a patrol, Audie Murphy was hit by a sniper. It felt like someone had sneaked up behind him and kicked him violently in the tail. Lying behind a log gritting his teeth against the pain, he waited for the sniper to stick his head up for another shot. When he did Audie sent a bullet crashing through his helmet. It was easier than shooting a Texas jackrabbit. But this time the wound was deep and serious, and he did not get back to his outfit until January 1945, when they were fighting in the Colmar Pocket.

The late afternoon of January 25, 1945, found Lieutenant Murphy lying in an icy foxhole staring across a snowy field at the enemy-held village of Holzwihr about a mile away. What was left of Company B, Fifteenth Infantry Regiment was dug in around him. Murphy was now the acting company commander of the outfit he had entered as a buck private in North Africa less than two years before. He was still a fugitive from the law of averages, and that enigmatic law was about to take another crack at him.

Company B was out there alone. A bridge had been blown up behind them after only two supporting tank destroyers had managed to cross. The orders were to hold the position until

reinforced. They had a fighting chance as long as the enemy did not bring up tanks.

About two o'clock the next afternoon the worst happened. Through his binoculars Audie Murphy watched white-clad figures begin moving toward them across the field from Holzwihr. Enemy infantry in white, snow clothing. Six enemy tanks fanned out on each side of the field, camouflaging themselves against the dark background of the forest. Murphy yelled for his men to get ready.

There was a sudden commotion from the road behind them as one of the two tank destroyers cranked up its engine, and began slipping and sliding on the icy road, trying to maneuver into firing position. Then the TD went out of control on the slick surface, skidding and sliding into the ditch, finally coming to rest at a drunken angle with its ninety millimeter gun pointing uselessly at the ground. The TD crew bailed out and headed for the rear.

Spreading his map on the icy ground Audie Murphy buzzed the field phone. "Attack shaping up," he said. "I need a round of smoke at coordinates 30.5-60. Make it fast."

They were deafened by an earsplitting scream ending in a resounding crash. The lone remaining tank destroyer erupted in a sudden mass of flame and smoke. Sprawled across the gun mount was the body of the tank destroyer officer, his hair and uniform on fire. Two crewmen, coughing convulsively and beating at flames on their uniforms, staggered from the burning vehicle and headed for the rear.

Just then the smoke shell Murphy had called for whistled over and burst in a streaming trail of black smoke behind the onrushing enemy. Using the marker as a base point, Murphy coolly called coordinates over the phone and asked for high-explosive shells. The American barrage was deadly accurate. Lines of enemy troops disappeared in geysers of exploding snow. But they kept on coming.

The enemy tanks were unstoppable. Rumbling in close, they went to work with their machine guns. Screams arose from the wounded and dying. Company B had really caught it. There were now only forty men left of the original hundred-odd. And their flanks were open.

Turning to his platoon sergeant, Murphy said, "Get the men back. I'm going to stay here with the phone as long as I can."

When the sergeant hesitated, Murphy shouted, "Get the hell out of here! That's an order." Reluctantly the men began falling back through the woods. "Let's have some more artillery!" Murphy yelled over the field phone.

Resting his carbine on the edge of the foxhole, he began firing methodically at the enemy infantry, now less than two hundred yards away. Then, out of ammunition, he threw down the carbine and, looking around for another weapon of some kind, noticed the perfectly good fifty-caliber machine gun on the turret of the burning tank destroyer. Dragging his telephone line behind him Murphy mounted the burning TD. He had to drag the body of the dead lieutenant out of the turret in order to get to the big machine gun. The gun felt hot to the touch, but seemed all right.

Murphy pressed the trigger of the machine gun, letting go a long chattering burst. A line of Germans staggered and fell in a ragged line. The tank destroyer shook violently with another terrific crash. Another direct hit from an eighty-eight. Fresh waves of black smoke billowed about the vehicle. Then as Murphy fed another belt of cartridges into the gun, the TD was hit again, and began to list like a sinking battleship. Murphy, bathed in a swirling cloud of smoke, coughed and rubbed his eyes. But the smoke was good cover. Every time the breeze blew a rift in the cloud, Murphy fired at everything that moved.

The enemy could not seem to get it through their Teutonic heads that the machine gun harassing them was actually mounted on the burning tank destroyer. From a distance the flames appeared unbearably hot. They feared to approach the burning wreck too closely lest the explosives and high-test gasoline on the vehicle blow up.

Then through a rift in the smoke Murphy saw a German patrol in a ditch not thirty yards away. As he slewed the gun around, he was engulfed in another wave of thick smoke. When it cleared suddenly, Murphy saw twelve Germans in the ditch. He pressed the trigger. Then the blinding cloud of smoke swirled back again, making him cough and rub his eyes. When the smoke cleared again he saw twelve twisted bodies in the ditch.

Coughing and choking he rang the phone again. "Correct fire. Fifty over."

"That's awful close to you, Murph."

"Fire!"

There was a brief interval of silence and then the barrage came, a rumbling chorus of aerial freight trains, the shells landing a bare fifty yards beyond the burning tank destroyer, squarely on top of the last infantry concentration. The German tanks hesitated uncertainly, then slewed around and headed back to Holzwihr. They did not want to brave the woods without infantry support.

The only Germans left were crawling about blindly in the ditch scarcely ten yards from the tank destroyer.

Murphy ground the handle of the phone. "This is my last chance. Correct fire. Fifty over."

"Murph, that's right on top of your own position!"

"Let her go, I'm leaving," said Murphy and leaped to the ground. He was almost to the bridge when the barrage roared in. The concussion knocked him flat. Picking himself up, he felt his arms and legs carefully. He seemed to be O. K., except that a dull pain throbbed in his right leg and there was blood on his trousers. He limped quickly back through the woods to his own lines.

In June 1945 the townspeople of Farmersville, Texas, population two thousand two hundred and six, held a reception in the town square for Audie Murphy and as a gesture of esteem presented him with $1750 in War Bonds. The temperature was ninety-eight degrees. First Lieutenant Audie Murphy, the poorwhite share-cropper's kid, expressed his thanks briefly and said, "I know you people don't want to stand in this hot sun any longer just to look at me."

One of the "unbelievables" winning the Army Medal of Honor during World War II was Private Rodger Wilton Young of Tiffin, Ohio. Rodger Young was a little skinny guy with goldrimmed spectacles, bearing a startling resemblance to the meek and owlish actor Wally Cox who became famous on TV as Mr. Peepers. Rodger Young probably should have been classified 4-F during World War II, as physically unfit for military duty. His eyesight and hearing were poor and he was too short to meet the minimum standards. Compared with such swaggering daredevils as John Basilone and Chuck Kelly, and such rugged he-men as Bobbie Brown and Herman Hanneken, Rodger

Young in the flesh seemed a pale hero. But Rodger became one of the immortal winners, a legend. He was the only winner whose life inspired a folk song, in the sense of Casey Jones and Floyd Collins. In 1945 you could hear this song on the juke boxes all over America:

> "Oh they've got no time for glory
>   in the Infantry—
> Oh they've got no time for praises
>   loudly sung—
> But in every soldier's heart in
>   all the Infantry
> Shines the name, shines the name of
>   Rodger Young . . ."

Why did they immortalize Rodger Young in song as they did Floyd Collins and Casey Jones? They honored him because he was a fine soldier and what he did that day on New Georgia in the Solomons was undeniably heroic, above and beyond the call of duty. . . .

Rodger Young was the typical small town boy-next-door. His father was an industrious mechanic and his mother a diligent church-worker. Rodger was born April 28, 1918, the third of five children. The whole family was musical and had a family orchestra. The father played the clarinet, the mother the piano, and the kids all played stringed instruments and accordions. During the long summer evenings in Tiffin you could hear the Young family rendering such old favorites as "Beautiful Ohio" and "The Blue Danube Waltz." Rodger played banjo, guitar and harmonica, and also carried a newspaper delivery route for the Toledo *News-Bee*. In 1934 he won a free trip to Toledo for selling more subscriptions than any other newsboy in Tiffin during the period of a year.

Rodger loved sports—football, baseball, basketball, track— in the way only a puny little guy with nothing to offer but a burning spirit can love sports. As a high school freshman play-ing on the scrub basketball team, he had his legs knocked out from under him during a game and landed on his head on the hardwood floor. He was unconscious for an hour or so, and when he regained consciousness at the hospital, there seemed to be no serious injury. But after a few months he became slightly deaf and the headaches began. His eyesight weakened and he was forced to put on the thick-lensed eyeglasses that gave him

such a marked resemblance to the latter-day Mr. Peepers. Study and classwork became a burden to him. He was so deaf and short-sighted that he needed to sit on the front row in class to get much out of what was going on. Because his name began with "Y" he was normally relegated to a rear seat alphabetically. Rodger hated to be continually asking for a front row seat. It embarrassed him to ask for favors. At the end of his second year, when he was sixteen years old, he dropped out of high school.

Rodger never became bitter about his injury. He remained devoted to sports. It was a family joke that if Rodger was starving and had a single nickel to his name, he would buy a paper for the sports page, rather than spend the nickel for food. He also liked to hunt and fish. Despite his tricky eyesight, he was a good shot with a rifle.

Rodger Young joined the Thirty-seventh "Buckeye" Division, Ohio National Guard, in 1940, before the Guard was federalized. The Guard needed men badly, and the doctors overlooked Rodger's deficiencies in eyesight and hearing.

Rodger was an enthusiastic soldier and despite the fact that he was the smallest man in his outfit he was soon promoted to squad leader with the rank of corporal. Then, soon after, he made sergeant.

The Thirty-seventh Division sailed for the Pacific in 1942, and during the overseas training period in the Russell Islands no noncom was more dedicated than Rodger in preparing his men for combat. But long hours on the firing range took a heavy toll of him, and after returning from the range his ears were full of buzzing and roaring. Plugging with cotton did not help. There were times when he had to strain mightily to hear ordinary conversation.

The recurrent deafness caused him to brood. In jungle warfare acute hearing was absolutely necessary for a squad leader. His deafness might cause some of his squad to get killed. With a deep sense of failure, he requested to be relieved as squad leader because of deafness and demoted to private.

The company commander, aware of Rodger's problem, regretfully ordered his reduction in rank.

On July 31, 1943, Rodger Young's platoon was in action against the enemy in the jungle near Munda on New Georgia Island. The platoon, several hundred yards ahead of the main

body of troops, was in danger of becoming cut off and isolated just as darkness was falling. The order came to fall back to the battalion perimeter.

As the platoon inched backward through the dense tangle of vines and jungle, an enemy machine gun opened up suddenly seventy-five yards away on the left flank, almost behind them, in a position to cut them off from the main body of troops. Pinned down, the platoon watched darkness fall with the full knowledge that night would bring their annihilation.

Suddenly a rifle cracked just fifty yards from the Jap machine-gun nest. It was Private Rodger Young, attacking single-handedly. He shouted back to the platoon sergeant. "Get the platoon out of here! I'll take care of this machine gun!"

Here was a command decision of the bitterest type. The sergeant had known Rodger since he was a kid back in Tiffin. He knew Rodger's family. But he had twenty other men to think of. The only way to save the platoon was to let Rodger go on alone. While the platoon fell back to the safety of the battalion line, the Jap fire concentrated on Rodger Young.

Wounded severely, Rodger continued crawling until he was barely fifteen yards from the enemy nest. Then he pulled the pin from a grenade and lobbed it high like a basketball at the nest. Nobody clipped his legs out from under him this time. The ball hit the bucket and the nest went up with a big roar. Rodger Young died there on the ground fifteen yards away.

Next morning the platoon, whose lives he had saved, snaked back through the undergrowth to find his body. They wrapped him in a shelter half and buried him in the soggy ground where he fell. Over his grave they erected a rough wooden cross.

Rodger Young was awarded the Congressional Medal of Honor posthumously. His parents received the award on his behalf from the President of the United States. He would have been proud to learn that after his death the Army named a baseball field on Bougainville after him. At last he had his name on the sport page of the services newspaper, *Stars and Stripes*.

The legend grew about Rodger Young, helped along by a lot of fantasy. He was soon better known than any other of the GI heroes. In March 1945, Fremont, Ohio, county seat of his home county, celebrated Rodger Young Day. At the high school they put on an exhibit of Rodger Young memorabilia in glass cases. On display were his banjo, guitar and harmonica, his ribbon for

winning the Toledo *News-Bee* trip in 1934, his ice skates, a few photos, and some of his letters home.

Everyone wanted to say they remembered Rodger, whether they actually did or not, because by this time he was a legend and in this life it is a distinction to have been personally acquainted with a legend. It is a weakness in all of us. Wouldn't you like to be able to say that you had known Casey Jones and Floyd Collins personally? Of course you would. It's human nature.

That was the way people felt about Rodger Young. The air waves were full of his plaintive ballad.

> "On the island of New Georgia in the
> Solomons
> Stands a simple wooden cross alone
> to tell
> That beneath the silent coral of the
> Solomons
> Sleeps a man, sleeps a man remembered
> well."

They remembered him all right. As long as there were soldiers to sing his song, Rodger Young would be remembered well.

XVIII

Majors and Bomber Pilots

DURING World War II the United States Air Force was still part of the Army. It did not become a separate branch until 1947. Thirty-eight of the total two hundred and ninety-two Army Medals of Honor awarded in World War II went to the Army Air Corps, and thirty-four of the thirty-eight went to officers.

The officers' Medals went to three brigadier generals, four colonels, two lieutenant colonels, nine majors, three captains,

six first lieutenants, six second lieutenants and one flight officer.

To win the Medal of Honor in the Air Corps in World War II you stood the best chance if you were a major and a pilot, preferably a bomber pilot. Twenty-nine of the Medals went to pilots: twenty-three to bomber and six to fighter pilots. Navigators got two, bombardiers got two, and one Medal went to an observer. Two of the Air Corps winners, Colonel Demas T. Craw and Major Pierpont M. Hamilton, received their Medals for volunteering for a special assignment with ground troops near Port Lyautey, Morocco, in 1942, an assignment which had nothing directly to do with flying; but both Craw and Hamilton were actually bomber pilots.

Traditionally it has been part of the pride of the Navy Air Corps that only Navy pilots could master take-offs from the teetering slippery decks of aircraft carriers. In Navy tradition other pilots are relegated to dry land, period. But the circumstances surrounding the winning of the first Medal of Honor by an Army Air Corps member in World War II refuted this idea.

On April 18, 1942, the huge new aircraft carrier *Hornet,* steaming in task force with another carrier and an escort of destroyers, bucked a rough sea just eight hundred miles off the coast of Japan. This was the closest to Japan that the United States fleet had ventured since the beginning of the war. Straining at their lashings on the unevenly rolling deck of the *Hornet* were sixteen Army Air Corps B-25 bombers. Their mission was a bombing raid on Japan itself.

By 8 A.M. that morning Lieutenant Colonel James H. Doolittle, command pilot of the raid, was warming the engines of his B-25 on the flight deck. A balding bantam-rooster type, he worked his controls grimly and stared through his rain-swept windshield. The *Hornet* was rolling but slightly, side to side, but she was pitching heavily foreward and aft. The drop-off into the choppy sea—just five hundred feet away at the end of the flight deck—was sickeningly close. There was another slight cause for uncertainty. Neither Jimmy Doolittle nor any other of his pilots had ever actually taken off from the deck of a carrier before.

As a Navy officer swung a checkered flag, Doolittle gunned the motors of the B-25 into high crescendo. As the flag dropped, he released the brakes. At full throttle with flaps full down,

thirty-one thousand pounds of loaded B-25 moved down the flight deck, like a fat lady lumbering with determination toward the end of a diving board.

As the bow of the *Hornet* rose majestically and was about to drop again, Doolittle lifted the bomber's nose delicately into the air, with over a hundred feet of runway to spare. Holding her almost straight up on the props, Doolittle fought the B-25 upward for altitude, and then swung around to circle the carrier.

In a small group of Navy pilots on the deck, one turned and muttered, "Jesus!" It was an admiring prayer.

Following the example of the leader, the remaining fifteen B-25s roared one at a time down the pitching flight deck and into the air.

Lieutenant Colonel James H. Doolittle was an ancient forty-five years of age when he led the famous bombing raid on Tokyo in 1942. His service in the Air Corps had bridged two wars; he first learned to fly on the old Spads, Jennies and Thomas Morse Scouts of World War I. He had been such an apt flying pupil that he was kept in the States as a flying instructor while World War I raged in Europe. It rankled that he had not seen combat in that war. He would have become a leading ace or died trying.

The reckless plan to bomb the Japanese home island with modified B-25 bombers, as a first installment in paying off Japan for the Pearl Harbor attack, was just to his liking. At first the top brass refused to let him go because of his age, but he managed to override that objection. He personally chose the men for the raid. All he told them at first was that they were going on an extremely important mission. For three months the group trained at a Navy airfield in Florida, practicing take-offs from space as short as an aircraft carrier's flight deck.

Five hours after take-off from the *Hornet* on the bombing mission, Doolittle and his crew sighted land. They skimmed the rooftops of Tokyo so low they could see the surprised faces of Japanese on the streets. They roared over a baseball park where a game was in progress, scattering the spectators, and then laid their fiery eggs on their target, an aircraft factory. They roared away amid the deadly black blossoms of anti-aircraft fire.

Leaving behind the damaged steel plants, powder factories,

machine works and railroad yards, the bombers now had to find their friendly field on the Chinese mainland. They ran into a severe storm. Bucking the strong winds depleted scanty gasoline reserves. Unknown to them, their homing aircraft, a C-47 full of radio equipment that was supposed to guide them to their field, had crashed that morning in take-off at Chungking. They had to grope for their field in the stormy darkness, and bail out in parachutes hoping to land in friendly territory.

Most of the crews landed in friendly territory, but two crews fell into the hands of the Japanese. Some of the captured crew members were summarily executed, and others suffered long periods in POW camps. The only plane to survive was one that fell into the hands of the Russians when the pilot landed at Vladivostok. This B-25 was never returned.

Doolittle and his crew made their parachute jump and landed safely. At first Doolittle was sure that he was going to be court-martialed and cashiered from the Air Corps for losing all sixteen of the planes. But, on the contrary, he was promoted to brigadier general and awarded the Medal of Honor. The daring raid of the sixteen little bombers had fired the spirits of all Americans. In a small measure, revenge had been obtained for the bombing of Pearl Harbor.

Another famous Air Corps raid of World War II was the one on Ploesti, Rumania, August 1, 1943. The target was the huge oil refineries which supplied almost a third of the oil required by Germany to wage the war. Five groups of American B-24 bombers from the Eighth and Ninth Air Force participated in this raid—a total of one hundred and seventy-six planes. Riding in the planes were one thousand, seven hundred and twenty-six airmen. It was a rough mission. The planes that finally made it back were riddled with flak from nose to tail. Five Medals of Honor were awarded for heroic actions on the raid.

One of the most unusual stories of the Medal of Honor winners of World War II was that of the redheaded Flight Officer John Cary Morgan. Morgan enlisted in the Royal Canadian Air Force in August 1941 and transferred over to the U.S. Air Force in England in March of 1943. He was assigned as a co-pilot of a B-17 bomber in the Eighth Bomber Command.

On July 28, 1943, Morgan's group was to fly a mission that

would be the deepest daylight penetration of the European continent by bombers, up to that time. The target was AGO Flugzeugwerk, a major manufacturer of Focke-Wulf 190 fighter planes, located in Ochersleben, ninety miles southwest of Berlin.

The main force of one hundred and twenty B-17s took off that morning and feinted in the direction of the heavily bombed Hamburg-Kiel area. At a strategic moment on the flight, Morgan's bomber and thirty-eight others, all specially equipped with long-range gasoline tanks, broke away from the main flight and headed for the fighter plant at Ochersleben. That flight became a bloody nightmare.

While still over the English Channel they met stiff fighter opposition. Wave after wave of the 190s roared in, firing machine guns, rockets and cannons.

Morgan's plane was one of the hardest hit from the beginning. The oxygen lines to tail, waist and radio gun positions were knocked out. Then a shell crashed through the windshield. Morgan's pilot slumped forward over the controls, blood streaming from his head. The windshield was completely gone and the wind whistled through the cabin. Clamping onto the steering wheel with both arms, the wounded pilot headed the B-17 downhill. By sheer strength Morgan pulled the pilot off the wheel and brought the plane back into its formation. Then Morgan began a weird struggle with the half-crazed pilot who was suicidally determined to freeze on the controls. After several frantic attempts to summon aid, Morgan realized with sick clarity that the interphone system was knocked out. No one could hear him. Suddenly, another body landed in the cabin. It was the top turret gunner. One of his arms was shot off and there was a gaping wound in his side. Grimly Morgan fought off the crazed pilot and managed to get a crude but effective tourniquet around the stump of the gunner's arm.

Despite the fact that the attack was continuing on the bomber formation, the guns of Morgan's B-17 were not answering. Struggling with the wounded gunner and maddened pilot, Morgan dared not leave the control cabin to summon the navigator to see what was wrong. Morgan was sure that the gunners, believing the pilot and co-pilot knocked out, had bailed out of the plane. What really happened was that the waist, tail and

radio gunners had lost consciousness due to lack of oxygen. And the navigator, completely oblivious that anything was seriously wrong, other than that the interphone was knocked out, went on navigating.

The wounded pilot continued his crazed fight to fly the plane. Morgan could not bring himself to bat him off the controls with the fire extinguisher, afraid he might kill him. The co-pilot had the choice of trying to pull out of the formation and return to base, or continuing on to the target and coming back with the outfit. Afraid that he could not fight off the pilot and successfully pull away from his position near the center of the group without crashing into another plane, Morgan decided to go on to the target. Of course, he could have bailed out himself but this he refused to do, because of the wounded pilot and gunner.

For the next two hours Morgan flew with one hand on the controls and the other holding off the struggling pilot. It was thus that the navigator found them. The navigator had been vainly trying to arouse the unconscious gunners. He took charge of the wounded, allowing Morgan to fly with nothing to worry about but the damaged controls and the attacking fighters. Morgan's citation for the Medal of Honor ended with the sentence, "The miraculous and heroic performance of Flight Officer Morgan on this occasion resulted in the successful completion of a vital bombing mission and the safe return of his airplane and crew."

One of the great fighter-pilot sagas of World War II was the contest between Majors Tommy McGuire and Dick Bong in scoring kills on Jap Zeros.

Richard Ira Bong, a stocky blondheaded kid from Poplar, Wisconsin, was the first ace of World War II to beat Rickenbacker's record of twenty-six kills, and when he got his twenty-seventh plane, Rickenbacker sent him a case of Scotch for breaking the record.

By January 1944 Dick Bong, with twenty-one victories, was the ranking ace in the Air Corps. Just behind him with twenty kills was Colonel Neel Kearby who had won the Medal of Honor for shooting down six enemy planes in a single action over Wewak in October 1943. Kearby was hot to beat Bong.

General Kenney, the Far East air commander, cautioned Kearby not to race with Bong. "He's too cool and collected," the general said. "Besides Dick Bong really doesn't give a damn who's top man. That's the big secret of his success. All he wants to do is kill Japs. Don't press your luck in trying to beat him."

But one day over Wewak, after getting two kills in a Jap formation, Kearby pressed his luck too far and came back for a third pass. Three Japs closed in and Kearby's P-47 took a long burst into the cockpit at close range. Kearby crashed in the jungle near the Jap airdrome of Dagua.

When Bong's score reached twenty-eight, General Kenney ordered him back to the States for a rest and to take a gunnery course. According to Kenney, Bong was not a very good shot, but was a good enough flyer to get too close to the Japs to miss. And so he went back to the States.

By this time Major Thomas B. McGuire, Jr. had twenty kills. It seemed to be his jinx that he always stayed eight kills behind Bong. When he got his first one, Bong already had nine. By the time McGuire had eleven, Bong had nineteen. And now that Bong had twenty-eight and was going back to the States, McGuire had twenty. Now was the time to break the jinx.

But fate took a hand. McGuire became afflicted with Pappy Boyington's malady, the disease known as "lackajaps." The Zeros hid out from the American fighters waiting for unprotected bombers. Then McGuire got dengue fever and recovering from that, had a bout with malaria. By the time McGuire was released from the hospital, Bong was back in the theater, his shooting polished from several weeks at gunnery school. McGuire was still eight kills behind him.

On October 14, 1944, McGuire, on his first post-hospital mission, scored a pair of kills and returned home happy that he was beginning to close the gap. He was greeted with the news that Bong had also scored two kills that day. The eight-kill lead seemed inescapable.

The aces continued the pace through November and December. McGuire would get one and Bong would match it. Then McGuire would get two and Bong would match those. By December 17, 1944, Dick Bong had a total of forty and had widened his margin over McGuire to nine. The thin intense McGuire was almost beside himself. The cards seemed stacked

in favor of his chunky opponent. Then suddenly on December 25 and 26, 1944, McGuire got seven kills in two days.

With the competition standing at forty–thirty-eight, General Kenney called a halt, recalling only too vividly the tragic case of Colonel Neel Kearby. On the morning of December 27th he summoned both officers into his office. Bong was wearing his new Medal of Honor ribbon, having received the award from General MacArthur earlier in the month. General Kenney grounded Major McGuire and ordered Bong back to the States, reasoning that Bong should go home as America's all-time leading fighter ace and that the tense and high-strung McGuire needed a rest after his two-day, seven-victory spurt.

When General Kenney was informed on January 6, 1945, that Dick Bong had arrived in the States, he called in McGuire and told him he was free to return to the aerial battles. But General Kenney warned McGuire not to press his luck too far. McGuire promised to be careful.

On January 7, 1945, Major Tommy McGuire was leading a sweep over Los Negros Island at two thousand feet altitude when a Jap Zero got on the tail of a squadron mate. To get at the enemy, McGuire whipped his P-38 around in a vertical bank without taking time to jettison the one-hundred-and-sixty-gallon auxiliary fuel tanks suspended from the wings. McGuire's plane shuddered into a high-speed stall, and before he could bail out, the plane crashed into the ground, killing him instantly. His all-time score remained at thirty-eight kills.

They named an Army airfield on Mindoro after McGuire and awarded him the Medal of Honor posthumously. He had not had a bullet hole in his plane for over a year, but he had pushed his luck too far. The great race was over.

Dick Bong went back to Poplar, Wisconsin, and married his sweetheart Marge Vattendahl. On August 6, 1945, the day the big bomb was dropped on Hiroshima, Dick Bong, America's leading ace, was killed when the engine of the Lockheed P-80 fighter he was flying "flamed-out" and quit, just after take-off. He was then twenty-four years old. His body was flown back to Wisconsin by Army transport, escorted by eighteen fighter planes. A one-hundred-man military police company and a thirty-piece military band were flown in from Chicago. All flags in Poplar flew at half-mast the day of the funeral. General Mac-

Arthur sent the widow his condolences. Luck had finally run out for the boy from Poplar, just the way it had for Neel Kearby and Tommy McGuire.

The awards of the Medal to Second Lieutenant Walter E. Truemper and Staff Sergeant Archibald Mathies were unusual for several reasons. Their case was the only instance in World War II of two crewmen on the same plane winning Medals of Honor. Truemper was one of the two navigators who received the Medal in World War II. Mathies was one of the four enlisted Air Corps winners. Their awards were posthumous. The citations were almost identical.

During a bombing mission over Germany January 20, 1944, the bomber on which Truemper was navigator and Mathies engineer and ball-turret gunner was attacked by a swarm of enemy fighters. As machine-gun bullets and cannon shells smashed into the bomber, both pilot and co-pilot slumped over the controls. The co-pilot died instantly. The pilot, seriously wounded, lost consciousness. Truemper, the navigator, took charge and he and Sergeant Mathies managed to right the crippled bomber and get it back on course for the home base. Circling unsteadily in the area of the home base, they contacted their tower to report their situation. They were ordered to jump from the plane in parachutes. Truemper and Mathies, refusing to leave the unconscious pilot, volunteered to stay on board and try to land the plane. Thereafter, all of the plane crew, except Truemper, Mathies and the unconscious pilot, bailed out. The field was cleared for an emergency landing, with ambulances and fire trucks standing by.

After making two unsuccessful passes at the field, they tried to land the crippled bomber in an open field across the road from the base. Something went wrong and they crashed in a cloud of smoke and flame. Lieutenant Truemper, Sergeant Mathies and the unconscious pilot were all killed.

The other navigator to win the Medal in World War II was Second Lieutenant Robert E. Femoyer, the navigator on a lone bomber trying to make it back to England from a raid on Merseburg, Germany, on November 2, 1944. Femoyer was severely wounded when his plane was hit over the target by anti-aircraft shells. Despite extreme pain and loss of blood, Femoyer refused a morphine injection. He wanted to keep his faculties

clear so that he could navigate the plane, fearing that none of the others could navigate the complicated course back home. Unable to rise from the floor, he had the crewmen prop him up so he could see his charts and instruments. For two and a half hours he suffered great pain but successfully navigated the course back to England. Only when the home field was in sight did he accept the morphine injection. He died shortly after being carried from the plane.

The first of two Medal-winning bombardiers was First Lieutenant Jack W. Mathis of San Angelo, Texas. On March 18, 1943, Mathis was leading bombardier of his squadron on a raid over Vegesack, Germany. Just as his plane was starting the initial run, he was hit by anti-aircraft fire. His right arm was shattered above the elbow and he had gaping wounds in his side and abdomen. The concussion blew him to the rear of the bombardier's compartment. Realizing that the success of the mission depended on the accurate sighting of the lead bombardier, Mathis dragged himself grimly back to his sights and released his bombs directly on the target. He died slumped over the bomb sights.

Bombardier David R. Kingsley won his Medal for heroic action during a raid on the ill-omened Ploesti oil fields on June 23, 1944. Kingsley gave up his parachute to a wounded tail-gunner after his bomber had received a mortal blow. After aiding all the wounded men to bail out, he was last seen by his mates standing on the bomb-bay catwalk. His body was later found in the wreckage of the plane.

The only aircraft observer winning the Medal was Second Lieutenant Joseph R. Sarnoski, who had formerly been an enlisted bombardier. He won his on June 16, 1943, while flying with a volunteer photographic mission over Buka in the Solomon Islands. When his lone photographic plane was attacked by twenty enemy fighters, Sarnoski manned the nose guns to great effect even after being mortally wounded. His defense of the plane was credited with making the vital photographic mission a success.

The other three enlisted Air Corps winners of World War II were Staff Sergeant Maynard H. Smith, Staff Sergeant Henry Erwin, and Technical Sergeant Forrest L. Vosler. All three survived. All three performed acts of heroism far above and beyond the call of duty while the bombers on which they were

crewmen were damaged and burning from enemy attack. Their stories were remarkably similar.

It should be noted that the case of Staff Sergeant Smith illustrates that the awarding the Medal of Honor in the Air Corps in World War II was completely divorced from promotion policy. In fact, it seemed to have been part of a demotion policy as far as Smith was concerned. Staff Sergeant Smith flew his first mission on May 1, 1943, over Saint-Nazaire, France. With the plane afire he managed to render first aid to wounded crewmen, man machine guns, and throw exploding ammunition overboard. Escaping oxygen made the fire so hot that the radio, gun mount and camera melted and ammunition began to explode. Smith stayed at his post and put out the fire. For this he was awarded the nation's highest decoration, the Medal of Honor. After four more combat missions, he was ordered before a medical board and found to be suffering from "operational exhaustion." The rigors of the first mission apparently had been too much for him. He was reassigned to non-combat clerical duties and reduced to buck private. He was still a buck private when discharged May 26, 1945. This seemed a peculiar situation. It would have been unthinkable for an officer winner to be reduced in rank because he suddenly became afflicted with "operational exhaustion" after winning the Medal. Several such cases were on record and no reduction in rank took place.

The case of Staff Sergeant Henry "Red" Erwin was a typical enlisted Air Corps saga of World War II. Enlisting for flight training on July 27, 1942, at twenty-one, he sweated out the next six months at his home in Birmingham, Alabama, anxiously awaiting orders. Finally, in February 1943, he was called to active duty as an aviation cadet. Then, midway in cadet training, he was washed out. Erwin joined the vast throng of enlisted crewmen who had not quite made it in cadets.

By April of 1945 Henry Erwin was a staff sergeant radio operator on a B-29 of the Fifty-second Bomber Group flying strikes against the Japanese home islands. On April 12 his crew flew as lead aircraft in a major raid against the chemical factories at Koriyama. What happened to him that day was starkly described in the citation for his Medal of Honor:

He was the radio operator of a B-29 airplane leading a group formation to attack Koriyama, Japan. He was charged with the

additional duty of dropping phosphoresce [sic] smoke bombs
to aid in assembling the group when the launching point was
reached. Upon entering the assembled area, anti-aircraft fire
and enemy fighter opposition was encountered. Among the
phosphoresce bombs launched by Sergeant Erwin, one proved
faulty, exploding in the launching chute, and shot back into
the interior of the aircraft striking him in the face. The burning phosphoresce obliterated his nose and completely blinded
him. Smoke filled the plane, obscuring the vision of the pilot.
Sergeant Erwin realized that the aircraft and crew would be lost
if the burning bomb remained in the plane. Without regard
for his own safety, he picked it up and, feeling his way, instinctively crawled around the gun turret and headed for the co-pilot's
window. He found the navigator's table obstructing his passage.
Grasping the burning bomb between his forearm and body, he
unleashed the spring lock and raised the table. Struggling
through the narrow passage, he stumbled forward into the
smoke-filled pilot's compartment. Groping with his burning
hands, he located the window and threw the bomb out. Completely aflame, he fell back upon the floor. The smoke cleared
and the pilot, at three hundred feet, pulled the airplane out of
its dive. Sergeant Erwin's gallantry and heroism above and beyond the call of duty saved the lives of his comrades.

Sergeant Red Erwin somehow survived and was rushed to
the States for medical care. In June 1945 he was awarded the
Medal of Honor and in October a grateful Army Air Force
promoted him to Master Sergeant. It was not until October
8, 1947, two and a half years after that flaming day over Koriyama, that he was discharged from Valley Forge General Hospital, Pennsylvania, and returned to his home at Birmingham,
Alabama. He was the only enlisted airman to win the Medal
in the Pacific Theater.

The ending of hostilities in 1945 witnessed an emotional
wave on the part of the public to express gratitude to military
leaders who had guided the armed forces successfully through
the greatest struggle in history. In 1945 there was a strong movement in Congress to award a special Medal of Honor to General Dwight D. Eisenhower, commander of the victorious Allied
forces in Europe. This Medal was disapproved by the War Department on the grounds that the award should be reserved for
gallantry in action with an armed enemy. General Eisenhower
expressed his agreement with the Department's opinion. The
War Department recommended that special gold medals be

voted by Congress in such cases of outstanding leadership. Congress concurred with the recommendation.

However, Congress did make a special award of the Medal during this period that is as unique in its own way as the award to Major General Adolphus W. Greely in the 1930's. This was the posthumous award to Major General William "Billy" Mitchell, voted by Congress in 1946 and presented to his son, William Mitchell, Jr., in 1948. Many doubts have been expressed as to whether this award was really a Medal of Honor or not. Since the official records of the United States Air Force carry the Mitchell award as a special Medal of Honor, along with the award to Charles A. Lindbergh, the award will be treated as a Medal of Honor in this book.

The similarity between the Greely and Mitchell cases is striking. Both awards were obvious attempts to make amends for past dishonors and were clearly motivated by a sense of guilt. The similarity is further enhanced by the fact that Mitchell and Greely had been colleagues and close personal friends.

When Billy Mitchell became a lieutenant in the Army Signal Corps at the beginning of the twentieth century, Major General Greely was Chief of the Signal Corps. Since there were only sixty officers in the entire corps, Greely knew them all. Greely was impressed with the young Mitchell and sent him on a special mission to build an important telegraph line in Alaska. Mitchell, for his part, became an ardent admirer of Greely and remained one for the rest of his life. Mitchell was one of the several influential individuals who petitioned Congress for the special award of the Medal of Honor for Greely in 1935.

By the end of World War I, Billy Mitchell, with the temporary rank of brigadier general, was the top-ranking officer of the Army Air Service. He was a flamboyant controversial individual, swaggering about Washington in his non-reg extralong British officer's blouse, brandishing a small gold-headed cane, telling the conservative old generals and admirals how obsolete they were.

In 1921 the Air Service asked for an appropriation of sixty million dollars, slightly more than the cost of a new battleship. During testimony before Congress in support of this request, Billy Mitchell stated bluntly that battleships were obsolete,

that any of them could be sent to the bottom with airplane bombs.

This statement raised such a furor with high-ranking Navy brass that tests were scheduled for later in the year. There was much test material available just then, such as ships from the captured German fleet which had to be sunk anyway.

The day before Mitchell brought his bombers over the first target, the five-thousand-ton cruiser *Frankfort,* Secretary of the Navy Josephus Daniels said facetiously he was not afraid to stand on the bridge of the target ship. Secretary Daniels probably felt like eating his words next day when Mitchell's bombers sank the *Frankfort* in thirty-five minutes with six-hundred-pound bombs.

The greatest test for bombers came against the twenty-seven-thousand-ton *Ostfriesland,* one of Germany's finest battleships. The *Ostfriesland* had a triple hull with eighty-five watertight compartments. During the Battle of Jutland she had survived twenty hits from twelve-inch and fourteen-inch navy guns and the explosion of a large sea-mine and still managed to escape under her own power. Mitchell led seven Martin bombers, each armed with a two-thousand-pound bomb, to the attack. The *Ostfriesland* went to the bottom in less than fifteen minutes. An old Navy officer, observing the action from a nearby cruiser, put his head in his arms and wept.

Even after such a dramatic demonstration the War and Navy Departments refused to go along with Mitchell's views. Mitchell kept berating his superiors for shortsightedness, his criticisms becoming more and more vitriolic as time went by. In one speech he prophesied the emergence of Japan as a strong air power and that Japan would strike American bases in the Pacific. Then in 1925 he accused the Navy and War Departments of "incompetency," "criminal negligence," and "treasonable administration of the national defense." It was too much. Mitchell was relieved of his command and court-martialed for "disrespect to his superiors and insubordination." Convicted, Mitchell was assessed a rather strange sentence. He was "to be suspended from rank, command and duty, with forfeiture of all pay and allowance for five years." Mitchell said that the object of the sentence was to deprive him of all rank, pay and so forth, and yet keep him in the Army so he would

keep his mouth shut. He resigned his commission in 1926 and spent the remaining ten years of his life writing his memoirs and a biography of his friend and mentor, Adolphus W. Greely. Billy Mitchell died of a heart attack in 1936.

In Washington in 1942 there was a great uproar to find scapegoats on whom to place blame for the bombing disaster at Pearl Harbor. People began to recall that Billy Mitchell had prophesied just such an attack by the Japanese eighteen years before, after demonstrating how vulnerable battleships were to air attack. Mitchell became a major prophet for military air power, posthumously. Everybody wanted to agree that Mitchell had been right.

In July 1946 Congress began the rather confusing chain of events that resulted in awarding Mitchell a special medal—a special medal that the Air Force carries on its records as a Medal of Honor. On July 25th the House of Representatives authorized a medal be presented on Mitchell's behalf to his sister, Mrs. Martin Fladoes, "in the name of the people of the United States in recognition of his outstanding pioneer service and foresight in the field of American military aviation." The next day the House decided that the medal should go to Mitchell's son, William Mitchell, Jr., rather than to his sister. The Senate concurred the following month.

During July 1947 Congress specified the design of the medal to be awarded Mitchell. This design bore no resemblance to the Gillespie design authorized for the Medal of Honor by the U.S. Army and Air Force. Because of this distinctive design, many newspapers stated flatly that the award to Mitchell was not a Congressional Medal of Honor, special or otherwise. The Mitchell medal was designed by Erwin Springweiler, a sculptor. On the face of the medal appeared Mitchell's name and his portrait, wearing a World War I pilot's flying helmet, goggles and scarf. On the reverse of the medal appeared a flying eagle and the inscription that the award was made by Congress on August 8, 1946.

On March 27, 1948, this medal was presented by General Carl Spaatz, Chief of Staff, U.S. Air Force, to William Mitchell, Jr. on behalf of his deceased father.

The award to Mitchell obviously was not the result of any World War II action on his part, since he died in 1936, but the

award was made because of World War II, in that the war proved Mitchell to have been correct in his views.

Medals of Honor, resulting from World War II actions, were awarded throughout the period of the late 1940's. The last Medal of Honor awarded for World War II service went in 1950 to Marine Colonel Justice Marion Chambers who was awarded the Medal for heroic action on the beachhead at Iwo Jima in February 1945. Colonel Chambers was recommended for the Medal of Honor in April 1945, after being evacuated from Iwo Jima seriously wounded. He had been awarded the Navy Cross instead. The Navy Cross was revoked on submission of additional evidence and a Medal of Honor awarded in its place by the President on November 1, 1950.

XIX

The Perfidy of Mousey Tongue

ONE hundred and thirty-one members of the Armed Forces won Medals of Honor for exploits during the Korean Conflict. Department of Defense figures show that a total of five million, seven hundred and twenty thousand personnel served in all branches during the war, the official dates of which were June 25, 1950, to July 27, 1953.

Most Americans recall the Korean Conflict as one of the most frustrating and inconclusive wars ever to engage this country. It was a half-war that cost the United States and the other members of the United Nations participating thousands of casualties. It was a war that shook the smug faith in an easy victory through push-button technology. In World War II the Americans brought in the big guns and heavy equipment and then tried to stand off and let the machines do the work. Korea was different. Old-fashioned hand-to-hand fighting returned to importance. The grenade and the bayonet were widely used in the ground fighting.

It was a half-war in that the fighting did not tear the fabric of society throughout the world. There was plenty of whisky, white shirts and cigarettes in the stores of the free world. People in the United States talked more about a new automobile called the Kaiser than they did about the "police action" in Korea. Tourists traveled regular schedules on their vacations to Europe. And world cruises carefully avoided the area of unpleasantness called Korea.

Doris Davis, wife of Lieutenant Colonel George A. Davis, who was one of the United States Air Force's four Medal of Honor winners of the Korean Conflict, voiced a typical reaction to the whole affair when she received her husband's posthumous Medal in May of 1954. "If I could feel that he lost his life for some good reason, I could feel better about it," she said.

This was the way the half-war came about. After World War II Korea was divided into two countries. A Communist dictatorship ruled north of the thirty-eighth parallel of latitude and a more or less democratic republic was formed south of the dividing line. On June 25, 1950, Communist troops from North Korea invaded the Republic of South Korea. The United Nations Security Council demanded that the North Koreans withdraw. The demand was refused. The UN asked that member nations enforce the demand. Fighting men came to Korea from all the free nations of the world—Great Britain, Australia, Turkey, Latin America—but mostly the troops were Americans.

During the hot summer of 1950, while Joe DiMaggio was playing his thirteenth and final year in the big leagues at home, the UN forces drove the North Koreans back across the thirty-eighth parallel and plunged on northward. The objective was the Yalu River, the boundary between Communist China and the Korean Peninsula. The American Eighth Army pushed up the west coast of Korea while the Tenth Corps drove up the center. The First Marine Division was part of the Tenth Corps. Air support at this time consisted mainly of Japan-based P-51s and B-26s of the United States Air Force.

North Korea is rugged terrain. Much of it is a nearly deserted land of hogback ridges, deep gulleys and conical peaks. The roads are tortuous and twisting. Yet despite the terrain, the invasion went smoothly until November. The weather turned suddenly cold and the UN troops were short on heavy clothing

and warming tents. The temperature dropped suddenly to twenty-five degrees below zero under the impact of a sudden, cold mass of air from Siberia. Oil became as thick as tar in the bitter cold and the well-oiled American weapons began to jam. The men themselves suffered intensely in the cold. With nothing to eat but cold rations they went into a state of shock. Their feet, sweating from marching during the days, froze at night when they failed to change to dry socks. Flesh wounds tended to develop gangrene in the bitter cold. But by November 23, 1950, forward units of the United States Seventh Division had planted the Stars and Stripes on the heights overlooking the frozen Yalu River and Marine units were strung out across a wide front behind and on the flanks of the Army division.

Unknown to the UN troops, they were about to feel the wrath of Red China's dictator, Mao Tse-tung, who later became referred to commonly by the GI's in Korea as "Old Mousey Tongue."

On the night of November 23rd brassy bugles suddenly blared in the icy night air along the Yalu and a violent artillery barrage slammed into the UN positions. Then a quarter of a million Red China infantrymen swarmed down the rugged hills of Manchuria and into North Korea.

While the GI's and Marines had been pushing northward across the terrible terrain of North Korea, battling the elements as well as a fleeing enemy, an army of Red Chinese "volunteers" had been secretly gathering in the mountain valleys of Manchuria.

The Chinese soldiers had an appearance that the GI's and Marines would later describe as "gookish." They wore brown or greenish-brown quilted uniforms of heavy cotton batting. Their pants were pegged at the ankles and their jackets hung loosely with the tail outside the pants. They wore heavy cotton caps with padded earflaps on their heads and they trotted along through the snow with green canvas rubber-soled sneakers on their feet. Each man had a blanket draped shawl-like across his shoulders and carried a Russian-made rifle or submachine gun. Each man carried his rations, ground rice or soybean meal, in a long cloth tube slung across his chest, in horseshoe roll. Food discipline was strict. The noncoms made the men in their squads tie knots in the roll to separate each day's ration.

The UN troops were to find that their attackers were driven

by two principal motives: hatred for American troops and fear of death for hanging back. Communist political commissars accompanying the troops were responsible for both motives.

The Chinese struck on a front extending across the entire Korean Peninsula. They died by the thousands. Army and Marine machine-gun crews piled up mountains of Chinese dead in front of their positions. Artillery and heavy mortar-fire decimated the attacking masses, killing up to thirty in single blasts. UN tactical aircraft strafed them unmercifully and burned them by the platoon with jellied gasoline. Still they came on, a human sea. It was thus that the American faith in technical know-how as a prime factor in winning a war began to be shaken; it was thus that the "police action" in Korea became an all-out war.

The Army awarded seventy-eight Medals of Honor during the Korean Conflict. Eighteen went to officers and sixty to enlisted men. Major General William F. Dean was the highest ranking military man to get the Medal during the Korean Conflict. He was captured by enemy troops after personally knocking out an enemy tank and was finally freed by the Communists in the course of operation Big Switch. The other Army officer awards were divided among the ranks as follows: two to lieutenant colonels, four to captains, eight to first lieutenants and three to second lieutenants. Eleven of the officer awards were posthumous.

The sixty Army enlisted awards went to nineteen privates and privates first class, eighteen corporals, and twenty-three sergeants of all grades. Forty-four of the sixty awards were posthumous.

The brunt of the Chinese attack across the Yalu on November 23, 1950, was borne by the veteran Twenty-seventh "Wolfhound" Infantry Regiment. By November 27th they had fought a successful rearguard action, covering the retreat of one hundred and fifty thousand United Nations troops, and were in the vicinity of a snow-capped hill north of the Chongchon River. It was Captain Reginald Desiderio, commanding officer of Company E, Second Battalion of the Wolfhounds, who noted the vital importance of that hill. If the Reds captured it, they could command the UN escape route, and there were still thirty thousand troops to run the gantlet south. Panting with haste,

he led Company E up the hill and had them dig in before darkness fell.

In the early hours before dawn Red artillery concentrated on the snow-covered hill, softening it up with thousands of rounds of cannon and mortar shells. Just before dawn five thousand screaming Chinese Red infantrymen in their shapeless uniforms stormed the hill. The chattering machine guns of the Wolfhounds knocked them down like Kewpie dolls. They fell in grotesque heaps, their blood staining the snowy slopes a dark red, but the ones behind kept charging forward, stomping and stumbling over the bodies of their dead companions.

Captain Desiderio scrambled from hole to hole, calming his jittery, frost-bitten troops, "Hold on until light," he urged them. "Just hold on until it gets to be daylight."

An enemy bullet struck Desiderio in the shoulder, knocking him down on the icy ground, but he got back to his feet and kept on making his rounds of the holes. Two more bullets struck him, one in each thigh. Then he crawled from position to position, dragging his crippled legs across the frozen ground behind him. At 3:35 A.M., a mortar shell whistled in, exploding near him and filling his back with fragments. Then another bullet hit him, this time in the left knee. Still he dragged himself from hole to hole, exhorting his men to stand fast.

When drawn broke, Company E was down to seventy-two men of the original two hundred and twenty, but the captain, wounded six times, had held them together. As the Chinese withdrew from their last attack, a final mortar shell came in and exploded in the crater Desiderio used as a command post. The captain was mortally wounded. He died in the arms of the company executive officer. "We've made it, Captain," the young lieutenant sobbed, "it's daylight and we're still holding on!"

Captain Reginald Desiderio was awarded the Medal of Honor posthumously. Company E of the Twenty-seventh Infantry Regiment received a Distinguished Unit Citation. Their stand on the hilltop had saved a United States task force. When the Quartermaster jeep came for the body of the dead captain, wrapped in a mattress cover, and took it to the rear, the men told themselves solemnly, "There'll never be another company commander like him in the regiment."

But fate has a way of tricking everyone. On occasion fate demonstrates that lightning can strike twice in the same place. Desiderio's replacement as company commander was Captain Lewis L. Millett.

Lewis L. Millett, a six-footer with a flaming red mustache from the state of Maine, was no stranger to Company E of the Wolfhounds. He was a World War II tank jockey, having served in North Africa and in Italy. In Italy he received a battlefield promotion to second lieutenant. He stayed in the Army and when the Korean Conflict began he was an artillery captain assigned to the Eighth Field Artillery which supported the Twenty-seventh Infantry. After Desiderio's death, Lew Millett wangled a transfer from the artillery to the infantry for the sole purpose of commanding Company E. Soon the veterans in the company were calling him "Captain Easy," because he was not.

Lew Millett had no faith in the push-button war. He drilled his men with bayonets and preached the gospel of using lots and lots of grenades. He drove the company hard, making the men double-time up and down the icy hills until they could run full-tilt with combat packs across the rough terrain like a herd of mountain goats.

On February 7, 1951, Company E reached the approaches to Hill 180, one of three knobby hills overlooking the route of march of the I Corps. Hill 180 was later named Bayonet Hill because of Captain "Easy" Millett and Company E. Leading his company with fixed bayonets up the hill in a straight up assault, he rammed his bayonet in an enemy soldier's face. As another reached for a grenade, Millett ripped his throat open with the cold steel. A third Chinese soldier, about to fire at the captain, was mortally slashed across the chest. Behind Millett came Company E, screaming and bayoneting. They left forty-seven dead Chinese on the hilltop, eighteen killed by bayonet thrusts. An observer, Brigadier General S. L. A. Marshall, termed Millett's action, "the greatest bayonet attack by U.S. soldiers since Cold Harbor . . ."

Lightning had struck twice in the same place. For a second time Company E of the Wolfhounds had a company commander with the Medal of Honor.

President Truman, the old World War I artilleryman, liked to honor Korean Conflict heroes by personally pinning on their Medals of Honor at the White House. On one such

occasion he pinned Medals on a group of three at one ceremony. The winners were First Lieutenant Carl H. Dodd, Master Sergeant Ernest R. Kouma, and Sergeant John A. Pittman. Pinning the Medal on Sergeant Pittman the President said, "Young man, I don't see how in the devil you can be alive."

Pittman's survival was indeed miraculous. A farm boy from Tallula, Mississippi, he had been a member of Company C, Twenty-third Infantry Regiment, on November 26, 1950, near Hamhung, Korea. With his company pinned down by fire from an enemy-held hill, Pittman volunteered to lead a squad to neutralize the strong point. The Chinese poured down a hail of burp gun and mortar fire. Pittman fell, wounded in the legs. When an enemy grenade sizzled down, landing in the middle of the squad, Pittman hurled himself on it, muffled the explosion with his body. He was carried away, his chest crushed and bleeding from the blast, yet somehow he survived to have the Medal pinned on by the President. President Truman was right in considering the feat unusual. During World War II, fourteen Army enlisted men received the Medal of Honor for the same feat and only one of the fourteen survived the ordeal.

The news of the Medal of Honor award caused quite a stir in Pittman's home town of Tallula, Mississippi. Tallula is in Issaquena County, Mississippi's smallest. In 1951 Issaquena had no schools and few telephones. Pittman's father, a farmer, got the news of his son's award from the sheriff of a nearby county, who drove up to the Pittman farmhouse with his siren blowing. Since Mr. Pittman could not read, the sheriff read the news of the award to him in the farmhouse kitchen by the light of a kerosene lamp. Mr. Pittman looked around at the gathering of friends and neighbors summoned by the sound of the sheriff's high siren. "Now, don't that beat the Dutch?" he said in a marveling tone of voice. "Don't that boy just really beat the Dutch?"

The exploit of Master Sergeant Ernest R. Kouma, a farm boy from Dwight, Nebraska, was similar to that of Audie Murphy of World War II. Kouma was a World War II tanker who had fought in the Battle of the Bulge and stayed on in the regular Army. On the night of August 31, 1950, commanding a tank of Company A, Seventy-second Tank Battalion, on the Naktong Line, his tank was suddenly surrounded by five hundred screaming North Koreans. While the infantry fell back to

regroup, he covered their retreat with cannon and machine-gun fire. Running out of cannon shells and thirty-caliber machine-gun ammunition, he crawled back to the fifty-caliber machine gun mounted on the rear deck of the tank and fired that gun until empty. Then he banged away with his forty-five automatic and threw grenades. Alone on the tank, he held out for an unbelievable nine hours. Then he drove the tank back to his own lines, leaving behind two hundred and fifty enemy dead on the ground.

"Those North Koreans are really not the greatest soldiers in the world," he modestly said later.

The third in the trio receiving Medals of Honor from President Truman that day was First Lieutenant Carl H. Dodd, a coal miner's son from Kenvir, Kentucky. Kenvir was a blackened coal-siding on the L & N Railroad in Harlan County, a county once aptly known as "Bloody Harlan." There was a grocery store where the miners never got out of debt, and a drug store where they bought green patent-medicine for one misery and red patent-medicine for another. There was a café —a narrow room with a greasy lunch-counter and a few wobbly tables decorated with blackening bottles of catsup. There was a small movie theater that ran third-run movies on holidays and weekends—a pink island of make-believe in the drab hamlet. There was a school house and four churches.

Carl Dodd spent his boyhood fishing and squirrel hunting, becoming a crack shot. Like every other man in town, he went into the mines when he was sixteen. There was no place else for a man to go. He twisted his foot in a mining accident. The injury was not noticeable but it hurt him when he walked a lot. Eighteen in 1943, Carl Dodd enlisted in the Army. He did not mention his twisted foot when he took his physical.

By the time he arrived in the Pacific Theater in 1945, the war was about over. He finished out his time in the Army as a sergeant on occupation duty in Korea. Back home in Kenvir he tried going down in the mines again, then several other jobs. Dissatisfied with civilian life, he re-enlisted in the Army.

It was almost like coming home when he returned to Korea, landing at Pusan with the Fifth Infantry on July 31, 1950. Soon after landing he won the Silver Star and a battlefield commission. On January 30, 1951, when his platoon was pinned down by machine-gun fire near Subuk, Carl Dodd charged the nest

singlehandedly and wiped it out with grenades. When other Chinese Reds on higher ground threw grenades down on him, he pitched them back, yelling for his men to come on. His platoon followed, and the Red soldiers broke and ran. Dodd and his platoon pursued, bayoneting the retreating enemy. They destroyed seven enemy machine-gun positions. When the first light came the next morning, the rest of the Fifth Infantry could see that Dodd and his platoon were dug in and the ridge was secure.

When the regimental commander later asked Dodd what had happened he grinned and said, "Why, we just went up and took the hilltop, sir!" He did not mention that his twisted foot was throbbing painfully from the uphill dash. He was afraid they might invalid him out and send him home.

If ever a soldier went to war with revenge in his mind it was Ronald Rosser. A quiet, well-behaved boy, five feet eight inches tall with brown hair, he came from the coal and pottery town of Crooksville, Ohio, population two thousand, nine hundred and fifty-six. He was a sort of latter-day Rodger Young, without the physical infirmities. Like Rodger Young he came from a large happy family and quit high school in his junior year to join the Army. That was 1946 and the peacetime doldrums were on. He did a three-year hitch, then came home to Crooksville to work in the Misco Mine. In February 1951, there was a black day when the word came that his younger brother Dick had been killed by the Chinese "volunteers" in Korea. Ronald Rosser resigned his job at the Misco Mine and enlisted in the Army. He did not have to go; he had been once before. But he grimly informed his parents and thirteen brothers and sisters how it was going to be. "I'm going over there to get even for what they did to Dick and I'm not going to take any prisoners." By the summer of 1951 he was in Korea, a member of Company L, Thirty-eighth Infantry Regiment.

Ronald Rosser was a man with a quiet deadly mission—to kill Chinese. He was always on the hunt and fretted when the enemy held back out of range or retreated before he could get in some shots with his carbine. He finally got in close and slaughtered enough to suit him near Ponggil-li. When his squad was trapped in the open by mortar machine-gun fire, Rosser charged up the slope at the enemy carrying his carbine and a

white phosphorous grenade. He leaped astride a trench and killed two Chinese with his carbine. Racing along the side of the trench he shot five more in quick succession. Crouching by a bunker, he pulled the pin and threw in the deadly white phosphorous grenade. Loud screams followed the violent blast. As two Chinese soldiers staggered out of the blazing bunker, Rosser gunned them down with his carbine. He was not taking any prisoners.

Running out of carbine clips, he raced back down the hill to his squad, with enemy bullets kicking up the dirt all around his feet. With his pockets full of loaded clips and carrying a bulging bag of grenades, Rosser led his squad back up the hill. While the rest of the squad dug in, Rosser ran around, throwing grenades and shooting Chinese soldiers. He seemed to bear a charmed life. When the action was over he found the only mark on him was a slight flesh wound in the hand. Slumped in his hole, he felt he had killed enough Chinese to avenge his brother Dick.

Back in Crooksville the home folks declared a Ronald Rosser Day and the Misco Mine and its employees chipped in to charter a bus for the Rosser family to go to Washington and see the boy get decorated with the Medal of Honor. Ronald's father, mother, wife and nineteen other relatives went to Washington on the bus.

Corporal Einar H. Ingman of Tomahawk, Wisconsin, son of a Swede mechanic and a German mother, joined the Army originally for the purpose of learning a trade. He never had a chance to learn much in the Army except combat and he had to have his face almost entirely rebuilt before he got out, but he won the Medal of Honor and acquired a brand new ear . . .

Einar went to a country school in Lincoln County, Wisconsin, where his family had a farm until he was in the eighth grade and then he quit. Schoolbooks were dull to Einar and classwork duller. Mechanics fascinated him. He liked to work on stalled tractors and farm machinery, and sometimes stood around in a country garage just watching while the mechanics worked on cars. Since there was not much opportunity in rural Lincoln County to learn that trade, Einar succumbed to the Army recruiting posters about the opportunities in the service. The year was 1948 and he was nineteen years old.

Early in 1949 he was sent to Japan and in September 1950 hit the beach at Inchon, Korea, with the rest of the Seventeenth Infantry Regiment. He was a corporal, assistant squad leader, in a rifle platoon. Wounded two weeks later north of Seoul, he stayed for several weeks in a hospital and returned to his platoon in November 1950.

The area around Maltavi in east Korea was wild, desolate country. The narrow road snaked through low rugged mountains, and clumps of brush clung to the slopes and the crests of the ominous ridges. The sky was gray and overcast and occasionally in the distance could be heard the brassy racket of the Chinese bugles. In February 1951 the Seventeenth Regiment was operating in that country, running a series of skirmishes with heavily armed bands of Chinese. When the leader of Einar Ingman's squad was killed, Einar took over and a few hours later when the squad leader of another squad was wounded and had to be evacuated, he took over that squad too.

As he led his double squad against a machine-gun nest dug in on a ridge, a grenade exploded in the air a foot from Einar about head high, blowing off his left ear, and knocking him flat. Einar staggered to his feet and charged the nest with his bayonet. He was hit directly in the face by a rifle bullet and fell down again, but got up, shook his head dazedly and leaped into the nest, killing ten Chinese with bullets and bayonet. Then he tottered away slowly and collapsed. When the squad carried him to the rear they thought he was done for. But Einar Ingman was tough.

The grenade had not only blown off his left ear, it also fractured his jaw. The bullet, hitting him in the face on the left side of his nose, smashed his upper teeth on one side and emerged behind the missing left ear. The left eardrum was destroyed. Plastic surgeons, with the use of lots of silver wire and skin grafts, made him a new face. They even made him a beautiful new left ear. The new ear had only one drawback—Einar could not hear out of it.

"I don't remember much about what happened after I got hit," he said later quite frankly. "That bullet through my head kind of made me quit thinking . . ."

Mitchell Red Cloud from Friendship, Wisconsin, had the blood of the painted Indian war chiefs in his veins. He quit

high school just before Pearl Harbor and joined the Marines, serving at Guadalcanal, Midway, and on several special missions with Carlson's Raiders. The islands of the South Pacific were hard on the red man from cool Wisconsin. He weighed a hundred and ninety-five when he joined the Marine Corps and only one hundred and fifteen pounds when he was mustered out in 1945. But he liked combat. He used to say, "There's no use being in the military service if there's no war going on."

When the Korean Conflict started, Mitchell Red Cloud joined up again, this time in the Army. In the early fall of 1950 he was in Korea as a BAR man in Company E of the Nineteenth Infantry Regiment. On November 5, the company was dug in along a ridge near Chonghyon when they were surprised by a massive attack of enemy troops from the heavy brush. Company E almost spooked and ran. Many were half out of their holes in terror when they were halted by the sudden chatter of Red Cloud's BAR in the forward hole. The deadly fire caused the charge to falter, and the rest of the GI's began blasting away at the enemy.

As Red Cloud stood half out of his hole firing his BAR, he was knocked down by the blast from a burp gun. Painfully he pulled himself erect on a stunted tree and, resting the BAR on a limb, continued to fire. "We got them on the run, you guys!" he yelled back at the company. "Go get them!" He slumped into the tree branches and died as the company thundered past, firing at the retreating enemy. Mitchell Red Cloud's last stand had inspired his company to charge the enemy and wrest victory from defeat.

In March of 1951, Mrs. Nellie Red Cloud, mother of Corporal Mitchell Red Cloud, a silent fifty-three-year-old Winnebago woman, was summoned by the Great White Father to Washington. President Truman hung the Medal of Honor around her neck, a posthumous award for her son. "He has joined the spirits of his forebears," said the President. "He will take his place among the other great Indian warriors who have died bravely on the field of battle."

In the summer of 1950 in Korea, Private First Class William Thompson, thin, hollow-eyed and quiet, continued his journey as always being one of the losers. Born out of wedlock in New York City, he had learned what it was to be unwanted from the

very beginning. As soon as he could he ran away from his grand-
mother and was brought up in a shelter for waifs. He never
asked anything from anybody except to be left alone. When he
was eighteen in 1945 he enlisted in the Army. Willie Thompson was a private all the time he was in the Army and knew that
he would never be anything but a private, but that was all right
with him. He was one of that peculiar breed of men who find a
home in the lowest rank of the Army, never seeking promotion
or favor, keeping a straight bunk and a tight pack.

Private Thompson was a member of the all-Negro Twenty-
fourth Infantry Regiment of the Twenty-fifth Division at
Masan, Korea, during August 1950 when the North Koreans
attacked in overwhelming strength. The situation became hope-
less and the lieutenant in charge of the platoon ordered a withdrawal. Thompson, firing his machine gun into the charging foe,
refused to leave. "I got nothing to go back for," he said. "I'll
just take a lot of these bastards with me." When his friends
tried to drag him back he fought them off savagely and returned
to his machine gun. When last seen by the retreating platoon
he was still firing the machine gun with enemy grenades exploding around him in a deadly shower.

Private William Thompson, born out of wedlock and raised
in a home for waifs, was the first Negro to win a Medal of Honor
since the Spanish-American War. Seven Negroes had won
Medals of Honor in 1898. Five of them won Army Medals as
members of the Tenth Cavalry Regiment making the historic
charge up San Juan Hill, and the other two Negroes won Navy
Medals.

The other Negro winner of the Korean War was Sergeant
Cornelius H. Charlton, also of the Twenty-fourth Infantry
Regiment. Cornelius was the eighth and biggest of Mr. and
Mrs. Van Charlton's seventeen babies, weighing almost sixteen
pounds when he was born. He was nicknamed "Connie" at an
early age because his sister Fairy Mae could not pronounce
Cornelius.

Van Charlton raised his big family on his wages as a miner in
Coalwood, West Virginia, working in mine shafts so low he had
to dig on his hands and knees. But he made his children go to
school during the week and took them to church on Sunday.
Connie's brothers served in the Marines and Army during
World War II and from an early age he yearned to be a soldier.

By 1945 he was only fifteen, but he was six feet tall and weighed a hundred and eighty pounds. He never drank, smoked or cursed, but he wanted to lie about his age and join the Army. His mother put her foot down on that. No lying, even to get into the Army. He waited until he was seventeen and then joined.

By 1951 Connie Charlton was a buck sergeant in the regular Army, acting sergeant major of an engineering battalion, a hundred miles back of the lines in Korea. His commanding officer was amazed one day when Sergeant Charlton requested transfer to the Twenty-fourth Infantry Regiment, on front line duty fighting the Chinese. "You're in line for master sergeant, Charlton," the officer said. "Why do you want to stick your neck out by transferring?"

"I just feel I could do more good up there," he said.

The battalion commander regretfully signed the transfer orders.

The engineers' loss was a definite gain for Captain Gordon E. Gullikson, the inactive reservist from World War II who was commanding Company C of the Twenty-fourth Infantry Regiment. Connie Charlton took over a squad his first day on the line and within three weeks was running a platoon. He was a first-class noncom; authority came naturally to him. Before every patrol he made his men take the grenades off their pack harnesses so that the pins could not be hooked out in the brush, made them tie double knots in their shoe laces so they did not trip on an untied shoe lace while running, and personally checked them for ammunition, full canteens, first-aid packs and live radio batteries. Connie Charlton was only twenty-one years old but he stood over six feet tall and wore a heavy black mustache that made him look older. He was big and easy-going, but when he stood in front of his platoon talking, there was silence in the ranks.

Connie Charlton had come to the Twenty-fourth Regiment as a sergeant in March of 1951. In May Captain Gullikson recommended him for a battlefield promotion to second lieutenant. But Connie never got to wear his bars.

On June 1, Charlton's platoon advanced on Hill 543, held by a large group of enemy troops. The lieutenant platoon leader was first to fall. Charlton immediately assumed command, moving to the front to spearhead the assault.

Captain Gullikson reported later, "The platoon was pinned down by intense fire, but three or four men followed Sergeant Charlton as he made a frontal attack on the first of the two enemy positions . . ."

Connie Charlton had seen it hard before, but this going was the hardest. The blast of a concussion grenade knocked him down. Picking himself up in a daze he threw one of his own grenades into the enemy hole and hugged the earth as it went off. When the Chinese survivors staggered out of the hole, Charlton shot them down with his carbine.

As he scrambled up the rocky hillside, an enemy machine-gun nest opened up and he staggered with a bad wound in his chest. Undaunted, he regrouped the few remaining survivors of his platoon and lunged on. At the top of the hill, he flung himself at the last gun emplacement, but not before an enemy grenade had wounded him mortally. Before he died he killed the rest of the Chinese on the hilltop with his carbine.

On Abraham Lincoln's birthday in 1952, President Harry S. Truman awarded posthumously a Medal of Honor to Sergeant Cornelius Charlton of the Twenty-fourth Infantry Regiment. Hill 543 in Korea, where he had given his life, was thereafter named Charlton Hill. Several weeks later, in a solemn ceremony on Governor's Island, New York, the United States Army Ferryboat No. 84 was christened the *Sergeant Cornelius H. Charlton*. He was probably the first Army Medal of Honor winner in history to have a sea-going vessel named after him. Colonel Henry C. Britt, West Pointer from Tifton, Georgia, and commander of the Twenty-fourth Infantry Regiment, wrote a letter to the parents which said in part, "I feel honored to have known a soldier like your boy. He was one of the best."

On April 25, 1951, the Seventh Infantry Regiment of the Third Infantry Division was fighting a vicious and disheartening rearguard action to cover the main body of retreating United Nations troops. Corporal Hiroshi H. Miyamura, of Gallup, New Mexico, personally killed over sixty Chinese soldiers who were harassing from the rear. Stunned by a concussion grenade, the skinny boyish-looking Nisei was captured by the enemy. Nothing was heard of him for two years.

In April 1953—over two years later—Miyamura, thin and

worn after a long imprisonment, was repatriated with other United Nations soldiers. As he stood in one of the big tents of Freedom Village awaiting a dash of DDT, a quick physical and a dish of ice cream, Brigadier General Ralph Osborne stopped him. "Corporal Hiroshi Miyamura?"

Miyamura, so startled he almost dropped his ice cream, nodded.

"Miyamura," said the general, "I am honored to tell you that you have been awarded the Medal of Honor!"

Corporal Hiroshi Miyamura was the second Japanese-American in history to win the Medal of Honor. The first had been Sadao S. Munemori who had died in Italy during World War II smothering a grenade with his body. The Army had cautiously refrained from announcing the award to Miyamura until after he was safely returned to his own countrymen for fear of reprisal against him if the news of the decoration became known to his Communist captors.

Later that same year, Freedom Village welcomed another Medal of Honor winner. The tall man coming through the line of repatriated prisoners that September day of 1953 was only fifty-four, but he looked ten years older. An ill-fitting suit hung on his gaunt frame and he wore a blue cap, thick-soled canvas sneakers, an orange shirt and a red necktie. He had been a prisoner of the North Koreans for three years. On being told that he was the winner of the first Medal of Honor awarded in the Korean War, Major General William F. Dean shook his head in disbelief. "I expected to be court-martialed," he said.

During the latter part of World War II—that proud war that had seen Dean promoted from an obscure regular Army major to a major general—Dean had commanded the Forty-fourth Infantry Division in the European Theater. When hostilities ended in 1945 he asked that a comprehensive casualty list be compiled for the division. The Forty-fourth had nine hundred and sixty-eight killed, four thousand three hundred and ninety wounded, three hundred and seventy-four missing in action and forty-two captured. Dean was especially proud of the low captured figure. "Nothing is worse than being taken prisoner," he informed his subordinates at the time. The truth of that statement was to be cruelly dramatized for him in Korea.

William Frische Dean was born in Carlyle, Illinois, the son of

a moderately successful dentist, just before the turn of the century. He wanted to go to West Point from the time he could talk. It was a cruel disappointment to him when he failed in the competitive examinations. But even in defeat he did not lapse into the comfort of rationalizing. "I just wasn't smart enough to pass the exams," he told his parents without rancor and enrolled at the University of California. He worked his way through college as a stevedore, a streetcar motorman, a short-order cook in a restaurant and finally as a policeman. After graduation from college in 1922, Dean eagerly accepted a commission as second lieutenant in the regular army. Promotion in the peacetime army was snail-like, especially for a mustang officer who had not attended the trade school. Dean was an infantry lieutenant for twelve years and a captain for five, but he was happy. He was a field soldier who loved the bivouacs and the maneuvers. In garrison he always had the sharpest, best turned-out company in the regiment. He was an obscure major in 1941 when World War II started.

After a stint in War Department Headquarters in Washington he went out as a brigadier general, assistant commander of the Forty-fourth Division in Europe. This was the action he craved. As assistant and later as commander of the Forty-fourth he acquired a reputation for recklessness, because he spent so much of his time up forward in the front lines. The corps commander cautioned him on several occasions for his disregard for his own safety. Dean promised to spend more time in the rear, but the next push would find him up front with the GI's slugging it out with the enemy. Then the war ended and he was just another two-star general division commander. And division commanders were really a dime a dozen after that war.

When the fighting started in Korea in June of 1950, Dean was commanding officer of the Twenty-fourth Infantry Division stationed in Japan. The Twenty-fourth was loaded with green troops, soft from garrison duty. Arriving in Korea with his division on July 4th, Dean spent the next sixteen days fighting delaying actions, trying to buy time for the Eighth Army which was unloading and building a firm perimeter around Pusan. On July 19th, when he was trying vainly to hold a position in Taejon against a horde of attacking troops, orders came from General MacArthur to hold the town for two more days. The situation in Taejon was critical. North Koreans, disguised

in baggy U.S. fatigues, infiltrated the ramshackle town. Snipers filled the streets with bullets, and gasoline dumps began exploding in columns of red flame and black smoke. On July 20th, after holding the required two days, Dean sent the bulk of his division south to dig in for a later delaying action and stayed with elements of the Nineteenth and Thirty-fourth Regiments to direct personally the last resistance in Taejon. In the house-to-house fighting, Dean was back in his element. Appropriating one of the new 3.5 rocket launchers just flown in by aircraft, Dean made good use of it in the burning town. "I got me a tank!" he told an aide gleefully.

Instead of the required two-day stand in Taejon, Dean made it three. Historians have agreed that the defense of Taejon was a pivotal point of the Korean War. If Dean and his division had not delayed the enemy at that point, the Pusan perimeter would have been overrun before it could have been fortified.

But by the time General Dean gave the retreat order, Taejon was surrounded by the enemy to a depth of three miles. Later, during his captivity, he would say with vain regret, "I stayed in Taejon twenty-four hours too long!" But those extra twenty-four hours proved invaluable to the landing forces at Pusan.

Leaving Taejon in a motor column July 21 on the narrow winding road that led back to Pusan and the sea, Dean turned over his jeep to seven wounded GI's and rode in the prime mover pulling a howitzer. The column was under constant attack. Finally, with the narrow road hopelessly clogged with stalled trucks, Dean headed his group south on foot.

It was rough in the darkness staggering along the road, trying to hold the column together and carry the wounded. At one point Dean dropped behind the column to get a canteen of water for a wounded man. The act of mercy had tragic consequences. Attempting to reach a nearby stream, Dean slipped and fell down a steep embankment, landing on his head and losing consciousness. When he awoke, he was all alone in the darkness. The rest of the column had stumbled on, unaware that he was missing. They made it back safely to the UN lines.

Finding himself separated from his group, Dean headed south on his own. But, due to his lack of a compass, he headed southwest instead of southeast and lost himself more completely than ever. For the next thirty-five days he wandered, eating raw rice, potatoes and green peaches, begging an oc-

casional meal from a Korean hut. He ate only six or seven real meals during this time and lost sixty pounds. Finally, the inevitable happened. Two Korean farmers betrayed him to the invaders for a reward the monetary equivalent of $5. That was on August 25th near Chinan in Chollapukdo Province. He was still fifty-five miles from UN lines.

The next three years were the bitterest of all for General Dean. At first he was relentlessly interrogated, once for sixty-eight hours at a stretch. His captors took away all his clothes but his underwear and he had to sit on his hands on the floor of an icy room. When he did not break under duress they offered him the command of a corps if he would defect. Dean laughed at them and told them where they could go. Finally they left him alone and there was nothing but the boredom of confinement.

When General William F. Dean finally walked through the line at Freedom Village in his outlandish civilian attire, he was not a broken man, but he was sadly bent. The Medal award did not bolster him much. He always stated he did not deserve the decoration and was reluctant to wear it. Back home for a visit in Carlyle, Illinois, he expressed his opinion with the rational brusqueness that was part of his personality. "Anybody who's dumb enough to get captured, doesn't deserve to be a hero," he said.

XX

Medics and Whirlybirds

THE Navy awarded forty-nine Medals of Honor to its heroes of the Korean Conflict. Seven went to blue-clad Navy and forty-two went to Marines, all members of the First Marine Division. The Korean Conflict was predominantly a ground-troops war, so naturally the Marines got the lion's share of the Medals. This point is dramatically emphasized when it is

pointed out that five of the seven awards to blue-clad Navy went to combat medics attached to Marine rifle companies. No seagoing Navy man nor airborne Marine got the Medal in Korea.

The other two Navy Medals went to flyers. One went to a helicopter pilot—the only helicopter pilot or crewman in history to receive the Medal. The other Navy flying award went to a Corsair pilot off the carrier *Leyte*. Both Navy pilot exploits had to do with combat rescue operations.

The Corsair pilot was Lieutenant (jg) Thomas J. Hudner, Jr., of Fall River, Massachusetts, an Annapolis graduate of 1946. After a tour as a junior officer on a cruiser, he entered flight training and received his wings as a Navy pilot in 1949. In November 1949 he joined Fighter Squadron Thirty-two, based on the carrier U.S.S. *Leyte*, for service in the Far East. Hudner was the first Navy man to receive the Medal of Honor in the Korean Conflict.

The first week of December 1950, the Corsairs off the *Leyte* were heavily engaged in flying daily sorties over Marines cut off in the Chosin Reservoir area of Korea. Booming in at treetop level over the rough terrain, they blasted away with machine guns and rockets at anything that moved. It was dangerous business. Ground fire inflicted numerous casualties on the low-flying planes.

On December 4th Ensign Jesse L. Brown, flying a Corsair off the *Leyte*, caught a direct hit from anti-aircraft fire as he roared over the rough terrain on a strafing run. He came down on a snow-covered rocky slope on the plane's belly, crashing and skittering to a halt. Black smoke began pouring from his engine.

Circling above, his fighter mates watched the ominous black smoke with sinking hearts. Jesse Brown had the distinction of being the first Negro flying officer in the United States Navy and his squadron mates were fond of him. He waved as they circled overhead, but did not climb from the cockpit. It was painfully clear that Brown was trapped in his wrecked and burning plane in hostile territory.

Brown had been Lieutenant Tom Hudner's wing man and Hudner felt responsible for him. Circling the wreck and throttling back to almost stalling speed, Hudner put his Corsair down in a deliberate wheels-up landing, bouncing and banging across the rough terrain to a safe stop. Running to Brown's plane, he

pounded frantically at the canopy. It was stuck fast. Brown, grinning weakly, was obviously alive. Hot flames were sweeping back from the engine. Hudner gathered armfuls of snow and packed it around the fuselage, the snow freezing his bare hands and turning them blue. Then he ran back to his own plane to get on the radio. He could see the tiny figures of enemy troops dodging about in the rocks on the hillsides but was not too worried as long as his squadron circled above as an umbrella.

"Brown's alive," he told his mates on the radio. "Send for a helicopter. Tell them to bring a big fire extinguisher, a crowbar and an axe." Then he turned and trotted back to the wrecked plane to pack more snow on the fuselage. It was a long wait, but finally came the welcome put-putting and the unwieldy whirlybird sailed down from the hills and settled to earth beside the two downed planes. The helicopter pilot was Marine Lieutenant Charles Ward. Ignoring the increasing enemy rifle-fire from the surrounding hills, Hudner and Ward lugged the fire extinguisher, axe and crowbar to Brown's plane.

Blood was now coming from Brown's mouth as they went to work with axe and crowbar, but the Negro pilot kept smiling weakly. With a splintering, rasping sound they finally ripped off the canopy. As they lifted Brown from the cockpit they found it was too late. The Negro pilot was dead. Silently, Hudner and Ward carried his body to the helicopter and took off. It was none too soon. As they rose, the reinforced enemy troops on the surrounding hills let them have a hail of bullets.

Hudner was awarded the Navy Medal of Honor for his fearless but futile attempt to save the life of his wing man. Hudner survived the Korean Conflict and lived to have the Medal pinned on him at the White House.

Because of the widespread use of the helicopter in hazardous rescue operations during the Korean Conflict it was almost inevitable that at least one of the daring whirlybird pilots would be awarded the Medal of Honor. One was. That man was Lieutenant (jg) John Kelvin Koelsch, USN, helicopter pilot off the U.S. carrier *Princeton*. It was an amusing coincidence that Koelsch was also a graduate of Princeton University. Born in London, England, of American parentage, he came to the United States at an early age and was educated here. Enlisting in the Navy as an aviation cadet in 1942, Koelsch was a non-combat

veteran of World War II, never leaving the States during the period of hostilities. But he became an expert torpedo-bomber pilot and decided to remain in the Navy after World War II was over.

In October 1950, Koelsch joined the U.S.S. *Princeton* as Officer in Charge of the Helicopter Detachment. The year before he had forsaken the piloting of planes to take up helicopters in answer to an urgent call for volunteers. Naturally enthusiastic about all phases of flying, he soon became an outstanding helicopter pilot. The rescue work in which he was engaged became so important to him that he voluntarily refused rotation to the States when his time came in order to continue his hazardous duties.

The supreme test for Koelsch and his whirlybird came on July 3, 1951. That afternoon Marine Captain James V. Wilkins led a flight of Corsairs on a reconnaissance mission along the east coast of Korea, fifteen miles inland and twenty miles south of Wonsan. A small town, apparently deserted, attracted his attention and Wilkins made several low-level passes over it. Fairly well satisfied that nothing unusual was going on in the town, Wilkins decided to make just one more pass and then head back for the carrier. Banking sharply he headed back for that one more pass. He never quite completed the turn. The Corsair lurched and quivered from three fast crashing blows. The prop disintegrated and flame burst from his engine cowling. Wilkins's next movements were instinctively precise. He flipped open the canopy hatch, unsnapped his safety belt and heaved himself out of the cockpit.

The parachute snapped open with a jerk, but he did not have far to fall, being less than eight hundred feet from the ground. After striking the ground with a numbing thump, Wilkins got out of the chute and started running for the sea. Within a few steps he fell down. Looking at his legs he saw with surprise that the trousers of his flight suit were burned off around his calves. Then he began to feel a sharp burning pain in his legs. The Corsair's fire wall must have blown in just before he jumped, scalding him with burning gasoline. While his squadron mates engaged the North Korean troops by strafing the road leading to the village, Wilkins painfully climbed to the top of a nearby hill. In the distance to the northeast he saw the sea. That's where I've got to go, he thought dully.

The word that the Marine Corsairs had a pilot down in enemy territory came to Lieutenant (jg) John Koelsch on the
Princeton, cruising in the Sea of Japan just off Wonsan Harbor. Quickly he and his crewman, Aviation Machinist's Mate
George M. Neal, a Negro from Greensboro, North Carolina,
stowed their gear in the big Vertol H.U.P. helicopter and took
off.

"He's in a bowl-shaped depression in a little hill," said
Koelsch tersely as they sailed in the sky landward above the
oily looking swells of the sea, "and enemy troops are right
across the road. The rest of the Corsair flight will stand by as
long as their fuel lasts to keep the gooks on their side of the
road."

Just at that moment Captain Wilkins, the downed pilot,
would not have given much for his chances of ever getting out.
In the distance he could see a fog bank advancing, a bank that
would effectively block off his air cover. From across the road he
could hear the North Koreans yelling at each other. The day
was warm and he dozed slightly, crouching under a scrubby
bush.

He was roused suddenly by the put-put sound of a whirlybird rotor. Leaping to his feet frenziedly he raced to the top of
the hill waving his arms. He could not believe it, but there it
was. The big bird came chugging in, just under the cloud
bank, calmly and steadily as a stork heading for a chimney.
She swept on past him, heading for the east-west road. "I've got
to get back to my parachute," Wilkins thought dully. "He
won't know where I am if I'm not near the chute." He began
running, slipping and sliding down the mountain to the place
where he had landed.

In the air, Koelsch tried to do a number of things all at once.
He had to fly low enough down into the bowl to look for the
pilot and yet avoid crashing into the rim. He had to avoid the
advancing fog bank. And there was the enemy ground-fire
which he tried to avoid by flying an erratic course. To top it
off he had to watch out his side of the helicopter for Wilkins,
while Neal covered the other side. Suddenly Koelsch saw the
downed pilot near his parachute. "There he is!" he yelled and
dropped the big helicopter down into the bowl.

"Winds too tricky to hover, George!" he yelled at the crewman. "Get the sling out. I'll spin her."

"Aye, aye, sir!" Neal began unreeling the sling cable from the winch. Flying in tight circles at fifty feet, the helicopter dropped its sling on the man below on the ground.

On the ground, Wilkins awaited the loop anxiously. Although it took only seconds in coming down, the seconds seemed an eternity. When it was finally down, he limped to the sling and slipped it over his head and under his arms.

As Wilkins dangled about ten feet off the ground, a UN Corsair boomed in under the fog ceiling and sprayed the enemy-held ridge across the road. As the Corsair zoomed back into the fog, the fire on the helicopter from the ridge burst forth in renewed fury. There was a grinding and tearing of metal as the whirlybird spun with the dangling man. Suddenly, something gave way and the put-putting contraption dropped out of the sky like a rock, straight down on top of Wilkins.

Wilkins recalled later that when he came to, his face was pressed down into the soft dirt with a heavy weight pressing down on the middle of his back. He could hear two voices shouting above him. Laboriously he twisted himself out from under the wreck and staggered to his feet. In the cockpit of the helicopter, Koelsch and Neal hung upside down from their safety belts, twisting to get free. "Are you all right?" Wilkins asked.

"Yes, we're O.K." said Koelsch as he and Neal dropped free to the ground.

Enemy fire from the ridge was kicking up the dirt all around the wrecked whirlybird. "We better get the hell out of here," Neal said.

With Wilkins stumbling in the lead they went back up the mountain. By the time they reached the first crest, Wilkins was ready to collapse from pain and fatigue. "Short . . . break," he gasped.

"Not yet," said Koelsch, taking command quietly, "let's make it to the summit."

At the summit Koelsch called a halt and they took inventory of their arms and rations. Wilkins had lost his thirty-eight caliber revolver, but Koelsch still had his, and they had the two carbines. All the ammunition they had were the fifteen-round clips in the carbines and the six rounds in the revolver. The ration situation was even more disheartening. They had two half-

canteens of water, an Oh Henry candybar from Neal's pocket, a signaling mirror, six flares and a small flask of brandy.

The trio spent a disheartening three days on the mountain, freezing at night and sweating during the day, weakening gradually from hunger. Corsairs came over several times and they fired flares, but apparently the planes missed them. On the third day, in the middle of a miserable drizzle, they spotted their first North Korean patrol, obviously looking for them. Koelsch faced the other two grimly. "I think we'd better forget about rescue and head for the sea while we've still got strength to make it," he said.

Then they began the slipping sliding descent down the mountain, Wilkins stumbling ahead grimly on his burned legs, with Neal or Koelsch helping him over extra-slippery spots. Somehow, without additional food and water, they made it six days later to a village by the sea. In a field outside the village they dug up and ate raw potatoes. They were captured next day in a hut by the sea. With their hands tied behind them with telephone wire, they were marched through the streets of a fishing village while the population lined the streets shouting threats and throwing filth at them. A North Korean soldier had taken Neal's rubber sneakers, giving him in return an oversized pair of shoepacs. The shoepacs cut his feet to ribbons and caused him much agony. Koelsch kept pointing at Wilkins's bandaged legs and shouting "Medicine!" at the captors. He was ignored.

Next day the three were separated. Wilkins and Neal, surviving the long period of imprisonment until the cease-fire, later were able to piece together the last phase of the saga of John Kelvin Koelsch.

In prison camp he categorically refused to answer all questions and refused to be interrogated. His example was a source of inspiration to the rest of the prisoners in the camp. His conduct later formed the basis of a new Navy manual on behavior in the hands of the enemy. Beaten and abused and never given a single break as a prisoner, he died of malnutrition on October 16, 1951. On August 3, 1955, President Eisenhower presented his mother, Mrs. Beulah Koelsch, with the Medal of Honor on behalf of her son.

Captain James Wilkins, the Marine flyer, said later, when describing how Koelsch drove his whirlybird like an uncon-

cerned stork through the merciless ground fire near Wonsan, "It was the greatest display of guts I've ever seen."

Five of the seven Medals of Honor awarded to blue-clad Navy men of the Korean Conflict went to Navy medics attached to Marine rifle companies. Four of the five awards were posthumous. Indistinguishable from the Marines in their battle dress, the medics carried a twelve-pound medical kit and a musette bag with twelve pints of medical whiskey, in addition to their other gear. Each also carried a forty-five caliber automatic pistol. The North Korean and Chinese troops made no pretense of observing the rules of the Geneva Convention and a medic ministering to the wounded on the battlefield was fair game for rifles and burp guns.

None of the Navy medics receiving the award were veterans of World War II. Their average age was just twenty-one years. Hospitalmen Richard DeWert, Taunton, Massachusetts; John E. Kilmer, Houston, Texas; and Francis C. Hammond, of Alexandria, Virginia, gave their lives while seriously wounded themselves. All three refused evacuation for medical treatment in order to stay with their wounded companions.

The case of Hospitalman Edward C. Benfold of Camden, New Jersey, was unusual because he fought the enemy in addition to bandaging the wounded. His citation read in part as follows:

> Leaving the protection of his sheltered position to treat the wounded when the platoon area in which he was working was attacked from both the front and rear, he moved forward to an exposed ridge line where he observed two Marines in a large crater. As he approached the two men to determine their condition, an enemy soldier threw two grenades into the crater while two other enemy charged the position. Picking up a grenade in each hand, Benfold leaped out of the crater and hurled himself against the onrushing hostile soldiers, pushing the grenades against their chests and killing both the attackers. Mortally wounded while carrying out this heroic act, Benfold, by his personal valor and resolute spirit of self-sacrifice in the face of almost certain death, was directly responsible for saving the lives of his two comrades.

The sole survivor of the five Navy medic winners was Hospital Corpsman Third Class William R. Charette of Luding-

ton, Michigan. Charette graduated from high school in Luding-ton in the spring of 1950, and joined the Navy the following January. After training in several Naval hospitals he was sent to Korea as a corpsman attached to the First Marine Division in February 1953.

On March 27, 1953, while attached to a rifle company as medic he moved about methodically in the midst of an intense barrage of enemy small-arms and mortar fire rendering assist-ance to wounded comrades. He was wearing a combat armored vest and occasionally an enemy bullet hit him directly and knocked him down. He always got up again and kept on mov-ing. When an enemy grenade landed a few feet from a Marine he was attending, Charette threw himself over the fallen Ma-rine, protecting the wounded man with his body. The blast was intense. The vest protected his body, but Charette's face was gashed from the blast and he was stunned momentarily from the concussion. His helmet and medical kit were torn off. Then he had to improvise emergency bandages by tearing up por-tions of his own clothing to continue bandaging the wounded. Unable to move one badly wounded man from an exposed po-sition, Charette took off his own battle vest and placed it on the helpless man.

Charette received the Medal of Honor from President Ei-senhower in ceremonies at the White House on January 12, 1954.

After the cessation of hostilities Charette remained in the Navy, making it his career. On May 26, 1958, he was selected for a special assignment. On that date he reported aboard the missile cruiser U.S.S. *Canberra* off the Virginia Capes and se-lected the Unknown Soldier of World War II by placing a wreath on one of two unidentified caskets. The casket he se-lected was later buried with the Unknown of Korea in Arling-ton National Cemetery near the grave of the Unknown Soldier of World War I.

XXI

A Good Marine Will Fight with Anything You Hand Him

FORTY-TWO members of the United States Marine Corps won the Medal of Honor in the Korean War. Twelve of the Medals went to officers and thirty to enlisted men. All winners were ground troops, members of the First Marine Division (Reinforced). No flying Marines got the Medal in Korea.

The highest ranking Marine to get the Medal in Korea was Lieutenant Colonel Raymond G. Davis of Goggins, Georgia. Lieutenant Colonel Davis, commanding officer of the First Battalion, Seventh Marines, First Marine Division, led his battalion in a bitter four-day attack against the invading Chinese in the Chosin Reservoir area in Korea from December 1 to 4, 1950. His action saved a rifle company from destruction and opened a vital mountain pass to enable two Marine regiments to escape annihilation. In the Marine awards in Korea, as well as Army awards, the name Chosin Reservoir figured with grim prominence.

Of the other Medal-winning Marine officers, one was a major, four were captains and the remaining six were first and second lieutenants. Most of the officers received the Medals for heroic actions directly connected with the command and leadership of troops. The award to Lieutenant Colonel Davis is a good example of a command award. Three of the officers, however, received the award for the traditional suicidal act of smothering grenades with their own bodies, thus saving the lives of the men around them. Five of the twelve officer awards were posthumous.

Most of the thirty Medals awarded to enlisted Marines in Korea went to noncommissioned officers. Eleven went to various grades of sergeants, and six to corporals. Privates and privates first class won thirteen. Twenty-three of the thirty enlisted awards were posthumous.

It is difficult to put the various exploits in categories, but in general it might be said that they fall into five general groups:

command exploits, one-man stands or assaults, grenade smothering with the body, throwing back hostile grenades, and the rescue or shielding of fallen comrades. There was only one citation of the last category for a Marine in Korea. That was the case of Private First Class Eugene A. Obregon of Los Angeles, California, age nineteen, an ammunition carrier of a machine-gun squad who shielded a fallen comrade with his own body at Seoul, Korea, on September 26, 1950, until he was mortally wounded by machine-gun fire. In addition to Obregon in this category, however, the exploits of the five Navy medical corpsmen serving with Marine ground troops must be recalled since all of their exploits had to do with rescue or shielding the wounded and these medic exploits were Marine exploits for all intents and purposes.

The first Marine to win the Medal in the Korean War was Second Lieutenant Henry A. Commiskey of Hattiesburg, Mississippi. He joined the Marine Corps in 1944, two days after his seventeenth birthday. He fought at Iwo Jima and was in the Marines with the rank of staff sergeant, serving as a DI in the Marine bootcamp at Parris Island in 1949 when accepted for officer training. He was commissioned second lieutenant on September 10, 1949. A year later he was in Korea with the First Marine Regiment. Commiskey's exploit was of the one-man assault variety. Armed with only a pistol, he charged up a steep hill on the outskirts of Seoul on September 20, 1950, and killed seven of the enemy in hand-to-hand combat. He survived and was presented his Medal at the White House.

Some of the one-man assaults executed by Marines seem almost as suicidal as leaping on live grenades. Corporal Charles G. Abrell, nineteen years old, of Terre Haute, Indiana, won the Medal on a hill near Hwachon on June 10, 1951. While his platoon was pinned down by strong enemy machine-gun fire from a fortified bunker, Abrell leaped to his feet and ran forward alone, firing at the emplacement. Wounded four times, he staggered grimly to the edge of the bunker, pulled the pin from a grenade and hurled himself bodily into the bunker, the grenade clutched in his hand. Abrell and the entire enemy gun-crew were killed in the resulting explosion.

Private First Class Walter C. Monegan, Jr., age nineteen, of Seattle, Washington, won his Medal near Seoul on September 17, 1950, by taking on six enemy tanks singlehandedly

with his 3.5 bazooka. Monegan had wanted to be a fighting man at an early age and had even enlisted in the Army in 1947 when he was sixteen. When his age was discovered, the Army discharged him, so he waited around until he was seventeen and joined the Marines. His outfit was dug in on a hill overlooking the main Seoul highway when six enemy tanks rumbled down the road in a predawn attack. Disregarding heavy small-arms fire, Monegan crawled forward with his bazooka to within fifty yards of the lead tank and scored a bull's eye on the advancing monster. The enemy tank commander flew upward from the turret like a disconnected jack-in-the-box. Black smoke boiled from the vents. When the sole surviving tankman tried to wriggle out the escape hatch, Monegan killed him with his carbine. Then Monegan laid two more rockets with deadly accuracy into the rest of the oncoming tanks, disorganizing the attacks and halting them so they were destroyed by Marine artillery.

Three days later, during the darkness of early morning on September 20th, Monegan seized his rocket launcher and charged down the slope to help break up another tank attack. He blinked and strained his eyes in the darkness. He could hear the tanks rumbling close by but he could not see them. Suddenly an illuminating shell burst overhead, flooding the area with a weird, white light. Three tanks stood starkly exposed on the road. Dropping to one knee, Monegan knocked out the first tank with a rocket, then reloaded. With his second rocket he destroyed the second tank, shooting through it from side to side, broadside. As the third tank turned tail to beat a retreat, Monegan stood upright to get better aim. Another star shell burst, silhouetting him against the sky. An enemy machine gun chattered and Monegan collapsed. He died trying to get that last tank.

A one-man stand reminiscent of that of Marine John Basilone of World War II was that of Private First Class Alford L. McLaughlin on an isolated Korean outpost in September 1952. Like Basilone, McLaughlin survived his Medal-winning exploit, receiving his decoration at the White House. While manning an outpost called Bunker Hill far in advance of his own lines, on his second volunteer tour of duty, he was attacked by hostile forces in battalion strength. Through the long night McLaughlin fought them off with his two machine guns, alter-

nating as the barrels grew dangerously hot. When individual enemies came too close, he fired at them with a carbine and threw grenades. As he stood to fire the machine guns from the hip, he was wounded several times and his hands were severely blistered from the hot guns. Somehow he managed to survive the fanatical attacks during the long night and when daylight came, over two hundred Chinese were found dead in front of his position. McLaughlin was invalided back to the States. Not because of the wounds, which were serious enough, but because of the condition of his hands, burned almost to the bone from shooting the hot guns.

Chosin Reservoir, lying in the desolate mountains of North Korea, is a frozen lake in winter, a lake swept by arctic winds from the Siberian wasteland to the north. The saga of the First Marine Division in the Chosin area began on November 27, 1950. Eleven of the Marine Medals of Honor went for heroic action in this area.

In November 1950, enemy resistance was so light that the Marine division took on the double mission of pushing on to the Yalu and also guarding its main supply line that stretched all the way back to Hungnam on the sea. On the night of November 27, the Marines were strung out in small units along the thirty-five miles of winding road between Chinhung-ni and Yudam-ni. Unknown to them and the rest of the UN forces, they were about to be assaulted from north of the Yalu by hordes of Oriental troops, unmatched in size and ferocity since the days of Genghis Khan. The Chinese troops streaming across the Yalu were tightly disciplined and led by experienced officers. They had come down into Korea through the mountain valleys of Manchuria, marching thirty miles each night through the bitter cold and hiding from aerial observation during the days. In their shapeless uniforms of quilted cotton, padded earflap caps and canvas sneaker-type shoes, they presented a grotesque and rather comical silhouette. There was nothing comical about their attitude. Political commissars had ground into them that all Americans, and particularly Marines, were professional murderers and war criminals. Kill Marines as you would snakes in your homes, were the orders. Of the entire Chinese force of two hundred and fifty thousand men a total of ten divisions (over one hundred thousand men), were

assigned the sole mission of annihilating the First Marine Division and then smashing on to the coast.

The hordes of grotesque little shapes scrambled to the attack in their rubber-soled shoes across the snow to the weird and brassy blare of bugles, whistles and cymbals. With deadly speed they infiltrated between the scattered Marine strong points, between battalions, companies, platoons and even squads. As the Marines struggled with their frozen rifles and machine guns they found themselves firing on each other in the howling melee. All they could do was pull back into tighter perimeters and keep blasting away at the enemy.

The Fifth and Seventh Regiments of Marines were stuck off by themselves at Yudam-ni, thirty-five miles north of the main Marine headquarters at Hagaru-ri. Staff Sergeant Robert S. Kennemore, a career Marine from Greenville, South Carolina, and veteran of the Tulagi-Guadalcanal campaign of World War II, won his Medal near Yudam-ni. Kennemore, leader of a machine-gun section, took over his platoon when the platoon commander was seriously wounded. During attacks on the nights of November 27 and 28, 1951, Kennemore and his group fought off the yelling attackers. On the second night the grenades came in thick and fast and Kennemore picked up several and threw them back before they exploded. Collapsing in the snow with wounded legs, he was lying there helpless in the midst of several wounded men when two more grenades came in. Without hesitation, Kennemore covered the grenades with his legs, smothering the blasts. He lost both legs as result of his action, but he survived to accept his Medal from President Harry Truman at the White House in 1952.

For some there was no perimeter to pull back to. On the morning of November 27, before the Chinese attack, Captain William E. Barber led Company F to defend Toktong Pass, a strategic point north of the Marine headquarters at Hagaru-ri. Barber was a tall Kentuckian who had played baseball and basketball in high school and college. He was a career Marine officer, a veteran of World War II, and had been in Korea since October. Making his own reconnaissance of the area, Barber chose to defend a steep-sided mountain that overlooked the pass with its winding road. Barber dug himself a foxhole in the frozen rocky ground along with the rest of the company and prepared for a long cold night. There was no time to pitch

tents and fire up oil stoves. The men huddled in their sleeping bags, mostly unzipped so they could be leaped from in a hurry. The night was clear and cold with stars twinkling in the black sky. The temperature dropped to twenty-five degrees below zero. Then there was sudden crackle of gunfire and someone yelled, "Here they come!"

Numb with cold the Marines leaped up to meet the enemy. When some of the frozen guns refused to fire, they threw grenades at the howling attackers. Cold weather even affected the grenades. Some failed to explode but others went off with big crashing explosions, tossing the dwarfish attackers about like ninepins, but still the horde came on. The most unfortunate Marines were those who had not left their sleeping bags unzipped. The Chinese burp gunners slaughtered them unmercifully as they lay in their cocoons.

Private Hector Cafferatta found himself the last man alive on the right flank of his platoon. Cafferatta had been a semi-pro football player in his home state of New Jersey and he was tough. Jumping out of his hole, he emptied his rifle into the oncoming enemy, marveling at how far a gook would bounce when hit by an M-1 slug. Exhausting his ammunition and all his grenades, he ran zigzagging across the frozen ground to the next platoon. Standing in front of a trench holding several wounded Marines, Cafferatta kept firing rifles loaded for him by the wounded. When an enemy grenade landed at his feet, he kicked it aside. It rolled down the mountain and exploded harmlessly. He kicked away a second one. Then a third one flew past him, landing in the trench with the wounded. Jumping back into the trench he grabbed the grenade and threw. It exploded just as it left his hand, wounding him but not putting him out of action.

At daybreak when the attackers finally broke off and withdrew, leaving nearly five hundred dead in front of F Company, the medics evacuated Cafferatta against his will, because of wounds in his chest and upper arm and a shattered hand from the grenade. Company F had suffered twenty killed and fifty-four wounded.

The second night Captain Barber was hit in the leg. He had it bandaged and kept hobbling around, encouraging the men. That night he lost five killed and twenty-nine wounded but F Company piled up two hundred more Chinese dead. After the

enemy drew off for the night, the Marines could hear the screams of the Chinese wounded in darkness, screams that grew weaker and weaker as they gradually froze to death.

The next night Barber was hit again, this time in the other leg. He continued as company commander from a stretcher, having himself carried about to the different positions, snapping out orders and encouragement as the situation demanded. Company F kept fighting off the attacking Chinese division for two days and nights, waiting hopefully for relief.

Lieutenant Colonel Raymond G. Davis, commanding the First Battalion, Seventh Marine Regiment, one of the units farthest north, received orders to lead his unit down the mountain road eight miles to join up with Captain Barber's isolated F Company, defend the pass and then clear the remaining six miles of road south to the Marine headquarters at Hagaru-ri. Colonel Davis, like Captain Barber, was a career Marine and a veteran of World War II. He had entered the Marines as a second lieutenant in 1938 after graduation from Georgia Tech. During World War II he saw action at Guadalcanal, Tulagi, New Guinea, Cape Gloucester and Peleliu. He was an old combat hand but he had never before fought under the bitter arctic conditions of the Korean winter. The orders to fall back and join up with Barber's group were welcome and logical to his thinking. There was one impediment. Davis was surrounded and fighting from a perimeter the same as every other Marine group. To join up with Barber he had to break the ring south along a road blocked by a regiment of Chinese.

Three times Marines assaulted the roadblock in company strength attacks and all three times they were repulsed. During these attacks on December 2, 1950, two enlisted Marines won Medals of Honor. Master Sergeant James E. Johnson of Pocatello, Idaho, was one of the winners. A veteran of the Peleliu and Okinawa campaigns of World War II, Johnson was a dyed-in-the-wool Marine. He won his Medal as a member of a provisional company in the Seventh Marine Regiment, but his regular outfit was the Eleventh Marines, a unit in which his father had served during World War I. Johnson was an artilleryman but his howitzer section was buried somewhere along the road and now he was fighting with a rifle. A good Marine will fight with anything you hand him. When the officer platoon leader was killed, it was natural for Johnson to take over. In Marine

history master sergeants have commanded companies and even battalions on occasion.

Personally directing his platoon's withdrawal after sustaining about fifty percent casualties in an assault on the roadblock, Johnson covered the rear, firing his rifle and throwing grenades into the following Chinese. As the battered remains of the platoon made it back to cover, their last view of Sergeant Johnson was of his head and shoulders rising above a swarm of howling Chinese, battering them down with his clubbed rifle. Johnson, overwhelmed in the wave of counterattacking enemy, received the Medal posthumously.

Staff Sergeant William G. Windrich of East Chicago, Indiana, was another of the old breed, having served in the Marines since 1940. He had fought on bloody Tarawa in World War II. As Sergeant Johnson fought his hand-to-hand battle with the Chinese, Windrich led a squad out to meet the counterattackers. Seven of his twelve men were wounded before they reached their forward positions. Windrich was hit in the head with a grenade fragment but staggered on grimly, blood streaming down his face. Rallying what was left of a platoon, Windrich led them against the yelling attackers. Wounded in both legs, he crawled about in the snow, urging his men to hold their ground and fight. When the aid men tried to bandage his legs and evacuate him, he brushed them aside. For over an hour he crawled about, commanding the defense. When the Chinese were finally beaten off, Windrich collapsed and died from loss of blood before he could be carried back to the aid station.

While the companies battered away at the roadblock, Colonel Davis led his battalion across the fields below the road and toward the mountains that separated him from beleaguered Barber's company at Toktong Pass. He had decided to flank the roadblock and fight through the ring on the snow-covered slopes. Mortars were the most reliable weapons in the extreme cold—the shells would generally fire but sometimes the base plates would split against the frozen ground—so extra mortar shells were carried on stretchers and each man carried a shell in addition to his own equipment.

The battalion met the enemy in strength on the crest of a hill just a thousand yards south of Yudam-ni. The icy slope was so steep that they had to climb it on their hands and knees and

then lock with the enemy hand-to-hand at the top. Somehow they took the ridge. As they staggered forward again, Colonel Davis saw at once a new danger. The men were soaked with sweat from the grinding climb and the frantic action at the summit, and now the sweat was freezing. Their eyebrows were already covered with icicles. If Davis let them stop to rest, they would freeze into icy lumps and never move again. As midnight approached and the men marched on across one ridge after another, the cold and fatigue began to gain control. When they staggered off the rocky path and attempted to sit down, Davis pushed them roughly back along the path, berating them caustically. At one point the leading element became confused and stopped to reset the course by compass. The halt was almost catastrophic. Almost to a man, the column slumped and collapsed in the snow. They had been fighting in the arctic temperature with insufficient food and rest for over three weeks. They were so exhausted they were quite ready to lie there and freeze to death.

Colonel Davis became like a madman, running about shouting and kicking the prostrate forms. "Get them up!" he yelled at the few officers and noncoms still standing. "Get them back on their feet!" The others started kicking and shoving on their own and soon the men were back on their feet, shambling along like sleepwalkers.

In a sheltered ravine Davis finally let the battalion rest, but before they could succumb to exhaustion he made each man take off his shoes and socks in the bitter cold, dry his feet and put on dry socks. Then he made them huddle together for warmth in unzipped sleeping bags. It was dangerous to bunch up like that, but it was a chance that had to be taken.

While the men slept, Colonel Davis reconnoitered the terrain ahead. He was convinced they were somewhere near F Company's position. Until the company was found, Colonel Davis would not sleep.

At daylight the battalion crawled out of its sacks and were ready to go. The two hours' rest had worked wonders. As the column crawled along across the hills, the Chinese attacked their rear and flanks in patrol strength but the column fought them off. In the middle of the morning, Davis was hailed by a messenger, "Colonel, we got Captain Barber on the radio!"

It was true. The voice on the field radio was scratchy and al-

most unintelligible but it was Barber. Colonel Davis almost wept with relief as he took down the coordinates of Barber's position. "But hold back a while, Colonel," said Barber. "The Aussies are going to give us an air strike in a few minutes and you don't want to be caught in the middle."

They began to hear the planes shortly thereafter. When the last plane had blasted the Chinese positions with bombs and rockets, Davis led his battalion up the slope, shooting and bayoneting the stunned enemy in their holes. They charged all the way to F Company's position.

The relief came none too soon for Barber's outfit. Out of a two-hundred-and-twenty-man company, only eighty-two men were still able to fight. Six of his seven officers were wounded. Barber himself was commanding from his stretcher.

After the main body of Marines moved down from Yudam-ni through the gap in the enemy lines blasted by Colonel Davis and his battalion, Davis took over the point on the southward march. Their objective was the Hagaru-ri perimeter where the Marine headquarters was digging in for a permanent stand. Enemy resistance followed them all the way. Overhead, observation planes flashed the word when enemy movements were sighted. Then the P-51s and Corsairs strafed the hills ahead and on the flanks, sending the dwarfish little minions of Mousey Tongue scurrying for cover.

A few hundred yards from the Hagaru-ri perimeter the column stopped and the wounded who were able to walk got off the trucks and lined up with the unwounded. They stood, faces bandaged, arms in slings, with drawn pale faces under their parka hoods, ready to march in like Marines. And march in they did. When the line at the perimeter parted to let them through, they marched in silently, shoulders back and in step. There were no shouts of greeting or witticism for the men who had fought their way through the white hell to relieve the company at Toktong Pass and then come on to Hagaru-ri. Some of the welcoming group wept unashamedly, their tears freezing on their cheeks.

Colonel Davis and Captain Barber ultimately received Medals of Honor for their command exploits in the Chosin area, although Navy boards mulled the decision for almost two years, influenced by the hidebound opinions of some that they had only done their duty.

Twelve Marines—three officers and nine enlisted men— won Medals for smothering grenades during the Korean War. The case of one of them, Staff Sergeant Robert S. Kennemore, has already been described. Kennemore, it will be recalled, did not leap bodily on a grenade, being incapacitated from leg wounds at the time, but covered two incoming grenades with his wounded legs. He lost both legs but survived the ordeal. Two other of the enlisted men survived the explosions. One of the survivors was Corporal Duane E. Dewey of Muskegon, Michigan. A leader of a machine-gun squad in the Fifth Marines, Dewey was wounded near Panmunjom on April 16, 1952. While being treated with a group of wounded by a medical corpsman, an enemy grenade dropped nearby. Pushing the corpsman roughly out of the way, Dewey shouted, "I got it in my hip pocket!" and flung himself on the grenade. The grenade went off with a muffled roar, lifting Dewey a foot into the air. Dewey was hospitalized for fifty days after the action and released from active duty for medical reasons in August 1952. Dewey was the first winner from any service to receive the Medal of Honor from President Dwight Eisenhower. "You must have a body of steel," the new President observed.

Another survivor was Private First Class Robert E. Simanek of Detroit, Michigan. When his unit was ambushed by the enemy he unhesitatingly flung himself on an incoming grenade. Simanek survived but he was so badly wounded he had to be medically retired from the service. He, too, received his award from President Eisenhower.

However, the survivors among the grenade smotherers were strictly exceptions to the rule. Mostly they died. Generally they were similar to the case of Private First Class William B. Baugh of Harrison, Ohio. Baugh was riding with his squad in a truck during the withdrawal to Hagaru-ri in the Chosin Reservoir area the night of November 29, 1950. As the truck stopped and the squad prepared to alight and assist in fighting off an enemy attack, an enemy grenade landed in the truck. Baugh shouted "Grenade!" and hurled himself on the bomb. He died almost instantly from the explosion, but the rest of the squad were unharmed.

First Lieutenant Baldomero Lopez died from one of his own grenades which he misthrew due to a wounded arm. Lopez was a platoon commander in the Fifth Marines during the Inchon

invasion in September 1950. Exposing himself to enemy fire, he crouched almost upright by a bunker and cocked his arm to throw a grenade into the next pillbox. Just as he was about to let fly, a burst from an enemy machine gun caught him in the right shoulder and chest, knocking him backward. As Lopez fell, the activated grenade flew from his hand. He dragged himself forward to retrieve the hissing grenade and threw it, but due to his wounded arm he could not grasp the bomb firmly. With a sweeping motion of his wounded right arm, Lopez cradled the grenade under him and absorbed the full impact of the explosion.

In several cases the act of covering or smothering the grenade was associated with attempting to throw it away or back toward the enemy. The case of Lieutenant Lopez involved that sort of an act. When he saw he could not get rid of the deadly bomb, he fell on it, the way a trapped quarterback will fall on a football. Private First Class Whitt L. Moreland performed a similar act. Moreland was one of many Marine reservists called to active duty in 1950 because of the Korean crisis. On May 29, 1951, while leading an attacking squad along a winding ridge, Moreland and his group were showered with enemy grenades. While the rest of his squad scattered for safety, Moreland leaped about kicking the sputtering bombs off the ridgeline so that they would explode harmlessly down the slope. Kicking away at one of them, Moreland slipped and fell. Aware that the grenade would explode before he could get to his feet and dispose of it, Moreland leaped on the bomb just before it exploded. He died as a result of the explosion.

Corporal David B. Champagne, a Rhode Islander, member of the Seventh Marines in Korea, was directing the fire of his squad from a trench on May 28, 1952, when an enemy grenade landed in the midst of his group. Champagne grabbed up the grenade and threw it back at the enemy. He was just a fraction of an instant too late. The grenade exploded just as it left his hand, hurling him backward from the trench. While lying exposed outside the trench, he was killed from an incoming mortar shell.

The forty-second Marine to be awarded the Medal of Honor in Korea was Staff Sergeant Ambrosio Guillen of El Paso, Texas. Guillen was cited for his heroic leadership of a platoon near Songuch-on, on July 25, 1953, just two days before the

cease-fire. Mortally wounded in a vicious night attack, Guillen refused medical aid and continued in command of his unit until the enemy was routed. A few hours later he died of his wounds. Sergeant Guillen was later buried in Fort Bliss National Cemetery overlooking the Rio Grande near El Paso. His was the last Medal of Honor awarded to a Marine in the Korean War.

XXII

The Ratio Was Fourteen to One

Two days after hostilities began in Korea, President Harry Truman ordered the United States Air Force, an independent branch of service since 1947, to fly cover and support for the forces defending the south. The Air Force dipped into mothballed reserves for the first of the Korean tactical aircraft. Prop-driven P-51 Mustang fighters and B-26 bombers, modified with cannons and rockets, flew the first missions. Then later came the jets, the F-80 Shooting Stars, the F-84 Thunderjets, and the bomber versions of the F-86 Sabrejet. The bombers flew their missions from Okinawa and Japan and the fighters from the Seoul and Pusan perimeters. Korea had few big industrial areas, so the main targets were the MSRs—the main supply routes—and the enemy troops.

At the beginning of the war the North Korean air force consisted of approximately one hundred and fifty obsolete Russian planes—mainly YAK 7s and 11s and IL 10s. The UN air forces attacked this group with such ferocity that by late in July 1950, when the war was scarcely a month old, the North Korean air force was reduced to eighteen aircraft. By August enemy air-resistance was almost nonexistent.

Then, on November 6, 1950, a bird of ill-omen appeared in the skies over Korea. A Russian-built MIG-15 jet fighter swooped over the lines briefly and then headed back north.

Four days later the first jet plane aerial combat in history took place when an Air Force F-80 Shooting Star shot down one of the enemy MIG-15s. The F-80 proved capable of mastering the supposedly better MIG-15, and the F-86, a later USAF fighter, proved to be vastly superior to the Russian jet, making a record of fourteen-to-one superiority in aerial combat over the MIGs.

The final score of the air war after thirty months of action in Korea was overwhelmingly in favor of the UN Air Force. Official statistics showed one thousand and twenty enemy aircraft destroyed, and one thousand and ten damaged. UN losses from all causes, operational accidents included, were four hundred and thirty-five jets, and three hundred and sixty-six prop-driven aircraft. UN Air Force casualty statistics showed four hundred and ninety dead, and seven hundred and seventy-eight missing in action. North Korean and Red Chinese casualty statistics have never been released.

The UN Air Force exacted a murderous toll in the destruction of ground targets. In five hundred thousand sorties, they destroyed fifty-five thousand motor vehicles, seven thousand five hundred railroad cars, six hundred bridges, seven hundred tunnels and one thousand tanks. The Air Force estimated its planes killed or wounded one hundred and eighty thousand enemy troops by bombing and ground strafing during the Korean War.

During the war the Air Force destroyed seven hundred MIGs under a peculiarly unfavorable handicap. After taking off from their fields in the south, the fighters had to fly several hundred miles north to the strip just below the Yalu River, the strip called aptly MIG Alley. Patrolling just south of the river the Air Force fighters could see the large Chinese airfields at Antung, Tatungkou, Takushan and Tapao, north of the river. The enemy planes were lined up row on row on their fields but the Air Force was forbidden to attack targets north of the Yalu. After flying all that distance the Air Force fighters had only ten to fifteen minutes of fighting fuel left, if they reserved enough to get home. Generally, on seeing the fighters, the Chinese squadrons would accept the challenge and come aloft for a fight. If an MIG pilot got in trouble he could glide home easily, secure in the knowledge that once he was north of the river he was safe. When an Air Force fighter got in trouble he had to

fight his crippled plane across miles of enemy-held territory to Pusan or ditch in the Yellow Sea and pray that rescue would pick him up before he froze in the icy water.

The Air Force awarded four Medals of Honor to its members during the Korean War. All four of these Medals were of the traditional Army design.

The Air Force winners of the Korean War Medals were all commissioned pilots. Two flew jets and two flew props. Three of the four were fighter pilots and one was the pilot of a B-26 bomber. They were a lieutenant colonel, two majors and a captain. All were veterans of World War II, and all died winning their Medals.

The first Air Force Medal of Honor hero of the Korean Conflict was Major Louis J. Sebille of Harbor Beach, Michigan, a P-51 pilot assigned to the Eighteenth Fighter-Bomber Group of the Fifth Air Force. His award came for an action which occurred less than two months after hostilities began.

Sebille, joining the Air Force as a flying cadet in 1941, barely got under the wire on the age qualification. By the time he started flight training he was two months past his twenty-sixth birthday. During World War II in Europe he flew sixty-eight missions in B-26 bombers and on his return to the States was ordered to the Command and General Staff School at Fort Leavenworth, Kansas. World War II ended in August 1945, and the following November Major Sebille returned to civilian life. Eight months as a civilian was enough. He went back on active duty with the Air Force in July of 1946, reporting to Barksdale Field, Louisiana. Later he transferred to the Far East. When the Korean Conflict broke out, Sebille was commanding officer of the Sixty-seventh Fighter-Bomber Squadron of the Eighteenth Group. The squadron was ordered to Japan to assist in the defense of South Korea. Upon arrival at Ashiya Air Base, Sixty-seventh Squadron, led by Major Sebille, began flying sorties in support of United Nations troops in Korea.

On August 5, 1950, Sebille led a strafing attack on a concentration of enemy troops, artillery, and armored vehicles near Hamchang, Korea. Anti-aircraft fire from a group of mobile flak-trucks was intense. Sebille's Mustang was hit as he pulled out of his run. The engine, spraying cooling fluid back over the canopy, began to overheat. The plane began to buck and throw smoke.

"Turn back, Lou," his wing man told him on the radio. "Turn back and head for the sea. We'll call a chopper."

The sea was far away, as Sebille well knew, and the terrain below was held by the enemy. "I'll never make it," said Sebille calmly. "I'm going back and get that bastard!" Then he aimed the crippled fighter at the concentration of anti-aircraft vehicles and dived into them, exploding in a great crash.

Major Louis Sebille was awarded the Medal of Honor for his act that day. Sebille's Medal was the forty-fourth awarded by the United States Air Force, the series having begun with the award to Frank Luke, Jr., during World War I. Sebille's Medal was the first awarded to a member of the Air Force in Korea and the first awarded by that service as a separate branch.

Perhaps the most deadly of the Air Force war-birds in Korea was Major George A. Davis, Jr., who received a posthumous promotion to lieutenant colonel, along with his Medal of Honor. Davis in his F-86 once shot down a million dollars' worth of Red aircraft in less than four minutes. He was the only one of four Medal of Honor winners to be shot down by enemy aircraft. The other three met their deaths from ground fire.

Davis was born on December 1, 1920, on a farm near Lubbock, Texas, and entered the Air Force as a cadet in 1942, after spending a year at Searcy College in Arkansas. During World War II in the Asiatic-Pacific Theater of Operations, from August 1943 to March 1945 he flew two hundred and sixty-six combat missions in P-47s and P-51s, downing seven enemy planes. After the war he decided to stay in the Air Force and made the round of the routine stateside assignments. He was a family man, having married Doris Forgason of Sudan, Texas, while on leave in 1943. By the time Davis landed in Korea in October of 1951, they had two children, a girl seven years old and a son nineteen months, and were expecting another child the following May.

Davis at thirty-one was a sort of un-Texan type Texan, being quiet and rather reticent. A dark-haired medium-sized officer, he had the reputation of being iceberg cool. His appearance was not especially impressive. The men of his outfit, the Fourth Fighter-Interceptor Group, always said that George Davis looked about as aggressive as Bugs Bunny. The Reds found that he was the deadliest bunny of them all, however.

When Davis arrived in Korea on October 21, 1951, the Red air strength was estimated at seven hundred MIG-15s. UN air strength in comparable fighters was one hundred and fifty F-86 Sabrejets. Davis flew ten missions as a wing man with the Fourth Fighter-Interceptor Group and in November was given his own squadron. Despite his meek appearance, Davis had practically every attribute necessary for an outstanding jet fighter-pilot. His reflexes were instantaneous and his eyesight was exceptionally sharp. He had a natural gift for shooting, perfected by long hours of practice. And his mental attitude toward flying a fighter aircraft was simple and direct. To Davis, an aircraft was nothing more or less than a flying gun-platform. Get the platform in position, then blast away with the guns. It was just that easy.

As squadron commander, Davis took over the aggressive initiative at once as a plane killer. He shot down two MIGs on November 28th. Two days later on November 30th, he shot down a million dollars' worth of Red aircraft in less than four minutes. Leading three clusters of Sabres on that date in the skies over Korea, he saw suddenly twelve twin-tail Red Bombers ten thousand feet below, obviously heading for a UN coast installation. The sharp-eyed Davis noted that MIG-15 fighters formed a wheeling cover over the bombers and Russian-built LA-9 prop fighters clung to the flanks. This was the largest flight of bombers Davis had seen in Korea.

With Davis in the lead, the Sabres rocketed down on the bombers. Davis made three passes through the Red formation, shooting down a bomber each time. After the third pass, as he was getting his outfit assembled again for the trip home, an MIG-15 came up to contest. Ordering the squadron to maintain formation, Davis peeled off and blasted the MIG out of the sky in one pass. That made four for the day for the pilot who looked about as aggressive as Bugs Bunny.

It went on like that. Davis shot down two MIGs on December 5, 1951, and then on December 13th he shot down four MIGs, two in the morning and two in the afternoon. That made a total of twelve Red aircraft in sixteen days. The news correspondents wrote it up big. "He's a natural," they said. At home Doris Davis read the news stories with foreboding.

The luck ran out for Major George A. Davis on February 10, 1952, over the Yalu River in Korea. Leading a flight of four

Sabrejets on a combat aerial patrol near the Manchurian border on that date, Davis noted one of the group flying erratically. "Out of oxygen," came the gasping message over the radio.

"You and your wing man take off for home," ordered Davis.

The oxygenless pilot and his wing man turned off for home
while George Davis and his wing man continued the patrol.

The Korean skies were clear that day, but the war was moving along nearer the ground. To the south low-flying UN P-51s
and B-26s were harassing ground installation, blasting away
at troop concentrations and supply lines. Part of the Davis
patrol mission was to look for enemy fighters that might appear
to attack the strafing aircraft.

Suddenly, Davis and his lone companion saw a flight of
twelve enemy MIGs speeding southward, obviously headed for
the area where the Red ground-troops were being attacked.
Without hesitation, Davis positioned his two aircraft—his flying gun-platforms—and dived at the enemy formation. Taking
the first MIG from the rear was easy, it blew up almost in
his face, but Davis swooshed on through the cloud of wreckage
to get a second, although the fire from enemy planes behind
him was hitting his own plane. When the second MIG blew up,
Davis, by all rules of logic, should have poured on the coal and
used the superior speed of his Sabrejet to get out of range. Instead he reduced speed and headed for another MIG. As he
concentrated on the third one, his Sabrejet sustained a direct
hit. He crashed into a mountain side, thirty miles south of the
Yalu River.

Davis was awarded the Medal posthumously two years later
in May 1954. His widow received the Medal on his behalf. At
that time she expressed a prevalent point of view about the
whole Korean affair. "If I could feel that he lost his life for
some good reason, I could feel better about it." But the reaction
might have been different from George A. Davis if he could
have spoken. He had been a regular Air Force officer, flying his
gun-platform against the forces of oppression, the enemies of
free people everywhere. At a ratio of fourteen to one, he had
found himself to be a very effective weapon against that enemy.
Perhaps that was enough for Major George A. Davis, Jr.

Charles J. Loring, Jr., an F-80 jet pilot, joined the Air Force
in his home town of Portland, Maine, in March 1942. He was a
combat fighter-pilot in the European Theater during World

War II, flying fifty-five missions in P-47s and P-51s. On Christmas Eve of 1944, his plane was hit by ground fire while he was on a strafing mission over Belgium. He managed to fight the bucking, smoking aircraft to sufficient altitude to allow him to bail out by parachute. Taken prisoner, he spent the rest of the war—until May 1945—in a POW stockade.

After the war Loring stayed in the Air Force. During this period he did several tours as an instructor on the staffs of the Army Information School at Carlisle Barracks, Pennsylvania, and the Air University at Maxwell Field, Alabama.

Major Loring did not arrive in the Korean Theater until June 1952, at which time he joined the Eighth Fighter-Bomber Group. He became squadron operations officer of an outfit, flying F-80 Shooting Stars.

On November 22, 1952, Major Loring was leading a flight of four F-80s on a close-support mission near Sniper Ridge in North Korea. Circling lazily at twelve thousand feet, Loring and his flight got their briefing by radio from a Mosquito reconnaissance plane flitting along the ridges below. "They're all along the ridgetop," the observer in the Mosquito chattered through the static. "It's a long run and there's lots of ack-ack down here. They nearly burned my tail for me a minute ago."

Loring rolled into his dive-bomb run, heading downward for the long humpbacked ridge that stretched for miles below.

The reconnaissance pilot had not been kidding. The black clouds of flak began exploding around him at six thousand feet. Grimly he dived on, aiming for the heaviest concentration. At four thousand feet, the F-80 shuddered in the air as though struck by a giant fist. A direct hit. The F-80 began falling away from the ridge. In one last grim effort, Loring turned his controls and poured on the power. The watchers above saw his plane turn approximately forty-five degrees to the left in a deliberate controlled maneuver and dive directly into the midst of the strongest concentration gun emplacements. The entire enemy position went up in a resounding crash.

Captain John S. Walmsley, a native of Baltimore, Maryland, was the only one of the four Air Force winners in Korea who had not flown combat air missions during World War II. He enlisted in the Air Force in 1942 and was commissioned as a pilot in 1943, but he spent practically the whole of World War II as an instructor at Turner Field, Georgia. Staying in the

States rankled, but what could he do about it? The same thing had happened to Jimmy Doolittle in World War I and he too went on to get the big Medal later.

Walmsley spent most of his time from 1946 to 1949 in Japan doing peacetime flying-duty as a pilot in a bombardment squadron, and was back in the States by the time the Korean Conflict broke out. He returned to Japan in June 1951, a member of the Eighth Bombardment Group. From then until the following September he participated in twenty-five night-intruder combat missions over Korea as pilot of a B-26 bomber.

On the night of September 14, 1951, Walmsley's crew was picked for a special mission, one designed to test some new night-bombing tactics.

Flying low over the railroad in a valley near Yongdok, Korea, Walmsley encountered an enemy supply-train. He roared down on the train blasting away with his cannon. An ammunition car on the train disintegrated in a huge red explosion, breaking the train in two and bringing both sections to a halt. Roaring back down on the train, Walmsley strafed with his machine guns and cursed with frustration. He was out of cannon ammunition. Circling for altitude, he called on the radio for another B-26 aircraft in the area.

"Where is the target?" the other B-26 wanted to know. It was a dark night and several other fires on the ground made it difficult to identify the burning train.

"Follow me and I'll lead you in," said Walmsley, snapping on the powerful searchlight mounted on his plane. With the searchlight blazing out a brilliant trail in front, Walmsley led the other B-26 at a low altitude along the valley, through intense anti-aircraft fire.

The trailing plane, with the target brightly illuminated, blasted away with rockets and cannon, wreaking great damage on the disabled train.

As they pulled up over the encircling rim of mountains out of the fire-filled valley, Walmsley got back on the air. "You didn't knock out the locomotive," he said. "Let's go back and start the run a little sooner and get the boiler."

"My Lord, John," said the other pilot, "they'll blow you out of the sky with that searchlight on."

"Let's get that locomotive," said Walmsley grimly and headed back along the valley, running interference with the

searchlight blazing. The other B-26, in the darkness behind, lined up on the locomotive and blew it up with an accurate rocket.

But as Walmsley roared along the valley, flying straight and true above the rails, his B-26 lurched violently, the right-hand engine coughing flame and smoke. He had taken a direct hit. With flames spreading toward the cockpit, Walmsley ordered the crew to bail out. Only the engineer made it, bailing out at an altitude of less than a thousand feet. As he dangled in the air from his chute, there was a terrific explosion from the stricken aircraft. The engineer could not tell whether the plane exploded in mid-air or crashed into the mountain side at the end of the valley. John Walmsley, Jr. never made it back to Baltimore.

XXIII

Do the Real Heroes Get the Medals?

In the olden days of chivalry the braveness of a knight was written on the dents and holes in his armor and the scars on his body. His baron gave him gold and land while the knight himself emblazoned his shield with his coat of arms and his motto. The western gunfighter kept his own score by notching the butt of his six-gun and some frontiersmen collected scalps.

The modern soldier may notch the stock of his carbine to record the number of his slain adversaries—as did Lieutenant Bobbie Brown of World War II—but may not, because of the conventions of modern warfare, remove the hair, ears or toes of slain enemies for commemorative purposes. The modern soldier must rely on the administrative processes of his branch of service to recognize his deeds with medals and decorations. How fallible are the administrative processes used to recognize and reward bravery?

Some critics say the processes are extremely fallible. One such critic is S. L. A. Marshall, Brigadier General, U.S. Army,

retired. General Marshall served as an Army historian in the European Theater during World War II and again in the Far East during the Korean conflict. A well-known writer in civilian life, General Marshall wrote up eight men for the Medal of Honor during his military career. All but two of these men received the top award. Six winners out of eight write-ups is a high percentage. But General Marshall feels that the two cases which missed the top award were the best of all!

General Marshall described the procedures used during World War II and the Korean Conflict to originate and pass on Medal of Honor recommendations. First the commanding officer of the man recommended wrote several pages of facts describing the deed and sent the report in to the division commander. Here was the first drawback. The initial recommendation could only be instituted by the man's own commanding officer. If a man did something heroic while separated from his own unit, he was out of luck.

Once launched, the recommendation rose tortuously upward through a series of awards boards: division board, corps board, army board, theater board and finally the Decorations Board of the Department of the Army. In the Navy and the Air Force recommendations had to make the same tortuous climb within those departments.

All recommendations for the Medal of Honor had to go ultimately all the way up to the top board of the Department, but any board along the way could recommend a lesser award. The top board would not generally overrule such a veto.

Human factors entered in. The higher boards were far far removed from the battle scene. The member officers, all detailed to perform decoration board duty in addition to other pressing duties, tended to slight the assignment. Some board members tended to haggle over trifles and technicalities. Many took the easy way out and would only approve acts they considered sure-fire, for example, such suicidal acts as grenade smothering.

Psychologists have long pondered whether certain suicidal acts of bravery, performed on the spur of a few seconds, are really bravery at all or rather expressions of an uncontrollable urge for self-destruction. It is not within the purview of this book to analyze the psychological implications of such suicidal acts as grenade smothering. They have long been acceptable as

exploits meriting the award of the Medal of Honor. They are simple acts, unquestionably far beyond the call of duty, and generally result in killing the performer. They also generally result in saving the lives of witnesses, who naturally feel an intense gratitude for the hero who made their own survivals possible. These witnesses are as a rule strongly motivated to furnish affidavits attesting to the heroism of the one who saved them and thereby push to get a decoration for him.

Sometimes, according to General Marshall, boards would be overcome by the sheer audacity of a deed and lose sight of the ultimate consequences. Then a Medal might be awarded for a reckless or foolhardy venture which resulted in the loss of other lives. It must be said in this regard that the Navy law says specifically that the deed involved must be performed "without detriment to the mission." Acts, no matter how brave, which irresponsibly endanger the lives of others or the success of the overall operation, are not supposed to be eligible for the Navy Medal of Honor.

Officers on the upper echelon boards have for years taken a dim view of awarding the Medal to officers for acts of outstanding leadership. Command acts traditionally have been downgraded because of a "he merely did his duty" attitude. The Medal of Honor award to Lieutenant Colonel Raymond G. Davis, USMC, in the Korean Conflict broke this tradition, but the top Navy boards kicked his recommendation around for two years before letting him have the Medal.

Many outstandingly heroic acts were passed completely unrecommended. There were many reasons for this happening. The most fundamental and widespread was the natural reticence on the part of most performers of heroic acts. It never occurred to them to push for a decoration or recognition. Acts tended to come in groups, during attacks, skirmishes, in the heat of sudden violent action. Many commanding officers were too preoccupied to think about writing them up, and even if they did think to, they were too busy to do so until much later.

General Marshall made the point that literary style was extremely important in the write-ups. When he wrote the Medal recommendation for Captain Lewis L. Millett, an Army winner of the Korean Conflict, the writing took him two and a half days with the full-time services of two stenographers.

General Marshall criticized the Army use of the "quota" sys-

tem in making the awards. The quota system reportedly limited to a definite figure the number of awards that could be in a certain army or theater during a stipulated period. The purpose of the Army policy was to restrict the number in order to prevent cheapening the award. General Marshall contended the only way the award could be cheapened was giving it to the wrong man. Every deserving act should rate a Medal of Honor, no matter how many there were. General Marshall suggested that recommendations should go no higher than the headquarters of an army in the field for approval. This would, in a sense, be a return to the Civil War system of awarding the Medal of Honor.

A divergent view was expressed by Samuel I. Parker, winner of the Medal of Honor at Soissons during World War I. Like most winners, Parker was of the citizen-soldier breed. After his World War I service he returned to civilian life to pursue a successful business career, retiring in 1956 as a vice-president of a large corporation. In the interim he returned to active duty in the Army during World War II as an instructor in the Infantry School at Fort Benning, Georgia. Mr. Parker, who now resides in Concord, North Carolina, is a past Secretary of the Congressional Medal of Honor Society of the United States of America, an organization formed to preserve the honor and dignity of the Medal of Honor. Mr. Parker too has definite personal views on how the Medal should be awarded.

He believes it should continue to be awarded only by the authority of the Secretary of the Department involved: Army, Navy or Air Force; and should be presented by the President in the name of Congress. He believes firmly that the Pyramid of Honor should be maintained to cover lesser acts of bravery and the Medal should remain at the peak of eminence.

Mr. Parker has this trenchant observation, however: "I know that there are many more men who deserve medals who do not get them than those who do receive them. The ones who get the medals are just lucky. It just so happens to the lucky ones that there is someone around who takes time out to see that a recommendation is executed. There is no reason for any medal holder to get a swelled head, when he thinks of the many who deserved them that did not get any recognition."

Another matter for controversy has been the name Congres-

sional Medal of Honor. Most military and naval sources prefer to call the decoration simply the Medal of Honor. They have a sound basis for this. In March 1944, the Secretaries of War and Navy met with White House officials and agreed to the shorter name. Congress never concurred. In Congressional indices legislation relating to the award is all alphabetized under "C" for "Congressional" Medal of Honor. Congress obviously feels that since this decoration was established by Congressional acts and is awarded "in the name of Congress" the word Congressional properly belongs in the name.

In its hundred-year history the Medal has been a democratic decoration. All ranks from privates and apprentice seamen through four-star generals and admirals have won it. The personality types of the winners range from the self-effacing bespectacled Rodger Young to the pugnacious bantam Pappy Boyington. The public press often notes the doings of many of them: Joe Foss, Eddie Rickenbacker, Jimmy Doolittle, "Wild Bill" Donovan, Douglas MacArthur. These are front page names, synonymous with success and prestige.

Sometimes the newspapers record their tragedies. On Friday December 1, 1961, you could read this story:

"Junior James Spurrier of Baltimore, whose World War II exploits earned him the nickname of 'One Man Army,' was sentenced Thursday to two years in the Maryland House of Correction. He was convicted . . . on charges stemming from a shooting after Spurrier and a friend quarreled while drinking. Spurrier, thirty-five, was awarded the Congressional Medal of Honor in 1945 while a member of the Thirty-sixth Division for single-handedly liberating a French town, Achain. He was credited with killing twenty-five Germans and capturing sixteen."

Thus was recorded the personal tragedy of one Medal of Honor winner.

The most recent laws pertaining to the decoration for the United States Army, Navy and Air Force were passed by Congress in 1956. These laws can be found in the United States Code, Title Ten, Sections beginning 3741, 6241 and 8741 respectively. In general they merely restate those which governed the awards during World War I, World War II and the Korean Conflict. The time limits for making the awards differ slightly between the services. The Army and Navy awards must be made within five years of the act or service for which the

Medal is recommended while the Air Force time limit is only three years. The Army and Air Force restrict the award to those acts performed "in conflict with the enemy," while the Navy still retains the extra proviso covering acts of heroism performed "in line of profession." However, the Navy has not awarded the Medal of Honor for such a non-conflict act since the *Squalus* affair in 1939, with the lone exception of the Medal to Owen F. P. Hammerberg, a Navy diver working in Pearl Harbor in 1945. All Navy Medals awarded during the Korean Conflict went for conflict with the enemy deeds.

In the 1956 laws and in service policies lie the reasons why America's space men are not considered for awards of the Medal of Honor. The law specifically bars non-combat acts for those who are members of the Air Force. Theoretically, however, Commander Alan Shepard and Marine Lieutenant Colonel John H. Glenn are eligible under the law for Navy Medals of Honor for space deeds. But Navy policy is such that they probably will never be considered for Medals of Honor. This is further evidence of the trend toward awarding special gold medals for deeds of great renown rather than making special awards of the Medal of Honor.

The 1956 laws provide no extra pay for either enlisted or commissioned winners, no monetary rewards, no promotion in rank. There is no provision in the 1956 law, or in any previous law for that matter, entitling enlisted winners to a salute or entitling sons of winners automatic appointment to West Point or Annapolis. Medal winners are entitled to free military air-transportation within the continental limits of the United States, space permitting, and to a special tax-free pension.

The law regarding payment of pensions to living Medal winners was revised by Congress in August 1961. At that time the amount of the pension was raised from $10 a month to $100 a month and the eligible age lowered from sixty-five to fifty years of age. In 1961 there were less than three hundred living winners of the Medal of Honor. Of these, less than half were old enough to be eligible for the pension.

Even in the so-called "easy award" era prior to 1918 when the Medal was the only military award for valor authorized, there were never a great many Medal-winners around. Even in the old days a man might spend thirty years in Army or Marine combat units or in fighting ships of the Navy and never see a

Medal of Honor winner, much less witness a Medal of Honor deed. Statistics graphically bear this out. Approximately two million eight hundred thousand men fought with the Union Army and Navy during the Civil War. Of these, one thousand five hundred and twenty-seven won Medals of Honor. (This number does not include the nine hundred and eleven Medal holders later stricken from the Army list.) The percentage of winners in the Civil War forces was therefore less than six hundredths of one percent. Even counting the nine hundred and eleven stricken, the percentage is less than one tenth of one percent.

After the 1918 legislation the percentage naturally became even more infinitesimal. During World Wars I and II the percentage was approximately three thousandths of one percent and in the Korean Conflict dropped to approximately two thousandths of one percent.

These figures point out the positive trend that the Medal is becoming harder and harder to win all the time.

The last Medals of Honor awarded went to the Unknowns of World War II and Korea on Memorial Day 1958, on the occasion of their interment in Arlington National Cemetery. President Eisenhower made the presentation. "On behalf of a grateful people I now present Medals of Honor to these two Unknowns who gave their lives for the United States of America."

It was in keeping with the trend that the last two Medals awarded should go to the dead. The time when the Medal was a decoration primarily for live heroes was long in the past. Since 1918 most people have had to die to win the award.

Present at the ceremony in 1958 were two hundred and twelve of the three hundred and twenty Medal winners then living. Some stood smartly at attention; others, crippled by wounds or age, sat straight in their wheel chairs. A few were blind. Of the other winners, many many lay under the green turf of that historic burial ground. Cannons boomed a thunderous twenty-one-gun salute in a solemn cadence. Then a bugler blew the sad and lonely notes of Taps, summoning the nation's heroes to the last mustering.

MEDALS OF HONOR
AWARDED BY PERIOD AND SERVICE SINCE 1862
(USAF Separate Branch Since 1947)

Period	Army	Navy	MC	CG	USAF	Total
Civil War (1861-65)	1200	310	17	0		1527
Indian Wars (1861-98)	416	117	8	0		541
Span-Am. War (1898)	30	66	15	0		111
Interim (1899-1917)	75	136	62	0		273
World War I (1917-18)	95	21	7	0		123
Interim (1920-40)	8	20	5	0		33
World War II (1941-45)	292	57	80	1		430
Interim (1946-50)	0	0	0	0	1	1
Korean Conflict (1950-53)	78	7	42	0	4	131
	2194	734	236	1	5	3170

(List includes five Army and nine Navy men who received award twice and all special awards by Congress. Special award to General Billy Mitchell included in USAF awards.)

MEDAL OF HONOR ALPHABETICAL INDEX

This list includes winners from all services—Army, Navy and Air Force—and all special awards. The winner's rank, organization, branch of service, and the war or campaign in which he won the Medal follow his name. In cases of certain Navy non-conflict awards and all special awards, the year the award was made is set forth. In some few cases, the date of the award is not known.

The wars and campaigns are abbreviated as follows:

Box	Boxer Rebellion
CRE	China Relief Expedition
CW	Civil War
Dom C	Dominican Campaign
Haiti	Haitian Campaigns
Ind	Indian Wars
KC	Korean Conflict (1950-53)
K-1871	Korean Campaign (1871)
Mex	Mexican Campaign (1911)
Nic C	Nicaraguan Compaign
PI	Philippine Insurrection
P-1911	Action Against Outlaws (Philippines 1911)
S-A	Spanish-American War
VC	Mexican Campaign (Vera Cruz) 1914
WW I	World War I
WW II	World War II

Asterisks mark the names of the five Army double-winners, the nine Navy double-winners and the five Marines who won both Army and Navy Medals.

Award	Entry
KC	ABRELL, CHARLES G., Cpl., USMC
Ind	ACHESAY, Sgt., Indian Scouts, USA
CW	ADAMS, JAMES F., Pvt., 1st W., Va. Cav., USA
CW	ADAMS, JOHN G. B., 2d Lt., 19th Mass. Inf., USA
CRE	ADAMS, JOHN MAPES, Sgt., USMC
WW II	ADAMS, LUCIAN, S/Sgt., 3d Inf. Div., USA
KC	ADAMS, STANLEY T. M/Sgt., 24 Inf. Div., USA
WW I	ADKISON, JOSEPH B., Sgt., 30th Div., USA
CRE	ADRIANCE, HARRY CHAPMAN, Cpl., USMC
WW II	AGERHOLM, HAROLD CHRIST, Pfc., USMCR
CW	AHEARN, MICHAEL, Paymaster's Steward, USN
1897	AHERN, WILLIAM, Watertender, USN
Ind	ALBEE, GEORGE E., 1st Lt., 41st U.S. Inf., USA
CW	ALBERT, FREDERICK, Pvt., Co. A, 17th Mich. Inf., USA
CW	ALBERT, CHRISTIAN, Pvt., 47th Ohio Inf., USA
CW	ALLEN, ABNER P., Cpl., 39th Ill. Inf., USA
CRE	ALLEN, EDWARD, Boatswain's Mate First Class, USN
CW	ALLEN, JAMES, Pvt., Co. F, 16th N.Y. Inf., USA
CW	ALLEN, NATHANIEL M., Cpl., 1st Mass. Inf., USA
Ind	ALLEN, WILLIAM, 1st Sgt., 23d U.S. Inf., USA
WW I	ALLEX, JAKE, Cpl., 33d Div., USA
WW I	ALLWORTH, EDWARD C., Capt., 5th Div., USA
CW	AMES, ADELBERT, 1st Lt., 5th U.S. Arty., USA
CW	AMMERMAN, ROBERT W., Pvt., 148th Pa. Inf., USA
PI	ANDERS, FRANK L., Cpl., 1st N. Dak. Vol. Inf., USA
CW	ANDERSON, AARON, Landsman, USN
WW II	ANDERSON, BEAUFORD T., S/Sgt., 96th Inf. Div., USA
CW	ANDERSON, BRUCE, Pvt., 142d N.Y. Inf., USA
CW	ANDERSON, CHARLES W., Pvt., 1st N.Y. (Lincoln) Cav., USA
VC	ANDERSON, EDWIN A. Capt., USN
CW	ANDERSON, EVERETT W., Sgt., 15th Pa. Cav., USA
CW	ANDERSON, FREDERICK C., Pvt., 18th Mass. Inf., USA
Ind	ANDERSON, JAMES, Pvt., 6th U.S. Cav., USA
WW I	ANDERSON, JOHANNES S., 1st Sgt., 33d Div., USA
CW	ANDERSON, MARION T., Capt., 51st Ind. Inf., USA
CW	ANDERSON, PETER, Pvt., 31st Wis. Inf., USA
WW II	ANDERSON, RICHARD BEATTY, Pfc., USMC
CW	ANDERSON, ROBERT, Quartermaster, USN
CW	ANDERSON, THOMAS, Cpl., 1st W. Va. Cav., USA
1878	ANDERSON, WILLIAM, Coxswain, USN
K-1871	ANDREWS, JOHN, Ordinary Seaman, USN

Award	Entry
CW	ANGLING, JOHN, Cabin Boy, USN
WW II	ANTOLAK, SYLVESTER, Sgt., 3d Inf. Div., USA
WW II	ANTRIM, RICHARD NOTT, Commander, USN
CW	APPLE, ANDREW O., Cpl., 12th W. Va. Inf., USA
CRE	APPLETON, EDWIN NELSON, Cpl., USMC
CW	APPLETON, WILLIAM H., 1st Lt., 4th U.S. Colored Troops, USA
CW	ARCHER, JAMES W., 1st Lt. and Adj., 59th Ind. Inf., USA
CW	ARCHER, LESTER, Sgt., 96th N.Y. Inf., USA
CW	ARCHINAL, WILLIAM, Cpl., 30th Ohio Inf., USA
CW	ARMSTRONG, CLINTON L., Pvt., 83d Ind. Inf., USA
CW	ARNOLD, ABRAHAM K., Capt., 5th U.S. Cav., USA
CW	ARTHUR, MATTHEW, Signal Quartermaster, USN
CW	ASTEN, CHARLES, Quarter Gunner, USN
Ind	ASTON, EDGAR R., Pvt., 8th U.S. Cav., USA
1898	ATKINS, DANIEL, Ship's Cook First Class, USN
WW II	ATKINS, THOMAS E., Pfc., 32nd Inf. Div., USA
CW	ATKINSON, THOMAS E., Yeoman, USN
1883	AUER, JOHN F., Ordinary Seaman Apprentice, USN
Ind	AUSTIN, WILLIAM G., Sgt., 7th U.S. Cav., USA
CW	AVERY, JAMES, Seaman, USN
CW	AVERY, WILLIAM B., Lt., 1st N.Y. Marine Arty., USA
CW	AYERS, DAVID, Sgt., 57th Ohio Inf., USA
Ind	AYERS, JAMES F., Pvt., 6th U.S. Cav., USA
CW	AYERS, JOHN G. K., Pvt., 8th Mo. Inf., USA
Ind	BABCOCK, JOHN B., 1st Lt., 5th U.S. Cav., USA
CW	BABCOCK, WILLIAM J., Sgt., 2d R.L. Inf., USA
CW	BACON, ELIJAH W., Pvt., 14th Conn. Inf., USA
1939	BADDERS, WILLIAM, Chief Machinist's Mate, USN
VC	BADGER, OSCAR CHARLES, Ensign, USN
WW I	BAESEL, ALBERT E., 2d Lt., 37th Div., USA
Ind	BAILEY, JAMES E., Sgt., 5th U.S. Cav., USA
WW II	BAILEY, KENNETH D., Major, USMC
CW	BAIRD, ABSALOM, Brig. Gen., U.S. Vol. USA
Ind	BAIRD, GEORGE W., 1st Lt. and Adj., 5th U.S. Inf., USA
WW II	BAKER, ADDISON E., Lt. Col., 93d Bomb Grp., USAAF
Ind	BAKER, BENJAMIN FRANKLIN, Coxswain, USN
S-A	BAKER, EDWARD L., Jr., Sgt. Maj., 10th U.S. Cav., USA
S-A	BAKER, HENRY, Quarter Gunner, USN
CW	BAKER, JOHN, Musician, 5th U.S. Inf., USA
WW II	BAKER, THOMAS A., Sgt., 27th Inf. Div., USA

Name, Rank, Unit	
BALCH, JOHN HENRY, Pharmacist's Mate First Class, USN	WW I
BALDWIN, CHARLES, Coal Heaver, USN	CW
*BALDWIN, FRANK D., Capt., 19th Mich. Inf., 1st Lt., 5th U.S. Inf., USA	CW, Ind
BALLEN, FREDERICK, Pvt., 47th Ohio Inf., USA	CW
BANCROFT, NEIL, Pvt., 7th U.S. Cav., USA	Ind
BANKS, GEORGE L., Sgt., 15th Ind. Inf., USA	CW
BARBER, JAMES A., Cpl., 1st R.I. Light Arty., USA	CW
BARBER, WILLIAM E., Cpl., USMC	KC
BARFOOT, VAN T., 2d Lt., 45th Inf. Div., USA	WW II
BARGER, CHARLES D., Pfc., 89th Div., USA	WW I
BARKELEY, DAVID B., Pvt., 89th Div., USA	WW I
BARKER, CHARLES H., Pvt., 7th Inf. Div., USA	KC
BARKER, NATHANIEL C., Sgt., 11th N.H. Inf., USA	CW
BARKLEY, JOHN L., Pfc., 3d Div., USA	WW I
BARNES, WILLIAM H., Pvt., 38th U.S. Colored Troops, USA	Ind
BARNUM, HENRY A., Col., 149th N.Y. Inf., USA	CW
BARNUM, JAMES, Boatswain's Mate, USN	CW
BARRELL, CHARLES L., 1st Lt., 102d U.S. Colored Troops, USA	CW
BARRETT, CARLTON W., Pvt., 1st Inf. Div., USA	WW II
BARRETT, EDWARD, Second Class Fireman, USN	1881
BARRICK, RICHARD, 1st Sgt., 1st U.S. Cav., USA	Ind
BARRINGER, JESSE, Cpl., 3d Minn. Inf., USA	CW
BARROW, DAVID D., Ordinary Seaman, USN	CW
BARRY, AUGUSTUS, Sgt. Major, 16th U.S. Inf., USA	S-A
BART, FRANK J., Pvt., 2d Div., USA	CW
BARTER, GURDON H., Landsman, USN	WW I
BARTON, THOMAS C., Seaman, USN	CW
BASILONE, JOHN, Sgt., USMC	WW II
BASS, DAVID L., Seaman, USN	CW
BATCHELDER, RICHARD N., Lt. Col. and Chief QM, 2d Corps, USA	CW
BATES, DELAVAN, Col., 30th U.S. Colored Troops, USA	CW
BATES, NORMAN F., Sgt., 4th Iowa Cav., USA	CW
BATSON, MATTHEW A., 1st Lt., 4th U.S. Cav., USA	PI, 1866
BAUER, HAROLD WILLIAM, Lt. Col., USMC	WW II
BAUGH, WILLIAM B., Pfc., USMC	KC
BAUSELL, LEWIS KENNETH, Cpl., USMC	WW II
BAYBUTT, PHILIP, Pvt., 2d Mass. Cav., USA	CW
BAZAAR, PHILIP, Ordinary Seaman, USN	CW
BEARSS, HIRAM IDDINGS, Col., USMC	PI
BEASLEY, HARRY C., Seaman, USN	VC
BEATTIE, ALEXANDER M., Capt., 3d Vt. Inf., USA	CW
BEATY, POWHATAN, 1st Sgt., 5th U.S. Colored Troops, USA	CW
BEAUDOIN, RAYMOND O., 1st Lt., 30th Inf. Div., USA	WW II
BEAUFORD, CLAY, 1st Sgt., 5th U.S. Cav., USA	Ind
BEAUFORT, JEAN J., Cpl., 2d La. Inf., USA	CW
BEAUMONT, EUGENE B., Major and Asst. Adj. Gen., Cav. Corps, Army of the Miss., USA	CW
BEBB, EDWARD J., Pvt., 4th Iowa Cav., USA	CW
BECKWITH, WALLACE A., Pvt., 21st Conn. Inf., USA	CW
BEDDOWS, RICHARD, Pvt., 34th N.Y. Batry., USA	CW
BEEBE, WILLIAM S., 1st Lt., Ord. Dept., USA	CW
BEECH, JOHN P., Sgt., 4th N.J. Inf., USA	CW
BEGLEY, TERRENCE, Sgt., 7th N.Y. Heavy Arty., USA	CW
BEHNKE, FREDERICK, Fireman First Class, USN	1905
BEHNKE, HEINRICH, Seaman First Class, USN	1905
BELCHER, THOMAS, Pvt., 9th Maine Inf., USA	CW
BELL, BERNARD P., T/Sgt., 36th Inf. Div., USA	WW II
BELL, DENNIS, Pvt., 10th U.S. Cav., USA	S-A
BELL, GEORGE, Captain of Afterguard, USN	CW
BELL, HARRY, Capt., 36th Inf., U.S. Vol., USA	PI
BELL, J. FRANKLIN, Col., 36th Inf., U.S. Vol., USA	PI
BELL, JAMES, Pvt., 7th U.S. Inf., USA	Ind
BELL, JAMES B., Sgt., 11th Ohio Inf., USA	CW
BELPITT, W. H., Captain of Afterguard, USN	1884
BENDER, STANLEY, S/Sgt., 7th Inf., 3d Inf. Div., USA	WW II
BENEDICT, GEORGE G., 2d Lt., 12th Vt. Inf., USA	CW
BENJAMIN, GEORGE, JR., Pfc., 77th Inf. Div., USA	WW II
BENJAMIN, JOHN F., Cpl., 2d N.Y. Cav., USA	CW
BENNETT, SAMUEL N., 1st Lt., 2d U.S. Arty., USA	CW
BENNETT, EDWARD A., Pfc., 90th Inf. Div., USA	WW II
BENNETT, EMORY L., Pfc., 3d Inf. Div., USA	KC
BENNETT, FLOYD, Machinist, USN	1926
BENNETT, JAMES H., Chief Boatswain's Mate, USN	S-A
BENNETT, ORREN, Pvt., 141st Pa. Inf., USA	CW

Name	Conflict
BENNETT, ORSON W., 1st Lt., 102d U.S. Colored Troops, USA	CW
BENNION, MERVYN SHARP, Capt., USN	WW II
BENSINGER, WILLIAM, Pvt., 21st Ohio Inf., USA	CW
BENSON, JAMES, Seaman, USN	1872
BENYAURD, WILLIAM H. H., 1st Lt., Engrs., USA	CW
BERG, GEORGE, 17th U.S. Inf., USA	S-A
BERGENDAHL, FREDERICK, Pvt., Band, 4th U.S. Cav., USA	Ind
BERKELEY, RANDOLPH CARTER, Major, USMC	VC
BERRY, CHARLES JOSEPH, Cpl., USMC	WW II
BETHAM, ASA, Coxswain, USN	CW
BERTOLDO, VETO R., Sgt., 42d Inf. Div., USA	WW II
BERTRAM, HEINRICH, Cpl., 8th U.S. Cav., USA	Ind
BESSEY, CHARLES A., Cpl., 3d U.S. Cav., USA	Ind
BETTS, CHARLES M., Lt. Col., 15th Pa. Cav., USA	CW
BEYER, ALBERT, Coxswain, USN	CW
BEYER, ARTHUR O., T/4, 603d T. D. Bn., USA	WW II
BEYER, HILLARY, 2d Lt., 90th Pa. Inf., USA	CW
BIANCHI, WILLIBALD C., 1st Lt., 45th Inf., Philippine Scouts	WW II
BIBBER, CHARLES J., Gunner's Mate, USN	CW
BICKFORD, HENRY H., Cpl., 8th N.Y. Cav., USA	CW
BICKFORD, JOHN F., Captain of Top, USN	CW
BICKFORD, MATTHEW, Cpl., 8th Mo. Inf., USA	CW
BICKHAM, CHARLES G., 1st Lt., 27th U.S. Inf., USA	PI
BIDDLE, MELVIN E., Pfc., 517th Para. Inf. Regt., USA	WW II
BIEGER, CHARLES, Pvt., 4th Mo. Cav., USA	CW
BIEGLER, GEORGE W., Capt., 28th Inf., U.S. Vol., USA	PI
BIGELOW, ELMER CHARLES, Watertender First Class, USNR	WW II
BINDER, RICHARD, Sgt., USMC	CW
BINGHAM, HENRY H., Capt., 140th Pa. Inf., USA	CW
BIRDSALL, HORATIO L., Sgt., 3d Iowa Cav., USA	CW
BIRKHIMER, WILLIAM E., Capt., 3d U.S. Arty., USA	PI
BISHOP, CHARLES FRANCIS, Quartermaster Second Class, USN	VC
BISHOP, DANIEL, Sgt., 5th U.S. Cav., USA	Ind
BISHOP, FRANCIS A., Pvt., 57th Pa. Inf., USA	CW
BJORKLUND, ARNOLD L., 1st Lt., 36th Inf. Div., USA	WW II
BJORKMAN, ERNEST H., Ordinary Seaman, USN	1903
BLACK, JOHN C., Lt. Col., 37th Ill. Inf., USA	CW
BLACK, WILLIAM P., Capt., 37th Ill. Inf., USA	CW
BLACKMAR, WILMON W., Lt., 1st W. Va. Cav., USA	CW
BLACKWELL, ROBERT L., Pvt., 119th Inf. 30th Div., USA	WW I
BLACKWOOD, WILLIAM R. D., Surgeon, 48th Pa. Inf., USA	CW
BLAGEEN, WILLIAM, Ship's Cook, USN	CW
BLAIR, JAMES, 1st Sgt., U.S. Cav., USA	Ind
BLAIR, ROBERT M., Boatswain's Mate, USN	CW
BLAKE, ROBERT, Contraband, USN	CW
BLANQUET, Indian Scout, USA	Ind
BLASDEL, THOMAS A., Pvt., 83d Ind. Inf., USA	CW
BLEAK, DAVID B., Sgt., 40th Inf. Div., USA	KC
BLECKLEY, ERWIN R., 2d Lt., 130th F.A. Obs., 50th Aero Sq., Air Serv., USA	WW I
BLICKENSDERFER, MILTON, Cpl., 126th Ohio Inf., USA	CW
BLISS, GEORGE N., Capt., 1st R.I. Cav., USA	CW
BLISS, ZENAS R., Col., 7th R.I. Inf., USA	CW
BLOCH, ORVILLE E., 1st Lt., 85th Inf. Div., USA	WW II
BLODGETT, WELLS H., 1st Lt., 37th Ill. Inf., USA	CW
BLUCHER, CHARLES, Cpl., 188th Pa. Inf., USA	CW
BLUME, ROBERT, Seaman, USN	S-A
BLUNT, JOHN W., 1st Lt., 6th N.Y. Cav., USA	CW
BOEHLER, OTTO, Pvt., 1st N. Dak. Volt. Inf., USA	PI
BOEHM, PETER M., 2d Lt., 15th N.Y. Cav., USA	CW
BOERS, EDWARD WILLIAM, Seaman, USN	1905
BOIS, FRANK, Quartermaster, USN	CW
BOLDEN, PAUL L., S/Sgt., 30th Inf. Div., USA	WW II
BOLTON, CECIL H., 1st Lt., 104th Inf. Div., USA	WW II
BOND, WILLIAM, Boatswain's Mate, USN	CW
BONEBRAKE, HENRY G., Lt., 17th Pa. Cav., USA	CW
BONG, RICHARD I., Major, USAAF	WW II
BONNAFFON, SYLVESTER, JR., 1st Lt., 99th Pa. Inf., USA	CW
BONNEY, ROBERT EARL, Chief Watertender, USN	1910
BONNYMAN, ALEXANDER, JR., 1st Lt., USMCR	WW II
BOODY, ROBERT M., Sgt., 40th N.Y. Inf., USA	CW
BOOKER, ROBERT D., Pvt., 34th Inf. Div., USA	WW II
BOON, HUGH P., Capt., 1st W. V. Cav., USA	CW
BOONE, JOEL THOMPSON, Lt. (Medical Corps), USN	WW I
BOQUET, NICHOLAS, Pvt., 1st Iowa Inf., USA	CW
BORDELON, WILLIAM JAMES, S/Sgt., USMC	WW II
BOSS, ORLANDO, Cpl., 25th Mass. Inf., USA	CW

BOURKE, JOHN G., Pvt., 15th Pa. Cav., USA — CW
BOURNE, THOMAS, Seaman, USN — CW
BOURY, RICHARD, Sgt., 1st W. Va. Cav., USA — CW
BOUTWELL, JOHN W., Pvt., 18th N.H. Inf., USA — CW
BOWDEN, SAMUEL, Cpl., 6th U.S. Cav., USA — Ind
BOWEN, CHESTER B., Cpl., 19th N.Y. Cav. (1st N.Y. Dragoons), USA
BOWEN, EMMER, Pvt., 127th Ill. Inf., USA — CW
BOWMAN, ALONZO, Sgt., 6th U.S. Cav., USA — Ind
BOWMAN, EDWARD R., Quartermaster, USN — CW
BOX, THOMAS J., Capt., 27th Ind. Inf., USA — CW
BOYCE, GEORGE W. G., JR., 2d Lt., 112th Cav. Regt. Combat Team, USA — WW II
BOYDSTON, ERWIN JAY, Pvt., USMC — CRE
BOYINGTON, GREGORY, Major, USMCR — WW II
BOYNE, THOMAS, Sgt., 9th U.S. Cav., USA — Ind
BOYNTON, HENRY V., Lt. Col., 35th Ohio Inf., USA — CW
BRADBURY, SANFORD, 1st Sgt., 8th U.S. Cav., USA — Ind
BRADLEY, ALEXANDER, Landsman, USN — 1872
BRADLEY, AMOS, Landsman, USN — CW
BRADLEY, CHARLES, Boatswain's Mate, USN — CW
BRADLEY, GEORGE, Chief Gunner, USN — VC
BRADLEY, THOMAS W., Sgt., 124th N.Y. Inf., USA — WW I
BRADLEY, WILLIS WINTER, JR., Commander, USN — WW I
BRADY, GEORGE F., Chief Gunner's Mate, USN — S-A
BRADY, JAMES, Pvt., 10th N.H. Inf., USA — CW
BRANAGAN, EDWARD, Pvt., 4th U.S. Cav., USA — Ind
BRANDLE, JOSEPH E., Pvt., 17th Mich. Inf., USA — CW
BRANNIGAN, FELIX, Pvt., 74th N.Y. Inf., USA — CW
BRANT, ABRAM B., Pvt., 7th U.S. Cav., USA — Ind
BRANT, WILLIAM, Lt., 1st N.J. Vet. Bn., USA — CW
BRAS, EDGAR A., Sgt., 8th Iowa Inf., USA — CW
BRATLING, FRANK, Cpl., 8th U.S. Cav., USA — Ind
BRAZELL, JOHN, Quartermaster, USN — CW
BREAULT, HENRY, Torpedoman Second Class, USN — 1923
BREEMAN, GEORGE, Seaman, USN — No data
BREEN, JOHN, Boatswain's Mate, USN — CW
BRENNAN, CHRISTOPHER, Seaman, USN — CW
BRESNAHAN, PATRICK FRANCIS, Watertender, USN — 1905
BREST, LEWIS F., Pvt., 57th Pa. Inf., USA — CW
BRETT, LLOYD M., 2d Lt., 2d U.S. Cav., USA — Ind
BREWER, WILLIAM J., Pvt., 2d N.Y. Cav., USA — CW

BREWSTER, ANDRE W., Capt., 9th U.S. Inf., USA — B
BREYER, CHARLES, Sgt., 90th Pa. Inf., USA — CW
BRIGGS, ELIJAH A., Cpl., 2d Conn. Heavy Arty., USA — CW
BRIGHT, GEORGE WASHINGTON, Coal Passer, USN — S-A
BRILES, HERSHEL F., S/Sgt., 899th T. D. Bn., USA — WW II
BRINGLE, ANDREW, Seaman, USN — CW
BRINN, ANDREW, Seaman, USN — CW
BRITT, MAURICE L., Capt., 3d Inf. Div., USA — WW II
BRITTIN, NELSON V., Sfc, 24th Inf. Div., USA — KC
BROCK, GEORGE F., Carpenter's Mate Second Class, USN — 1905
BROGAN, JAMES, Sgt., 6th U.S. Cav., USA — Ind
BRONNER, AUGUST F., Pvt., 1st N.Y. Arty., USA — CW
BRONSON, DEMING, 1st Lt., 364th Inf. 91st Div., USA — WW I
BRONSON, JAMES H., 1st Sgt., 5th U.S. Colored Troops, USA — CW
BROOKIN, OSCAR, Pvt., 17th U.S. Inf., USA — S-A
BROPHY, JAMES, Pvt., 8th U.S. Cav., USA — Ind
BROSNAN, JOHN, Sgt., 164th N.Y. Inf., USA — CW
BROSTROM, LEONARD C., Pfc., 7th Inf. Div., USA — WW II
BROUSE, CHARLES W., Capt., 100th Ind. Inf., USA — CW
BROWN, BENJAMIN, Sgt., 24th U.S. Inf. (Ind.), USA — Ind
BROWN, BOBBIE E., Capt., 1st Inf. Div., USA — WW II
BROWN, CHARLES, Cpl., USMC — K-1871
BROWN, CHARLES, Sgt., 50th Pa. Inf., USA — CW
BROWN, EDWARD, JR., Cpl., 62d N.Y. Inf., USA — CW
BROWN, HENRI LEFEVRE, Sgt., 72d N.Y. Inf., USA — CW
BROWN, JAMES, Quartermaster, USN — CW
BROWN, JAMES, Sgt., 5th U.S. Cav., USA — Ind
BROWN, JEREMIAH Z., Capt., 148th Pa. Inf., USA — CW
BROWN, JOHN, Captain of Afterguard, USN — 1866
BROWN, JOHN, Captain of Forecastle, USN — CW
BROWN, JOHN H., 1st Sgt., 47th Ohio Inf., USA — CW
BROWN, JOHN H., Capt., 12th Ky. Inf., USA — CW
BROWN, LORENZO D., Pvt., 7th U.S. Inf., USA — Ind
BROWN, MELVIN L., Pfc., 1st Cav. Div., USA — KC
BROWN, MORRIS, JR., Capt., 126th N.Y. Inf., USA — CW
BROWN, ROBERT, Captain of Top, USN — CW
BROWN, ROBERT B., Pvt., 15th Ohio Inf., USA — CW
BROWN, URIAH, Pvt., 30th Ohio Inf., USA — CW
BROWN, WILLIAM H., Landsman, USN — CW
BROWN, WILSON, Pvt., 21st Ohio Inf., USA — CW
BROWN, WILSON, Landsman, USN — CW

BROWNELL, FRANCIS E., Pvt., 11th N.Y. Inf., USA — CW
BROWNEL, WILLIAM P., Coxswain, USN — CW
BRUNER, LOUIS J., Pvt., 5th Ind. Cav., USA — Ind
BRUSH, GEORGE W., Lt., 34th U.S. Colored Troops, USA — CW
BRUTON, CHRISTOPHER C., Capt., 22d N.Y. Cav., USA — CW
BRUTSCHE, HENRY, Landsman, USN — CW
BRYANT, WILLIAM C., Hosp. Steward, USA — CW
BRYANT, ANDREW S., Sgt., 46th Mass. Inf., USA — CW
BUCHANAN, ALLEN, Lt. Commander, USN — VC
BUCHANAN, DAVID M., Apprentice, USN — 1879
BUCHANAN, GEORGE A., Pvt., 148th N.Y. Inf., USA — CW
BUCK, F. CLARENCE, Cpl., 21st Conn. Inf., USA — CW
BUCKINGHAM, DAVID E., 1st Lt., 4th Del. Inf., USA — CW
BUCKLES, ABRAM J., Sgt., 19th Ind. Inf., USA — CW
BUCKLEY, DENIS, Pvt., 136th N.Y. Inf., USA — CW
BUCKLEY, HOWARD MAJOR, Pvt., USMC — PI
BUCKLEY, JOHN C., Sgt., 4th Va. Inf., USA — CW
BUCKLEY, JOHN K., 1st Lt., 1st R.I. Light Arty., USA — CW
BUFFINGTON, JOHN E., Sgt., 6th Md. Inf., USA — CW
BUFFUM, ROBERT, Pvt., 21st Ohio Inf., USA — CW
BUHRMAN, HENRY G., Pvt., 54th Ohio Inf., USA — CW
BULKELEY, JOHN DUNCAN, Lt. Commander, USN — WW II
BUMGARNER, WILLIAM, Sgt., 4th Va. Inf., USA — CW
BURBANK, JAMES H., Sgt., 4th R.I. Inf., USA — CW
BURGER, JOSEPH, Pvt., 2d Minn. Inf., USA — CW
BURK, MICHAEL, Pvt., 125th N.Y. Inf., USA — CW
BURK, THOMAS, Sgt., 97th N.Y. Inf., USA — CW
BURKARD, OSCAR, Pvt., Hosp. Corps, USA — Ind
BURKE, DANIEL W., 1st Sgt., 2d U.S. Inf., USA — CW
BURKE, FRANK, 1st Lt., 3d Inf Div., USA — WW II
BURKE, LLOYD L., 1st Lt., 1st Cav. Div., USA — KC
BURKE, PATRICK J., Farrier, 8th U.S. Cav., USA — Ind
BURKE, RICHARD, Pvt., 5th U.S. Inf., USA — Ind
BURKE, THOMAS, Seaman, USN — 1866
BURNES, JAMES, Pvt., USMC — CW
BURNETT, GEORGE R., 2d Lt., 9th U.S. Cav., USA — CRE
BURNS, JAMES M., Sgt., 1st W. Va. Inf., USA — Ind
BURNS, JOHN M., Seaman, USN — CW
BURR, ELMER J., 1st Sgt., 127th Inf. 32d Inf. Div., USA — WW II
BURR, HERBERT H., S/Sgt., 11th Armd. Div., USA — WW II

BURRIS, TONY K., Sfc, 2d Inf. Div., USA — KC
BURRITT, WILLIAM W., Pvt., 113th Ill. Inf., USA — CW
BURT, JAMES M., Capt., 2d Armd. Div., USA — WW II
BURTON, ALBERT, Seaman, USN — CW
BUSH, RICHARD EARL, Cpl., USMCR — WW II
BUSH, ROBERT EUGENE, Hospital Apprentice First Class, USNR — WW II
BUTLER, EDMOND, Capt., 5th U.S. Inf., USA — Ind
*BUTLER, SMEDLEY DARLINGTON, Major, USMC — VC, Haiti
BUTTERFIELD, DANIEL, Brig. Gen., U.S. Vol., USA — CW
BUTTERFIELD, FRANK G., 1st Lt., 6th Vt. Inf., USA — CW
BUTTON, WILLIAM ROBERT, Cpl., USMC — Haiti
BUTTS, GEORGE, Gunner's Mate, USN — CW
BUTTS, JOHN E., 2d Lt., 9th Inf. Div., USA — WW II
BUZZARD, ULYSSES G., Pvt., 17th U.S. Inf., USA — S-A
BYRD, RICHARD EVELYN, Commander, USN — 1926
BYRNE, BERNARD A., Capt., 6th U.S. Inf., USA — PI
BYRNES, DENIS, Sgt., 5th U.S. Inf., USA — Ind
BYRNES, JAMES, Boatswain's Mate, USN — CW

CABLE, JOSEPH A., Pvt., 5th U.S. Inf., USA — Ind
CADDY, WILLIAM ROBERT, Pfc., USMCR — WW II
CADWALLADER, ABEL G., Cpl., 1st Md. Inf., USA — CW
CADWELL, LUMAN L., Sgt., 2d N.Y. Vet. Cav., USA — CW
CAFFERATA, HECTOR A., JR., Pfc., USMC — KC
CAHEY, THOMAS, Seaman, USN — 1901
CALDWELL, DANIEL, Sgt., 13th Pa. Cav., USA — CW
CALKIN, IVERS S., 1st Sgt., 2d N.Y. Cav., USA — CW
CALL, DONALD M., Cpl., 344th Bn., Tank Corps, USA — WW I
CALLAHAN, DANIEL JUDSON, Rear Admiral, USN — WW II
CALLAHAN, JOHN H., Pvt., 122d Ill. Inf., USA — CW
CALLAN, THOMAS J., Pvt., 7th U.S. Cav., USA — Ind
CALUGAS, JOSE, Sgt., 88th F. A., Philippine Scouts, USA — WW II
CALVERT, JAMES S., Pvt., 5th U.S. Inf., USA — Ind
CAMP, CARLTON N., Pvt., 18th N.H. Inf., USA — CW
CAMPBELL, JAMES A., Pvt., 2d N.Y. Cav., USA — CW
CAMPBELL, WILLIAM, Pvt., 30th Ohio Inf., USA — CW
CAMPBELL, ALBERT RALPH, Pvt., USMC — CRE
CAMPBELL, DANIEL, Pvt., USMC — S-A
CAMPBELL, WILLIAM, Boatswain's Mate, USN — CW
CANFIELD, HETH, Pvt., 2d U.S. Cav., USA — Ind
CANN, TEDFORD H., Seaman, USN — WW I

CANNON, GEORGE HAM, 1st Lt., USMC — WW II
CANTRELL, CHARLES P., Pvt., 10th U.S. Inf., USA — S-A
CAPEHART, CHARLES E., Major, 1st W. Va. Cav., USA — CW
CAPEHART, HENRY, Col., 1st W. Va. Cav., USA — CW
CAPRON, HORACE, JR., Sgt., 8th Ill. Cav., USA — CW
CAREY, ALVIN, S/Sgt., 2d Inf. Div., USA — WW II
CAREY, CHARLES F., JR., T/Sgt., 100th Inf. Div., USA — WW II
CAREY, HUGH, Sgt., 82d N.Y. Inf., USA — CW
CAREY, JAMES, Seaman, USN — No data
CAREY, JAMES L., Sgt., 10th N.Y. Cav., USA — CW
CARLISLE, CASPER, Pvt., Ind. Pa. Light Arty., USA — CW
CARMAN, WARREN, Pvt., 1st N.Y. (Lincoln) Cav., USA — CW
CARMIN, ISAAC H., Cpl., 48th Ohio Inf., USA — CW
CARNEY, WILLIAM H., Sgt., 54th Mass. Colored Inf., USA — CW
CARPENTER, LOUIS H., Col., 10th U.S. Cav., USA — CW
CARR, EUGENE A., Col., 3d Ill. Cav., USA — Ind
CARR, FRANKLIN, Cpl., 124th Ohio Inf., USA — CW
CARR, JOHN, Pvt., 8th U.S. Cav., USA — Ind
CARR, WILLIAM LOUIS, Pvt., USMC — CRE
CARR, WILLIAM M., Master-at-Arms, USN — CW
CARROLL, THOMAS, Pvt., 8th U.S. Cav., USA — Ind
CARSON, ANTHONY J., Cpl., 43d Inf. U.S. Vol., USA — PI
CARSON, WILLIAM J., Musician, 15th U.S. Inf., USA — CW
CASWELL, HORACE S., JR., Major, 308th Bomb. Grp., USAAF — WW II
CART, JACOB, Pvt., 7th Pa. Res. Corps, USA — CW
CARTER, GEORGE, Pvt., 8th U.S. Cav., USA — Ind
CARTER, JOHN J., 2d Lt., 33d N.Y. Inf., USA — CW
CARTER, JOSEPH E., Blacksmith, USN — S-A
CARTER, JOSEPH F., Capt., 3d Md. Inf., USA — CW
CARTER, MASON, 1st Lt., 5th U.S. Inf., USA — Ind
CARTER, ROBERT G., 2d Lt., 4th U.S. Cav., USA — Ind
CARTER, WILLIAM H., 1st Lt., 6th U.S. Cav., USA — Ind
CARUANA, ORLANDO E., Pvt., 51st N.Y. Inf., USA — CW
CARY, ROBERT WEBSTER, Lt. Commander, USN — 1915
CASEY, DAVID, Pvt., 25th Mass. Inf., USA — CW
CASEY, HENRY, Pvt., 20th Ohio Inf., USA — CW
CASEY, JAMES S., Capt., 5th U.S. Inf., USA — Ind
CASSIDY, MICHAEL, Landsman, USN — CW
CASTLE, FREDERICK W., Brig. Gen., 4th Bomb. Wing, 8th AF, USAAF — WW II

CASTLE, GUY WILKINSON STUART, Lt., USN — VC
CATHERWOOD, JOHN, Ordinary Seaman, USN — P-1911
CATLIN, ALBERTUS WRIGHT, Major, USMC — VC
CATLIN, ISAAC S., Col., 109th N.Y. Inf., USA — CW
CAVANAUGH, THOMAS, Fireman First Class, USN — S-A
CAWETZKA, CHARLES, Pvt., 30th Inf., U.S. Vol., USA — PI
CAYER, OVILA, Sgt., 14th U.S. Inf., USA — CW
CECIL, JOSEPHUS S., 1st Lt., 19th U.S. Inf., USA — PI
CHADWICK, LEONARD, Apprentice First Class, USN — S-A
CHAMBERLAIN, JOSHUA L., Col., 20th Maine Inf., USA — CW
CHAMBERLAIN, ORVILLE T., 2d Lt., 74th Ind. Inf., USA — CW
CHAMBERS, JOSEPH B., Pvt., 100th Pa. Inf., USA — CW
CHAMBERS, JUSTICE K., Lt. Col., USMCR — WW II
CHAMPAGNE, DAVID B., Cpl., USMC — KC
CHANDLER, HENRY F., Sgt., 59th Mass. Inf., USA — CW
CHANDLER, JAMES B., Coxswain, USN — CW
CHANDLER, STEPHEN E., Qm. Sgt., 24th N.Y. Cav., USA — CW
CHANDRON, AUGUST, Seaman Apprentice Second Class, USN — 1885
CHAPIN, ALARIC B., Pvt., 142d N.Y. Inf., USA — CW
CHAPMAN, JOHN, Pvt., 1st Maine Heavy Arty., USA — CW
CHAPUT, LOUIS G., Landsman, USN — CW
CHARETTE, GEORGE, Gunner's Mate First Class, USN — S-A
CHARLTON, CORNELIUS H., Sgt., 25th Inf. Div., USA — KC
CHASE, JOHN F., Pvt., 5th Btry., Maine Light Arty., USA — CW
CHATHAM, JOHN PURNELL, Gunner's Mate Second Class, USN — CRE
CHEEVER, BENJAMIN H., JR., 1st Lt., 6th U.S. Cav., USA — Ind
CHELI, RALPH, Major, USAAF — WW II
CHILD, BENJAMIN H., Cpl., 1st R.I. Light Arty., USA — CW
CHILDERS, ERNEST, 2d Lt., 45th Inf. Div., USA — WW II
CHILES, MARCELLUS H., Capt., 89th Div., USA — WW I
CHIQUITO, Indian Scout, USA — Ind
CHRISMAN, WILLIAM W., Pvt., 83d Ind. Inf., USA — CW
CHOATE, CLYDE L., S/Sgt., 601st T. D. Bn., USA — WW II
CHOLISTER, GEORGE ROBERT, Boatswain's Mate First Class, USN — 1924
CHRISTENSEN, DALE ELDON, 2d Lt., 112th Cav. Regt., USA — WW II
CHRISTIAN, HERBERT F., Pfc., 3d Inf. Div., USA — WW II

DAVIS, CHARLES P., Pvt., 1st N.D. Vol. Inf., USA — PI
DAVIS, CHARLES W., Major, 25th Inf. Div., USA — WW II
DAVIS, FREEMAN, Sgt., 80th Ohio Inf., USA — CW
DAVIS, GEORGE A., Lt. Col., 5th AF, USAF — KC
DAVIS, GEORGE E., 1st Lt., 10th Vt. Inf., USA — CW
DAVIS, GEORGE FLEMING, Commander, USN — WW II
DAVIS, HARRY, Pvt., 56th Ohio Inf., USA — CW
DAVIS, JOHN, Quarter Gunner, USN — CW
DAVIS, JOHN, Gunner's Mate Third Class, USN — S-A
DAVIS, JOHN, Ordinary Seaman, USN — 1881
DAVIS, JOHN, Pvt., 17th Ind. Mtd. Inf., USA — CW
DAVIS, JOSEPH, Cpl., 104th Ohio Inf., USA — CW
DAVIS, JOSEPH H., Landsman, USN — 1886
DAVIS, MARTIN K., Sgt., 116th Ill. Inf., USA — CW
DAVIS, RAYMOND E., Quartermaster Third Class, USN — 1905
DAVIS, RAYMOND G., Col., USMC — KC
DAVIS, SAMUEL W., Ordinary Seaman, USN — CW
DAWSON, MICHAEL, Trumpeter, 6th U.S. Cav., USA — Ind
DAY, CHARLES, Pvt., 210th Pa. Inf., USA — CW
DAY, DAVID F., Pvt., 57th Ohio Inf., USA — CW
DAY, MATTHIAS W., 2d Lt., 9th U.S. Cav., USA — Ind
DAY, WILLIAM L., 1st Sgt., 5th U.S. Cav., USA — Ind
DEALEY, CHARLES, Boatswain's Mate, USN — CW
DEALEY, SAMUEL DAVID, Commander, USN — WW II
DEAN, WILLIAM F., Maj. Gen., 24th Inf. Div., USA — KC
DEANE, JOHN M., Major, 29th Mass. Inf., USA — CW
DeARMOND, WILLIAM, Sgt., 5th U.S. Inf., USA — Ind
DEARY, GEORGE, Sgt., 5th U.S. Cav., USA — Ind
De BLANC, JEFFERSON JOSEPH, Capt., USMCR — WW II
DeCASTRO, JOSEPH H., Cpl., 19th Mass. Inf., USA — CW
DeCESNOLA, LOUIS P., Col., 4th N.Y. Cav., USA — CW
DECKER, PERCY A., Boatswain's Mate Second Class, USN — VC
DEETLINE, FREDERICK, Pvt., 7th U.S. Cav., USA — Ind
De FRANZO, ARTHUR F., S/Sgt., 1st Inf. Div., USA — WW II
DeGLOPPER, CHARLES N., Pfc., 325th Glider Inf., 82d Airborne Div., USA — WW II
DEIGNAN, OSBORN, Coxswain, USN — S-A
DeLACEY, PATRICK, 1st Sgt., 143d Pa. Inf., USA — CW
DELAND, FREDERICK N., Pvt., 40th Mass. Inf., USA — CW
DELANEY, JOHN C., Sgt., 107th Pa. Inf., USA — CW
DeLAVIE, HIRAM H., Sgt., 11th Pa. Inf., USA — CW

DELEAU, EMILE, JR., Sgt., 36th Inf. Div., USA — WW II
DEMMING, LORENZO, Landsman, USN — CW
DEMPSEY, JOHN, Seaman, USN — 1875
DEMPSTER, JOHN, Coxswain, USN — CW
DENEEF, MICHAEL, Capt. of Top, USN — 1875
DENHAM, AUSTIN, Seaman, USN — 1872
DENIG, J. HENRY, Sgt., USMC — CW
DENNIS, RICHARD, Boatswain's Mate, USN — CW
DENNY, JOHN, Sgt., 9th U.S. Cav., USA — Ind
DENSMORE, WILLIAM, Chief Boatswain's Mate, USN — CW
DePUY, CHARLES H., 1st Sgt., 1st Mich. Sharpshooters, USA — CW
DERVISHIAN, ERNEST H., 2d Lt., 34th Inf. Div., USA — WW II
DESIDERIO, REGINALD, Capt., 25th Inf. Div., USA — KC
De SOMER, ABRAHAM, Chief Turret Capt., USN — VC
DeSWAN, JOHN F., Pvt., 21st U.S. Inf., USA — S-A
DEWEY, DUANE E., Cpl., USMC — KC
DeWITT, RICHARD W., Cpl., 47th Ohio Inf., USA — CW
DIAMOND, JAMES H., Pfc., 24th Inf. Div., USA — WW II
DICKENS, CHARLES H., Cpl., 8th U.S. Cav., USA — Ind
DICKEY, WILLIAM D., Capt., 15th N.Y. Heavy Arty., USA — CW
DICKIE, DAVID, Sgt., 97th Ill. Inf., USA — CW
DIETZ, ROBERT H., S/Sgt., 7th Armd. Div., USA — WW II
DIGGINS, BARTHOLOMEW, Ordinary Seaman, USN — CW
DILBOY, GEORGE, Pfc., 26th Div., USA — WW I
DILLON, HUBERT, Capt., 1st Ohio Light Arty., USA — CW
DILLON, MICHAEL A., Pvt., 2d N.H. Inf., USA — CW
DITZENBACK, JOHN, Quartermaster, USN — CW
DOCKUM, WARREN C., Pvt., 121st N.Y. Inf., USA — CW
DODD, CARL H., 1st Lt., 24th Inf. Div., USA — KC
DODD, ROBERT F., Pvt., 27th Mich. Inf., USA — CW
DODDS, EDWARD E., Sgt., 21st N.Y. Cav., USA — CW
DODGE, FRANCIS S., Capt., 9th U.S. Cav., USA — Ind
DOHERTY, THOMAS M., Cpl., 21st U.S. Inf., USA — S-A
DOLLOFF, CHARLES W., Cpl., 1st Vt. Inf., USA — CW
DONAHUE, JOHN L., Pvt., 8th U.S. Cav., USA — Ind
DONALDSON, JOHN, Sgt., 4th Pa. Cav., USA — CW
DONALDSON, MICHAEL A., 42d Div., USA — WW I
DONAVAN, CORNELIUS, Sgt., 8th U.S. Cav., USA — Ind
DONOVAN, WILLIAM JOSEPH, Lt. Col., 42d Div., USA — WW I
DONELLY, JOHN S., Pvt., 5th U.S. Inf., USA — Ind
DONOGHUE, TIMOTHY, Pvt., 69th N.Y. Inf., USA — CW

DONNELLY, JOHN, Ordinary Seaman, USN — CW
DOODY, PATRICK, Cpl., 164th N.Y. Inf., USA — CW
DOOLEN, WILLIAM, Coal Heaver, USN — CW
DOOLITTLE, JAMES H., Brig. Gen., USAAF — WW II
DORAN, JOHN J., Boatswain's Mate Second Class, USN — S-A
DORE, GEORGE H., Sgt., 126th N.Y. Inf., USA — CW
DORLEY, AUGUST, Pvt., 1st La. Cav., USA — CW
DORMAN, JOHN, Seaman, USN — CW
DORSEY, DANIEL, Cpl., 33d Ohio Inf., USA — CW
DORSEY, DECATUR, Sgt., 39th U.S. Colored Troops, USA — CW
DOSS, DESMOND T., Pfc., Med. Det., 77th Inf. Div., USA — WW II
DOUGALL, ALLAN H., 1st Lt. and Adj., 88th Ind. Inf., USA — CW

DOUGHERTY, JAMES, Pvt., USMC — K-1871
DOUGHERTY, MICHAEL, Pvt., 13th Pa. Cav., USA — CW
DOUGHERTY, PATRICK, Landsman, USN — CW
DOUGHERTY, WILLIAM, Blacksmith, 8th U.S. Cav., USA — Ind
DOW, GEORGE P., Sgt., 7th N.H. Inf., USA — CW
DOW, HENRY, Boatswain's Mate, USN — CW
DOWLING, JAMES, Cpl., 8th U.S. Cav., USA — Ind
DOWNEY, WILLIAM, Pvt., 4th Mass. Cav., USA — CW
DOWNS, HENRY W., Sgt., 8th Vt. Inf., USA — CW
DOWNS, WILLIS H., Pvt., 1st N.D. Vol. Inf., USA — PI
DOZIER, JAMES C., 1st Lt., 30th Div., USA — WW I
DRAKE, JAMES M., 2d Lt., 9th N.J. Inf., USA — CW
DREXLER, HENRY CLAY, Ensign, USN (Spec. Award) — 1924
DROWLEY, JESSIE R., S/Sgt., American Inf. Div., USA — WW II
DRURY, JAMES, Sgt., 4th Vt. Inf., USA — CW
DRUSTRUP, GUNNER NIELS, Lt., USA — VC
DUKE, RAY E., Sfc., 24th Inf. Div., USA — KC
DUFFEY, JOHN, Pvt., 4th Mass. Cav., USA — CW
Du MOULIN, FRANK, Apprentice, USN — 1867
DUNCAN, ADAM, Boatswain's Mate, USN — CW
DUNCAN, JAMES K. L., Ordinary Seaman, USN — CW
DUNHAM, RUSSELL E., T/Sgt., 3d Inf. Div., USA — WW II
DUNLAP, ROBERT HUGO, Capt., USMCR — WW II
DUNLAVY, JAMES, Pvt., 3d Iowa Cav., USA — CW
DUNN, PARKER F., Pfc., 78th Inf. Div., USA — WW I
DUNN, WILLIAM, Quartermaster, USN — CW
DUNNE, JAMES, Cpl., Chicago Mercantile Btry., Ill. Light Arty., USA — CW
DUNPHY, RICHARD D., Coal Heaver, USN — CW

DuPONT, HENRY A., Capt., 5th U.S. Arty., USA — CW
DURHAM, JAMES R., 2d Lt., 12th W. Va. Inf., USA — CW
DURHAM, JOHN S., Sgt., 1st Wis. Inf., USA — CW
DURNEY, AUSTIN J., Blacksmith, USN — S-A
DUTKO, JOHN W., Pfc., 3d Inf. Div., USA — WW II
DYER, JESSE FARLEY, Capt., USMC — VC
DYESS, AQUILLA JAMES, Lt. Col., USMCR — WW II

EADIE, THOMAS, Chief Gunner's Mate, USN — 1927
ECKES, JOHN N., Pvt., 47th Ohio Inf., USA — CW
EDDY, SAMUEL E., Pvt., 37th Mass. Inf., USA — CW
EDGERTON, NATHAN H., Lt. and Adj., 6th U.S. Colored Troops, USA — CW
EDSON, MERRITT AUSTIN, Col., USMC — WW II
EDWARDS, DANIEL R., Pfc., 1st Div., USA — WW I
EDWARDS, DAVID, Pvt., 146th N.Y. Inf., USA — CW
EDWARDS, JOHN, Capt. of Top, USN — CW
EDWARDS, JUNIOR D., Sfc., 2nd Inf. Div., USA — KC
EDWARDS, WALTER ATLEE, Lt. Commander, USN — 1922
EDWARDS, WILLIAM D., 1st Sgt., 7th U.S. Inf., USA — Ind
EGGERS, ALAN LOUIS, Sgt., 27th Div., USA — WW I
EGLIT, JOHN, Seaman, USN — S-A
EHLE, JOHN WALTER, Fireman First Class, USN — S-A
EHLERS, WALTER D., S/Sgt., 1st Inf. Div., USA — WW II
EILERS, HENRY A., Gunner's Mate, USN — 1892
ELDRIDGE, GEORGE H., Sgt., 6th U.S. Cav., USA — Ind
ELLIOTT, ALEXANDER, Sgt., 1st Pa. Cav., USA — CW
ELLIOTT, MIDDLETON STUART, Surgeon, USN — VC
ELLIOTT, RUSSELL C., Sgt., 3d Mass. Cav., USA — CW
ELLIS, HORACE, Pvt., 7th Wis. Inf., USA — CW
ELLIS, WILLIAM B., Sgt., 28th Inf., 1st Div., USA — WW I
ELLIS, WILLIAM, 1st Sgt., 3d Wis. Cav., USA — CW
ELLSWORTH, THOMAS F., Capt., 55th Mass. Inf., USA — CW
ELMORE, WALTER, Landsman, USN — CW
ELROD, HENRY TALMAGE, Capt., USMC — WW II
ELSATSOOSU, Cpl., Indian Scouts, USA — Ind
ELSON, JAMES M., Sgt., 9th Iowa Inf., USA — CW
ELWOOD, EDWIN L., Pvt., 8th U.S. Cav., USA — CW
EMBLER, ANDREW H., Capt., 59th N.Y. Inf., USA — CW
EMMET, ROBERT TEMPLE, 2d Lt., 9th U.S. Cav., USA — Ind
ENDERLIN, RICHARD, Musician, 73d Ohio Inf., USA — CW
ENDL, GERALD L., S/Sgt., 32d Inf. Div., USA — WW II

ENGLE, JAMES E., Sgt., 97th Pa. Inf., USA — CW
ENGLISH, EDMUND, 1st Sgt., 2d N.J. Inf., USA — CW
ENGLISH, THOMAS, Signal Quartermaster, USN — CW
ENNIS, CHARLES D., Pvt., 1st R.I. Light Arty., USA — CW
ENRIGHT, JOHN, Landsman, USN — 1886
EPPERSON, HAROLD GLENN, Pfc., USMCR — WW II
EPPS, JOSEPH L., Pvt., 33d Inf. U.S. Vol., USA — PI
ERICKSON, JOHN P., Capt. of Forecastle, USN — CW
ERICKSON, NICK, Coxswain, USN — S-A
ERWIN, HENRY E., S/Sgt., 20th A.F., USAAF — WW II
ESSEBAGGER, JOHN, JR., Cpl., 3d Inf. Div., USA — KC
ESTES, LEWELLYN G., Capt. and Asst. Adj. Gen., Vol., USA
EUBANKS, RAY E., Sgt., 503d Para. Inf., USA — CW
EVANS, CORON D., Pvt., 3d Ind. Cav., USA — WW II
EVANS, ERNEST EDWIN, Commander, USN — CW
EVANS, IRA H., Capt., 116th U.S. Colored Troops, USA — WW II
EVANS, JAMES R., Pvt., 62d N.Y. Inf., USA — CW
EVANS, THOMAS, Pvt., 54th Pa. Inf., USA — CW
EVANS, WILLIAM, Pvt., 7th U.S. Inf., USA — CW
EVERETTS, JOHN, Gunner's Mate First Class, USN — Ind
EVERHART, FORREST E., T/Sgt., 90th Inf. Div., USA — 1898
EVERSON, ADELBERT, Pvt., 185th N.Y. Inf., USA — WW II
EWING, JOHN C., Pvt., 211th Pa. Inf., USA — CW

FACTOR, POMPEY, Pvt., Indian Scouts, USA — Ind
FADDEN, HARRY D., Coxswain, USN — 1903
FAITH, DON C., JR., Lt. Col., 7th Inf. Div., USA — KC
FALCONER, JOHN A., Cpl., 17th Mich. Inf., USA — Ind
FALCOTT, HENRY, Sgt., 8th U.S. Cav., USA — Ind
FALL, CHARLES S., Sgt., 26th Mich. Inf., USA — CW
FALLON, THOMAS T., Pvt., 37th N.Y. Inf., USA — CW
FALLS, BENJAMIN F., Color Sgt., 19th Mass. Inf., USA — CW
FANNING, NICHOLAS, Pvt., 4th Iowa Cav., USA — CW
FARDY, JOHN PETER, Cpl., USMC — WW II
FARLEY, WILLIAM, Boatswain's Mate, USN — CW
FARNSWORTH, HERBERT E., Sgt. Maj., 10th N.Y. Cav., USA
FARQUHAR, JOHN M., Sgt. Maj., 89th Ill. Inf., USA — CW
FARREN, DANIEL, Pvt., 8th U.S. Cav., USA — Ind
FASNACHT, CHARLES H., Sgt., 99th Pa. Inf., USA — CW
FASSETT, JOHN B., Capt., 23d Pa. Inf., USA — CW

FASSEUR, ISAAC L., Ordinary Seaman, USN — 1884
FEASTER, MOSHEIM, Pvt., 7th U.S. Cav., USA — Ind
FEGAN, JAMES, Sgt., 3d U.S. Inf., USA — Ind
FEMOYER, ROBERT E., 2d Lt., 711th Hvy. Bomb. Sq., USAAF — WW II
FERGUSON, ARTHUR M., 1st Lt., 36th Inf., U.S. Vol., USA — PI
FERNALD, ALBERT E., 1st Lt., 20th Maine Inf., USA — CW
FERRARI, GEORGE, Cpl., Co. D, 8th U.S. Cav., USA — Ind
FERRELL, JOHN H., Pilot, USN — CW
FERRIER, DANIEL T., Sgt., 2d Ind. Cav., USA — CW
FERRIS, EUGENE W., 1st Lt. and Adj., 30th Mass. Inf., USA — CW
FESQ, FRANK, Pvt., 40th N.J. Inf., USA — CW
FICHTER, HERMANN, Pvt., 3d U.S. Cav., USA — Ind
FIELD, OSCAR WADSWORTH, Pvt., USMC — S-A
FIELDS, JAMES H., 1st Lt., 4th Armd. Div., USA — WW II
FINKENBINER, HENRY S., Pvt., 107th Ohi Inf., USA — CW
FINN, JOHN WILLIAM, Lt., USN — WW II
FISHER, ALMOND E., 2d Lt., 45th Inf. Div., USA — WW II
FISHER, FREDERICK THOMAS, Gunner's Mate First Class, USN — PI
FISHER, HARRY, Pvt., USMC — CRE
FISHER, JOHN H., 1st Lt., 55th Ill. Inf., USA — CW
FISHER, JOSEPH, Cpl., 61st Pa. Inf., USA — CW
FITZ, JOSEPH, Ordinary Seaman, USN — PI
FITZGERALD, JOHN, Pvt., USMC — S-A
FITZPATRICK, THOMAS, Coxswain, USN — CW
FLAHERTY, FRANCIS C., Ensign, USNR — WW II
FLANAGAN, AUGUSTIN, Sgt., 55th Pa. Inf., USA — CW
FLANNAGAN, JOHN, Boatswain's Mate, USN — CW
FLANNIGAN, JAMES, Pvt., 2d Minn. Inf., USA — 1878
FLEETWOOD, CHRISTIAN A., Sgt. Maj., 4th U.S. Colored Troops, USA — CW
FLEMING, RICHARD E., Capt., USMCR — WW II
FLETCHER, FRANK FRIDAY, Rear Admiral, USN — VC
FLETCHER, FRANK JACK, Lt., USN — VC
FLOOD, THOMAS, Boy, USN — CW
FLOYD, EDWARD, Boilermaker, USN — 1905
FLUCKEY, EUGENE BENNETT, Commander, USN — WW II
FLYNN, CHRISTOPHER, Cpl., 14th Conn. Inf., USA — CW
FLYNN, JAMES E., Sgt., 6th Mo. Inf., USA — CW

GARVIN, WILLIAM, Capt. of Forecastle, USN — CW
GARY, DONALD ARTHUR, Lt. (jg), USN — WW II
GASSON, RICHARD, Sgt., 47th N.Y. Inf., USA — CW
GATES, GEORGE, Bugler, 8th U.S. Cav., USA — Ind
GAUGHAN, PHILIP, Sgt., USMC — S-A
GAUJOT, ANTOINE A., Cpl., 27th Inf., U.S. Vol., USA — PI
GAUJOT, JULIEN E., Capt., 1st U.S. Cav., USA — Mex
GAUNT, JOHN C., Pvt., 104th Ohio Inf., USA — CW
GAUSE, ISAAC, Cpl., 2d Ohio Cav., USA — CW
GAY, THOMAS H., Pvt., 8th U.S. Cav., USA — Ind
GAYLORD, LEVI B., Sgt., 29th Mass. Inf., USA — CW
GEDEON, LOUIS, Pvt., 19th U.S. Inf., USA — PI
GEIGER, GEORGE, Sgt., 7th U.S. Cav., USA — Ind
GEORGE, CHARLES, Pfc., 45th Inf. Div., USA — KC
GEORGE, DANIEL G., Ordinary Seaman, USN — CW
GEORGIAN, JOHN, Pvt., 8th U.S. Cav., USA — Ind
GERBER, FREDERICK W., Sgt. Maj., U.S. Eng., USA — CW
GERE, THOMAS P., 1st Lt. and Adj., 5th Minn. Inf., USA — Ind
GERSTUNG, ROBERT E., T/Sgt., 79th Inf. Div., USA — WW II
GESCHWIND, NICHOLAS, Capt., 116th Ill. Inf., USA — CW
GIBBONS, MICHAEL, Oiler, USN — S-A
GIBBS, WESLEY, Sgt., 2d Conn. Heavy Arty., USA — CW
GIBSON, EDWARD H., Sgt., 27th Inf., U.S. Vol., USA — PI
GIBSON, ERIC G., T/5, 3d Inf. Div., USA — WW II
GIDDINGS, CHARLES, Seaman, USN — 1876
GIFFORD, BENJAMIN, Pvt., 121st N.Y. Inf., USA — CW
GIFFORD, DAVID L., Pvt., 4th Mass. Cav., USA — CW
GILE, FRANK S., Landsman, USN — CW
GILL, FREEMAN, Gunner's Mate First Class, USN — S-A
GILLENWATER, JAMES R., Cpl., 36th Inf., U.S. Vol., USA
GILLESPIE, GEORGE L., 1st Lt., Corps of Eng., USA — PI
GILLICK, MATTHEW, Boatswain's Mate, USN — 1883
GILLIGAN, EDWARD L., 1st Sgt., 88th Pa. Inf., USA — CW
GILLILAND, CHARLES L., Cpl., 3d Inf. Div., USA — KC
GILMORE, HOWARD WALTER, Commander, USN — WW II
GILMORE, JOHN C., Maj., 16th N.Y. Inf., USA — CW
GINLEY, PATRICK, Pvt., 1st N.Y. Light Arty., USA — CW
GION, JOSEPH, Pvt., 74th N.Y. Inf., USA — CW
GIRANDY, ALPHONSE, Seaman, USN — 1901
GISBURNE, EDWARD A., Electrician Third Class, USN — VC
GIVEN, JOHN J., Cpl., 6th U.S. Cav., USA — Ind

GLAVINSKI, ALBERT, Blacksmith, 3d U.S. Cav., USA — Ind
GLOVER, T. B., Sgt., 2d U.S. Cav., USA — Ind
GLOWIN, JOSEPH ANTHONY, Cpl., USMC — Dom C
GLYNN, MICHAEL, Pvt., 5th U.S. Cav., USA — Ind
GODFREY, EDWARD S., Capt., 7th U.S. Cav., USA — Ind
GODLEY, LEONIDAS M., 1st Sgt., 22d Iowa Inf., USA — CW
GOETTEL, PHILIP, Pvt., 149th N.Y. Inf., USA — CW
GOETTLER, HAROLD ERNEST, 1st Lt., Pilot, 50th Aero Sq., Air Serv., USA — WW I
GOHEEN, CHARLES A., 1st Sgt., 8th N.Y. Cav., USA — CW
GOLDEN, PATRICK, Sgt., 8th U.S. Cav., USA — Ind
GOLDIN, THEODORE W., Pvt., 7th U.S. Cav., USA — Ind
GOLDSBERY, ANDREW E., Pvt., 127th Ill. Inf., USA — CW
GOMEZ, EDWARD, Pfc., USMC — KC
GONZALES, DAVID M., Pfc., 32d Inf. Div., USA — WW II
GANSALVES, HAROLD, Pfc., USMCR — WW II
GOODALL, FRANCIS H., 1st Sgt., 11th N.H. Inf., USA — CW
GOODBLOOD, CLAIR, Cpl., 3d Inf. Div., USA — KC
GOODMAN, DAVID, Pvt., 8th U.S. Cav., USA — Ind
GOODMAN, WILLIAM E., 1st Lt., 147th Pa. Inf., USA — CW
GOODRICH, EDWIN, 1st Lt., 9th N.Y. Cav., USA — CW
GOTT, DONALD J., 1st Lt., 8th A.F., USAAF — WW II
GORDON, NATHAN GREEN, Lt., USNR — WW II
GOULD, CHARLES G., Capt., 5th Vt. Inf., USA — CW
GOULD, NEWTON T., Pvt., 113th Ill. Inf., USA — CW
GOURAUD, GEORGE E., Capt. and Aide-de-Camp, U.S. USA — CW
GOWAN, WILLIAM H., Boatswain's Mate, USN — 1909
GRABIARZ, WILLIAM J., Pfc., 1st Cav., Div., USA — WW II
GRACE, H. PATRICK, Chief Quartermaster, USN — K-1871
GRACE, PETER, Sgt., 83d Pa. Inf., USA — CW
GRADY, JOHN, Lt., USN — VC
GRAHAM, ROBERT, Landsman, USN — CW
GRAHAM, THOMAS N., 2d Lt., 15th Ind. Inf., USA — CW
GRANT, GABRIEL, Surgeon, U.S. Vol., USA — CW
GRANT, GEORGE, Sgt., 18th U.S. Inf., USA — Ind
GRANT, LEWIS A., Col., 5th Vt. Inf., USA — CW
GRAUL, WILLIAM, Cpl., 188th Pa. Inf., USA — CW
GRAVES, ORA, Seaman, USN — WW I
GRAVES, THOMAS J., Pvt., 17th U.S. Inf., USA — S-A
GRAY, JOHN, Pvt., 5th Ohio Inf., USA — CW
GRAY, ROBERT A., Sgt., 21st Conn. Inf., USA — CW

HANFORD, EDWARD R., Pvt., 2d U.S. Cav., USA — CW
HANKS, JOSEPH, Pvt., 37th Ohio Inf., USA — CW
HANLEY, RICHARD P., Sgt., 7th U.S. Cav., USA — Ind
HANNA, MARCUS A., Sgt., 50th Mass. Inf., USA — CW
HANNA, MILTON, Cpl., 2d Minn. Inf., USA — CW
HANNEKEN, HERMAN HENRY, 2nd Lt., USMC — Haiti C
HANSCOM, MOSES C., Cpl., 19th Maine Inf., USA — CW
HANSEN, DALE MERLIN, Pvt., USMCR — WW II
HANSEN, HANS A., Seaman, USN — CRE
HANSON, JACK G., Pfc., 7th Inf. Div., USA — KC
HANSON, ROBERT MURRAY, 1st Lt., USMCR — WW II
HAPEMAN, DOUGLAS, Lt. Col., 104th Ill. Inf., USA — CW
HARBOURNE, JOHN H., Pvt., 29th Mass. Inf., USA — CW
HARCOURT, THOMAS, Ordinary Seaman, USN — CW
HARDAWAY, BENJAMIN F., 1st Lt., 17th U.S. Inf., USA — S-A
HARDENBERGH, HENRY M., Pvt., 39th Ill. Inf., USA — CW
HARDING, MOSHER A., Blacksmith, 8th U.S. Cav., USA — Ind
HARDING, THOMAS, Capt. of Forecastle, USN — CW
HARLEY, BERNARD, Ordinary Seaman, USN — CW
HARMON, AMZI D., Cpl., 211th Pa. Inf., USA — CW
HARMON, ROY W., Sgt., 91st Inf. Div., USA — WW II
HARNER, JOSEPH GABRIEL, Boatswain's Mate 2nd Class, USN — VC
HARR, HARRY R., Cpl., 31st Inf. Div., USA — WW II
HARRELL, WILLIAM GEORGE, Sgt., USMC — WW II
HARRINGTON, DANIEL, Landsman, USN — CW
HARRINGTON, DAVID, 1st Class Fireman, USN — 1884
HARRINGTON, EPHRAIM W., Sgt., 2d Vt. Inf., USA — CW
HARRINGTON, JOHN, Pvt., 6th U.S. Cav., USA — Ind
HARRIS, CHARLES D., Sgt., 8th U.S. Cav., USA — Ind
HARRIS, DAVID W., 7th U.S. Cav., USA — Ind
HARRIS, GEORGE W., Pvt., 148th Pa. Inf., USA — CW
HARRIS, JAMES H., Sgt., 38th U.S. Colored Troops, USA — CW
HARRIS, JAMES L., 2d Lt., 756th Tank Bn., USA — WW II
HARRIS, JOHN, Capt. of Forecastle, USN — CW
HARRIS, MOSES, 1st Lt., 1st U.S. Cav., USA — CW
HARRIS, SAMPSON, Pvt., 30th Ohio Inf., USA — CW
HARRIS, WILLIAM M., Pvt., 7th U.S. Cav., USA — Ind
HARRISON, BOLDEN REUSH, Seaman, USN — P-1911
HARRISON, GEORGE H., Seaman, USN — CW
HARRISON, WILLIAM KELLY, Commander, USN — VC

HART, JOHN W., Sgt., 6th Pa. Res., USA — CW
HART, WILLIAM, Machinist 1st Class, USN — S-A
HART, WILLIAM E., Pvt., 8th N.Y. Cav., USA — CW
HARTELL, LEE R., 1st Lt., 2nd Inf. Div., USA — KC
HARTIGAN, CHARLES CONWAY, Lt., USN — VC
HARTRANFT, JOHN F., Col., 4th Pa. Militia, USA — CW
HARTZOG, JOSHUA B., Pvt., 1st U.S. Arty., USA — IND
HARVEY, HARRY, Sgt., USMC — CRE
HARVEY, HARRY, Cpl., 22d N.Y. Cav., USA — CW
HARVEY, RAYMOND, Capt., 7th Inf. Div., USA — KC
HASKELL, FRANK W., Sgt. Maj., 3d Maine Inf., USA — CW
HASKELL, MARCUS M., Sgt., 35th Mass. Inf., USA — CW
HASTINGS, JOE R., Pfc., 97th Inf. Div., USA — WW II
HASTINGS, SMITH H., Capt., 5th Mich. Cav., USA — CW
HATCH, JOHN P., Brig. Gen., U.S. Vol., USA — CW
HATHAWAY, EDWARD W., Seaman, USN — CW
HATLER, M. WALDO, Sgt., 89th Div., USA — WW I
HAUGE, LOUIS JAMES, JR., Cpl., USMCR — WW II
HAUPT, PAUL, Cpl., 8th U.S. Cav., USA — Ind
HAVRON, JOHN H., Sgt., 1st R.I. Light Arty., USA — CW
HAWK, JOHN D., Sgt., 90th Inf. Div., USA — WW II
HAWKINS, CHARLES, Seaman, USN — CW
HAWKINS, GARDNER C., 1st Lt., 3d Vt. Inf., USA — CW
HAWKINS, MARTIN J., Cpl., 33d Ohio Inf., USA — CW
HAWKINS, THOMAS, Sgt. Maj., 6th U.S. Colored Troops, USA — CW
HAWKINS, WILLIAM DEAN, 1st Lt., USMCR — CW
HAWKS, LLOYD C., Pfc., Med. Det., 3d Inf. Div., USA — WW II
HAWTHORN, HARRIS S., Cpl., 121st N.Y. Inf., USA — WW II
HAWTHORNE, HARRY L., 2d Lt., 2d U.S. Arty., USA — CW
HAY, FRED S., Sgt., 5th U.S. Inf., USA — Ind
HAYDEN, CYRUS, Carpenter, USN — Ind
HAYDEN, DAVID E., Apprentice 1st Class, USN — K-1871
HAYDEN, JOHN, Apprentice, USN — WW I
HAYDEN, JOSEPH B., Quartermaster, USN — 1879
HAYES, JOHN, Coxswain, USN — CW
HAYES, THOMAS, Coxswain, USN — CW
HAYES, WEBB C., Lt. Col., 31st Inf., U.S. Vol., USA — PI
HAYNES, ASBURY F., Cpl., 17th Maine Inf., USA — CW
HAYS, GEORGE PRICE, 1st Lt., 3d Div., USA — WW I
HAYS, JOHN H., Pvt., 4th Iowa Cav., USA — CW
HEALEY, GEORGE W., Pvt., 5th Iowa Cav., USA — CW

HEARD, JOHN W., 1st Lt., 3d U.S. Cav., USA — S-A
HEARTERY, RICHARD, Pvt., 6th U.S. Cav., USA — Ind
HEDGES, JOSEPH, 1st Lt., 4th U.S. Cav., USA — CW
HEDRICK, CLINTON M., T/Sgt., 17th Airborne Div., USA — WW II
HEERMANCE, WILLIAM L., Capt., 6th N.Y. Cav., USA — CW
HEISE, CLAMOR, Pvt., 8th U.S. Cav., USA — Ind
HEISCH, HENRY WILLIAM, Pvt., USMC — CRE
HELLER, HENRY, Sgt., 66th Ohio Inf., USA — CW
HELMS, DAVID H., Pvt., 83d Ind. Inf., USA — CW
HELMS, JOHN HENRY, Sgt., USMC — 1901
HENDERSON, JOSEPH, Sgt., 6th U.S. Cav., USA — PI
HENDRIX, JAMES R., S/Sgt., 4th Armd. Div., USA — WW II
HENRECHON, GEORGE FRANCIS, Machinist's Mate 2nd Class, USN — P-1911
HENRICKSON, HENRY, Seaman, USN — S-A
HENRY, FREDERICK F., 1st Lt., 2d Inf. Div., USA — KC
HENRY, GUY V., Col., 40th Mass. Inf., USA — CW
HENRY, JAMES, Sgt., 113th Ill. Inf., USA — CW
HENRY, JOHN, 1st Sgt., 3d U.S. Cav., USA — CW
HENRY, ROBERT T., Pvt., 1st Inf. Div., USA — WW II
HENRY, WILLIAM W., Col., 10th Vt. Inf., USA — CW
HERINGTON, PITT B., Pvt., 11th Iowa Inf., USA — CW
HERIOT, JAMES D., Cpl., 30th Div., USA — WW I
HERNANDEZ, RODOLFO P., Cpl., 187th Abn. Regtl. Combt. Team, USA — KC
HERRERA, SILVESTRE S., Pfc., 36th Inf. Div., USA — WW II
HERRING, RUFUS G., Lt., USNR — WW II
HERRON, FRANCIS J., Lt. Col., 9th Iowa Inf., USA — CW
HERRON, LEANDER, Cpl., 3d U.S. Cav., USA — Ind
HESSELTINE, FRANCIS S., Col., 13th Maine Inf., USA — CW
HEYL, CHARLES H., 2d Lt., 23d U.S. Inf., USA — Ind
HIBSON, JOSEPH C., Pvt., 48th N.Y. Inf., USA — CW
HICKEY, DENNIS W., Sgt., 2d N.Y. Cav., USA — CW
HICKMAN, JOHN, Fireman 2nd Class, USN — CW
HICKOK, NATHAN E., Cpl., 8th Conn. Inf., USA — CW
HIGBY, CHARLES, Pvt., 1st Pa. Cav., USA — CW
HIGGINS, THOMAS J., Sgt., 99th Ill. Inf., USA — CW
HIGGINS, THOMAS P., Pvt., 8th U.S. Cav., USA — Ind
HIGH, FRANK C., Pvt., 2d Oreg. Vol. Inf., USA — PI
HIGHLAND, PATRICK, Cpl., 23d Ill. Inf., USA — CW
HILL, EDWARD, Capt., 16th Mich. Inf., USA — CW
HILL, EDWIN JOSEPH, Chief Boatswain, USN — WW II

HILL, FRANK, Pvt., USMC — S-A
HILL, FRANK E., Ship's Cook 1st Class, USN — 1905
HILL, FRANK E., Sgt., 5th U.S. Cav., USA — Ind
HILL, HENRY, Cpl., 50th Pa. Inf., USA — CW
HILL, JAMES, Sgt., 14th N.Y. Heavy Arty., USA — CW
HILL, JAMES, 1st Lt., 21st Iowa Inf., USA — CW
HILL, JAMES M., 1st Sgt., 5th U.S. Cav., USA — Ind
HILL, JOHN, Chief Quarter Gunner, USN — 1872
HILL, RALYN, Cpl., 33d Div., USA — WW I
HILL, WALTER NEWELL, Capt., USMC — VC
HILL, WILLIAM L., Capt. of Top, USN — 1881
HILLIKER, BENJAMIN F., Musician, 7th U.S. Cav., USA — Ind
HILLOCK, MARVIN C., Pvt., 7th U.S. Cav., USA — Ind
HILLS, WILLIAM G., Pvt., 9th N.Y. Cav., USA — CW
HILTON, ALFRED B., Sgt., 4th U.S. Colored Troops, USA — CW
HILTON, RICHMOND H., Sgt., 30th Div., USA — WW I
HIMMELSBACK, MICHAEL, Pvt., 2d U.S. Cav., USA — Ind
HINCKS, WILLIAM B., Sgt. Maj., 14th Conn. Inf., USA — CW
HINEMANN, LEHMANN, Sgt., 1st U.S. Cav., USA — Ind
HINNEGAN, WILLIAM, Fireman 2nd Class, USN — CW
HOBAN, THOMAS, Coxswain, USN — S-A
HOBDAY, GEORGE, Pvt., 7th U.S. Cav., USA — Ind
HOBSON, RICHMOND PEARSON, Naval Constructor, USN — S-A
HODGES, ADDISON J., Pvt., 47th Ohio Inf., USA — CW
HOFFMAN, HENRY, Cpl., 2d Ohio Inf., USA — CW
HOFFMAN, THOMAS W., Capt., 208th Pa. Inf., USA — CW
HOGAN, FRANKLIN, Cpl., 35th Pa. Inf., USA — CW
*HOGARTY, WILLIAM P., Pvt., 23d N.Y. Inf., USA — CW
HOLCOMB, DANIEL I., Pvt., 41st Ohio Inf., USA — CW
HOLDEN, HENRY, Pvt., 7th U.S. Cav., USA — Ind
HOLDERMAN, NELSON M., Capt., 77th Div., USA — WW I
HOLEHOUSE, JAMES, Pvt., 7th Mass. Inf., USA — CW
HOLLAND, DAVID, Cpl., 5th U.S. Inf., USA — Ind
HOLLAND, LEMUEL F., Cpl., 104th Ill. Inf., USA — CW
HOLLAND, MILTON M., Sgt. Maj., 5th U.S. Colored Troops, USA — CW
HOLLAT, GEORGE, 3rd Class Boy, USN — CW
HOLMES, LOVILO N., 1st Sgt., 2d Minn. Inf., USA — CW
HOLMES, WILLIAM T., Pvt., 3d Ind. Inf., USA — PI
HOLT, GEORGE, Quarter Gunner, USN — 1871
HOLTON, CHARLES M., 1st Sgt., 7th Mich. Cav., USA — CW

HOLTON, EDWARD A., 1st Sgt., 6th Vt. Inf., USA — CW
HOLTZ, AUGUST, Chief Watertender, USN — 1910
HOLYOKE, WILLIAM E., Boatswain's Mate 1st Class, USN — CRE
HOMAN, CONRAD, Color Sgt., 29th Mass. Inf., USA — CW
HOOKER, GEORGE, Pvt., 5th U.S. Cav., USA — Ind
HOOKER, GEORGE W., 1st Lt., 4th Vt. Inf., USA — CW
HOOPER, WILLIAM B., Cpl., 1st N.J. Cav., USA — CW
HOOVER, SAMUEL, Bugler, 1st U.S. Cav., USA — Ind
HOPKINS, CHARLES F., Cpl., 1st N.J. Inf., USA — CW
HORAN, THOMAS, Sgt., 72d N.Y. Inf., USA — CW
HORNADAY, SIMPSON, Pvt., 6th U.S. Cav., USA — Ind
HORNE, SAMUEL B., Capt., 11th Conn. Inf., USA — CW
HORNER, FREEMAN V., S/Sgt., 30th Inf. Div., USA — WW II
HORSFALL, WILLIAM H., Drummer, 1st Ky. Inf., USA — CW
HORTON, JAMES, Gunner's Mate, USN — CW
HORTON, JAMES, Capt. of Top, USN — 1879
HORTON, LEWIS A., Seaman, USN — CW
HORTON, WILLIAM CHARLIE, Pvt., USMC — CRE
HOTTENSTINE, SOLOMON J., Pvt., 107th Pa. Inf., USA — CW
HOUGH, IRA, Pvt., 8th Ind. Inf., USA — CW
HOUGHTON, CHARLES H., Capt., 14th N.Y. Arty., USA — CW
HOUGHTON, EDWARD J., Ordinary Seaman, USN — CW
HOUGHTON, GEORGE L., Pvt., 104th Ill. Inf., USA — CW
HOULTON, WILLIAM, Commissary Sgt., 1st W. Va. Cav., USA — CW
HOWARD, HENDERSON C., Cpl., 11th Pa. Res., USA — CW
HOWARD, HIRAM R., Pvt., 11th Ohio Inf., USA — CW
HOWARD, JAMES, Sgt., 158th N.Y. Inf., USA — CW
HOWARD, JAMES H., Lt. Col., USAAF — WW II
HOWARD, MARTIN, Landsman, USN — CW
HOWARD, OLIVER O., Brig. Gen., U.S. Vol., USA — CW
HOWARD, PETER, Boatswain's Mate, USN — CW
HOWE, SQUIRE E., 1st Sgt., 8th Vt. Inf., USA — CW
HOWE, ORION P., Musician, 55th Ill. Inf., USA — CW
HOWE, WILLIAM H., Sgt., 29th Mass. Inf., USA — CW
HOWZE, ROBERT L., 2d Lt., 6th U.S. Cav., USA — Ind
HUBBARD, THOMAS, Pvt., 2d U.S. Cav., USA — Ind
HUBBELL, WILLIAM S., Capt., 21st Conn. Inf., USA — CW
HUBER, WILLIAM RUSSELL, Machinist's Mate, USN — 1923
HUDSON, AARON R., Pvt., 17th Ind. Mtd. Inf., USA — CW
HUDSON, MICHAEL, Sgt., USMC — CW
HUFF, JAMES W., Pvt., 1st U.S. Cav., USA — Ind

HUFF, PAUL B., Cpl., 509th Parachute Inf. Bn., USA — WW II
HUGGINS, ELI L., Capt., 2d U.S. Cav., USA — Ind
HUGHES, JOHN ARTHUR, Capt., USMC — VC
HUGHES, LLOYD H., 2d Lt., 9th A.F., USAAF — WW II
HUGHEY, JOHN, Cpl., 2d Ohio Cav., USA — CW
HUGHS, OLIVER, Cpl., 12th Ky. Inf., USA — CW
HUIDEKOPER, HENRY S., Lt. Col., 150th Pa. Inf., USA — CW
HULBERT, HENRY LEWIS, Pvt., USMC — PI
HULL, JAMES L., Fireman 1st Class, USN — S-A
HUMPHREY, CHARLES F., 1st Lt., 4th U.S. Arty., USA — Ind
HUNT, FRED O., Pvt., 5th U.S. Inf., USA — Ind
HUNT, LEWIS T., Pvt., 6th Mo. Inf., USA — CW
HUNT, MARTIN, Pvt., USMC — CRE
HUNTER, CHARLES A., Sgt., 34th Mass. Inf., USA — CW
HUNTERSON, JOHN C., Pvt., 3d Pa. Cav., USA — CW
HUNTSMAN, JOHN A., Sgt., 36th Inf., U.S. Vol., USA — PI
HUSE, HENRY McCLAREN PINCKNEY, Capt., USN — VC
HUSKEY, MICHAEL, Fireman, USN — CW
HUTCHINS, CARLTON BARMORE, Lt., USN — 1938
HUTCHINS, JOHNNIE DAVID, Seaman 1st Class, USNR — WW II
HUTCHINSON, RUFUS D., Sgt., 7th U.S. Cav., USA — Ind
HYATT, THEODORE, 1st Sgt., 127th Ill. Inf., USA — CW
HYDE, HENRY J., Sgt., 1st U.S. Cav., USA — Ind
HYDE, THOMAS W., Major, 7th Maine Inf., USA — CW
HYLAND, JOHN, Seaman, USN — CW
HYMER, SAMUEL, Capt., 115th Ill. Inf., USA — CW

IAMS, ROSS LINDSEY, Sgt., USMC — Haiti C
ILGENFRITZ, CHARLES H., Sgt., 207th Pa. Inf., USA — CW
IMMELL, LORENZO D., Cpl., 2d U.S. Arty., USA — CW
INGALLS, LEWIS J., Pvt., 8th Vt. Inf., USA — CW
INGMAN, EINAR H., Sgt., 7th Inf. Div., USA — KC
INGRAM, JONAS HOWARD, Lt. (jg), USN — VC
INGRAM, OSMOND K., Gunner's Mate 1st Class, USN — WW I
INSCHO, LEONIDAS H., Cpl., 12th Ohio Inf., USA — CW
IRSCH, FRANCIS, Capt., 45th N.Y. Inf., USA — CW
IRLAM, JOSEPH, Seaman, USN — CW
IRVING, JOHN, Coxswain, USN — CW
IRVING, THOMAS, Coxswain, USN — CW
IRWIN, BERNARD J. D., Asst. Sur., USA — Ind
IRWIN, NICHOLAS, Seaman, USN — CW
IRWIN, PATRICK, 1st Sgt., 14th Mich. Inf., USA — CW

ITRICH, FRANZ ANTON, Chief Carpenter's Mate, USN — S-A
IZAC, EDOUARD VICTOR MICHAEL, Lt., USN — WW I

JACKSON, ARTHUR J., Pfc., USMC — WW II
JACKSON, FREDERICK R., 1st Sgt., 7th Conn. Inf., USA — CW
JACKSON, JAMES, Capt., 1st U.S. Cav., USA — Ind
JACOBSON, DOUGLAS THOMAS, Pfc., USMCR — WW II
JACOBSON, EUGENE P., Sgt. Maj., 74th N.Y. Inf., USA — CW
JAMES, ISAAC, Pvt., 110th Ohio Inf., USA — CW
JAMES, JOHN, Cpl., 5th U.S. Inf., USA — Ind
JAMES, JOHN H., Capt. of Top, USN — CW
JAMIESON, MILES, Cpl., 36th U.S. Colored Troops, USA — CW
JAMIESON, WALTER, 1st Sgt., 139th N.Y. Inf., USA — CW
*JANSON, ERNEST AUGUST, Gunnery Sgt., USMC — WW I
JARDINE, ALEXANDER, Fireman 1st Class, USN — S-A
JARDINE, JAMES, Sgt., 54th Ohio Inf., USN — CW
JARRETT, BERRIE H., Seaman, USN — VC
JARVIS, FREDERICK, Sgt., 1st U.S. Cav., USA — Ind
JECELIN, WILLIAM R., Sgt., 25th Inf. Div., USA — KC
JELLISON, BENJAMIN H., Sgt., 19th Mass. Inf., USA — CW
JENKINS, THOMAS, Seaman, USN — CW
JENNINGS, JAMES T., Pvt., 56th Pa. Inf., USA — CW
JENSEN, GOTFRED, Pvt., N. Dak. Vol. Inf., USA — PI
JERSTAD, JOHN L., Maj., USAAF — WW II
JETTER, BERNHARD, Sgt., 7th U.S. Cav., USA — Ind
JEWETT, ERASTUS W., 1st Lt., 9th Vt. Inf., USA — CW
JIM, Sgt., Indian Scouts, USA — Ind
JOHANNESSEN, JOHANNES J., Chief Watertender, USN — 1905
JOHANSON, JOHN P., Seaman, USN — S-A
JOHANSSON, JOHAN J., Ordinary Seaman, USN — S-A
JOHN, WILLIAM, Pvt., 37th Ohio Inf., USA — CW
JOHNDRO, FRANKLIN, Pvt., 118th N.Y. Inf., USA — CW
JOHNS, HENRY T., Pvt., 49th Mass. Inf., USA — CW
JOHNSEN, HANS, Chief Machinist, USN — S-A
JOHNSON, ANDREW, Pvt., 116th Ill. Inf., USA — CW
JOHNSON, ELDEN H., Pvt., 3d Inf. Div., USA — WW II
JOHNSON, FOLLETT, Cpl., 60th N.Y. Inf., USA — CW
JOHNSON, HENRY, Seaman, USN — CW
JOHNSON, HENRY, Sgt., 9th U.S. Cav., USA — Ind
JOHNSON, JAMES E., Sgt., USMC — KC
JOHNSON, JOHN, Seaman, USN — 1872
JOHNSON, JOHN, Pvt., 2d Wis. Inf., USA — CW

JOHNSON, JOSEPH E., 1st Lt., 58th Pa. Inf., USA — CW
JOHNSON, LEON W., Col., 9th A.F., USAAF — WW II
JOHNSON, LEROY, Sgt., 32d Inf. Div., USA — WW II
JOHNSON, OSCAR G., JR., Sgt., 91st Inf. Div., USA — WW II
JOHNSON, PETER, Fireman 1st Class, USN — S-A
JOHNSON, RUEL M., Maj., 100th Ind. Inf., USA — CW
JOHNSON, SAMUEL, Pvt., 9th Pa. Res., USA — CW
JOHNSON, WALLACE W., Sgt., 6th Pa. Res., USA — CW
JOHNSON, WILLIAM, Cooper, USN — 1879
JOHNSON, WILLIAM P., Landsman, USN — CW
JOHNSTON, DAVID, Pvt., 8th Mo. Inf., USA — CW
JOHNSTON, EDWARD, Cpl., 5th U.S. Inf., USA — Ind
JOHNSTON, GORDON, 1st Lt., U.S. Sig. Corps, USA — PI
JOHNSTON, HAROLD I., Pfc., 89th Div., USA — WW I
JOHNSTON, RUFUS ZENAS, Lt., USN — VC
JOHNSTON, WILLIAM J., Pfc., 45th Inf. Div., USA — WW II
JOHNSTON, WILLIE, Musician, 3d Vt. Inf., USA — CW
JONES, ANDREW, Chief Boatswain's Mate, USN — CW
JONES, CLAUD ASHTON, Commander, USN — 1916
JONES, DAVID, Pvt., 54th Ohio Inf., USA — CW
JONES, HERBERT CHARPIOT, Ensign, USNR — WW II
JONES, JOHN, Landsman, USN — CW
JONES, JOHN E., Quartermaster, USN — CW
JONES, THOMAS, Coxswain, USN — CW
JONES, WILLIAM, Capt. of Top, USN — CW
JONES, WILLIAM, 1st Sgt., 73d N.Y. Inf., USA — CW
JONES, WILLIAM H., Farrier, 2d U.S. Cav., USA — Ind
JORDAN, ABSALOM, Cpl., 3d Ind. Cav., USA — CW
JORDAN, GEORGE, Sgt., 9th U.S. Cav., USA — Ind
JORDAN, ROBERT, Coxswain, USN — CW
JORDAN, THOMAS, Quartermaster, USN — CW
JORDAN, WILLIAM R., Pfc., 24th Inf. Div., USA — KC
JOSSELYN, SIMEON T., 1st Lt., 13th Ill. Inf., USA — CW
JUDGE, FRANCIS W., 1st Sgt., 79th N.Y. Inf., USA — CW
JULIAN, JOSEPH RODOLPH, Platoon Sgt., USMCR — WW II

KAISER, JOHN, Sgt., 2d U.S. Arty., USA — CW
KALTENBACH, LUTHER, Cpl., 12th Iowa Inf., USA — CW
KANDLE, VICTOR L., 1st Lt., 3d Inf. Div., USA — WW II
KANE, JOHN, Cpl., 100th N.Y. Inf., USA — CW
KANE, JOHN R., Col., USAAF — WW II
KANE, THOMAS, Capt. of the Hold, USN — CW

Name	Conflict
KANELL, BILLIE G., Pvt., 25th Inf. Div., USA	KC
KAPPESSER, PETER, Pvt., 149th N.Y. Inf., USA	CW
KARABERIS, CHRISTOS H., Sgt., 85th Inf. Div., USA	WW II
KARNES, JAMES E., Sgt., 30th Div., USA	WW I
KARPELES, LEOPOLD, Sgt., 57th Mass. Inf., USA	CW
KATES, THOMAS WILBUR, Pvt., USMC	CRE
KATZ, PHILIP C., Sgt., 91st Div., USA	WW I
KAUFMAN, BENJAMIN, 1st Sgt., 77th Div., USA	WW I
KAUFMAN, LOREN R., Sfc., 2d Inf. Div., USA	KC
KAY, JOHN, Pvt., 8th U.S. Cav., USA	CW
KAYS, AUGUST, Cpl., 15th N.Y. Heavy Arty., USA	Ind
KEARBY, NEEL E., Col., USAAF	WW II
KEARNEY, MICHAEL, Pvt., USMC	S-A
KEATHLEY, GEORGE D., S/Sgt., 85th Inf. Div., USA	WW II
KEATING, DANIEL, Cpl., 6th U.S. Cav., USA	Ind
KEEFER, PHILIP B., Coppersmith, USN	S-A
KEELE, JOSEPH, Sgt. Maj., 182d N.Y. Inf., USA	CW
KEEN, JOSEPH S., Sgt., 13th Mich. Inf., USA	CW
KEENAN, BARTHOLOMEW T., Trumpeter, 1st U.S. Cav., USA	Ind
KEENAN, JOHN, Pvt., 8th U.S. Cav., USA	Ind
KEENE, JOSEPH, Pvt., 26th N.Y. Inf., USA	CW
KEFURT, GUS, S/Sgt., 3d Inf. Div., USA	WW II
KELLER, WILLIAM, Pvt., 10th U.S. Inf., USA	S-A
KELLEY, ANDREW J., Pvt., 17th Mich. Inf., USA	CW
KELLEY, CHARLES, Pvt., 1st U.S. Cav., USA	Ind
KELLEY, GEORGE V., Capt., 104th Ohio Inf., USA	CW
KELLEY, JOHN, Fireman 2nd Class, USN	CW
KELLEY, JONAH E., S/Sgt., 78th Inf. Div., USA	WW II
KELLEY, LEVERETT M., Sgt., 36th Ill. Inf., USA	CW
KELLEY, OVA A., Pvt., 96th Inf. Div., USA	WW II
KELLY, ALEXANDER, 1st Sgt., 6th U.S. Colored Troops, USA	CW
KELLY, CHARLES E., Cpl., 36th Inf. Div., USA	WW II
KELLY, DANIEL, Sgt., 8th N.Y. Cav., USA	CW
KELLY, FRANCIS, Watertender, USN	S-A
KELLY, JOHN D., T/Sgt., 79th Inf. Div., USA	WW II
KELLY, JOHN D., Pfc., USMC	KC
*KELLY, JOHN JOSEPH, Pvt., USMC	WW I
KELLY, JOHN J. H., Cpl., 5th U.S. Inf., USA	Ind
KELLY, THOMAS, Pvt., 6th N.Y. Cav., USA	CW
KELLY, THOMAS, Pvt., 5th U.S. Inf., USA	Ind
KELLY, THOMAS J., Cpl., Med. Det., 7th Armd. Div., USA	WW II
KELSAY, Indian Scout, USA	Ind
KELSO, JACK W., Pvt., USMC	KC
KEMP, JOSEPH, 1st Sgt., 5th Mich. Inf., USA	CW
KENDALL, WILLIAM W., 1st Sgt., 49th Ind. Inf., USA	CW
KENDRICK, THOMAS, Coxswain, USN	CW
KENNA, BARNETT, Quartermaster, USN	CW
KENNEDY, JOHN, Pvt., 2d U.S. Arty., USA	PI
KENNEDY, JOHN T., 2d Lt., 6th U.S. Cav., USA	Ind
KENNEDY, PHILIP, Pvt., 5th U.S. Inf., USA	Ind
KENNEMORE, ROBERT S., T/Sgt., USMC	KC
KENTON, CHARLES, Fireman, USN	CW
KENYON, JOHN S., Sgt., 3d N.Y. Cav., USA	CW
KENYON, SAMUEL P., Pvt., 24th N.Y. Cav., USA	CW
KEOUGH, JOHN, Capt., 67th Pa. Inf., USA	CW
KEPHART, JAMES, Pvt., 13th U.S. Inf., USA	CW
KEPPLER, REINHARDT JOHN, Boatswain's Mate 1st Class, USN	WW II
KERR, JOHN B., Capt., 6th U.S. Cav., USA	Ind
KERR, THOMAS R., Capt., 14th Pa. Cav., USA	CW
KERRIGAN, THOMAS, Sgt., 6th U.S. Cav., USA	Ind
KERSEY, THOMAS, Ordinary Seaman, USN	1876
KERSTETTER, DEXTER J., Pfc., 33d Inf. Div., USA	WW II
KESSLER, PATRICK L., Pfc., 3d Inf. Div., USA	WW II
KIDD, ISAAC CAMPBELL, Rear Admiral, USN	WW II
KIGGINS, JOHN, Sgt., 149th N.Y. Inf., USA	CW
KILBOURNE, CHARLES E., 1st Lt., Sig. C., U.S. Vol., USA	PI
KILLACKEY, JOSEPH, Landsman, USN	CRE
KILMARTIN, JOHN, Pvt., 3d U.S. Cav., USA	Ind
KIMBALL, JOSEPH, Pvt., 2d W. Va. Cav., USA	CW
KIMBRO, TRUMAN, T/4, 2d Inf. Div., USA	WW II
KINDIG, JOHN M., Cpl., 63d Pa. Inf., USA	CW
KINER, HAROLD G., Pvt., 30th Inf. Div., USA	WW II
KING, HORATIO C., Maj. & Qm., U.S. Vol., USA	CW
KING, HUGH, Ordinary Seaman, USN	1871
*KING, JOHN, Chief Watertender, USN	1901, 1909
KING, ROBERT H., Landsman, USN	CW
KING, RUFUS, JR., 1st Lt., 4th U.S. Arty., USA	CW
KINGSLEY, DAVID R., 2d Lt., USAAF	WW II
KINNAIRD, SAMUEL W., Landsman, USN	CW

KINNE, JOHN B., Pvt., 1st N. Dak. Inf., USA — PI
KINSER, ELBERT LUTHER, Sgt., USMCR — WW II
KINSEY, JOHN, Cpl., 45th Pa. Inf., USA — CW
KIRBY, DENNIS T., Maj., 8th Mo. Inf., USA — CW
KIRK, JOHN, 1st Sgt., 6th U.S. Cav., USA — Ind
KIRK, JONATHAN C., Capt., 20th Ind. Inf., USA — CW
KIRKWOOD, JOHN A., Sgt. 3d U.S. Cav., USA — CW
KISTERS, GERRY H., 2d Lt., 2d Armd. Div., USA — WW II
KITCHEN, GEORGE K., Sgt., 6th U.S. Cav., USA — Ind
KLEIN, ROBERT, Chief Carpenter's Mate, USN — 1904
KLINE, HARRY, Pvt., 40th N.Y. Inf., USA — CW
KLOTH, CHARLES H., Pvt., Chicago Mercantile Btry., Ill. Light Arty., USA
KNAAK, ALBERT, Pvt., 8th U.S. Cav., USA — Ind
KNAPPENBERGER, ALTON W., Pfc., 3d Inf. Div., USA — WW II
KNIGHT, CHARLES H., Cpl., 9th N.H. Inf., USA — CW
KNIGHT, JACK L., 1st Lt., 124th Cav. Reg., USA — WW II
KNIGHT, JOSEPH F., Sgt., 6th U.S. Cav., USA — CW
KNIGHT, NOAH O., Pfc., 3d Inf. Div., USA — KC
KNIGHT, RAYMOND L., 1st Lt., USAAF — WW II
KNOWLES, ABIATHER J., Pvt., 21st Ohio Inf., USA — CW
KNOX, EDWARD M., 2d Lt., 2d Maine Inf., USA — CW
KNOX, JOHN W., Cpl., 15th N.Y. Btry., USA — CW
*KOCAK, MATEJ, Sgt., USMC — WW I
KOELPIN, WILLIAM, Sgt., 5th U.S. Inf., USA — Ind
KOOGLE, JACOB, 1st Lt., 7th Md. Inf., USA — CW
KOSOHA, Indian Scout, USA — Ind
KOUMA, ERNEST R., M/Sgt., 2d Inf. Div., USA — KC
KOUNTZ, JOHN S., Musician, 37th Ohio Inf., USA — CW
KRAMER, FRANZ, Seaman, USN — CW
KRAMER, THEODORE L., Pvt., 188th Pa. Inf., USA — S-A
KRAUS, RICHARD EDWARD, Pfc., USMCR — WW II
KRAUSE, ERNEST, Coxswain, USN — CW
KREHER, WENDELIN, 1st Sgt., 5th U.S. Inf., USA — S-A
KRETSINGER, GEORGE, Pvt., Chicago Mercantile Btry., Ill. Light Arty., USA — Ind
KROTIAK, ANTHONY L., Pfc., 37th Inf. Div., USA — CW
KRYSYZOWSKI, EDWARD C., Capt., 2d Inf. Div., USA — WW II
KUCHNEISTER, HERMANN WILLIAM, Pvt., USMC — KC
KUDER, ANDREW, 2d Lt., 8th N.Y. Cav., USA — S-A
KUDER, JEREMIAH, Lt., 74th Ind. Inf., USA — CW

KYLE, DARWIN K., 2d Lt., 3d Inf. Div., USA — KC
KYLE, JOHN, Cpl., 5th U.S. Cav., USA — Ind
KYLE, PATRICK J., Landsman, USN — 1879

LA BELLE, JAMES DENNIS, Pfc., USMCR — WW II
LABILL, JOSEPH S., Pvt., 6th Mo. Inf., USA — CW
LADD, GEORGE, Pvt., 22d N.Y. Cav., USA — CW
LAFFEY, BARTLETT, Seaman, USN — CW
LAING, WILLIAM, Sgt., 158th N.Y. Inf., USA — CW
LAKIN, DANIEL, Seaman, USN — CW
LAKIN, THOMAS, Seaman, USN — 1874
LANDIS, JAMES P., Chief Bugler, 1st Pa. Cav., USA — CW
LANE, MORGAN D., Pvt., Sig. C., USA — CW
LANFARE, AARON S., 1st Lt., 1st Conn. Cav., USA — CW
LANGBEIN, J. C. JULIUS, Musician, 9th N.Y. Inf., USA — VC
LANGHORNE, CARY DeVALL, Surgeon, USN — CW
LANN, JOHN S., Landsman, USN — CW
LANNON, JAMES PATRICK, Lt., USN — VC
LARIMER, SMITH, Cpl., 2d Ohio Cav., USA — Ind
LARKIN, DAVID, Farrier, 4th U.S. Cav., USA — CW
LARRABEE, JAMES W., Cpl., 55th Ill. Inf., USA — WW II
LATHAM, JOHN CRIDLAND, Sgt., 27th Div., USA — WW I
LAVERTY, JOHN, Fireman, USN — CW
LAVERTY, JOHN, Fireman 1st Class, USN — 1881
LAWLEY, WILLIAM R., JR., 1st Lt., 8th A.F., USAAF — WW II
LAWRENCE, JAMES, Pvt., 8th U.S. Cav., USA — Ind
LAWS, ROBERT E., S/Sgt., 43d Inf. Div., USA — WW II
LAWSON, GAINES, 1st Sgt., 4th E. Tenn. Inf., USA — CW
LAWSON, JOHN, Landsman, USN — CW
LAWTON, HENRY W., Capt., 30th Ind. Inf., USA — CW
LAWTON, JOHN S., Sgt., 5th U.S. Cav., USA — CW
LAWTON, LOUIS B., 1st Lt., 9th U.S. Inf., USA — Box
LEAHY, CORNELIUS J., Pvt., U.S. Vol., USA — PI
LEAR, NICHOLAS, Quartermaster, USN — CW
LEE, DANIEL W., 1st Lt., 117th Cav. Rcn. Sq., USA — WW II
LEE, FITZ, Pvt., 10th U.S. Cav., USA — S-A
LEE, HUBERT L., M/Sgt., 2d Inf. Div., USA — KC
LEE, JAMES H., Seaman, USN — CW
LEIMS, JOHN HAROLD, 2nd Lt., USMCR — WW II
LEJEUNE, EMILE, Seaman, USN — 1876
LELAND, GEORGE W., Gunner's Mate, USN — CW
LEMERT, Milo, 1st Sgt., 30 Div., USA — WW I

LENIHAN, JAMES, Pvt., 5th U.S. Cav., USA — Ind
LEON, PIERRE, Capt. of Forecastle, USN — CW
LEONARD, EDWIN, Sgt., 37th Mass. Inf., USA — CW
LEONARD, JOSEPH, Pvt., USMC — PI
{*LEONARD, PATRICK, Cpl., 23d U.S. Inf., USA — Ind
{*LEONARD, PATRICK, Sgt., 2d U.S. Cav., USA — Ind
LEONARD, TURNEY W., 1st Lt., 893d T. D. Bn., USA — WW II
LEONARD, WILLIAM, Pvt., 2d U.S. Cav., USA — Ind
LEONARD, WILLIAM E., Pvt., 85th Pa. Inf., USA — CW
LESLIE, FRANK, Pvt., 4th N.Y. Cav., USA — CW
LESTER, FRED FAULKNER, Hosp. Apprentice, 1st Class, USNR — WW II
LEVERY, WILLIAM, Apprentice 1st Class, USN — S-A
LEVY, BENJAMIN, Pvt., 40th N.Y. Inf., USA — CW
LEWIS, De WITT CLINTON, Capt., 97th Pa. Inf., USA — CW
LEWIS, HENRY, Cpl., 47th Ohio Inf., USA — CW
LEWIS, SAMUEL E., Cpl., 1st R.I. Light Arty., USA — CW
LEWIS, WILLIAM B., Sgt., 3d U.S. Cav., USA — Ind
LIBAIRE, ADOLPHE, Capt., 9th N.Y. Inf., USA — CW
LIBBY, GEORGE D., Sgt., 24th Inf. Div., USA — KC
LILLEY, JOHN, Pvt., 205th Pa. Inf., USA — CW
LINDBERGH, CHARLES A., Capt., A. C. Res., USA (Spec. Award) — 1927
LINDSEY, DARRELL R., Capt., USAAF — WW II
LINDSEY, JAKE W., T/Sgt., 1st Inf. Div., USA — WW II
LINDSTROM, FLOYD K., Pfc., 3d Inf. Div., USA — WW II
LIPSCOMB, HARRY, Watertender, USN — 1910
LITTLE, HENRY F. W., Sgt., 7th N.H. Inf., USA — CW
LITTLE, THOMAS, Bugler, 8th U.S. Cav., USA — Ind
LITTLEFIELD, GEORGE H., Cpl., 1st Maine Inf., USA — CW
LITTLETON, HERBERT A., Pfc., USMC — KC
LIVINGSTON, JOSIAH O., 1st Lt. and Adj., 9th Vt. Inf., USA — CW

LLOYD, BENJAMIN, Coal Heaver, USN — CW
LLOYD, EDGAR H., 1st Lt., 80th Inf. Div., USA — WW II
LLOYD, JOHN W., Coxswain, USN — CW
LOBAUGH, DONALD R., Pvt., 32d Inf. Div., USA — WW II
LOCKE, LEWIS, Pvt., 1st N.J. Cav., USA — CW
LOGAN, HUGH, Capt. of Afterguard, USN — CW
LOGAN, JAMES M., Sgt., 36th Inf. Div., USA — WW II
LOGAN, JOHN A., Maj., 33d Inf., U.S. Vol., USA — PI
LOHNES, FRANCIS W., Pvt., 1st Nebr. Vet. Cav., USA — Ind

LOMAN, BERGER, Pvt., 33d Div., USA — WW I
LONERGAN, JOHN, Capt., 13th Vt. Inf., USA — CW
LONG, CHARLES R., Sgt., 2nd Inf. Div., USA — KC
LONG, OSCAR F., 2d Lt., 5th U.S. Inf., USA — Ind
LONGFELLOW, RICHARD M., Pvt., 1st N. Dak. Vol. Inf., USA — PI
LONGSHORE, WILLIAM H., Pvt., 30th Ohio Inf., USA — CW
LONSWAY, JOSEPH, Pvt., 20th N.Y. Cav., USA — CW
LOPEZ, BALDOMERO, 1st Lt., USMC — KC
LOPEZ, JOSE M., Sgt., 2d Inf. Div., USA — WW II
LORD, WILLIAM, Musician, 40th Mass. Inf., USA — CW
LORING, CHARLES J., JR., Major, 5th A.F., USAF — KC
LORISH, ANDREW J., Commissary Sgt., 19th N.Y. Cav. (1st N.Y. Dragoons), USA — CW
LOVE, GEORGE M., Col., 116th N.Y. Inf., USA — CW
LOVERING, GEORGE M., 1st Sgt., 4th Mass. Inf., USA — CW
LOW, GEORGE, Seaman, USN — 1881
LOWER, CYRUS B., Pvt., 13th Pa. Res., USA — CW
LOWER, ROBERT A., Pvt., 55th Ill. Inf., USA — CW
LOWRY, GEORGE MAUS, Ensign, USN — VC
LOWTHERS, JAMES, Pvt., 6th U.S. Cav., USA — Ind
LOYD, GEORGE, Sgt., 7th U.S. Cav., USA — Ind
LOYD, GEORGE, Pvt., 122d Ohio Inf., USA — CW
LUCAS, GEORGE W., Pvt., 3d Mo. Cav., USA — CW
LUCAS, JACKLYN HARRELL, Pfc., USMCR — WW II
LUCE, MOSES A., Sgt., 4th Mich. Inf., USA — CW
LUCY, JOHN, 2nd Class Boy, USN — 1876
LUDGATE, WILLIAM, Capt., 59th N.Y. Vet. Inf., USA — CW
LUDWIG, CARL, Pvt., 34th N.Y. Btry., USA — CW
LUKE, FRANK, JR., 2d Lt., Air Serv., USA — WW I
LUKES, WILLIAM F., Landsman, USN — K-1871
LUMMUS, JACK, 1st Lt., USMCR — WW II
LUNT, ALPHONSO M., Sgt., 38th Mass. Inf., USA — CW
LUTHER, FRANKLIN W., Cpl., 111th N.Y. Inf., USA — CW
LUTHER, JAMES H., Pvt., 7th Mass. Inf., USA — CW
LUTY, GOTLIEB, Cpl., 75th N.Y. Inf., USA — CW
LYELL, WILLIAM F., Cpl., 7th Inf. Div., USA — KC
LYLE, ALEXANDER GORDON, Lt. Commander, Dental Corps, USN — WW I
LYMAN, JOEL H., Qm. Sgt., 9th N.Y. Cav., USA — CW
LYON, EDWARD E., Pvt., 2d Oreg. Vol. Inf., USA — PI
LYON, FREDERICK A., Cpl., 1st Vt. Cav., USA — CW

McALWEE, BENJAMIN F., Sgt., 3d Md. Inf., USA — CW
McANALLY, CHARLES, Lt., 69th Pa. Inf., USA — CW
McBRIDE, BERNARD, Pvt., 8th U.S. Cav., USA — Ind
McBRYAR, WILLIAM, Sgt., 10th U.S. Cav., USA — Ind
McCABE, WILLIAM, Pvt., 4th U.S. Cav., USA — Ind
McCALL, THOMAS E., S/Sgt., 36th Inf. Div., USA — WW II
McCAMMON, WILLIAM W., 1st Lt., 24th Mo. Inf., USA — CW
McCAMPBELL, DAVID, Commander, USN — WW II
McCANDLESS, BRUCE, Commander, USN — WW II
McCANN, BERNARD, Pvt., 22d U.S. Inf., USA — Ind
McCARD, ROBERT HOWARD, Gunnery Sgt., USMC — WW II
McCARREN, BERNARD, Pvt., 1st Del. Inf., USA — CW
McCARTER, LLOYD G., Pvt., 503d Para. Inf. Regt., USA — WW II
McCARTHY, JOSEPH JEREMIAH, Capt., USMCR — WW II
McCARTHY, MICHAEL, 1st Sgt., 1st U.S. Cav., USA — Ind
McCARTON, JOHN, Ship's Printer, USN — 1882
McCAUSLIN, JOSEPH, Pvt., 12th W. Va. Inf., USA — CW
McCLEARY, CHARLES H., 1st Lt., 72d Ohio Inf., USA — CW
McCLELLAND, JAMES M., Pvt., 30th Ohio Inf., USA — CW
McCLERNAND, EDWARD J., 2d Lt., 2d U.S. Cav., USA — Ind
*McCLOY, JOHN, Chief Boatswain, USN — CRE, VC
McCONNELL, JAMES, Pvt., 33d Inf., U.S. Vol., USA — PI
McCONNELL, SAMUEL, Capt., 119th Ill. Inf., USA — CW
McCOOL, RICHARD MILES, JR., Lt., USN — WW II
McCORMICK, MICHAEL, Boatswain's Mate, USN — CW
McCORMICK, MICHAEL, Pvt., 5th U.S. Inf., USA — Ind
McCORNACK, ANDREW, Pvt., 127th Ill. Inf., USA — CW
McCULLOCK, ADAM, Seaman, USN — CW
McDONALD, FRANKLIN M., Pvt., 11th U.S. Inf., USA — Ind
McDONALD, GEORGE E., Pvt., 1st Conn. Heavy Arty., USA — CW
McDONALD, JAMES, Cpl., 8th U.S. Cav., USA — Ind
McDONALD, JAMES HARPER, Chief Metalsmith, USN — 1939
McDONALD, JOHN, Boatswain's Mate, USN — CW
McDONALD, JOHN WADE, Pvt., 20th Ill. Inf., USA — CW
McDONALD, ROBERT, 1st Lt., 5th U.S. Inf., USA — Ind
McDONNELL, EDWARD ORRICK, Ensign, USN — VC
McELHINNY, SAMUEL O., Pvt., 2d W. Va. Cav., USA — CW
McENROE, PATRICK H., Sgt., 6th N.Y. Cav., USA — CW
McFALL, DANIEL, Sgt., 17th Mich. Inf., USA — CW
McFARLAND, JOHN, Capt. of Forecastle, USN — CW

McGAHA, CHARLES L., M/Sgt., 25th Inf. Div., USA — WW II
McGANN, MICHAEL A., 1st Sgt., 3d U.S. Cav., USA — Ind
McGAR, OWEN, Pvt., 5th U.S. Inf., USA — Ind
McGARITY, VERNON, S/Sgt., 99th Inf. Div., USA — WW II
McGEE, WILLIAM D., Pvt., Med. Det., 76th Inf. Div., USA — WW II
McGILL, TROY A., Sgt., 1st Cav. Div., USA — WW II
McGINN, EDWARD, Pvt., 54th Ohio Inf., USA — CW
McGONAGLE, WILSON, Pvt., 30th Ohio Inf., USA — CW
McGONNIGLE, ANDREW J., Capt. and Asst. Qm., U.S. Vol., USA — CW
McGOUGH, OWEN, Cpl., 5th U.S. Arty., USA — CW
McGOVERN, ROBERT M., 1st Lt., 1st Cav. Div., USA — KC
McGOWAN, JOHN, Quartermaster, USN — CW
McGRATH, HUGH J., Capt., 4th U.S. Cav., USA — PI
McGRAW, FRANCIS X., Pfc., 1st Inf. Div., USA — WW II
McGRAW, THOMAS, Sgt., 23d Ill. Inf., USA — CW
McGUIRE, FRED HENRY, Hosp. Apprentice, USN — P-1911
McGUIRE, PATRICK, Pvt., Chicago Mercantile Btry., Ill. Light Arty., USA — CW
McGUIRE, THOMAS B., Maj., 13th A.F., USAAF — WW II
McGUNIGAL, PATRICK, Shipfitter 1st Class, USN — WW II
McHALE, ALEXANDER U., Cpl., 26th Mich. Inf., USA — CW
McHUGH, JOHN, Pvt., 5th U.S. Inf., USA — Ind
McHUGH, MARTIN, Seaman, USN — CW
McINTOSH, JAMES, Capt. of Top, USN — CW
McKAY, CHARLES W., Sgt., 154th N.Y. Inf., USA — CW
McKEE, GEORGE, Color Sgt., 89th N.Y. Inf., USA — CW
McKEEN, NINEVEH S., 1st Lt., 21st Ill. Inf., USA — CW
McKEEVER, MICHAEL, Pvt., 5th Pa. Cav., USA — CW
McKENZIE, ALEXANDER, Boatswain's Mate, USN — K-1871
McKINLEY, DANIEL, Pvt., 8th U.S. Cav., USA — Ind
McKINNEY, JOHN R., Sgt., 33d Inf. Div., USA — WW II
McKINNEY, WILLIAM, Coxswain, USN — CW
McKOWN, NATHANIEL A., Sgt., 58th Pa. Inf., USA — CW
McLAUGHLIN, ALFORD L., Sgt., USMC — KC
McLENNON, JOHN, Musician, 7th U.S. Inf., USA — Ind
McLEOD, JAMES, Capt. of Foretop, USN — CW
McLOUGHLIN, MICHAEL, Sgt., 5th U.S. Inf., USA — Ind
McMAHON, MARTIN T., Capt. and Aide-de-Camp, U.S. Vol., USA — CW
McMASTERS, HENRY A., Cpl., 4th U.S. Cav., USA — Ind
McMILLAN, ALBERT W., Sgt., 7th U.S. Cav., USA — Ind

MIZE, OLA L., M/Sgt., 3d Inf. Div., USA — KC
MOFFETT, WILLIAM A., Commander, USN — VC
MOFFITT, JOHN H., Cpl., 16th N.Y. Inf., USA — CW
MOLBONE, ARCHIBALD, Sgt., 1st R.I. Light Arty., USA — CW
MOLLOY, HUGH, Ordinary Seaman, USN — CW
MONAGHAN, PATRICK, Cpl., 48th Pa. Inf., USA — CW
MONEGAN, WALTER C., JR., Pfc., USMC — KC
MONSSEN, MONS, Chief Gunner's Mate, USN — 1904
MONTAGUE, DANIEL, Chief Master-at-Arms, USN — S-A
MONTEITH, JIMMIE W., JR., 1st Lt., 1st Inf. Div., USA — WW II
MONTGOMERY, JACK C., 1st Lt., 45th Inf. Div., USA — WW II
MONTGOMERY, ROBERT WILLIAM, Capt. of After Guard, USN — CW
MONTROSE, CHARLES H., Pvt., 5th U.S. Inf., USA — CW
MOON, HAROLD H., JR., Pvt., 5th U.S. Inf., USA — Ind
MOORE, ALBERT, Pvt., USMC — Ind
MOORE, CHARLES, Landsman, USN — CRE
MOORE, CHARLES, Seaman, USN — CW
MOORE, DANIEL B., Cpl., 11th Wis. Inf., USA — CW
MOORE, FRANCIS, Boatswain's Mate, USN — 1882
MOORE, GEORGE, Seaman, USN — CW
MOORE, GEORGE G., Pvt., 11th W. Va. Inf., USA — CW
MOORE, PHILIP, Seaman, USN — 1880
MOORE, WILBUR F., Pvt., 117th Ill. Inf., USA — CW
MOQUIN, WILLIAM, Boatswain's Mate, USN — CW
MORAN, GEORGE, Cpl., 5th U.S. Cav., USA — Ind
MORAN, JOHN, Pvt., 8th U.S. Cav., USA — Ind
MORAN, JOHN E., Capt., 37th Inf., U.S. Vol., USA — PI
MORELOCK, STERLING, Pfc., USMC — KC
MOREY, DELANO, Pvt., 82d Ohio Inf., USA — WW I
MORFORD, JEROME, Pvt., 55th Ill. Inf., USA — CW
MORGAN, GEORGE H., 2d Lt., 3d U.S. Cav., USA — CW
MORGAN, JAMES H., Capt. of Top, USN — Ind
MORGAN, JOHN C., 2d Lt., USAAF — WW II
MORGAN, LEWIS, Pvt., 4th Ohio Inf., USA — CW
MORGAN, RICHARD H., Cpl., 4th Iowa Cav., USA — CW
MORIARTY, JOHN, Sgt., 8th U.S. Cav., USA — Ind
MORRILL, WALTER G., Capt., 20th Maine Inf., USA — CW
MORIN, WILLIAM H., Boatswain's Mate 2nd Class, USN — S-A
MORRIS, JAMES L., 1st Sgt., 8th U.S. Cav., USA — Ind
MORRIS, JOHN, Cpl., USMC — 1881

MORRIS, WILLIAM, Sgt., 1st N.Y. Cav., USA — CW
MORRIS, WILLIAM W., Cpl., 6th U.S. Cav., USA — Ind
MORRISON, FRANCIS, Pvt., 85th Pa. Inf., USA — CW
MORRISON, JOHN G., Coxswain, USN — CW
MORSE, BENJAMIN, Pvt., 3d Mich. Inf., USA — CW
MORSE, CHARLES E., Sgt., 62d N.Y. Inf., USA — CW
MORSE, WILLIAM, Seaman, USN — 1880
MORTON, CHARLES W., Boatswain's Mate, USN — CW
MOSHER, LOUIS C., 2d Lt., Philippine Scouts, USN — PI
MOSKALA, EDWARD J., Pfc., 96th Inf. Div., USA — WW II
MOSTOLLER, JOHN W., Pvt., 54th Pa. Inf., USA — CW
MOTT, JOHN, Sgt., 3d U.S. Cav., USA — Ind
MOWER, CHARLES E., Sgt., 24th Inf. Div., USA — WW II
MOYER, DONALD R., Sfc., 25th Inf. Div., USA — KC
MOYLAN, MYLES, Capt., 7th U.S. Cav., USA — Ind
MULHOLLAND, ST. CLAIR A., Maj., 116th Pa. Inf., USA — CW
MULLER, JOSEPH E., Sgt., 77th Inf. Div., USA — WW II
*MULLER, PATRICK, Boatswain's Mate, USN — CW
MULLER, FREDERICK, Mate, USN — S-A
MULLIN, HUGH P., Seaman, USN — PI
MUNDELL, WALTER L., Cpl., Co. E, 5th Mich. Inf., USA — CW
MUNEMORI, SADAO S., Pfc., 442d Combat Team, USA — WW II
MUNRO, DOUGLAS ALBERT, Signalman 1st Class, USCG — WW II
MUNSELL, HARVEY M., Sgt., 99th Pa. Inf., USA — CW
MURPHY, AUDIE L., 1st Lt., 3d Inf. Div., USA — WW II
MURPHY, CHARLES J., 1st Lt. & Qm., 38th N.Y. Inf., USA — CW
MURPHY, DANIEL, Sgt., 19th Mass. Inf., USA — CW
MURPHY, DENNIS J. F., Sgt., 14th Wis. Inf., USA — CW
MURPHY, EDWARD, Pvt., 1st U.S. Cav., USA — Ind
MURPHY, EDWARD F., Cpl., 5th U.S. Cav., USA — Ind
MURPHY, FREDERICK C., Pfc., Med. Det., 65th Inf. Div., USA — WW II
MURPHY, JAMES T., Pvt., 1st Conn. Arty., USA — CW
MURPHY, JEREMIAH, Pvt., 3d U.S. Cav., USA — Ind
MURPHY, JOHN ALPHONSUS, Drummer, USMC — CRE
MURPHY, JOHN EDWARD, Coxswain, USN — S-A
MURPHY, JOHN P., Pvt., 5th Ohio Inf., USA — CW
MURPHY, MICHAEL C., Lt. Col., 170th N.Y. Inf., USA — CW
MURPHY, PATRICK, Boatswain's Mate, USN — CW
MURPHY, PHILIP, Cpl., 8th U.S. Cav., USA — Ind
MURPHY, RAYMOND G., Capt., USMC — KC

MURPHY, ROBINSON B., Musician, 127th Ill. Inf., USA — CW
MURPHY, THOMAS, Cpl., 8th U.S. Cav., USA — Ind
MURPHY, THOMAS, Cpl., 158th N.Y. Inf., USA — CW
MURPHY, THOMAS C., Cpl., 31st Ill. Inf., USA — CW
MURPHY, THOMAS J., 1st Sgt., 146th N.Y. Inf., USA — CW
MURRAY, CHARLES P., JR., 1st Lt., 3d Inf. Div., USA — WW II
MURRAY, THOMAS, Sgt., 7th U.S. Cav., USA — Ind
MURRAY, WILLIAM H., Pvt., USMC — CRE
MYERS, FRED, Sgt., 6th U.S. Cav., USA — Ind
MYERS, GEORGE S., Pvt., 101st Ohio Inf., USA — CW
MYERS, REGINALD R., Lt. Col., USMC — KC
MYERS, WILLIAM H., Pvt., Co. A, 1st Md. Cav., USA — CW

NANNASADDIE, Indian Scout, USA — Ind
NANTAJE, Indian Scout, USA — Ind
NASH, HENRY, Cpl., 47th Ohio Inf., USA — CW
NASH, JAMES J., Pvt., 10th U.S. Inf., USA — CW
NAYLOR, DAVID, Landsman, USN — S-A
NEAHR, ZACHARIAH C., Pvt., 142d N.Y. Inf., USA — CW
NEAL, SOLON D., Pvt., 6th U.S. Cav., USA — Ind
NEDER, ADAM, Cpl., 7th U.S. Cav., USA — Ind
NEE, GEORGE H., Pvt., 21st U.S. Inf., USA — S-A
NEIBAUR, THOMAS C., Pvt., 42d Div., USA — WW I
NEIL, JOHN, Quarter Gunner, USN — CW
NEILON, FREDERICK S., Sgt., 6th U.S. Cav., USA — Ind
NELSON, LAURITZ, Sailmaker's Mate, USN — S-A
NELSON, OSCAR FREDERICK, Machinist's Mate 1st Class, USN — 1905
NELSON, WILLIAM L., Sgt., 9th Inf. Div., USA — WW II
NEPPEL, RALPH G., Sgt., 83d Inf. Div., USA — WW II
NETT, ROBERT P., Capt., 77th Inf. Div., USA — WW II
NEVILLE, EDWIN M., Capt., 1st Conn. Cav., USA — CW
NEVILLE, WENDELL CUSHING, Lt. Col., USMC — VC
NEW, JOHN DURY, Pfc., USMC — WW II
NEWLAND, WILLIAM, Ordinary Seaman, USN — CW
NEWMAN, BERYL R., 1st Lt., 34th Inf. Div., USA — WW II
NEWMAN, HENRY, 1st Sgt., 5th U.S. Cav., USA — Ind
NEWMAN, MARCELLUS L., Pvt., 111th Ill. Inf., USA — CW
NEWMAN, WILLIAM H., Lt., 86th N.Y. Inf., USA — CW
NIBBE, JOHN H., Quartermaster, USN — CW
NICHOLS, HENRY C., Capt., 73d U.S. Colored Troops, USA — CW

NICHOLS, WILLIAM, Quartermaster, USN — CW
NICKERSON, HENRY NEHEMIAH, Boatswain's Mate, USN — VC
NIHILL, JOHN, Pvt., 5th U.S. Cav., USA — Ind
NININGER, ALEXANDER R., JR., 2d Lt., Philippine Scouts, USA — WW II
NISPEROS, JOSE B., Pvt., Philippine Scouts, USA — PI
NIVEN, ROBERT, 2d Lt., 8th N.Y. Cav., USA — CW
NOBLE, JOHN, Landsman, USN — CW
NOIL, JOSEPH B., Seaman, USN — 1872
NOLAN, JOHN J., Sgt., 8th N.H. Inf., USA — CW
NOLAN, JOSEPH A., Artificer, 45th Inf., U.S. Vol., USA — PI
NOLAN, RICHARD J., Farrier, 7th U.S. Cav., USA — Ind
NOLL, CONRAD, Sgt., 20th Mich. Inf., USA — CW
NORDSIEK, CHARLES LUERS, Ordinary Seaman, USN — VC
NORDSTROM, ISIDOR, Chief Boatswain, USN — 906
NORRIS, J. W., Landsman, USN — 1883
NORTH, JASPER N., Pvt., 4th Va. Inf., USA — CW
NORTON, ELLIOTT M., 2d Lt., 6th Mich. Cav., USA — CW
NORTON, JOHN R., Lt., 1st N. Y. Cav., USA — CW
NORTON, LLEWELLYN P., Sgt., 10th N.Y. Cav., USA — CW
NOYES, WILLIAM W., Pvt., 2d Vt. Inf., USA — CW
NUGENT, CHRISTOPHER, Orderly Sgt., USMC — CW
NUTTING, LEE, Capt., 61st N.Y. Inf., USA — CW

OAKLEY, WILLIAM, Gunner's Mate 2nd Class, USN — S-A
O'BEIRNE, JAMES R., Capt., 37th N.Y. Inf., USA — CW
OBREGON, EUGENE A., Pfc., USMC — KC
O'BRIEN, GEORGE H., JR., Capt., USMC — KC
O'BRIEN, HENRY D., Cpl., 1st Minn. Inf., USA — CW
O'BRIEN, OLIVER, Coxswain, USN — CW
O'BRIEN, PETER, Pvt., 1st N.Y. Cav., USA — CW
O'BRIEN, WILLIAM J., Lt. Col., 27th Inf. Div., USA — WW II
O'CALLAGHAN, JOHN, Sgt., 8th U.S. Cav., USA — Ind
O'CALLAHAN, JOSEPH TIMOTHY, Commander, USNR — WW II
O'CONNELL, THOMAS, Coal Heaver, USN — CW
O'CONNOR, JAMES F., Landsman Engineer's Force, USN — 1880
O'CONNOR, ALBERT, Sgt., 7th Wis. Inf., USA — CW
O'CONNOR, TIMOTHY, Pvt., 1st U.S. Cav., USA — CW
O'DEA, JOHN, Pvt., 8th Mo. Inf., USA — CW
O'DONNELL, MENOMEN, 1st Lt., 11th Mo. Inf., USA — CW
O'DONOGHUE, TIMOTHY, Seaman, USN — CW

OGDEN, CARLOS C., Capt., 79th Inf. Div., USA	WW II
O'HARE, EDWARD HENRY, Lt., USN	WW II
OHMSEN, AUGUST, Master-at-Arms, USN	1884
O'KANE, RICHARD HETHERINGTON, Commander, USN	WW II
OLIVER, CHARLES, Sgt., 100th Pa. Inf., USA	Ind
OLIVER, FRANCIS, 1st Sgt., 1st U.S. Cav., USA	CW
OLIVER, PAUL A., Capt., 12th N.Y. Inf., USA	S-A
OLSEN, ANTON, Ordinary Seaman, USN	WW II
OLSON, ARLO L., 3d Inf. Div., USA	WW II
OLSON, TRUMAN O., Sgt., 3d Inf. Div., USA	1872
O'NEAL, JOHN, Boatswain's Mate, USN	WW I
O'NEILL, RICHARD W., Sgt., 42d Div., USA	CW
O'NEILL, STEPHEN, Cpl., 7th U.S. Inf., USA	CW
OPEL, JOHN N., Pvt., 7th Ind. Inf., USA	CW
ORBANSKY, DAVID, Pvt., 58th Ohio Inf., USA	Ind
O'REGAN, MICHAEL, Pvt., 8th U.S. Cav., USA	WW II
ORESKO, NICHOLAS, T/Sgt., 94th Inf. Div., USA	WW I
ORMSBEE, FRANCIS EDWARD, JR., Chief Machinist's Mate, USN	WW II
ORNDOFF, HARRY WESTLEY, Pvt., USMC	CRE
ORR, CHARLES A., Pvt., 187th N.Y. Inf., USA	CW
ORR, MOSES, Pvt., 1st U.S. Cav., USA	Ind
ORR, ROBERT L., Maj., 61st Pa. Inf., USA	CW
ORTEGA, JOHN, Seaman, USN	CW
ORTH, JACOB G., Cpl., 28th Pa. Inf., USA	CW
OSBORNE, JOHN, Seaman, USN	1876
OSBORNE, WEEDON E., Lt. (jg), Dental Corps, USN	WW I
OSBORNE, WILLIAM, Sgt., 1st U.S. Cav., USA	Ind
OSBORNE, WILLIAM H., Pvt., 29th Mass. Inf., USA	CW
OSEPINS, CHRISTIAN, Seaman, USN	1882
O'SHEA, THOMAS E., Cpl., 27th Div., USA	WW I
OSS, ALBERT, Pvt., 11th N.J. Inf., USA	CW
OSTERMANN, EDWARD ALBERT, 1st Lt., USMC	Haiti
O'SULLIVAN, JOHN, Pvt., 4th U.S. Cav., USA	Ind
OUELLETTE, JOSEPH R., Pfc., 2d Inf. Div., USA	KC
OVERTURF, JACOB H., Pvt., 83d Ind. Inf., USA	CW
OVIATT, MILES M., Cpl., USMC	CW
OWENS, MICHAEL, Pvt., USMC	K-1871
OWENS, ROBERT ALLEN, Sgt., USMC	WW II
OZBOURN, JOSEPH WILLIAM, Pvt., USMCR	WW II
PACKARD, LORON F., Pvt., 5th N.Y. Cav., USA	CW
PAGE, JOHN U. D., Lt. Col., X Corps Art., USA	KC
PAIGE, MITCHELL, Platoon Sgt., USMC	WW II
PAINE, ADAM, Pvt., Indian Scouts, USA	Ind
PALMER, GEORGE H., Musician, 1st Ill. Cav., USA	CW
PALMER, JOHN G., Cpl., 21st Conn. Inf., USA	CW
PALMER, WILLIAM J., Col., 15th Pa. Cav., USA	CW
PARKER, ALEXANDER, Boatswain's Mate, USN	1876
PARKER, JAMES, Lt. Col., 45th Inf., U.S. Vol., USA	PI
PARKER, POMEROY, Pvt., USMC	S-A
PARKER, SAMUEL I., 2d Lt., 1st Div., USA	WW I
PARKER, THOMAS, Cpl., 2d R.I. Inf., USA	CW
PARKER, WILLIAM, Capt. of Afterguard, USN	CW
PARKS, GEORGE, Capt. of Forecastle, USN	CW
PARKS, JAMES W., Cpl., 11th Mo. Inf., USA	CW
PARKS, JEREMIAH, Pvt., 9th N.Y. Cav., USA	CW
PARLE, JOHN JOSEPH, Ensign, USNR	WW II
PARNELL, WILLIAM R., 1st Lt., 1st U.S. Cav., USA	Ind
PARRISH, LAVERNE, T/4, Med. Det., 25th Inf. Div., USA	WW II
PARROTT, JACOB, Pvt., 33d Ohio Inf., USA	CW
PARSONS, JOEL, Pvt., 4th Va. Inf., USA	CW
PATTERSON, JOHN H., 1st Lt., 11th U.S. Inf., USA	
PATTERSON, JOHN T., Principal Musician, 122d Ohio Inf., USA	
PAUL, WILLIAM H., Pvt., 90th Pa. Inf., USA	CW
PAY, BYRON E., Pvt., 2d Minn. Inf., USA	CW
PAYNE, IRVIN C., Cpl., 2d N.Y. Cav., USA	CW
PAYNE, ISAAC, Trumpeter, Indian Scouts, USA	Ind
PAYNE, THOMAS H. L., 1st Lt., 37th Ill. Inf., USA	CW
PEARSALL, PLATT, Cpl., 30th Ohio Inf., USA	CW
PEARSON, ALFRED L., Col., 155th Pa. Inf., USA	CW
PEASE, HARL, JR., Capt., USAAF	WW II
PEASE, JOACHIM, Seaman, USN	CW
PECK, ARCHIE A., Pvt., 77th Div., USA	WW I
PECK, CASSIUS, Pvt., 1st U.S. Sharpshooters, USA	CW
PECK, OSCAR E., 2nd Class Boy, USN	CW
PECK, THEODORE S., 1st Lt., 9th Vt. Inf., USA	CW
PEDEN, FORREST E., T/5, 3d Inf. Div., USA	WW II
PEIRSOL, JAMES K., Sgt., 13th Ohio Cav., USA	CW
PELHAM, WILLIAM, Landsman, USN	CW
PENDLETON, CHARLES F., Cpl., 3d Inf. Div., USA	KC
PENDLETON, JACK J., S/Sgt., 30th Inf. Div., USA	WW II
PENGALLY, EDWARD, Pvt., 8th U.S. Cav., USA	Ind

PENN, ROBERT, Fireman 1st Class, USN — S-A
PENNSYL, JOSIAH, Sgt., 6th U.S. Cav., USA — Ind
PENNYPACKER, GALUSHA, Col., 97th Pa. Inf., USA — CW
PENTZER, PATRICK H., Capt., 97th Ill. Inf., USA — CW
PEREGORY, FRANK D., T/Sgt., 29th Inf. Div., USA — WW II
PEREZ, MANUEL, JR., Pfc., 11th Airborne Div., USA — WW II
PERKINS, MICHAEL J., Pfc., 26th Div., USA — WW I
PERRY, THOMAS, Boatswain's Mate, USN — CW
PESCH, JOSEPH, Pvt., 1st Mo. Light Arty., USA — CW
PETERS, ALEXANDER, Boatswain's Mate 1st Class, USN — KC
PETERS, GEORGE J., Pvt., 17th Airborne Div., USA — WW II
PETERS, HENRY C., Pvt., 47th Ohio Inf., USA — 1904
PETERSEN, CARL EMIL, Chief Machinist, USN — CRE
PETERSON, ALFRED, Seaman, USN — CW
PETERSON, GEORGE, S/Sgt., 1st Inf. Div., USA — WW II
PETERSON, OSCAR VERNER, Chief Watertender, USN — WW II
PETRARCA, FRANK J., Pfc., Med. Det., 37th Inf. Div.,USA — WW II
PETTY, ORLANDO HENDERSON, Lt., Med. Corps, USNRF — WW I
PETTY, PHILIP, Sgt., 136th Pa. Inf., USA — CW
PFEIFER, LOUIS FRED, Pvt., USMC — 1901
PFISTERER, HERMAN, Musician, 21st U.S. Inf., USA — S-A
PHARRIS, JACKSON CHARLES, Lt., USN — WW II
PHELPS, CHARLES E., Col., 7th Md. Inf., USA — CW
PHELPS, WESLEY, Pfc., USMCR — WW II
PHIFE, LEWIS, Sgt., 8th U.S. Cav., USA — Ind
PHILIPSEN, WILHELM O., Blacksmith, 5th U.S. Cav., USA — Ind
PHILLIPS, GEORGE, Pvt., USMCR — WW II
PHILLIPS, GEORGE F., Machinist 1st Class, USN — S-A
PHILLIPS, JOSIAH, Pvt., 148th Pa. Inf., USA — CW
PHILLIPS, LEE H., Cpl., USMC — KC
PHILLIPS, REUBEN JASPER, Cpl., USMC — CRE
PHINNEY, SAMUEL D., Pvt., 2d U.S. Cav., USA — Ind
PHINNEY, WILLIAM, Boatswain's Mate, USN — CW
PHISTERER, FREDERICK, 1st Lt., 18th U.S. Inf., USA — CW
PHOENIX, EDWIN, Cpl., 4th U.S. Cav., USA — Ind
PICKLE, ALONZO H., Sgt., 1st Minn. Inf., USA — CW
PIERCE, CHARLES H., Pvt., 22d U.S. Inf., USA — PI
PIERCE, FRANCIS JUNIOR, Pharm. Mate 1st Class, USN — WW II
PIKE, EDWARD M., 1st Sgt., 33d Ill. Inf., USA — CW
PIKE, EMORY J., Lt. Col., 82d Div., USA — WW I
PILE, RICHARD, Ordinary Seaman, USN — 1872

PIILAAU, HERBERT K., Pfc., 2d Inf. Div., USA — KC
PINDER, JOHN J., T/5, 1st Inf. Div., USA — WW II
PINGREE, SAMUEL E., Capt., 3d Vt. Inf., USA — CW
PINKHAM, CHARLES H., Sgt. Maj., 57th Mass. Inf., USA — CW
PINN, ROBERT, 1st Sgt., 5th U.S. Colored Troops, USA — CW
PIPES, JAMES M., Capt., 140th Pa. Inf., USA — CW
PITMAN, GEORGE J., Sgt., 1st N.Y. (Lincoln) Cav., USA — CW
PITTINGER, WILLIAM, Sgt., 2d Ohio Inf., USA — CW
PITTMAN, JOHN A., Sgt., 2nd Inf. Div., USA — KC
PLANT, HENRY E., Cpl., 14th Mich. Inf., USA — CW
PLATT, GEORGE C., Pvt., 6th U.S. Cav., USA — CW
PLATTEN, FREDERICK, Sgt., 6th U.S. Cav., USA — Ind
PLIMLEY, WILLIAM, 1st Lt., 120th N.Y. Inf., USA — CW
PLOWMAN, GEORGE H., Sgt. Maj., 3d Md. Inf., USA — CW
PLUNKETT, THOMAS, Sgt., 21st Mass. Inf., USA — CW
POLOND, ALFRED, Pvt., 10th U.S. Inf., USA — S-A
POMEROY, RALPH E., Pfc., 7th Inf. Div., USA — KC
POND, GEORGE F., Pvt., 3d Wis. Cav., USA — CW
POND, JAMES B., 1st Lt., 3d Wis. Cav., USA — CW
POOLE, WILLIAM B., Quartermaster, USN — CW
POPE, EVERETT PARKER, Capt., USMC — WW II
POPE, THOMAS A., Cpl., 33d Div., USA — WW I
POPPE, JOHN A., Sgt., 5th U.S. Cav., USA — Ind
PORTER, AMBROSE, Commissary Sgt., 12th Mo. Cav., USA — CW
PORTER, DAVID DIXON, Col., USMC — PI
PORTER, DONN F., Sgt., 25th Inf. Div., USA — KC
PORTER, HORACE, Capt., Ord. Department, USA — CW
PORTER, JOHN R., Pvt., 21st Ohio Inf., USA — CW
PORTER, SAMUEL, Farrier, 6th U.S. Cav., USA — Ind
PORTER, WILLIAM, Sgt., 1st N.J. Cav., USA — CW
POST, PHILIP SIDNEY, Col., 59th Ill. Inf., USA — CW
POSTLES, JAMES PARKS, Capt., 1st Del. Inf., USA — CW
POTTER, GEORGE W., Pvt., 1st R.I. Light Arty., USA — CW
POTTER, NORMAN F., 1st Sgt., 149th N.Y. Inf., USA — CW
POWELL, WILLIAM H., Maj., 2d W. Va. Cav., USA — CW
POWER, ALBERT, Pvt., 3d Iowa Cav., USA — CW
POWER, JOHN VINCENT, 1st Lt., USMCR — WW II
POWERS, JOHN JAMES, Lt., USN — WW II
POWERS, LEO J., Pfc., 34th Inf. Div., USA — WW II
POWERS, THOMAS, Cpl., 1st U.S. Cav., USA — Ind
POWERS, WESLEY J., Cpl., 147th Ill. Inf., USA — CW
POYNTER, JAMES L., Sgt., USMC — KC

PRANCE, GEORGE, Capt. of Maintop, USN — CW
PRATT, JAMES, Blacksmith, 4th U.S. Cav., USMC — Ind
PRENDERGAST, THOMAS FRANCIS, Cpl., USMC — PI
PRENTICE, JOSEPH R., Pvt., 19th U.S. Inf., USA — CW
PRESTON, ARTHUR MURRAY, Lt., USNR — WW II
PRESTON, HERBERT IRVING, Pvt., USMC — CRE
PRESTON, JOHN, Landsman, USN — CW
PRESTON, NOBLE D., 1st Lt. & Commissary, 10th N.Y. Cav., USA —
PRICE, EDWARD, Coxswain, USN — CW
PROVINCE, GEORGE, Ordinary Seaman, USN — CW
*PRUITT, JOHN HENRY, Cpl., USMC — WW I
PRUSSMAN, ERNEST W., Pfc, 8th Inf. Div., USA — WW II
PUCKET, DONALD D., 1st Lt., USAAF — WW II
PURCELL, HIRAM W., Sgt., 104th Pa. Inf., USA — CW
PURMAN, JAMES J., Lt., 140th Pa. Inf., USA — Ind
PURVIS, HUGH, Pvt., USMC — K-1871
PUTNAM, EDGAR P., Sgt., 9th N.Y. Cav., USA — CW
PUTNAM, WINTHROP D., Cpl., 77th Ill. Inf., USA — CW
PYM, JAMES, Pvt., 7th U.S. Cav., USA — Ind
PYNE, GEORGE, Seaman, USN — CW

QUAY, MATTHEW S., Col., 134th Pa. Inf., USA — CW
QUICK, JOHN HENRY, Sgt., USMC — S-A
QUICK, JOSEPH, Coxswain, USN — 1902
QUINLAN, JAMES, Maj., 88th N.Y. Inf., USA — CW
QUINN, ALEXANDER M., Sgt., 13th U.S. Inf., USA — S-A
QUINN, PETER H., Pvt., 4th U.S. Cav., USA — PI

RAERICK, JOHN, Pvt., 8th U.S. Cav., USA — Ind
RAFFERTY, PETER, Pvt., 69th N.Y. Inf., USA — CW
RAGNAR, THEODORE, 1st Sgt., 7th U.S. Cav., USA — Ind
RAMAGE, LAWSON PATERSON, Commander, USN — WW II
RAMER, GEORGE H., 2d Lt., USMC — KC
RAND, CHARLES F., Pvt., 12th N.Y. Inf., USA — CW
RANKIN, WILLIAM, Pvt., 4th U.S. Cav., USA — Ind
RANNEY, GEORGE E., Asst. Surgeon, 2d Mich. Cav., USA — CW
RANNEY, MYRON H., Pvt., 13th N.Y. Inf., USA — CW
RANNAHAN, JOHN, Cpl., USMC — CW
RANSBOTTOM, ALFRED, 1st Sgt., 97th Ohio Inf., USA — CW
RATCLIFF, EDWARD, 1st Sgt., 38th U.S. Colored Troops, USA — CW

RAUB, JACOB F., Asst. Surgeon, 210th Pa. Inf., USA — CW
RAY, BERNARD J., 1st Lt., 4th Inf. Div., USA — WW II
RAY, CHARLES W., Sgt., 22d U.S. Inf., USA — PI
RAYMOND, WILLIAM H., Cpl., 108th N.Y. Inf., USA — CW
READ, CHARLES, Ordinary Seaman, USN — CW
READ, CHARLES A., Coxswain, USN — CW
READ, GEORGE E., Seaman, USN — CW
READ, MORTON A., Lt., 8th N.Y. Cav., USA — CW
REBMANN, GEORGE F., Sgt., 119th Ill. Inf., USA — CW
RED CLOUD, MITCHELL, JR., Cpl., 24th Inf. Div., USA — KC
REDDICK, WILLIAM H., Cpl., 33d Ohio Inf., USA — CW
REED, AXEL H., Sgt., 2d Minn. Inf., USA — CW
REED, CHARLES W., Bugler, 9th Independent Btry., Mass. Light Arty., USA —
REED, GEORGE W., Pvt., 11th Pa. Inf., USA — CW
REED, JAMES C., Pvt., 8th U.S. Cav., USA — CW
REED, WILLIAM, Pvt., 8th Mo. Inf., USA — Ind
REEDER, CHARLES A., Pvt., 12th W. Va. Inf., USA — CW
REEM, ROBERT D., 2d Lt., USMC — KC
REESE, JAMES W., Pvt., 1st Inf. Div., USA — WW II
REESE, JOHN N., JR., Pfc., 37th Inf. Div., USA — WW II
REEVES, THOMAS J., Chief Radioman, USN — WW II
REGAN, JEREMIAH, Quartermaster, USN — CW
REGAN, PATRICK, 2d Lt., 29th Div., USA — WW I
REGAN, PATRICK, Ordinary Seaman, USN — 1873
REID, GEORGE CROGHAN, Major, USMC — VC
REID, PATRICK, Chief Watertender, USN — 1910
REIGLE, DANIEL P., Cpl., 87th Pa. Inf., USA — CW
REISINGER, J. MONROE, Cpl., 150th Pa. Inf., USA — CW
RENNINGER, LOUIS, Cpl., 37th Ohio Inf., USA — CW
RESSLER, NORMAN W., Cpl., 17th U.S. Inf., USA — S-A
REYNOLDS, GEORGE, Pvt., 9th N.Y. Cav., USA — CW
RHODES, JULIUS D., Pvt., 5th N.Y. Cav., USA — CW
RHODES, SYLVESTER D., Sgt., 61st Pa. Inf., USA — CW
RICE, EDMUND, Maj., 19th Mass. Inf., USA — CW
RICH, CARLOS H., 1st Sgt., 4th Vt. Inf., USA — CW
RICHARDS, LOUIS, Quartermaster, USN — CW
RICHARDSON, WILLIAM R., Pvt., 2d Ohio Cav., USA — CW
RICHEY, WILLIAM E., Cpl., 15th Ohio Inf., USA — CW
RICHMAN, SAMUEL, Pvt., 8th U.S. Cav., USA — Ind
RICHMOND, JAMES, Pvt., 8th Ohio Inf., USA — CW

RICKENBACKER, EDWARD V., 1st Lt., Air Serv., USA — WW I
RICKETTS, MILTON ERNEST, Lt., USN — WW II
RICKSECKER, JOHN H., Pvt., 104th Ohio Inf., USA — CW
RIDDELL, RUDOLPH L., Lt., 61st N.Y. Inf., USA — CW
RILEY, THOMAS, Pvt., 1st La. Cav., USA — S-A
RILEY, JOHN PHILLIP, Landsman, USN — CW
RINGOLD, EDWARD, Coxswain, USN — CW
RIORDAN, PAUL F., 2d Lt., 34th Inf. Div., USA — WW II
RIPLEY, WILLIAM Y. W., Lt. Col., 1st U.S. Sharpshooters, USA — CW
RICE, CHARLES, Coal Heaver, USN — CW
ROACH, HAMPTON M., Cpl., 5th U.S. Cav., USA — Ind
ROAN, CHARLES HOWARD, Pfc., USMCR — WW II
ROANTREE, JAMES S., Sgt., USMC — CW
ROBB, GEORGE S., 1st Lt., 93d Inf., USA — WW I
ROBBINS, AUGUSTUS J., 2d Lt., 2d Vt. Inf., USA — CW
ROBBINS, MARCUS M., Pvt., 6th U.S. Cav., USA — Ind
ROBERTS, CHARLES CHURCH, Machinist's Mate 1st Class, USN — 1910
ROBERTS, CHARLES D., 2d Lt., 17th U.S. Inf., USA — S-A
ROBERTS, HAROLD W., Cpl., 344th Bn., Tank Corps, USA — WW I
ROBERTS, JAMES, Seaman, USN — CW
ROBERTS, OTIS O., Sgt., 6th Maine Inf., USA — CW
ROBERTSON, MAUCUS W., Pvt., 2d Oreg. Vol. Inf., USA — PI
ROBERTSON, ROBERT S., 1st Lt., 93d N.Y. Inf., USA — CW
ROBERTSON, SAMUEL, Pvt., 33d Ohio Inf., USA — CW
ROBIE, GEORGE F., Sgt., 7th N.H. Inf., USA — CW
ROBINSON, ALEXANDER, Boatswain's Mate, USN — CW
ROBINSON, CHARLES, Boatswain's Mate, USN — CW
ROBINSON, ELBRIDGE, Pvt., 122d Ohio Inf., USA — CW
ROBINSON, JAMES E., JR., 1st Lt., 63d Inf. Div., USA — WW II
ROBINSON, JAMES H., Pvt., 3d Mich. Cav., USA — CW
ROBINSON, JOHN, Pvt., 19th Mass. Inf., USA — CW
ROBINSON, JOHN, Capt. of the Hold, USN — 1867
ROBINSON, JOHN C., Brig. Gen., U.S. Vol., USA — CW
ROBINSON, JOSEPH, 1st Sgt., 3d U.S. Cav., USA — Ind
ROBINSON, ROBERT GUY, Gunnery Sgt., USMC — WW I
ROBINSON, THOMAS, Pvt., 81st Pa. Inf., USA — CW
ROBINSON, THOMAS, Capt. of Afterguard, USN — 1866
ROCHE, DAVID, 1st Sgt., 5th U.S. Inf., USA — Ind
ROCK, FREDERICK, Pvt., 37th Ohio Inf., USA — CW
ROCKEFELLER, CHARLES M., Lt., 178th N.Y. Inf., USA — CW

RODENBOUGH, THEOPHILUS F., Capt., 2d U.S. Cav., USA — CW
RODENBURG, HENRY, Pvt., 5th U.S. Inf., USA — Ind
RODRIGUEZ, CLETO, Pfc., 37th Inf. Div., USA — WW II
RODRIGUEZ, JOSEPH C., Sgt., 7th Inf. Div., USA — KC
ROEDER, ROBERT E., Capt., 88th Inf. Div., USA — WW II
ROGAN, PATRICK, Sgt., 7th U.S. Inf., USA — Ind
ROGERS, SAMUEL F., Quartermaster, USN — K-1871
ROHM, FERDINAND F., Chief Bugler, 16th Pa. Cav., USA — CW
ROMEYN, HENRY, 1st Lt., 5th U.S. Inf., USA — Ind
ROOD, OLIVER P., Pvt., 20th Ind. Inf., USA — CW
ROOKS, ALBERT HAROLD, Capt., USN — WW II
ROONEY, EDWARD, Pvt., 5th U.S. Inf., USA — Ind
ROOSEVELT, GEORGE W., 1st Sgt., 26th Pa. Inf., USA — CW
ROOSEVELT, THEODORE, JR., Brig. Gen., USA — WW II
ROSE, GEORGE, Seaman, USN — CRE
ROSS, DONALD KIRBY, Lt. Commander, USN — WW II
ROSS, FRANK F., Pvt., 1st N. Dak. Vol. Inf., USA — PI
ROSS, MARION A., Sgt. Maj., 2d Ohio Inf., USA — CW
ROSS, WILBURN K., Pfc., 3d Inf. Div., USA — WW II
ROSSBACH, VALENTINE, Sgt., 34th N.Y. Btry., USA — CW
ROSSER, RONALD E., Cpl., 2d Inf. Div., USA — KC
ROTH, PETER, Pvt., 6th U.S. Cav., USA — Ind
ROUGHT, STEPHEN, Sgt., 141st Pa. Inf., USA — CW
ROUH, CARLTON ROBERT, 1st Lt., USMCR — WW II
ROUNDS, LEWIS A., Pvt., 8th Ohio Inf., USA — CW
ROUNING, JOHANNES, Ordinary Seaman, USN — 1882
ROUNTRY, JOHN, 1st Class Fireman, USN — CW
ROUSH, J. LEVI, Cpl., 6th Pa. Res., USA — CW
ROWALT, JOHN F., Pvt., 8th U.S. Cav., USA — Ind
ROWAND, ARCHIBALD H., JR., Pvt., 1st W. Va. Cav., USA — CW
ROWDY, Sgt., Indian Scouts, USA — CW
ROWE, HENRY W., Pvt., 11th N.H. Inf., USA — Ind
ROY, STANISLAUS, Sgt., 7th U.S. Cav., USA — CW
RUD, GEORGE WILLIAM, Chief Machinist's Mate, USN — Ind
RUDOLPH, DONALD E., 2d Lt., 6th Inf. Div., USA — 1916
RUHL, DONALD JACK, Pfc., USMCR — WW II
RUIZ, ALEJANDRO RENTERIA, Pfc., 27th Inf. Div., USA — WW II
RUNDLE, CHARLES W., Pvt., 116th Ill. Inf., USA — WW II
RUSH, JOHN, 1st Class Fireman, USN — CW
RUSH, WILLIAM REES, Capt., USN — VC

RUSSELL, CHARLES L., Cpl., 93d N.Y. Inf., USA	CW
RUSSELL, HENRY P., Landsman, USN	S-A
RUSSELL, JAMES, Pvt., 1st U.S. Cav., USA	Ind
RUSSELL, JOHN, Seaman, USN	1880
RUSSELL, MILTON, Capt., 51st Ind. Inf., USA	CW
RUTHERFORD, JOHN T., 1st Lt., 9th N.Y. Cav., USA	CW
RUTTER, JAMES M., Sgt., 143d Pa. Inf., USA	CW
RYAN, DAVID, Pvt., 5th U.S. Inf., USA	Ind
RYAN, DENNIS, 1st Sgt., 6th U.S. Cav., USA	Ind
RYAN, FRANCIS T., Coxswain, USN	CRE
RYAN, PETER J., Pvt., 11th Ind. Inf., USA	CW
RYAN, RICHARD, Ordinary Seaman, USN	1876
RYAN, THOMAS JOHN, Ensign, USN	1923
SACRISTE, LOUIS J., 1st Lt., 116th Pa. Inf., USA	CW
SADLER, WILLIAM, Capt. of Top, USN	1881
SADOWSKI, JOSEPH J., Sgt., 4th Armd. Div., USA	WW II
SAGE, WILLIAM H., Capt., 23d U.S. Inf., USA	PI
SAGELHURST, JOHN C., Sgt., 1st N.J. Cav., USA	CW
SALE, ALBERT, Pvt., 8th U.S. Cav., USA	Ind
SAMPLER, SAMUEL M., Cpl., 36th Div., USA	WW I
SANCRAINTE, CHARLES F., Pvt., 15th Mich. Inf., USA	CW
SANDLIN, WILLIE, Sgt., 33d Div., USA	WW I
SANDS, WILLIAM, 1st Sgt., 88th Pa. Inf., USA	CW
SANFORD, JACOB, Pvt., 55th Ill. Inf., USA	CW
SAPP, ISAAC, Seaman, Engineers' Force, USN	1871
SARGENT, JACKSON, Sgt., 5th Vt. Inf., USA	CW
SARNOSKI, JOSEPH R., 2d Lt., USAAF	WW II
SARTWELL, HENRY, Sgt., 123d N.Y. Inf., USA	CW
SAUNDERS, JAMES, Quartermaster, USN	CW
SAVACOOL, EDWIN F., Capt., 1st N.Y. Cav., USA	CW
SAVAGE, AUZELLA, Ordinary Seaman, USN	CW
SAWELSON, WILLIAM, Sgt., 78th Div., USA	WW I
SAXTON, RUFUS, Brig. Gen., U.S. Vol., USA	CW
SAYERS, FOSTER J., Pfc, 90th Inf. Div., USA	WW II
SCANLAN, PATRICK, Pvt., 4th Mass. Cav., USA	CRE
SCANNELL, DAVID JOHN, Pvt., USMC	WW II
SCHAEFER, JOSEPH E., S/Sgt., 1st Inf. Div., USA	WW II
SCHAFFNER, DWITE H., 1st Lt., 77th Div., USA	WW I
SCHAUER, HENRY, Pfc., 3d Inf. Div., USA	WW II
SCHEIBNER, MARTIN E., Pvt., 90th Pa. Inf., USA	CW
SCHENCK, BENJAMIN W., Pvt., 116th Ill. Inf., USA	CW
SCHEPKE, CHARLES S., Gunner's Mate 1st Class, USN	1904
SCHILLER, JOHN, Pvt., 158th N.Y. Inf., USA	CW
SCHILT, CHRISTIAN FRANK, 1st Lt., USMC	Nic C
SCHLACHTER, PHILIPP, Pvt., 73d N.Y. Inf., USA	CW
SCHMAL, GEORGE W., Blacksmith, 24th N.Y. Cav., USA	CW
SCHMAUCH, ANDREW, Pvt., 30th Ohio Inf., USA	CW
SCHMIDT, CONRAD, 1st Sgt., 2d U.S. Cav., USA	CW
SCHMIDT, OSCAR, JR., Chief Gunner's Mate, USN	WW I
SCHMIDT, OTTO DILLER, Seaman, USN	1905
SCHMIDT, WILLIAM, Pvt., 37th Ohio Inf., USA	CW
SCHNEIDER, GEORGE, Sgt., 3d Md. Vet. Inf., USA	CW
SCHNELL, CHRISTIAN, Cpl., 37th Ohio Inf., USA	CW
SCHNEPEL, FRED JURGEN, Ordinary Seaman, USN	VC
SCHNITZER, JOHN, Wagoner, 4th U.S. Cav., USA	Ind
SCHOFIELD, JOHN M., Maj., 1st Mo. Inf., USA	CW
SCHONLAND, HERBERT EMERY, Commander, USN	WW II
SCHOONMAKER, JAMES M., Col., 14th Pa. Cav., USA	CW
SCHOONOVER, DAN D., Cpl., 7th Inf. Div., USA	KC
SCHORN, CHARLES, Chief Bugler, 1st W. Va. Cav., USA	CW
SCHOU, JULIUS, Cpl., 22d U.S. Inf., USA	Ind
SCHOWALTER, EDWARD R., JR., 1st Lt., 7th Inf. Div., USA	KC
SCHROEDER, HENRY F., Sgt., 16th U.S. Inf., USA	PI
SCHROETER, CHARLES, Pvt., 8th U.S. Cav., USA	Ind
SCHUBERT, MARTIN, Pvt., 26th N.Y. Inf., USA	CW
SCHUTT, GEORGE, Coxswain, USN	CW
SCHWAB, ALBERT EARNEST, Pfc., USMCR	WW II
SCHWAN, THEODORE, 1st Lt., 10th U.S. Inf., USA	CW
SCHWENK, MARTIN, Sgt., 6th U.S. Cav., USA	CW
SCOFIELD, DAVID H., Qm. Sgt., 5th N.Y. Cav., USA	CW
SCOTT, ALEXANDER, Cpl., 10th Vt. Inf., USA	CW
SCOTT, GEORGE, Pvt., 7th U.S. Cav., USA	Ind
SCOTT, JOHN M., Sgt., 21st Ohio Inf., USA	CW
SCOTT, JOHN W., Capt., 157th Pa. Inf., USA	CW
SCOTT, JOSEPH FRANCIS, Pvt., USMC	WW II
SCOTT, JULIAN A., Drummer, 3d Vt. Inf., USA	CW
SCOTT, NORMAN, Rear Admiral, USN	WW II
SCOTT, ROBERT B., Pvt., 8th U.S. Cav., USA	Ind
SCOTT, ROBERT R., Machinist's Mate 1st Class, USN	WW II
SEACH, WILLIAM, Ordinary Seaman, USN	WW II
SEAMAN, ELISHA B., Pvt., 66th Ohio Inf., USA	CW

SEANOR, JAMES, Master-at-Arms, USN — CW
SEARS, CYRUS, 1st Lt., Ohio Light Arty., USA — CW
SEAVER, THOMAS O., Col., 3d Vt. Inf., USA — CW
SEBILLE, LOUIS J., Maj., 5th A.F., USAF — KC
SEIBERT, LLOYD M., Sgt., 91st Div., USA — WW I
SEITZINGER, JAMES M., Pvt., 116th Pa. Inf., USA — CW
SELLERS, ALFRED J., Maj., 90th Pa. Inf., USA — CW
SEMPLE, ROBERT, Chief Gunner, USN — VC
SESTON, CHARLES H., Sgt., 11th Ind. Inf., USA — CW
SEWARD, GRIFFIN, Wagoner, 8th U.S. Cav., USA — CW
SEWARD, RICHARD, Paymaster's Steward, USN — CW
SEWELL, WILLIAM J., Col., 5th N.J. Inf., USA — CW
SHACKLETTE, WILLIAM SIDNEY, Hospital Steward, USN — 1905
SHAFFER, WILLIAM, Pvt., 8th U.S. Cav., USA — Ind
SHAFTER, WILLIAM R., 1st Lt., 7th Mich. Inf., USA — CW
SHAHAN, EMISIRE, Cpl., 1st W. Va. Cav., USA — CW
SHALER, ALEXANDER, Col., 65th N.Y. Inf., USA — CW
SHAMBAUGH, CHARLES, Cpl., 11th Pa. Reserves, USA — CW
SHANAHAN, PATRICK, Chief Boatswain's Mate, USN — PI
SHANES, JOHN, Pvt., 14th W. Va. Inf., USA — CW
SHAPLAND, JOHN, Pvt., 104th Ill. Inf., USA — CW
SHARP, HENDRICK, Seaman, USN — CW
SHARPLESS, EDWARD C., Cpl., 6th U.S. Cav., USA — Ind
SHAW, GEORGE C., 1st Lt., 27th U.S. Inf., USA — PI
SHAW, THOMAS, Sgt., 8th U.S. Cav., USA — Ind
SHEA, CHARLES W., 2d Lt., 88th Inf. Div., USA — WW II
SHEA, JOSEPH H., Pvt., 92d N.Y. Inf., USA — CW
SHEA, RICHARD T., JR., 1st Lt., 7th Inf. Div., USA — KC
SHEERIN, JOHN, Blacksmith, 8th U.S. Cav., USA — Ind
SHELLENBERGER, JOHN S., Cpl., 85th Pa. Inf., USA — CW
SHELTON, GEORGE M., Pvt., 23d U.S. Inf., USA — PI
SHEPARD, IRWIN, Cpl., 17th Mich. Inf., USA — CW
SHEPARD, LOUIS C., Ordinary Seaman, USN — CW
SHEPHERD, WARREN J., Cpl., 17th U.S. Inf., USA — S-A
SHEPHERD, WILLIAM, Pvt., 3d Ind. Cav., USA — CW
SHEPPARD, CARL V., Pfc., 5th U.S. Inf., USA — Ind
SHERIDAN, JAMES, Quartermaster, USN — WW II
SHERMAN, MARSHALL, Pct., 1st Minn. Inf., USA — CW
SHIEL, JOHN, Cpl., 90th Pa. Inf., USA — CW
SHIELDS, BERNARD, Pvt., 2d W. Va. Cav., USA — CW

SHIELS, GEORGE F., Surgeon, U.S. Vol., USA — PI
SHILLING, JOHN, 1st Sgt., 3d Del. Inf., USA — CW
SHINGLE, JOHN H., 1st Sgt., 3d U.S. Cav., USA — Ind
SHIPLEY, ROBERT F., Sgt., 140th N.Y. Inf., USA — CW
SHIPMAN, WILLIAM, Coxswain, USN — CW
SHIVERS, JOHN, Pvt., USMC — CW
SHOCKLEY, WILLIAM R., Pfc., 32d Inf. Div., USA — WW II
SHOEMAKER, LEVI, Sgt., 1st W. Va. Cav., USA — CW
SHOMO, WILLIAM A., Maj., 82d Tactical Rcn. Sq., USAAF — WW II
SHOPP, GEORGE J., Pvt., 191st Pa. Inf., USA — CW
SHOUP, CURTIS F., S/Sgt., 87th Inf. Div., USA — WW II
SHOUP, DAVID MONROE, Col., USMC — WW II
SHUBERT, FRANK, Sgt., 43d N.Y. Inf., USA — CW
SHUCK, WILLIAM E., JR., S/Sgt., USA — KC
SHUTES, HENRY, Capt. of Forecastle, USN — CW
SICKLES, DANIEL E., Maj. Gen., U.S. Vol., USA — CW
SICKLES, WILLIAM H., Sgt., 7th Wis. Inf., USA — CW
SIDMAN, GEORGE D., Pvt., 16th Mich. Inf., USA — CW
SIEGEL, JOHN OTTO, Boatswain's Mate 2nd Class, USN — WW I
SIGLER, FRANKLIN EARL, Pvt., USMCR — WW II
SILK, EDWARD A., 1st Lt., 100th Inf. Div., USA — WW II
SILVA, FRANCE, Pvt., USMC — CRE
SIMANEK, ROBERT E., Pfc., USMC — KC
SIMKINS, LEBBEUS, Coxswain, USN — CW
SIMMONS, JOHN, Pvt., 2d N.Y. Heavy Arty., USA — CW
SIMMONS, WILLIAM T., Lt., 11th Mo. Inf., USA — CW
SIMONDS, WILLIAM E., Sgt. Maj., 25th Conn. Inf., USA — CW
SIMONS, CHARLES J., Sgt., 9th N.H. Inf., USA — CW
SIMPSON, HENRY, Fireman 1st Class, USN — 1877
SINGLETON, FRANK, Sgt., 6th U.S. Cav., USN — Ind
SINNETT, LAWRENCE C., Seaman, USN — VC
SITMAN, WILLIAM S., Sfc., 2d Inf. Div., USA — KC
SITTER, CARL L., Maj., USMC — KC
SIVEL, HENRY, 1st Sgt., 2d Md. Vet. Inf., USA — CW
SJOGREN, JOHN C., S/Sgt., 40th Inf. Div., USA — WW II
SKAGGS, LUTHER, JR., USMCR — WW II
SKELLIE, EBENEZER, Cpl., 112th N.Y. Inf., USA — CW
SKINNER, ALEXANDER R., Capt., 35th Div., USA — WW I
SKINNER, JOHN O., Contract Surgeon, USA — Ind
SLACK, CLAYTON K., Pvt., 33d Div., USA — WW I
SLADEN, JOSEPH A., Pvt., 33d Mass. Inf., USA — CW

SLAGLE, OSCAR, Pvt., 104th Ill. Inf., USA — CW
SLATON, JAMES D., Cpl., 45th Inf. Div., USA — WW II
SLAVENS, SAMUEL, Pvt., 33d Ohio Inf., USA — CW
SLETTELAND, THOMAS, Pvt., 1st N. Dak. Inf., USA — PI
SLOAN, ANDREW J., Pvt., 12th Iowa Inf., USA — CW
SLUSHER, HENRY C., Pvt., 22d Pa. Cav., USA — CW
SMALLEY, REUBEN, Pvt., 83d Ind. Inf., USA — CW
SMALLEY, REUBEN S., Pvt., 104th Ill. Inf., USA — CW
SMITH, ALBERT JOSEPH, Pvt., USMC — 1921
SMITH, ALONZO, Sgt., 7th Mich. Inf., USA — CW
SMITH, ANDREW J., Sgt., 8th U.S. Cav., USA — Ind
SMITH, CHARLES E., Cpl., 6th U.S. Cav., USA — Ind
SMITH, CHARLES H., Coxswain, USN — CW
SMITH, CHARLES H., Col., 1st Maine Cav., USA — CW
SMITH, CORNELIUS C., Cpl., 6th U.S. Cav., USA — Ind
SMITH, DAVID L., Sgt., 1st N.Y. Light Arty., USA — CW
SMITH, DAVID M., Pfc., 2d Inf. Div., USA — KC
SMITH, EDWIN, Ordinary Seaman, USN — CW
SMITH, EUGENE P., Chief Watertender, USN — 1915
SMITH, FRANCIS M., 1st Lt., & Adj., 1st Md. Inf., USA — CW
SMITH, FRANK ELMER, Oiler, USN — CRE
SMITH, FRED E., Lt. Col., 77th Div., USA — WW I
SMITH, FURMAN L., Pvt., 34th Inf. Div., USA — WW II
SMITH, GEORGE W., Pvt., 6th U.S. Cav., USA — Ind
SMITH, HENRY I., 1st Lt., 7th Iowa Inf., USA — CW
SMITH, JAMES, Pvt., 2d Ohio Inf., USA — CW
SMITH, JAMES, Capt. of Forecastle, USN — CW
SMITH, JAMES, Seaman, USN — 1872
SMITH, JAMES, Landsman, USN — CRE
SMITH, JOHN, Capt. of Forecastle, USN — CW
SMITH, JOHN, 2nd Capt. of Top, USN — CW
SMITH, JOHN, Seaman, USN — 1880
SMITH, JOHN LUCIAN, Maj., USMC — WW II
SMITH, JOSEPH S., Lt. Col. & Commissary, 2d Army Corps, USA — CW
SMITH, MAYNARD H., Sgt., 432d Bomb Sq., USAAF — WW II
SMITH, OLOFF, Coxswain, USN — CW
SMITH, OTIS W., Pvt., 95th Ohio Inf., USA — CW
SMITH, OTTO, Pvt., 8th U.S. Cav., USA — Ind
SMITH, RICHARD, Pvt., 95th N.Y. Inf., USA — CW
SMITH, ROBERT, Pvt., 3d U.S. Inf., USA — Ind
SMITH, S. RODMOND, Capt., 4th Del. Inf., USA — CW

SMITH, THADDEUS S., Cpl., 6th Pa. Res. Inf., USA — CW
SMITH, THEODORE F., Pvt., 1st U.S. Cav., USA — Ind
SMITH, THOMAS, Seaman, USN — CW
SMITH, THOMAS, Pvt., 1st U.S. Cav., USA — Ind
SMITH, THOMAS, Seaman, USN — 1878
SMITH, THOMAS J., Pvt., 1st U.S. Cav., USA — Ind
SMITH, WALTER, Ordinary Seaman, USN — CW
SMITH, WILHELM, Gunner's Mate 1st Class, USN — 1916
SMITH, WILLARD M., Cpl., USMC — CW
SMITH, WILLIAM, Quartermaster, USN — CW
SMITH, WILLIAM, Pvt., 8th U.S. Cav., USA — Ind
SMITH, WILLIAM H., Pvt., 1st U.S. Cav., USA — Ind
SMITH, WILSON, Cpl., 3d N.Y. Light Arty., USA — CW
SNEDDEN, JAMES, Musician, 54th Pa. Inf., USA — CW
SNOW, ELMER A., Trumpeter, 3d U.S. Cav., USA — Ind
SNYDER, WILLIAM E., Chief Electrician, USN — 1910
SODERMAN, WILLIAM A., Pfc., 2d Inf. Div., USA — WW II
SORENSON, RICHARD KEITH, Pvt., USMCR — WW II
SOUTHARD, DAVID, Sgt., 1st N.J. Cav., USA — CW
SOVA, JOSEPH E., Saddler, 8th N.Y. Cav., USA — CW
SOWERS, MICHAEL, Pvt., 4th Pa. Cav., USA — CW
SPALDING, EDWARD B., Sgt., 52d Ill. Inf., USA — CW
SPECKER, JOE C., Sgt., 48th Engr. Bn., USA — WW II
SPENCE, ORIZOBA, Pvt., 8th U.S. Cav., USA — Ind
SPERRY, WILLIAM J., Maj., 6th Vt. Inf., USA — CW
SPEICHER, CLIFTON T., Cpl., 40th Inf. Div., USA — KC
SPICER, WILLIAM, Gunner's Mate 1st Class, USN — S-A
SPILLANE, TIMOTHY, Pvt., 16th Pa. Cav., USA — CW
SPRAGUE, BENONA, Cpl., 116th Ill. Inf., USA — CW
SPRAGUE, JOHN W., Col., 63d Ohio Inf., USA — CW
SPRINGER, GEORGE, Pvt., 1st U.S. Cav., USA — Ind
SPROWLE, DAVID, Orderly Sgt., USMC — CW
SPURLING, ANDREW B., Lt. Col., 2d Maine Cav., USA — CW
SPURRIER, JUNIOR J., S/Sgt., 35th Inf. Div., USA — WW II
SQUIRES, JOHN C., Sgt., 3d Inf. Div., USA — WW II
STACEY, CHARLES, Pvt., 55th Ohio Inf., USA — CW
STACY, WILLIAM B., Seaman, USN — 1866
STAHEL, JULIUS, Maj. Gen., U.S. Vol., USA — CW
STANCE, EMANUEL, Sgt., 9th U.S. Cav., USA — Ind
STANLEY, DAVID S., Maj. Gen. U.S. Vol., USA — CW
STANLEY, EBEN, Pvt., 5th U.S. Cav., USA — Ind
STANLEY, EDWARD, Cpl., 8th U.S. Cav., USA — Ind

STANLEY, ROBERT, Hosp. Apprentice, USN — CRE
STANLEY, WILLIAM A., Shell Man, USN — CW
STANTON, THOMAS, Chief Machinist's Mate, USN — 1910
STARKINS, JOHN H., Sgt., 34th N.Y. Btry., USA — CW
STATON, ADOLPHUS, Lt., USN — VC
STAUFFER, RUDOLPH, 1st Sgt., 5th U.S. Cav., USA — Ind
STEELE, JOHN W., Maj. & Aide-de-Camp, U.S. Vol., USA — CW
STEIN, TONY, Cpl., USMCR — WW II
STEINER, CHRISTIAN, Saddler, 8th U.S. Cav., USA — Ind
STEINMETZ, WILLIAM, Pvt., 83d Ind. Inf., USA — CW
STEPHENS, WILLIAM G., Pvt., Chicago Mercantile Btry., Ill. Light Arty., USA — CW
STERLING, JAMES E., Coal Heaver, USN — CW
STERLING, JOHN T., Pvt., 11th Ind. Inf., USA — CW
STEVENS, DANIEL D., Quartermaster, USN — CW
STEVENS, HAZARD, Capt. & Asst. Adj. Gen., U.S. Vol., USA — CW
STEVENS, THOMAS W., Pvt., 7th U.S. Cav., USA — Ind
STEWART, BENJAMIN F., Pvt., 7th U.S. Cav., USA — Ind
STEWART, GEORGE E., 2d Lt., 19th U.S. Inf., USA — PI
STEWART, GEORGE W., 1st Sgt., 1st N.J. Cav., USA — CW
STEWART, JAMES A. Cpl., USMC — 1872
STEWART, JOSEPH, Pvt., 1st Md. Inf., USA — CW
STEWART, PETER, Gunnery Sgt., USMC — CRE
STICKLES, JOSEPH, Sgt., 83d Ohio Inf., USA — CW
STOCKOFFER, JULIUS H., Saddler, 8th U.S. Cav., USA — CW
STICKNEY, HERMAN OSMAN, Commander, USN — VC
STOCKHAM, FRED W., Gunnery Sgt., USMC — WW I
STOCKMAN, GEORGE H., 1st Lt., 6th Mo. Inf., USA — CW
STODDARD, JAMES, Seaman, USN — CW
STOKES, ALONZO, 1st Sgt., 6th U.S. Cav., USA — Ind
STOKES, GEORGE, Pvt., 122d Ill. Inf., USA — CW
STOKES, JOHN, Chief Master-at-Arms, USN — PI
STOLTENBERG, ANDREW V., Gunner's Mate 2nd Class, USN — PI
STOLZ, FRANK, Pvt., 83d Ind. Inf., USA — CW
STONE, JAMES L., 1st Lt. 1st Cav. Div., USA — KC
STOREY, JOHN H. R., Sgt., 109th Pa. Inf., USA — CW
STORY, LUTHER H., Pfc., 2d Inf. Div., USA — KC
STOUT, RICHARD, Landsman, USN — CW
STRAHAN, ROBERT, Capt. of Top, USN — CW
STRAUB, PAUL F., Surgeon, U.S. Vol., USA — PI

STRAUSBAUGH, BERNARD A., 1st Sgt., 3d Md. Inf., USA — CW
STRAYER, WILLIAM H., Pvt., 3d U.S. Cav., USA — Ind
STREET, GEORGE LEVICK, III, Commander, USN — WW II
STREILE, CHRISTIAN, Pvt., 1st N.J. Cav., USA — CW
STRIVSON, BENONI, Pvt., 8th U.S. Cav., USA — Ind
STRONG, JAMES N., Sgt., 49th Mass. Inf., USA — CW
STRYKER, STUART S., Pfc., 17th Airborne Div., USA — WW II
STUPKA, LADDIE, Fireman 1st Class, USN — 1903
SUDUT, JEROME A., 2d Lt., 25th Inf. Div., USA — KC
STURGEON, JAMES K., Pvt., 46th Ohio Inf., USA — CW
SULLIVAN, DANIEL AUGUSTUS JOSEPH, Ensign, USNRF — WW I
SULLIVAN, EDWARD, Pvt., USMC — S-A
SULLIVAN, JAMES, Ordinary Seaman, USN — CW
SULLIVAN, JAMES F., Boatswain's Mate, USN — 1882
SULLIVAN, JOHN, Seaman, USN — CW
SULLIVAN, THOMAS, Pvt., 1st U.S. Cav., USA — Ind
SULLIVAN, THOMAS, Pvt., 7th U.S. Cav., USA — Ind
SULLIVAN, TIMOTHY, Coxswain, USN — CW
SUMMERS, JAMES C., Pvt., 4th W. Va. Inf., USA — CW
SUMMERS, ROBERT, Chief Quartermaster, USN — CW
SUMNER, JAMES, Pvt., 1st U.S. Cav., USA — Ind
SUNDQUIST, AXEL, Chief Carpenter's Mate, USN — S-A
SUNDQUIST, GUSTAV A., Ordinary Seaman, USN — S-A
SURLES, WILLIAM H., Pvt., 2d Ohio Inf., USA — CW
SUTHERLAND, JOHN A., Cpl., 8th U.S. Cav., USA — Ind
SUTTON, CLARENCE EDWIN, Sgt., USMC — CRE
SWAN, CHARLES A., Pvt., 4th Iowa Cav., USA — CW
SWANSON, JOHN, Seaman, USN — CW
SWAP, JACOB E., Pvt., 83d Pa. Inf., USA — CW
SWATTON, EDWARD, Seaman, USN — CW
SWAYNE, WAGER, Lt. Col., 43d Ohio Inf., USA — CW
SWEARER, BENJAMIN, Seaman, USN — CW
SWEATT, JOSEPH S. G., Pvt., 6th Mass. Inf., USA — CW
SWEENEY, JAMES, Pvt., 1st Vt. Cav., USA — CW
*SWEENEY, ROBERT, Ordinary Seaman, USN — 1881, 1883
SWEENEY, WILLIAM, Landsman Engineer's Force, USN — 1880
SWEGHEIMER, JACOB, Pvt., 54th Ohio Inf., USA — CW
SWETT, JAMES ELMS, 1st Lt., USMCR — WW II
SWIFT, FREDERIC W., Lt. Col., 17th Mich. Inf., USA — CW
SWIFT, HARLAN J., 2d Lt., 2d N.Y. Militia Regt., USA — CW
SYPE, PETER, Pvt., 47th Ohio Inf., USA — CW

VOKES, LEROY H., 1st Lt., 3d U.S. Cav., USA	Ind
VOLZ, JACOB, Carpenter's Mate, USN	P-1911
VOLZ, ROBERT, Seaman, USN	S-A
VON MEDEM, RUDOLPH, Sgt., 5th U.S. Cav., USA	Ind
VON SCHLICK, ROBERT H., Pvt., 9th U.S. Inf., USA	Box
VON VEGESACK, ERNEST, Maj. and Aide-de-Camp, U.S. Vol., USA	CW
VOSLER, FORREST L., T/Sgt., USAAF	WW II
WAALER, REIDAR, Sgt., 27th Div., USA	WW I
WAGEMAN, JOHN H., Pvt., 60th Ohio Inf., USA	CW
WAGG, MAURICE, Coxswain, USN	CW
WAGNER, JOHN W., Cpl., 8th Mo. Inf., USA	CW
WAHLEN, GEORGE EDWARD, Pharmacist's Mate 2nd Class, USN	WW II
WAINWRIGHT, JOHN, 1st Lt., 97th Pa. Inf., USA	CW
WAINWRIGHT, JONATHAN M., Gen., USA	WW II
WAINWRIGHT, RICHARD, JR., Lt., USN	VC
WALKER, ALLEN, Pvt., 3d U.S. Cav., USA	Ind
WALKER, EDWARD ALEXANDER, Sgt., USMC	CRE
WALKER, FRANK O., Pvt., 46th Inf., U.S. Vol., USA	PI
WALKER, JAMES C., Pvt., 31st Ohio Inf., USA	CW
WALKER, JOHN, Pvt., 8th U.S. Cav., USA	Ind
WALKER, KENNETH N., Brig. Gen., USAAF	WW II
WALL, JERRY, Pvt., 126th N.Y. Inf., USA	CW
WALLACE, GEORGE W., 2d Lt., 9th U.S. Inf., USA	PI
WALLACE, HERMAN C., Pfc., 76th Inf. Div., USA	WW II
WALLACE, WILLIAM, Sgt., 5th U.S. Cav., USA	Ind
WALLAR, FRANCIS A., Cpl., 6th Wis. Inf., USA	CW
WALLEY, AUGUSTUS, Pvt., 9th U.S. Cav., USA	Ind
WALLING, WILLIAM H., Capt., 142d N.Y. Inf., USA	CW
WALMSLEY, JOHN S., JR., Capt., 5th A.F., USAAF	KC
WALSH, JAMES A., Seaman, USN	VC
WALSH, JOHN, Cpl., 5th N.Y. Cav., USA	CW
WALSH, KENNETH AMBROSE, 1st Lt., USMC	WW II
WALSH, MICHAEL, Chief Machinist, USN	1903
WALSH, WILLIAM GARY, Sgt., USMCR	WW II
WALTON, GEORGE W., Pvt., 97th Pa. Inf., USA	CW
WAMBSGAN, MARTIN, Pvt., 90th N.Y. Inf., USA	CW
WANTON, GEORGE H., Pvt., 10th U.S. Cav., USA	S-A
WARD, CALVIN J., Pvt., 30th Div., USA	WW I
WARD, CHARLES H., Pvt., 1st U.S. Cav., USA	Ind
WARD, JAMES, Quarter Gunner, USN	CW
WARD, JAMES, Sgt., 7th U.S. Cav., USA	Ind
WARD, JAMES RICHARD, Seaman 1st Class, USN	WW II
WARD, JOHN, Sgt., Indian Scouts, USA	Ind
WARD, NELSON W., Pvt., 11th Pa. Cav., USA	CW
WARD, THOMAS J., Pvt., 116th Ill. Inf., USA	CW
WARD, WILLIAM H., Capt., 47th Ohio Inf., USA	CW
WARDEN, JOHN, Cpl., 55th Ill. Inf., USA	CW
WARE, KEITH L., Lt. Col., 3d Inf. Div., USA	WW II
WARFEL, HENRY C., Pvt., 1st Pa. Cav., USA	CW
WARNER, HENRY F., Cpl., 1st Inf. Div., USA	WW II
WARREN, DAVID, Coxswain, USN	CW
WARREN, FRANCIS, E., Cpl., 49th Mass. Inf., USA	CW
WARRINGTON, LEWIS, 1st Lt., 4th U.S. Cav., USA	Ind
WATKINS, LEWIS G., S/Sgt., USMC	KC
WATKINS, TRAVIS E., M/Sgt., 2d Inf. Div., USA	KC
WATSON, JAMES C., Cpl., 6th U.S. Cav., USA	Ind
WATSON, JOSEPH, Pvt., 8th U.S. Cav., USA	Ind
WATSON, WILSON DOUGLAS, Pvt., USMCR	WW II
WAUGH, ROBERT T., 1st Lt., 85th Inf. Div., USA	WW II
WAYBUR, DAVID C., 1st Lt., 3d Inf. Div., USA	WW II
WEAHER, ANDREW J., Pvt., 8th U.S. Cav., USA	Ind
WEAVER, AMOS, Sgt., 36th Inf., U.S. Vol., USA	PI
WEBB, ALEXANDER S., Brig. Gen., U.S. Vol., USA	CW
WEBB, JAMES, Pvt., 5th N.Y. Inf., USA	CW
WEBBER, ALASON P., Musician, 86th Ill. Inf., USA	CW
WEBSTER, HENRY S., Landsman, USN	CW
WEEKS, CHARLES H., Capt. of Foretop, USN	CW
WEEKS, JOHN H., Pvt., 152d N.Y. Inf., USA	CW
WEICHT, ELLIS R., Sgt., 36th Inf. Div., USA	WW II
WEINERT, PAUL H., Cpl., 1st U.S. Arty., USA	Ind
WEIR, HENRY C., Capt. and Asst. Adj. Gen., U.S. Vol., USA	CW
*WEISBOGEL, ALBERT, Capt. of Mizzen Top, USN	1874, 1876
WEISS, ENOCH R., Pvt., 1st U.S. Cav., USA	Ind
WEISSEL, ADAM, Ship's Cook, USN	1881
WELBORN, IRA C., 2d Lt., 9th U.S. Inf., USA	S-A
WELCH, CHARLES H., Sgt., 7th U.S. Cav., USA	Ind
WELCH, GEORGE W., Pvt., 11th Mo. Inf., USA	CW
WELCH, MICHAEL, Sgt., 6th U.S. Cav., USA	Ind
WELCH, RICHARD, Cpl., 37th Mass. Inf., USA	CW
WELCH, STEPHEN, Sgt., 154th N.Y. Inf., USA	CW

WELD, SETH L., Cpl., 8th U.S. Inf., USA	PI
WELLS, HENRY S., Pvt., 148th N.Y. Inf., USA	CW
WELLS, THOMAS M., Chief Bugler, 6th N.Y. Cav., USA	CW
WELLS, WILLIAM, Quartermaster, USN	CW
WELSH, WILLIAM, Maj., 1st Vt. Cav., USA	CW
WELSH, EDWARD, Pvt., 54th Ohio Inf., USA	CW
WELSH, JAMES, Pvt., 4th R.I. Inf., USA	CW
WENDE, BRUNO, Pvt., 17th U.S. Inf., USA	S-A
WEST, CHESTER H., 1st Sgt., 91st Div., USA	WW I
WEST, ERNEST E., Pfc., 25th Inf. Div., USA	KC
WEST, FRANK, 1st Lt., 6th U.S. Cav., USA	CW
WEST, WALTER SCOTT, Pvt., USMC	S-A
WESTA, KARL, Chief Machinist's Mate, USN	1910
WESTERHOLD, WILLIAM, Sgt., 52d N.Y. Inf., USA	CW
WESTERMARK, AXEL, Seaman, USN	CRE
WESTON, JOHN F., Maj., 4th Ky. Cav., USA	CW
WETHERBY, JOHN C., Pvt., 4th U.S. Inf., USA	CW
WETZEL, WALTER C., Pfc., 8th Inf. Div., USA	WW II
WHEATON, LOYD, Lt. Col., 8th Ill. Inf., USA	CW
WHEELER, DANIEL D., 1st Lt., 4th Vt. Inf., USA	CW
WHEELER, GEORGE HOWARD, Shipfitter 1st Class, USN	P-1911
WHEELER, HENRY W., Pvt., 2d Maine Inf., USA	CW
WHERRY, WILLIAM M., 1st Lt., 3d U.S. Res. Mo. Inf., USA	CW
WHITAKER, EDWARD W., Capt., 1st Conn. Cav., USA	CW
WHITE, ADAM, Cpl., 11th W. Va. Inf., USA	CW
WHITE, EDWARD, Pvt., 20th Kans. Vol. Inf., USA	PI
WHITE, J. HENRY, Pvt., 90th Pa. Inf., USA	CW
WHITE, JOSEPH, Coxswain, USN	CW
WHITE, PATRICK H., Capt., Chicago Mercantile Btry., Ill. Light Arty., USA	CW
WHITEHEAD, JOHN M., Chaplain, 15th Ind. Inf., USA	CW
WHITEHEAD, PATTON G., Pvt., 5th U.S. Inf., USA	Ind
WHITELEY, ELI, 1st Lt., 3d Inf. Div., USA	WW II
WHITFIELD, DANIEL, Quartermaster, USN	CW
WHITMAN, FRANK M., Pvt., 35th Mass. Inf., USA	CW
WHITMORE, JOHN, Pvt., 119th Ill. Inf., USA	CW
WHITNEY, WILLIAM G., Sgt., 11th Mich. Inf., USA	CW
WHITTIER, EDWARD N., 1st Lt., Maine Light Arty., USA	CW
WHITTINGTON, HULON B., Sgt., 2d Armd. Div., USA	WW II
WHITTLESEY, CHARLES W., Maj., 77th Div., USA	WW I
WICKERSHAM, J. HUNTER, 2d Lt., 89th Div., USA	WW I
WIDICK, ANDREW J., Pvt., 116th Ill. Inf., USA	CW
WIDMER, JACOB, 1st Sgt., 5th U.S. Cav., USA	Ind
WIEDORFER, PAUL J., Pvt., 80th Inf. Div., USA	WW II
WIGLE, THOMAS W., 2d Lt., 34th Inf. Div., USA	WW II
WILBUR, WILLIAM H., Col., Western Task Force, North Africa, USA	WW II
WILCOX, FRANKLIN L., Ordinary Seaman, USN	CW
WILCOX, WILLIAM H., Sgt., 9th N.H. Inf., USA	CW
WILDER, WILBER E., 1st Lt., 4th U.S. Cav., USA	Ind
WILEY, JAMES, Sgt., 59th N.Y. Inf., USA	CW
WILHELM, GEORGE, Capt., 56th Ohio Inf., USA	CW
WILKE, JULIUS A. R., Boatswain's Mate 1st Class, USN	S-A
WILKENS, HENRY, 1st Sgt., 2d U.S. Cav., USA	Ind
WILKES, HENRY, Landsman, USN	CW
WILKIN, EDWARD G., Cpl., 45th Inf. Div., USA	WW II
WILKINS, LEANDER A., Sgt., 9th N.H. Inf., USA	CW
WILKINS, RAYMOND H., Maj., USAAF	WW II
WILKINSON, THEODORE STARK, Ensign, USN	VC
WILL, WALTER J., 1st Lt., 1st Inf. Div., USA	WW II
WILLCOX, ORLANDO B., Col., 1st Mich. Inf., USA	CW
WILLEY, CHARLES H., Machinist, USN	1916
WILLIAMS, ANTHONY, Sailmaker's Mate, USN	CW
WILLIAMS, ANTONIO, Seaman, USN	1877
WILLIAMS, AUGUSTUS, Seaman, USN	CW
WILLIAMS, ELLWOOD N., Pvt., 28th Ill. Inf., USA	CW
WILLIAMS, ERNEST CALVIN, 1st Lt., USMC	Dom C
WILLIAMS, FRANK, Seaman, USN	S-A
WILLIAMS, GEORGE C., Sgt., 14th U.S. Inf., USA	CW
WILLIAMS, HENRY, Carpenter's Mate, USN	1879
WILLIAMS, HERSHEL WOODROW, Cpl., USMCR	WW II
WILLIAMS, JACK, Pharmacist's Mate 3rd Class, USNR	WW II
WILLIAMS, JAY, Coxswain, USN	CRE
WILLIAMS, JOHN, Seaman, USN	CW
WILLIAMS, JOHN, Capt. of Maintop, USN	CW
WILLIAMS, JOHN, Boatswain's Mate, USN	CW
WILLIAMS, LEROY, Sgt., 8th N.Y. Heavy Arty., USA	CW
*WILLIAMS, LOUIS, Capt. of Top, USN	1883, 1884
WILLIAMS, MOSES, 1st Sgt., 9th U.S. Cav., USA	Ind
WILLIAMS, PETER, Seaman, USN	CW
WILLIAMS, ROBERT, Signal Quartermaster, USN	CW
WILLIAMS, WILLIAM, Landsman, USN	CW

WILLIAMS, WILLIAM H., Pvt., 82d Ohio Inf., USA	CW
WILLIAMSON, JAMES A., Col., 4th Iowa Inf., USA	CW
WILLIS, GEORGE, Coxswain, USN	1873
WILLIS, JOHN HARLAN, Pharmacist's Mate 1st Class, USN	WW II
WILLIS, RICHARD, Coxswain, USN	CW
WILLISTON, EDWARD B., 1st Lt., 2d U.S. Arty., USA	CW
WILLS, HENRY, Pvt., 8th U.S. Cav., USA	Ind
WILSON, ALFRED L., T/5, 26th Inf. Div., USA	WW II
WILSON, ARTHUR H., 2d Lt., 6th U.S. Cav., USA	PI
WILSON, AUGUST, Boilermaker, USN	1897
WILSON, BENJAMIN, Pvt., 6th U.S. Cav., USA	Ind
WILSON, BENJAMIN F., 1st Lt., 7th Inf. Div., USA	KC
WILSON, CHARLES E., Sgt., 5th U.S. Inf., USA	Ind
WILSON, CHARLES E., Sgt., 1st N.J. Cav., USA	CW
WILSON, CHRISTOPHER W., Pvt., 73d N.Y. Inf., USA	CW
WILSON, FRANCIS A., Cpl., 95th Pa. Inf., USA	CW
WILSON, HAROLD E., Ch. War. Ofcr., USMC	KC
WILSON, JOHN, Sgt., 1st N.J. Cav., USA	CW
WILSON, JOHN A., Pvt., 21st Ohio Inf., USA	CW
WILSON, JOHN M., 1st Lt., U.S. Engr., USA	CW
WILSON, LOUIS HUGH, JR., Capt., USMC	WW II
WILSON, MILDEN H., Sgt., 7th U.S. Inf., USA	Ind
WILSON, RICHARD G., Pfc., 11th Abn. Div., USA	KC
*WILSON, ROBERT LEE, Pfc., USMC	WW II
WILSON, WILLIAM, Sgt., 4th U.S. Cav., USA	Ind
WILSON, WILLIAM O., Cpl., 9th U.S. Cav., USA	Ind
WINANS, ROSWELL, 1st Sgt., USMC	Dom C
WINDOLPH, CHARLES, Pvt., 7th U.S. Cav., USA	Ind
WINDRICH, WILLIAM G., S/Sgt., USMC	KC
WINDUS, CLARON A., Bugler, 6th U.S. Cav., USA	Ind
WINEGAR, WILLIAM W., Lt., 19th N.Y. Cav., USA	CW
WINTERBOTTOM, WILLIAM, Sgt., 6th U.S. Cav., USA	Ind
WISE, HOMER L., S/Sgt., 36th Inf. Div., USA	WW II
WISNER, LEWIS S., 1st Lt., 124th N.Y. Inf., USA	CW
WITCOME, JOSEPH, Pvt., 8th U.S. Cav., USA	Ind
WITEK, FRANK PETER, Pfc., USMCR	WW II
WITHINGTON, WILLIAM H., Capt., 1st Mich. Inf., USA	CW
WOLD, NELS, Pvt., 35th Div., USA	WW I
WOLLAM, JOHN, Pvt., 33d Ohio Inf., USA	CW
WOMACK, BRYANT H., Pfc., 25th Inf. Div., USA	KC
WOOD, H. CLAY, 1st Lt., 1st U.S. Inf., USA	CW
WOOD, LEONARD, Asst. Surgeon, USA	Ind
WOOD, MARK, Pvt., 21st Ohio Inf., USA	CW
WOOD, RICHARD H., Capt., 97th Ill. Inf., USA	CW
WOOD, ROBERT B., Coxswain, USN	CW
WOODALL, ZACHARIAH, Sgt., 6th U.S. Cav., USA	Ind
WOODBURY, ERI D., Sgt., 1st Vt. Cav., USA	CW
WOODFILL, SAMUEL, 1st Lt., 5th Div., USA	WW I
WOODFORD, HOWARD E., S/Sgt., 33d Inf. Div., USA	WW II
WOODRUFF, ALONZO, Sgt., 1st U.S. Sharpshooters, USA	CW
WOODRUFF, CARLE A., 1st Lt., 2d U.S. Arty., USA	CW
WOODS, BRENT, Sgt., 9th U.S. Cav., USA	Ind
WOODS, DANIEL A., Pvt., 1st Va. Cav., USA	CW
WOODS, SAMUEL, Seaman, USN	CW
WOODWARD, EVAN M., 1st Lt. and Adj., 2d Pa. Res. Inf., USA	CW
WOOD, JOHN, Boatswain's Mate, USN	CW
WORAM, CHARLES B., Seaman, USN	CW
WORTICK, JOSEPH, Pvt., 8th Mo. Inf., USA	CW
WORTMAN, GEORGE G., Sgt., 8th U.S. Cav., USA	Ind
WRAY, WILLIAM J., Sgt., 1st Vet. Res. Corps, USA	CW
WRIGHT, ALBERT D., Capt., 43d U.S. Colored Troops, USA	CW
WRIGHT, EDWARD, Quartermaster, USN	CW
WRIGHT, ROBERT, Pvt., 14th U.S. Inf., USA	CW
WRIGHT, SAMUEL, Cpl., 2d Minn. Inf., USA	CW
WRIGHT, SAMUEL C., Pvt., 29th Mass. Inf., USA	CW
WRIGHT, WILLIAM, Yeoman, USN	CW
YEAGER, JACOB F., Pvt., 101st Ohio Inf., USA	CW
YORK, ALVIN C., Cpl., 82d Div., USA	WW I
YOUNG, ANDREW J., Sgt., 1st Pa. Cav., USA	CW
YOUNG, CALVARY M., Sgt., 3d Iowa Cav., USA	CW
YOUNG, CASSIN, Commander, USN	WW II
YOUNG, EDWARD B., Coxswain, USN	CW
YOUNG, FRANK ALBERT, Pvt., USMC	CRE
YOUNG, HORATIO N., Seaman, USN	CW
YOUNG, JAMES M., Pvt., 72d N.Y. Inf., USA	CW
YOUNG, BENJAMIN F., Cpl., 1st Mich. Sharpshooters, USA	CW
YOUNG, ROBERT H., Pfc, 1st Cav. Div., USA	KC
YOUNG, RODGER W., Pvt., 37th Inf. Div., USA	WW II
YOUNG, WILLIAM, Boatswain's Mate, USN	CW

YOUNKER, JOHN L., Pvt., 12th U.S. Inf., USA   CW
YOUNT, JOHN P., Pvt., 3d U.S. Cav., USA   Ind

ZEAMER, JAY, JR., Maj., USAAF   WW II
ZIEGNER, HERMANN, Pvt., 7th U.S. Cav., USA   Ind
ZION, WILLIAM, Pvt., USMC   CRB
ZUIDERVELD, WILLIAM, Hospital Appren. 1st Class, USN   VC
ZUSSMAN, RAYMOND, 2d Lt., 756th Tank Bn., USA   WW II